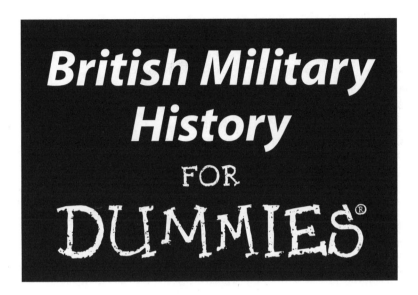

British Military History

for

DUMMIES®

by Bryan Perrett

BICENTENNIAL
1807
WILEY
2007
BICENTENNIAL

John Wiley & Sons, Ltd

British Military History For Dummies®

Published by
John Wiley & Sons, Ltd
The Atrium
Southern Gate
Chichester
West Sussex
PO19 8SQ
England

E-mail (for orders and customer service enquires): cs-books@wiley.co.uk

Visit our Home Page on www.wiley.com

For general information on our other products and services, please contact our Customer Care Department within the U.S. at 800-762-2974, outside the U.S. at 317-572-3993, or fax 317-572-4002.

For technical support, please visit www.wiley.com/techsupport.

Wiley also publishes its books in a variety of electronic formats. Some content that appears in print may not be available in electronic books.

British Library Cataloguing in Publication Data: A catalogue record for this book is available from the British Library

ISBN: 978-0-470-03213-8

Printed and bound in Great Britain by Bell & Bain Ltd, Glasgow

10 9 8 7 6 5 4 3 2 1

WILEY

About the Author

Bryan Perrett was educated at Liverpool College. He served for nineteen years in Regular and Territorial Regiments of the Royal Armoured Corps before deciding to take up the pen professionally. His numerous books include *Seize and Hold,* a study of the *coup de main,* and *Iron Fist,* containing case studies of classic armoured engagements, which was selected by the Royal United Services Institute for Defence Studies for its book option. His more recent works include *The Real Hornblower,* a biography of Admiral Sir James Gordon, believed to be the officer upon whom C.S. Forester based his immortal character Horatio Hornblower, and *For Valour: Victoria Cross and Medal of Honor Battles.* During the Falklands and First Gulf Wars he served as Defence Correspondent to the *Liverpool Echo.*

Dedication

To my wife Anne for her astonishing patience while I worked my way through 2000 years of military history.

Publisher's Acknowledgements

We're proud of this book; please send us your comments through our Dummies online registration form located at www.dummies.com/register/.

Some of the people who helped bring this book to market include the following:

Acquisitions, Editorial, and Media Development

Special Projects Coordinator: Daniel Mersey

Project Editor: Simon Bell

Content Editor: Steve Edwards

Development Editors: Sally Lansdell, Daniel Mersey

Commissioning Editor: Alison Yates

Technical Editor: Michael Rayner

Executive Editor: Jason Dunne

Executive Project Editor: Martin Tribe

Cover Photos: Cromwell: © Time Life Pictures/ Getty Images; Marlborough: © Getty Images; Wellington: © Mary Evans Picture Library; Roberts: © Getty Images; Victoria Cross: © Peter Russell/The Military Picture Library; Kitchener: © Time Life Pictures/Getty Images; Tank: © Mary Evans Picture Library; First World War soldiers: © Getty Images; Montgomery: © Getty Images; Second World War soldiers: © F4689/Imperial War Museum; Blues and Royals: © Grant Faint/ Getty Images; Iraq: © Getty Images

Cartoons: Rich Tennant (www.the5thwave.com)

Composition Services

Project Coordinator: Jennifer Theriot

Layout and Graphics: Carl Byers, Brooke Graczyk, Stephanie Jumper, Erin Zeltner

Special Art:

Proofreader: Laura Albert, Dwight Ramsey

Indexer: Aptara

Special Help

Brand Reviewer: Rev Mengle

Publishing and Editorial for Consumer Dummies

    Diane Graves Steele, Vice President and Publisher, Consumer Dummies

    Joyce Pepple, Acquisitions Director, Consumer Dummies

    Kristin A. Cocks, Product Development Director, Consumer Dummies

    Michael Spring, Vice President and Publisher, Travel

    Kelly Regan, Editorial Director, Travel

Publishing for Technology Dummies

    Andy Cummings, Vice President and Publisher, Dummies Technology/General User

Composition Services

    Gerry Fahey, Vice President of Production Services

    Debbie Stailey, Director of Composition Services

Contents at a Glance

Table of Contents

Introduction

You come across them everywhere. Not always in the flesh, of course. Their names are inscribed on the walls of temples and the badges of their old regiments are carved into rock faces around the world. I mean British soldiers, of course, who have served on every continent. At one time they policed one-quarter of the earth's surface, which is a remarkable achievement for a comparatively small group of men (and these days, women) born in an insignificant group of offshore islands. They were heroes and cowards, wise men and fools, good men and bad. Their story is one of triumph and tragedy, victory and sometimes defeat, hard living and laughter. Strong bonds of comradeship, a sense of family, and pride in the soldier's regiment have always existed, as well as traditions that aren't found to the same extent in any other army. When times are at their worst, these things provide a tremendous source of strength.

The British – by which I mean the English, Welsh, Scots, Irish, and Manx – were fighting among themselves long, long before the Regular Army was established in the seventeenth century, and when they weren't doing that they were fighting the French! The story of the British army is a long one that I hope you enjoy reading as much as I have enjoyed telling it.

About This Book

On the way through the book you meet all sorts of people, from King Arthur to Field Marshal Viscount Montgomery of Alamein. One of the most important people you meet is called Tommy Atkins, the universal name for the British soldier that even his enemies use. He's a rather likeable sort, a good ambassador for his country, slow to anger, stubborn as a mule, and someone to avoid when his temper's up. He's as brave as anyone, but because of his training, discipline, and regimental spirit, he tends to be braver for five minutes longer. One French general described him as a very bad soldier who didn't seem to understand that he'd lost the battle and went on fighting until the French (who of course were better soldiers) realised they had lost and sensibly withdrew. In addition, in the book you get to know something about weapons, tactics, battles, and the army's part in creating and defending the British Empire.

What I've written in this book represents my own opinions. Other people may not agree or may differ in their interpretation of details, but the thing to remember about military history, as Sir Basil Liddell Hart said, is that no one can know more than a fraction of anything, and every day there is something fresh to discover. It's fun.

Conventions Used in This Book

First, dates. I have stuck to BC *(Before Christ)* and AD *(Anno Domini, the year of our Lord)* because that is how dates are recorded in all but a tiny percentage of the reference books you may wish to consult.

Second, I refer to military formations. Not everyone is familiar with the structures the army uses, so here they are:

- ✔ An **army group** consists of two or more armies.
- ✔ An **army** usually consists of two or more corps.
- ✔ A **corps** normally consists of two or more divisions.
- ✔ A **division** consists of two or more brigades.
- ✔ A **brigade** consists of three infantry battalions or cavalry regiments.

This is representative and varies according to circumstances. Although British infantry regiments may consist of several battalions (of between 500 and 1,000 soldiers), it was unusual for them to serve together prior to the World Wars.

In military history, the written conventions employed to identify formations are:

- ✔ **Army Group:** Arabic numerals, for example 21st Army Group
- ✔ **Army:** Roman letters, for example Eighth Army
- ✔ **Corps:** Roman numerals, for example XXX Corps
- ✔ **Divisions:** Arabic numerals, for example 1st Division. If other than infantry a designation is added, such as 1st Cavalry Division, 1st Armoured Division
- ✔ **Brigades:** As divisions. Recent convention is to omit 'st, nd, rd, th' from the numeral, for example 123 Brigade.

When you get to the smaller units, things can become a little confusing. For the same of simplicity I have used regiments' numbers, such as 24th. When a regiment had two battalions, I have indicated which one we're talking about, such as 1/24th or 2/24th.

What You're Not to Read

From time to time in this book I've used icons called Technical Stuff. These are necessary because warfare is a technical business and I've recorded the introduction of new weapons systems and other developments separately from the main narrative. The same is true of sidebars, which contain interesting info that you can skip if you just want to read the main narrative. You don't have to read either to understand what is happening.

Foolish Assumptions

I've made some assumptions about *you* when writing this book. I'm assuming that one or more of the following is true:

- ✔ You did a bit of military history at school, perhaps relating to the Second World War, but had difficulty placing all the information into context.
- ✔ You may have studied other aspects, like the Napoleonic Wars, but have become a bit hazy about who did what and when.
- ✔ You enjoy reading a good story in which some of your not-so-distant ancestors are bound to have taken part.

How This Book Is Organised

I've organised the book in a modular way. It consists of a number of parts, each of which stands on its own so you don't need to read the book cover to cover (unless you want to!). If your interest is in ancient and medieval warfare or the Napoleonic Wars, for example, go straight to the relevant part. Each part contains chapters with information about the British involvement in the wars of that period. The following sections describe the type of information you can find in each part.

Part 1: Ancient and Medieval Warfare

When the Roman Legions invaded the island they called *Britannia*, they found themselves fighting fierce blue tribesmen egged on by wild women and weird Druids. The Romans won, but after they had gone, Angles, Saxons, and Jutes invaded the island. If you read this part you find out about the rough-and-tumble punch-ups between the Saxon kingdoms, admire Offa and his smart new dyke, cheer on Alfred as he batters the Danes, and make the acquaintance of Canute, owner of the original float-away throne. Then, if you've got time, you can make friends with William the Conqueror, or discover how to build a castle or two and really oppress people. You may well agree that the Scots deserved their independence after Edward II's dreadful performance at Bannockburn, and that the snobby French nobility asked for the regular hidings they got from English archers.

Part II: The Arrival of Gunpowder

Suddenly, all the rules changed. Why? Because of an unstable black powder that has a tendency to explode anywhere, any time, given the slightest encouragement. That means that guns, muskets, and pistols are in. And that means a complete new look for the infantry. The cavalry didn't adapt too well at first, but they gradually got the hang of things, as did the chaps who designed fortifications. The British weren't really into land warfare at this time, so when Charles I and his Parliament came to blows they did so with amateur armies. Charles II realised that he needed a regular standing army. In this part, you discover how that army was formed, what it consisted of, and how it operated.

Part III: Wars of Succession, Independence, and Revolution

The British army spent most of the eighteenth century, and some years after, fighting the French. They fought other people too, but mostly the French. In fact, some people grew up believing that fighting the French was what you did when you left school. During the early years of the century, the Duke of Marlborough won a series of stunning victories that established the army's reputation. India was an area of constant squabbling where the Honourable East India Company looked after British interests. Another area of continual friction was North America, where Canada in the north and Louisiana in the south menaced the 13 British colonies. Then some of the American colonists rebelled and declared their independence. France declared war on Great Britain, little realising that the two countries would still be fighting 22 years later when the French had a pushy general called Bonaparte.

Part IV: Nineteenth-Century Wars

In India, the jewel of the expanding Empire, threats developed requiring the armed services to protect British interests. Even the Crimean War, the British army's only European involvement during the period, was fought to prevent Imperial Russia expanding its influence into the Mediterranean and so posing a threat to British India. In fact, what became known as the 'Great Game', the nineteenth-century equivalent of the Cold War, played out between Great Britain and Russia in Central Asia. Other European nations were eager to enhance their status by acquiring colonies, mainly in Africa, and this meant that the British acquired additional colonies they did not want, simply to prevent them being used by potentially hostile powers. Improved weapons systems completely altered the way wars were fought and hinted at the industrialised killing that would take place during the twentieth century.

Part V: The First World War

In 1914 the young men of Europe rushed eagerly to war, hoping that they were not too late to miss an adventure that would, they thought, be over by Christmas. Their reward was four long years of horror and killing. The only thing that broke the deadlock was the tank, a British invention. The war engulfed much of Europe, the Middle East, and Africa. The British Empire expanded a little further, but at a cost of one million casualties and a damaged economy.

Part VI: The Second World War (and Beyond)

Years of political neglect left the British army unprepared for the Second World War. The only area in which Great Britain maintained a lead was in the theoretical application of armoured warfare; the German army absorbed these ideas practically. Following the defeat of the French army in 1940, the British Expeditionary Force had to be evacuated from mainland Europe. The Japanese had captured Hong Kong, Malaya, and Singapore and occupied most of Burma. But from 1943 onwards the British army and its allies began to make real progress. They defeated the enemy in North Africa, Sicily, Italy, Normandy, and North West Europe, as well as finally winning against the Japanese. Postwar, the army's tasks included policing an orderly withdrawal from the Empire, a commitment to its NATO allies during the European Cold War, and a number of wars as well as internal security and peacekeeping tasks.

Part VII: The Part of Tens

This part contains information worth remembering when it comes to any discussion on British military history. As you can gather from this book, British military history goes back a great distance and lots of things have happened that most people have long since forgotten. So the lists in this part contain ten important battles, ten of the best generals, and ten military museums worth visiting, together with my reasons for thinking they are the best. Even if you don't agree with my selections, they may give you food for thought.

Icons Used in This Book

History – especially military history – isn't just about telling stories. What you really want to know about campaigns, battles, and weapons is highlighted by icons indicating something special about the text they appear with:

Military history is full of good stories, not all of which are necessarily true. Check them out for yourself!

The good, the bad, and the ugly of the British army and its enemies. This icon highlights the most influential warriors in the book.

This icon gets down to the nitty-gritty of the main event – how campaigns were planned and how battles were fought. This icon signifies the hottest action.

These are key points to remember for making sense of the action that follows on the battlefield.

Want to know how armies were equipped, what tactics they used, and what weapons systems were operated? Then this icon is for you! Memorise a few and show off (but feel free to skip over them if you're not such a military techie)!

Where to Go from Here

You don't have to start on the first page and read right through the book. You know what interests you best; just look in the Table of Contents to find it. You don't have to read the chapter before or the chapter after if you don't want to. Not like school at all, is it?

Part I
Ancient and Medieval Warfare

The 5th Wave   By Rich Tennant

"Who knows what day it is?"

In this part . . .

The Romans put Britain on the map, militarily speaking. During their period of occupation those areas of the mainland that became England and Wales enjoyed an unequalled period of peace and prosperity. When the legions left, wave after wave of invaders took their place: Angles, Saxons, Jutes, Vikings, Danes, and finally the Normans.

The Normans established a strong central government in England, controlling the land with numerous castles and armoured knights. In turn, they became absorbed into the population. During the later Middle Ages, British battles were dominated by English or Welsh archers, armed with a deadly longbow that sent continental nobility tumbling by the score. The longbow was also used during the Wars of the Roses, which saw the English aristocracy come close to wiping each other out.

Chapter 1

Small Islands with Lots of Clout

The British Isles may be geographically small on the world stage, but they have packed some serious clout over the centuries. This opening chapter looks at some of the reasons behind this, offering up some of the themes you can read about by delving further into this book.

The British (historically the English, Scottish, Welsh, Irish, and Manx) live in a small group of islands off the west coast of Europe. They have a reputation for being courteous, considerate, fair minded, law abiding, stolid, a little reserved, and gifted with an ironic sense of humour. In general this picture holds true, although visitors may not think so if they penetrate the centres of some metropolitan areas on a Saturday night! There, they can see a ritual that forms part of the mating game. Phase I involves lots of alcoholic drink. Phase II, which can be optional, involves fisticuffs and shouting. Phase III involves the actual acquisition of a mate. It's all a little raucous and 'twas ever thus. Had it been otherwise, Sir Robert Peel would not have founded the police force. This kind of event probably reminds visitors that the British do have a robust history. As you can read in Chapter 2, the first general historical record of Britons involves a scrap or two with Julius Caesar and his Roman boys. Since then, the British appear to have fought among themselves, gone on to fight everyone else, and left their bones on every one of the world's continents.

Checking Out Britain's Wars Through the Ages

Ready for a whistle-stop tour of action seen by British soldiers over the centuries? If you want to find out more about the historical build-up or aftermath of these campaigns, a useful companion volume is Sean Lang's *British History For Dummies* (Wiley) – although the basics you need to know are outlined in this book. OK, here goes with the action.

Part I of this book shows you that apart from squabbles between neighbouring kingdoms, the first British wars were against invaders, including the Romans, the Saxons, the Vikings, and the Danes. Then William and his Normans did a bit of conquering of the British Isles, and the Middle Ages really got into their stride with a lot of dynastic wars, mainly with the French, although the Scots, Welsh, and Irish came in for trouble, too. The Gunpowder Revolution (detailed in Chapter 5) more or less coincided with the wars of religion on the continent, in which the British played a comparatively minor role, save at sea. On the other hand, the residue of these spilled over into the British Civil Wars (see Chapter 6). In their turn, these indicated the need for a British Regular Army (the formation of which is outlined in Chapter 7). The eighteenth century found that army entangled in several dynastic wars on the continent and in various places around the world, including the West Indies, North America, and India (covered in Chapter 8). Most of these involved fighting the French, but other opponents existed too, including Jacobite rebels at home and American colonists across the Atlantic (see Chapter 9).

The French Revolution triggered 22 years of war, with one short break (more on the Revolution and Napoleonic Wars in Chapters 10 and 11). During these years the British army fought in the Low Countries, Ireland, Egypt, Spain, Portugal, France, North and South America, and South Africa. The long series of victories that Wellington won during the Peninsula War and at Waterloo improved the army's popularity at home and enhanced its reputation abroad.

On the other side of the world was another British army, but this one belonged to a commercial organisation: In India the Honourable East India Company ran its own army, subdivided into the Bombay, Madras, and Bengal armies. These consisted mainly of regiments composed of Indian soldiers, plus a handful of European regiments, which were as near as the British ever got to having their own foreign legion. During the middle of the nineteenth century the British Empire began to expand at an unprecedented rate. The Honourable East India Company fought wars in Afghanistan, Scinde, and the Punjab (see Chapter 12). The mutiny of most of the Bengal army's Indian regiments resulted in savage fighting and atrocities committed by both sides, but was finally crushed (as explained in Chapter 14). After this the British government assumed responsibility for India and reorganised the Indian army. It fought another major war in Afghanistan and a large part of its strength was always deployed on the restless North West Frontier (see Chapter 15).

The Crimean War was the only occasion when the British army was committed to a European war during the nineteenth century. This war was notable for the bravery and fortitude of the troops and for the bungling of the government departments responsible for running the army (outlined in Chapter 13). The war was also the first occasion on which war correspondents were able to report what was taking place at the front, and saw the appearance of the war photographer.

The army was almost continuously employed in various parts of Africa from 1868 until 1902 (more on this in Chapter 16). It fought the Zulus in South Africa, the Ashanti on the west coast of the continent, the Egyptians in Egypt, and the dervishes in the Sudan. Some people may think that because the British were fighting poorly equipped native armies their task was an easy one. It was not. Both in Africa and other parts of the world, the British army was invariably outnumbered by a very wide margin, fought its battles far from any possible source of help, and knew that if it lost the best its survivors faced was to be massacred on the spot. Britain was also involved in two wars against the Boers, who had their own ideas about how wars should be fought: The first war was short and sharp and resulted in a Boer victory; the second was prolonged and involved considerable effort on the part of the British Empire before the Boers submitted.

During the First World War the British army expanded to many times its former size. It fought on the Western Front, the Dardanelles, in Egypt, Palestine, Mesopotamia, Italy, Salonika, and Germany's former colonies (Part V). It sustained horrific casualties, but solved many of the problems of industrialised warfare by inventing the tank, and it finally led the Allied advance that broke German resistance on the Western Front in 1918.

Political neglect ensured that the army entered the Second World War under strength and ill-equipped. In fact, it did not reach a condition capable of tackling a first-class enemy until mid-1942. The first phase of the war ended with the humiliation of the British army being evacuated from Norway, Dunkirk, Greece, and Crete. It subsequently fought successful campaigns in North Africa, the Middle East, Tunisia, Sicily, Italy, Normandy, and northwest Europe. In the Far East, preparations for war were even less satisfactory. The easy victories that the Japanese won in Hong Kong, Malaya, Singapore, and Burma damaged British prestige so seriously that even the subsequent complete destruction of the Japanese army group in Burma did not quite make up for them. This proved to be a factor in the transition from Empire to Commonwealth (read more in Part VI).

Moving with the Times: Key Strategies through History

Weapons, of course, play a major part in the way wars are fought, and the British army has seen many changes in both weapons and tactics. In more than 2000 years, the British have managed to produce their fair share of innovations. As you can find out in Chapter 2, Caesar didn't like the Britons' chariots one bit. The longbow (put through its paces in Chapter 4) was a uniquely British battle winner and in some ways actually a better weapon than the musket that took its place. Its rate of fire was certainly faster and it was more accurate. The effect of an arrow storm on packed enemy ranks was devastating. So why bother to change? Here are some reasons:

- ✔ Artillery outranged the archers.
- ✔ Muskets also had a longer range than longbows, even if they were less accurate.
- ✔ The kinetic energy stored in a musket ball was sufficient to fell a man or a horse or punch a hole through the best plate armour.

As the quality of the musket improved, the British army developed its own approach to infantry firepower. The infantry of other nations formed a three-deep battle line or attacked in *column* (see Part III), but the British preferred to fight in a two-rank *line* enabling more muskets to be deployed on the additional frontage. They also preferred to deliver precise volleys at close quarters, then charge with the bayonet while the enemy was disordered. When attacked by cavalry, they formed *squares* four ranks deep, bristling with bayonets. These were almost impossible to break and emphasised the stubborn streak of those forming them.

When it came to inventing the tank in the early twentieth century, the British beat the French by a short head (read more about tank development in Part V). The tank changed the nature of land warfare altogether, a fact that British governments of the 1920s and early 1930s completely ignored. They starved the army of funds and, apart from the development of a few prototypes, tank production stagnated. Far-sighted officers like Major General J.F.C. Fuller continued to promote their theories on mechanised warfare, which the Germans gratefully put into practice (as discovered in Chapter 20). When the government of the day finally accepted that Hitler was a dangerous maniac bent on reversing the verdict of the First World War, it embarked on a tank production programme that was too little too late and none too cleverly thought out. Instead of concentrating on one general-purpose tank for mass production, it decided it needed three different types:

- ✔ The *light tank* for colonial warfare and reconnaissance
- ✔ The *cruiser tank* intended to equip the armoured divisions
- ✔ The *infantry tank*, heavily armoured and slow to support infantrymen

By the end of the Second World War British tank production had caught up with itself. Indeed, in the field of assault engineering Major General Sir Percy Hobart's 79th Armoured Division, the largest division in the army, actually led the world (mentioned in Chapter 23).

Other factors that influence the way the army fights its battles are terrain and climate. Over the centuries, for the British army these have included the:

- ✔ Forests of North America
- ✔ Jungles of the Far East
- ✔ Mountains of the North West Frontier
- ✔ Temperate landscapes of Europe
- ✔ Veldt of South Africa
- ✔ Wastes of the Western Desert

In all of these places, and many more, it has been forced to adapt its skills and operate in temperatures that fry the brain or freeze it.

Remembering the Regiment: Traditions and Spirit

One highly prized and much admired asset possessed by the British and some Commonwealth armies is an intangible quality defined as *regimental spirit*. It is rooted in many things – a sense of family, comradeship, geographical background, tradition, pride in achievement, continuity, uniform, and a conviction that however good other regiments may seem, one's own is better.

The army encourages regimental spirit in a number of ways. It holds regimental days to commemorate famous battles. The officers' and sergeants' *messes* (quarters) contain portraits, paintings of battles, silverware donated by past members, trophies, scrapbooks, and photograph albums. In addition, the officers' mess houses the regimental *Colours* (flags) and the caskets containing the illuminated Freedom scrolls that towns and cities in the regiment's recruiting area present, confirming their citizens' esteem for the regiment and granting it the privilege of marching through with Colours flying, drums beating, and bayonets fixed.

Regimental spirit is tribal, and intentionally so. It has been proven time and time again that a regiment that fought well at Blenheim or Minden or Waterloo or any other hard-fought battle instinctively fights just as well when the going gets rough elsewhere. To put the concept at its simplest, the lad – or these days, the lady – needs to prove he's as good as his dad.

Realising the Army's Role in the Modern World

Since 1945 the British army has played a number of roles, often simultaneously. During this time of 'peace', the British army has:

- Overseen an orderly withdrawal from Empire
- Played a major part in the Cold War against the communist bloc in Europe
- Fought major wars in Korea, the Falkland Islands, the Persian Gulf, and Iraq
- Conducted successful jungle campaigns in Malaya and Borneo
- Carried out protracted counter-terrorist operations in Ulster
- Been involved in peace-keeping operations in the Balkans and elsewhere

Chapter 25 considers the army's role since the Second World War.

Chapter 2

Swords, Sandals, and Geometry: The Romans

*T*he earliest warriors in Britain wouldn't have been an army as we now recognise it. They didn't fight for the 'British army' – they fought for their own tribes and chiefs – and they didn't wear a recognised uniform as such (although being a fierce chap with a spear and a shield may have suggested to others exactly what his occupation was!). Fighting among themselves was one thing, but in the first century BC, a whole new way of war came to the British Isles – the Roman way of war.

The Roman army was the finest in the world in its time and experienced no real difficulty in conquering and holding down much of the British mainland. The Britons, however, were no slouches at fighting and made the Romans pay a high price for their success. Nevertheless, when the dust settled and Roman and Briton had learned to live together, for three centuries the island enjoyed a happy and comfortable lifestyle.

British armies fought the battles detailed in this chapter with the following troop types (for more on the Roman armies facing the British, see the later sidebar, 'The Roman army'):

✔ **Nobles:** The ultimate in barbaric chic, British nobles dressed well for battle. Many wore mail coats (capable of deflecting sword blows), sported helmets, and carried shields for protection. Some fought mounted, others in chariots, hurling spears and using skilful swordplay.

✔ **Warriors:** Armed with spears, shields, and swords, the bulk of British armies comprised warriors who charged fiercely towards their enemies, hoping to break their ranks at the first, violent clash.

✔ **Skirmishers:** A skirmisher's job was to harry the enemy, rushing forward and throwing javelins, or hurling stones from a sling. The Britons did not seem fond of the bow at this time.

Fighting from the Start: The Ancient Britons

Ugg (as I call my 'average' ancient Briton) lived long, long ago in what people call the mists of time. Ugg and his chums were not just brilliant engineers, able to construct such immense structures as Stonehenge and Silbury Hill. They were also capable of advanced mathematical calculations and laid out stone circles (ovals actually) with such accuracy that they functioned as calendars. Many circles still exist today (see Sean Lang's *British History For Dummies* for more information). However, Ugg's contemporaries have left us no written records, so we have to guess much of what went on. As far as fighting was concerned, Ugg learned very quickly that the family unit produced better results than individuals, and that lots of families working together overcame a single family. In this way the *tribe* was born and its best fighters led it into battle. In due course, neighbouring tribes joined together to form local kingdoms.

As the centuries passed, stone weapons became bronze ones, and then iron (each progressively sharper or stronger than the last). Table 2-1 gives a breakdown of the broad dates of these eras (along with the Roman period). Excavations at royal grave sites have unearthed swords, spears, helmets, and shields crafted to an extremely high standard, but the ordinary folk had to make do with whatever they could get.

Table 2-1	The Earliest Periods in British History
Years	*Period*
c12000–c2750 BC	Stone Age (*Neolithic*)
c2750–c750 BC	Bronze Age
c750 BC–43 AD	Iron Age
43–c410 AD	Roman Age

One uniquely British weapon system of the Iron Age, long discarded as obsolete in the Middle East, was the chariot, made from wicker and drawn by two horses. Chariots were the property of the nobility and, handled properly, could be remarkably effective (as the Romans were to find out – see 'Caesar Seizes an Opportunity'). Nor were the psychological aspects of warfare forgotten. Warriors covered their faces and bodies with strange patterns made with a blue vegetable dye called *woad*. Even hardened professionals like the Romans found themselves taken aback by their appearance.

The one element of Iron Age warfare still visible today are the *hill forts*. These consist of a concentric series of ditches and banks, the latter surmounted by stout fences, enclosing the summit of a large hill. Sometimes, the entrance followed a winding route through the banks to expose an attacker to a constant rain of missiles. The largest such fort in Europe is Maiden Castle, near Dorchester in Dorset, which is still an impressive sight.

Caesar Seizes an Opportunity

Unlike the Britons, the Romans had a written history, and we know that Julius Caesar (in the first century BC) described the Britons as a wild, hairy lot. Those Britons living closest to the Continent were the most civilised, he felt, while the tribes living in the interior lived on milk and meat and still dressed in skins.

The first recorded mention of Britons in battle comes from Julius Caesar, who wrote of encountering Britons while trying to conquer Gaul (modern-day France). A priesthood known as the *Druids*, who exercised immense influence in Britain and Gaul, had sent these Britons. The Druids collected and stored severed heads in the same way modern people collect postage stamps. For a real treat they constructed huge wicker men, stuffing live criminals into the limbs and torso, then setting fire to them. The British population feared, respected, and honoured the Druids, who regularly adjudicated in tribal disputes.

The Druids, well aware that Rome did not tolerate an alternative power in any land it conquered, violently opposed Caesar. They arranged for British tribes to support the Gauls in every way possible, including the provision of fighting men. In so doing, they placed Britain on the military historian's map for the first time, for during the summer of 55 BC Julius Caesar decided to cross the Channel and teach the Britons a lesson.

Caesar's first raid, 55 BC

Caesar took with him two Roman legions (see the sidebar 'The Roman army' for information about the strength of a legion). His first landfall across the English Channel was a narrow beach between two cliffs, from which the assembled Britons could hurl javelins and other missiles on to troops below, so Caesar moved the invasion fleet seven miles along the coast to an open shore. The enemy, led by their chariots and cavalry, followed him.

The Romans, shaken by the appearance of the wild, blue-painted Britons, attempted to disembark on a deeply shelving seabed and found themselves at an immediate disadvantage. Caesar ordered his war galleys to close in on the Britons' right flank. Unused to the strange craft and subjected to the fire of Roman archers, slingers, and powerful bolt-firing catapults known as *ballistae*, the Britons withdrew a little way. Seeing this, the Eagle bearer of the Roman 10th Legion (the legion's standard bearer) jumped down into the water, shouting for his comrades to follow if they didn't want to be involved in the disgrace of losing their standard. Caesar ordered the warships' boats to support them. Gradually more and more troops came ashore and formed a coherent line. As order had replaced confusion, the legions charged. When the Britons broke and fled, Caesar regretted that he was unable to mount a proper pursuit as his cavalry was still at sea.

Some days later, a gale seriously damaged many of the Roman ships and prevented the cavalry from landing. Shortly after, the 7th Legion left camp to cut corn and while its men were working in scattered parties, British cavalry and chariots attacked. The legion was barely holding its own when Caesar arrived with a relief force, enabling the legion to disengage and withdraw safely.

The Britons were well aware that Caesar had a limited number of troops at his disposal. The fact that he was nearing the end of his supplies and that his ships were still being repaired was also apparent. The Britons despatched messengers in every direction, expressing confidence that they could capture the Roman camp and organise booty galore for everyone. Some days later, having assembled a huge force of infantry and cavalry, they approached the camp. Caesar drew up both legions in battle formation and after a brief fight the Britons fled. The legionaries, lacking cavalry, conducted their pursuit on foot as far as they were able, killed a number of their opponents, and set fire to every building over a wide area.

Later in the day, the British leaders hurriedly asked for peace (they'd tried this earlier in the campaign, too, later going back on their word). Caesar demanded twice the number of hostages offered, to secure lasting peace. What he did not tell the Britons was that, worried by the prospect of further gales, he had already decided to re-embark his troops that very night. Setting sail shortly after midnight, the invasion fleet reached the continent without incident. End of round one.

Caesar made a number of very interesting observations regarding the Britons' use of chariots, which had unsettled his soldiers. Manned by a warrior and a driver, they operated at speed over the steepest hillsides. They could halt suddenly, enabling the warrior to run along the pole, stand on the yoke, and hurl a spear at the enemy. Alternatively, several warriors jumped down from the chariot and fought on foot while the drivers waited close by to pick them up if things began to go wrong. In this way, Caesar commented, they combined the mobility of cavalry with the staying power of infantry. These are the virtues of mounted infantry, but it was the better part of two millennia before they became apparent again (see Chapter 7 for more information).

Caesar's second raid, 54 BC

For his next expedition to Britain, Caesar assembled no fewer than five legions and 2000 cavalrymen. Landing unopposed in the area of modern Sandwich in Kent, locals told him that the Britons had assembled to prevent him getting ashore, but had dispersed in alarm on seeing the size of his invasion fleet.

Unfortunately, Caesar's account of subsequent operations is briefer than one would wish, given that he penetrated much deeper into Britain. He established a fortified camp and started marching inland. British horsemen and chariots emerged from the wooded countryside to harass the legions, but the Roman cavalry drove them off.

Many Britons retired into a hill fort on rising ground near Canterbury, Kent (see 'Fighting from the Start: The Ancient Britons', earlier in this chapter, for more on hill forts). The veteran Roman 7th Legion formed a *testudo* (meaning 'tortoise') by locking shields to provide protection, and beneath this built up a ramp of timber, earth, and brushwood against the fort's defences. Simultaneously, a barrage of ballista (catapult) bolts, arrows, and sling shots forced the defenders to keep their heads down. Once the ramp was high enough, the legion rushed the defences and stormed the fort.

Caesar learned that one of the most powerful British kings, Cassivelaunus, had taken charge of the forces opposing him. Cassivelaunus, unwilling to engage in a pitched battle, retreated steadily but ambushed the Roman columns on every possible occasion, causing some loss. Caesar recognised that he would have to follow the Briton into his own territory, which lay north of the river Thames. We do not know the precise site where the legions forded the river. Wherever it was, the legionaries must have crossed at low tide, and even then the water came up to their necks. Cassivelaunus asked the Kentish tribes to launch an attack on Caesar's base camp. Some did, but the Romans beat them off without difficulty.

The Roman army

The backbone of the Roman army was its legions. A legion had a nominal strength of 6000 men, although 4,800 was nearer to the real strength of most legions. Each legion had its own number, name, badge, and traditions, just like a modern regiment, and possessed a strong *esprit de corps*. A legion was under the command of six tribunes, who were often young sprigs of the nobility required to perform a period of military service before entering politics. The legion's internal organisation consisted of 60 *centuries*, each of 80 men commanded by a *centurion*. Two centuries made up a *maniple* and three maniples made up a *cohort*. The six centuries of the first cohort contained the legion's administrative and specialist personnel, so possessed more men than the other cohorts. The centurion commanding the 1st century of No 1 cohort was the legion's senior soldier, and generals and military tribunes regularly sought the opinions of senior centurions and were wise to respect them. On duty centurions carried a short club, serving as a badge of office and a means of enforcing discipline.

The *legionary* was a long-service regular soldier. He wore a reddish, knee-length tunic and a matching cloak or blanket. His leather-mounted strip armour buckled on above the tunic, around the body, and across the shoulders. Each legion wore its own type of helmet. The legionary protected his legs with *greaves* (rather like soccer shinpads) and carried an oblong, convex shield. His weapons included the *pilum* (a throwing spear that bent when it stuck in an opponent's shield, making it impossible to remove effectively), and a short, two-edged stabbing sword slung on the right of the body, called a gladius. Nothing pleased a legionary more than a barbarian enemy who slashed with his weapons, for as he raised his right arm he left his side unprotected against a very rapid Roman stab that was more often fatal than not. In peacetime the legionary trained constantly with weapons twice the weight of those he fought with, and on route marches he carried twice the weight he carried on campaign. He was, in short, the ideal professional soldier – highly trained, fit, hard, disciplined, and proud of his legion.

Other elements within the legion included a mounted detachment about 40 strong, and a ballista detachment. The mounted men were despatch riders, escorts, and prisoner guards rather than cavalry in the true sense. The *ballista* was a light catapult that fired bolts over a distance and provided what we now call fire support when attacking an enemy position. It was powered by twisted rope and carried in a cart.

The Roman army also contained a large number of *auxiliary* cohorts and cavalry units, recruited from the non-Roman peoples of the Roman Empire for their particular skills. For example, Cretan archers and slingers were recruited from the Balearic Islands. Other men were recruited among strong swimmers from Batavia, present-day Holland.

By now, the legions had reached Cassivelaunus's stronghold, a hill fort near present-day Wheathampstead in Hertfordshire, and they stormed the fort from two directions. This was too much for Cassivelaunus, who asked for peace terms. He had to hand over hostages, agree to pay an annual tribute to the Roman government, and promise not to harass other British tribes who were on good terms with Rome. Satisfied with subduing the Britons, Caesar marched his troops back to the coast and embarked for the continent.

The Roman Invasion, AD 43

It was 97 years after Caesar's second raid that the Roman army returned to Britain. By this time, the middle of the first century AD, a number of reasons existed for wanting to add Britain to the Roman Empire. These included:

✔ The British Isles carried potential wealth, including valuable deposits of tin, copper, and lead.

✔ The southeastern corner of the island, closest to the continent, had become the powerful kingdom of the Cantiaci – and a powerful kingdom so close to the empire wasn't a threat to ignore.

✔ Malcontents from the Empire found refuge in Britain and used it as a base for their own activities.

✔ The glory of the Emperor.

Enough was enough, the Romans decided to act.

Harvesting a landing

A general named Aulus Plautius was tasked with the invasion of AD 43. His invasion force numbered four legions with 25,000 men, plus an equal number serving in auxiliary units. They crossed the Channel in three divisions, landing at Richborough, Dover, and Lympne. The Britons did not oppose the landing, because while they had anticipated the Romans' arrival and actually assembled to meet them, the invasion was so long delayed that the Britons dispersed to bring in the harvest. When the Romans did eventually land, the British leaders, two princes named Tugodumnus and Caratacus, sons of the late King Cunobelinus (Shakespeare's Cymbeline), had to get everyone together again.

The three Roman divisions joined together and marched west. They found the Britons drawn up in strength on the far bank of the river Medway, close to the site of modern Rochester, in Kent. During the night, Plautius sent his Batavian swimmers (see sidebar 'The Roman army', earlier in this chapter) across the river, downstream of the enemy. At dawn, the startled Britons streamed out of their camp to attack, led by their chariots. A hail of javelins and arrows met them, aimed not at the men but at their horses. The attack broke down in such confusion that the campaign's Roman historian commented, 'not even the charioteers could save themselves'. For the rest of the day the Britons contented themselves with containing the bridgehead. That night, the 2nd Legion under the command of Flavius Vespasian (a future Emperor) crossed the river upstream, using boats and locally built rafts. When the bridgehead was secure, the legionary engineers constructed a bridge. By dawn, two legions and some auxiliary units were in the bridgehead and had formed a line of battle facing downstream, while a third was crossing the bridge, and the fourth was marching towards it. Realising that the Romans had tricked them, the Britons launched a furious attack. For a while the issue hung in the balance, but the Batavians in their rear unsettled the Britons and finally they broke. The battle had offered the Britons their best chance of defeating the invaders and that opportunity was never repeated. In addition, Tugodumnus sustained mortal wounds.

Bring on the elephants!

The Romans established a camp and in due course the Emperor Claudius joined them, bringing with him part of the 8th Legion as reinforcements and a personal escort provided by his own bodyguard, the Praetorian Guard. If all this did not impress the Britons, they must have marvelled at the elephants the emperor brought with him, probably the first ever to set foot on British soil. Claudius remained in Britain for just 16 days. Having inspected his new domain and shown its inhabitants who would be running things from then on, he departed, and the process of conquest resumed.

The legions fanned out to the west and north. Vespasian's 2nd Legion stormed Maiden Castle near Dorchester, and in Essex other Roman troops stormed Camulodunum (Colchester). Like a rising tide, the area under Roman rule spread steadily. By AD 49 it extended as far north as Lincoln and Chester.

Caratacus, the first British hero

Caratacus (King Cunobelinus's son) survived the defeat on the Medway and the subsequent fighting north of the Thames, but the Romans drove him from his lands. We know very little about him save that he was an implacable enemy of Rome and possessed a charismatic personality, attracting followers and enabling him to wage a sustained guerrilla war for years, mainly from the mountains of Wales. Finally, in AD 50, he made the mistake of fighting a pitched battle against the Romans rather than sticking to his successful guerrilla tactics. The site of this is uncertain, but it may have taken place somewhere on the Welsh border in Shropshire.

The Romans, now under the command of Ostorius Scapula, won a decisive victory, forcing Caratacus to seek protection with Queen Cartimandua of the Brigantes, the large tribe inhabiting most of northern England. The presence of Caratacus, however, meant big trouble with the Romans that Cartimandua just didn't need, and she handed him over. He and his family went to Rome in chains, but his dignity and courage in adversity won sincere respect. The Emperor Claudius granted Caratacus his life and freedom, although he had to spend the rest of his days in Rome. Tales of his deeds live on in Wales, as does the Welsh version of his name, Caradoc.

Setting London Ablaze: The Boudiccan Rebellion

The Druids were still active throughout Britain and were a constant source of trouble (see the earlier section 'Caesar Seizes an Opportunity' for why they were so troublesome). Their power base was the island of Anglesey, off the coast of North Wales, and in AD 61 the Governor of Britain, Suetonius Paulinus, decided to eliminate them once and for all. He marched across North Wales with the 14th and 20th Legions and auxiliary units. Lining the shore of the island was a dense armed mass, including black-robed women with dishevelled hair and flaming torches, screaming their heads off while the Druids raised their hands to heaven and called down all manner of unpleasant curses. They rained missiles on the legionaries, who found the prospect of fighting women unsettling. The centurions urged them on, shields locked, and the legions waded ashore.

The Britons put up frenzied resistance but were no match for disciplined infantry. The Romans showed no mercy to the Druids or their womenfolk. They hacked down the island's sacred groves of trees and overturned the sacrificial altars. This broke the power of the Druids for good – but at the very moment of victory a mud-splattered messenger arrived with dreadful news. The Iceni tribe of East Anglia had risen in revolt. They were killing every Roman they found and burning every Roman settlement they came across. Unless Suetonius acted quickly, the rebellion would spread to the rest of Britain. The legions promptly recrossed the Straits and set out for East Anglia.

Boudicca led the Iceni revolt. Her problems began when her husband, the king of the Iceni, died; the Romans flogged her for protesting at their high-handed methods of government. To ram home the message that she was no longer in charge, they also raped her daughters and deprived local chiefs of their hereditary lands. Boudicca, a tall woman of fierce expression and hair that flowed to her waist, became the immediate focus of a violent rebellion.

The rebels (Boudicca's Iceni tribe and the neighbouring Trinovantes) marched south towards the prosperous settlement of Colchester, which was virtually defenceless. A 2000-strong detachment from the 9th Legion, based at Lincoln, tried to deal with the situation, but the Iceni ambushed them and wiped them out. The rebels burned Colchester to the ground and slaughtered its inhabitants. The newly established port and business centre, London, suffered the same fate, as did the smaller settlement of Verulamium (St Albans). It began to look as though Boudicca was unstoppable.

In the meantime, Suetonius had been marching rapidly south along the line of the present A5 trunk road. He picked up such reinforcements as he could along the way and was kept informed as to Boudicca's whereabouts and movements. By now, she was moving northwest and the two armies met somewhere in the Midlands. Just where, no one is quite sure, although the Roman historian Tacitus tells us that Suetonius chose a position in a defile with a wood behind him. *Defile* could mean the space between two rivers or two hills, but it was probably the former as this would prevent Boudicca's much larger army working round the Roman flanks.

When the Britons swarmed to the attack, the legions adopted wedge formations, compressing the Britons so tightly that their superior numbers were wasted and many were unable to use their weapons. A fearful slaughter ensued. One source claims that as many as 80,000 Britons were killed, but this is almost certainly a wild exaggeration. Roman losses included 400 killed and twice that number wounded. Rather than suffer further humiliation or capture, Boudicca and her daughters took poison. The Romans had decisively crushed the rebellion, but the British had their first heroine and the Romans had learned a painful lesson.

Policing Roman Britain

The Romans had come to stay. They covered Britain with a network of paved roads that ran straight for mile after mile, up hill and down dale. Most can be traced to this day and some form the foundation of modern trunk roads. The Romans dotted the countryside with small forts and built great legionary fortresses such as Lincoln, Caerleon, Chester, and York that are still important towns and cities. Indeed, any modern place name that includes the element *-chester, -caster,* or *-cester* indicates the site of a Roman camp or fortification. This network helped to keep the Britons peaceful.

It wasn't all plain sailing for the Romans; in total, the conquest of Britain took 41 years:

✔ In AD 74–77 Petilius Cerealis, one of Emperor Vespasian's ablest generals, conquered the troublesome Silures in South Wales and the Brigantes in northern England.

✔ In AD 77 Gnaeus Julius Agricola succeeded Cerealis and during a series of campaigns, some of which the Roman fleet supported, advanced north into Scotland (then known as Caledonia). The decisive battle was in AD 83 at Mons Graupius, probably some miles northwest of Aberdeen, which resulted in a shattering defeat for an alliance of Caledonian tribes.

The most enduring reminder of the Roman presence in Britain is Hadrian's Wall, stretching coast to coast for 73 miles from Bowness-on-Solway to Wallsend-on-Tyne. Work on the wall commenced under Emperor Hadrian in AD 122. Its construction took advantage of every cliff, crag, and steep hill on its course, but where necessary a ditch fronted it. A milecastle, providing

The mystery of Legio IX Hispana

In AD 117 the 9th Legion marched north from its base at York to deal with a tribal uprising in Caledonia. After that date it vanishes altogether from the Roman army's records. Some 1,800 years later, archaeologists digging at the Roman city of Silchester in Berkshire discovered its Eagle, with its wings stripped off. Was the legion massacred somewhere in Scotland? And, if so, how was its Eagle saved and carried into southern England? If the Legion was destroyed, why have later tiles bearing its stamp turned up in Nijmegen? And what about later funerary altars erected in memory of members of the Legion? Do these fragments prove its continued existence after AD 117?

Rosemary Sutcliff provides one answer in her fiction book *The Eagle of the Ninth*. In her story the Legion has become badly disciplined and is massacred. On learning that its Eagle is now housed in a barbarian temple, the hero sets out to recover it, which he succeeds in doing after many adventures.

What is certain is that the 6th Legion was shipped over from the continent to garrison York. This happened shortly after the 9th marched north and suggests that some sort of disaster occurred for the 6th to be drafted in. Some of the 9th may have survived whatever took place, as someone took steps to preserve the Eagle – the very symbol of the Legion's honour – in its final resting place in Silchester. Alternatives to massacre are mutiny provoked by bad leadership and flight in the face of the enemy. The punishment for mutiny and cowardice was decimation of the Legion, disbandment, dispersion, removal from the army's list, and withdrawal of the Eagle. In this case the stripping of the Eagle's wings looks like an intentional slight, similar to the ceremonial breaking of a disgraced officer's sword.

If this happened, the 9th's survivors were dispersed to other units. Those sent to Nijmegen, probably from the Legion's rear party in York, may have defiantly continued to use the tile stamp to emphasise their own innocence in the affair. That's the best solution I can come up with, and if you can think of a better one I'd like to hear it!

accommodation for 30 men, was situated every Roman mile along the wall's length, and equally spaced between the milecastles were two turrets. These posts provided a complete signals system. Large fortified camps such as Housesteads and Chesters were later established close behind the wall. The wall was originally intended as a police and customs line, but it was capable of acting as a springboard for vigorous counter-offensives to the north. It was overwhelmed by the northern tribes in AD 197, 296, and 367, and extensive repairs were required after each re-occupation. The Wall was finally abandoned when the Romans left Britain but its most dramatic sections, including much of the fort at Housesteads, still exist.

By advancing further into Scotland, the Romans established a shorter frontier than Hadrian's Wall (requiring fewer troops to man it) between the Firths of Clyde and Forth. They started this in AD 139, and also constructed a comparable but less durable defence line known as the Antonine Wall. The area between the two walls was known as the province of Valentia. The problem was that not only were the inhabitants far from friendly, the uplands produced less revenue than required to administer the province, and the garrison of the new wall was difficult to supply. In AD 158 Hadrian's Wall became the frontier again, and the Antonine Wall was abandoned.

The Legions Depart

Following the disappearance of the 9th Legion (see the sidebar, 'The mystery of Legio IX Hispana') the permanent garrison of Britain was set at three legions at Caerleon, York, and Chester, plus a large number of auxiliary units, making it the largest in the Roman Empire. The only other province to boast three legions was Judea, a noted trouble spot. We can be sure that if Britain had not paid its way, the Romans would have abandoned it. In fact, the military governorship of the province was regarded as one of the Roman army's plum jobs.

As the generations passed and the benefits of living within the empire became apparent, the Roman army was seen less as an army of occupation, and simply as an army. Eventually, Britons were permitted to enlist, and some British auxiliary units went to serve in other parts of the Empire.

Latterly, the Roman Empire outgrew its ability to defend itself, as empires do. In Britain, pressure from sea-borne raiders from across the North Sea added to pressure from the Caledonian tribes (there's more on those pesky North Sea raiders in Chapter 3). An officer entitled the Count of Saxon Shore became responsible for the defence of the east coast and built a chain of forts and signal stations for the purpose (a fine example of a Roman coastal fort exists at Portchester on the south coast, incorporating a medieval castle that was subsequently built within the defences).

Towards the end of the Roman period, mobility to counter raiders became important, and cavalry replaced infantry as the most important part of the Roman army.

In the end barbarian pressure on the empire's European frontiers became too much to withstand. In AD 407, Emperor Constantine III began withdrawing troops from Britain. Within a couple of years, the last of them had gone and Roman Britain was no more.

Chapter 3

Arthur, Alfred, and Aethelstan: The Dark Ages

. . . .

In This Chapter

▶ The English invasions: 450–500

▶ The battles of King Arthur: 516–537

▶ The emergence of England: 716–796

▶ The Viking wars: c800–1035

. . . .

*T*he six centuries following the departure of the Roman legions (see Chapter 2) witnessed the virtual extinction of Roman culture in the British Isles, which successive waves of invaders swamped. This era – known as the Dark Ages – saw little military knowledge gained in Britain, and much that had been learned from the Romans was lost.

Britons during the Dark Ages were just one tribe fighting to control the islands – Saxons, Angles, and Jutes; Picts and Caledonians; and Irish armies all fought to control the British mainland. The Dark Ages was the era in which tribal groupings formed the small kingdoms that later evolved into the kingdoms of England (populated by Saxons), Scotland (the artists formerly known as the Picts and Caledonians), Ireland, and Wales (the last stronghold of the Britons, who became known to the Saxons as the Welsh).

British armies in the Dark Ages (along with their enemies) consisted of local kings, their retainers and family, and men of military age, armed according to their status. Not everything stood still though – chariots were no longer used, and generally horses were used to convey men to the battlefield rather than as cavalry mounts.

(Not) Welcoming New Arrivals: Angles, Saxons, and Jutes

When the Romans left at the start of the fifth century AD, the problems facing the *Romano-Britons* (Britons living in the Roman way after the legions left) were numerous:

- ✔ They lacked a central authority with the ability to raise taxes to use to establish a standing army.
- ✔ They did not agree on the best way to govern themselves.
- ✔ They were unable to defend themselves, after centuries of soft living under Roman protection.

Meanwhile, Saxons continued to raid at will (they had started back in Chapter 2!) and were joined by three more groups, the Angles from north-western Europe, the Jutes from the Jutland peninsula, and the Picts from the north. The Romano-Britons had to do something very quickly.

Among those who had risen to the top of the Romano-British pile was an influential leader named Vortigern. In about AD 450 he decided to invite two Saxon chiefs, Hengist and Horsa, to provide protection against the raiders in exchange for permission to settle in Kent. This was rather like asking professional criminals to look after the family silver. On arrival in Kent, Hengist and Horsa promptly reached the conclusion that life in Britain was good and that Britain was there for the taking. They invited large numbers of their chums to join them and turned on their hosts. But they encountered some resistance and in AD 455 the Romano-Britons killed Horsa at the Battle of Aylesford, on the river Medway.

Such isolated successes were too few to hold back the Saxon flood sweeping across southeastern England. The raiders eagerly stripped Romano-British towns of their riches and burned them down. Anyone unwilling to submit they killed or drove off their land, while the inhabitants of towns and villages took refuge in the ancient hill forts (see Chapter 2) and made them defensible again. As farmers, the Saxons were not interested in towns save as a source of plunder. Consequently, the towns crumbled to ruins and even when quieter times returned, many centuries passed before they recovered anything like their original population.

By the end of the century, the Saxons controlled all of southeastern England. They already possessed Kent and their later acquisitions provided the names for future counties: Essex (the East Saxons); Middlesex (the Middle Saxons); and Sussex (the South Saxons). Add to this Surrey and Hampshire, the latter forming the basis of the powerful West Saxon kingdom of Wessex, and you can see how tight was the Saxon hold on the southeast of the island.

Meanwhile, the Jutes had established themselves on the Isle of Wight and the Angles had taken over in what became Norfolk and Suffolk (respectively the North and South Folk).

Riding to the Rescue: King Arthur

With the Saxons and their chums on the up (see the preceding section), the future looked wretched for the Romano-Britons. Few suspected that they were about to produce a leader of legendary fame.

Yet little doubt exists that a Romano-British leader of real military ability did live at about this time. In the early part of the ninth century a monk named Nennius compiled a book called *Historia Britonum*. He drew on many earlier sources from all over England, Wales, and Ireland. He tells us that a certain Arthur became the Britons' *dux bellorum* (war leader) and that he was the victor in 12 major battles against the Saxons; significantly, Nennius does not refer to Arthur as 'king'. Of Arthur's victories, Mount Badon, fought in AD 517 near Badbury in Wiltshire, is the best known and seems to have halted the Saxon advance for the better part of a generation.

In all probability Arthur was a charismatic leader who managed to persuade other leaders from various parts of Britain that their only hope of survival lay in cooperation. He probably created an alliance of equals, hence the reference to the Round Table that has filtered down the years. For an alliance between leaders in different parts of Britain, it made sense to form a strategic mounted reserve to deploy from one threatened area to another, particularly as the sites of Nennius's 12 battles range across a wide area, including one fought in Scotland. This may be the original version of King Arthur's knights. Nothing is certain, however, not even the name Arthur, for our sources rely on the misty realm of Welsh and Cornish folk memory.

Following Arthur's death in about AD 534 (at the hands of his blood relative, Mordred, according to legend), the Saxons renewed their inexorable advance across Britain. The Romano-Britons were forced steadily west until all they possessed were Cornwall, Wales, Cumbria, and Strathclyde. Small wonder that they spoke wistfully of Good King Arthur's golden days and promised each other that one day he would return.

Carving Up Saxon England

One reason the Saxon invaders did not press on into the western extremities of the mainland was that the land was less fertile in these regions. Another was that they had established kingdoms of their own in the conquered territory and were too busy squabbling among themselves. There were seven such kingdoms, known as the *Heptarchy:* Kent, Sussex, Wessex, Essex, East Anglia, Mercia, and Northumbria. Figure 3-1 shows their whereabouts.

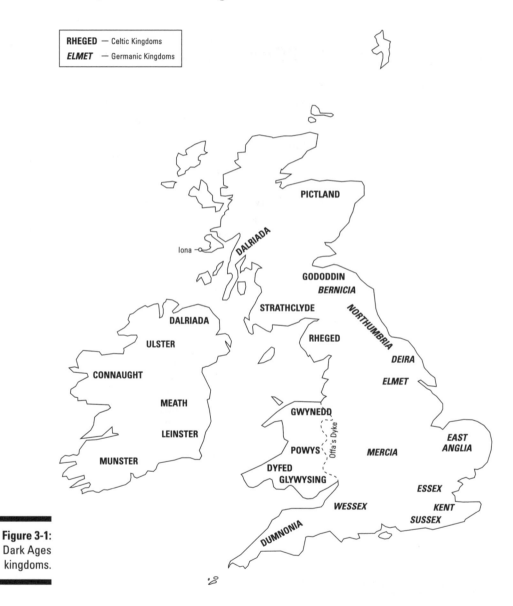

RHEGED — Celtic Kingdoms	
ELMET — Germanic Kingdoms	

PICTLAND

DALRIADA

Iona

GODODDIN
BERNICIA

STRATHCLYDE

NORTHUMBRIA

DALRIADA

RHEGED

ULSTER

DEIRA

CONNAUGHT

ELMET

MEATH

GWYNEDD

LEINSTER

POWYS

Offa's Dyke

MERCIA

EAST ANGLIA

DYFED

MUNSTER

GLYWYSING

ESSEX

WESSEX

KENT

SUSSEX

DUMNONIA

Figure 3-1:
Dark Ages
kingdoms.

The troubled seventh century saw the following military action take place as part of the on-going politicking:

606 Aethelfrith of Northumbria defeats a Scottish invasion.

615 Aethelfrith defeats the Britons at the Battle of Chester, separating the Britons in north Wales from their kinsmen in Cumbria.

617 Redwald of East Anglia defeats Aethelfrith of Northumbria. Edwin becomes the first Christian king of Northumbria. He defeats the Britons of North Wales.

633 An alliance consisting of the British king Cadwallon and Penda, the Saxon king of Mercia, defeats and kills Edwin at the Battle of Hatfield Chase.

633 Oswald, Edwin's successor, defeats and kills Cadwallon at the Battle of Rowley Water, driving the Britons right out of northwest England.

641 Penda defeats Oswald at the Battle of Maserfeld. He has Oswald tied to a tree and shot full of arrows. The site becomes the town of Oswestry.

654 Oswy, Oswald's younger brother, defeats and kills Penda at the Battle of Winwaed.

685 Oswy's successor, Ecgfrith, invades Scotland but is defeated and killed at the Battle of Dunnichen Moss. This battle ensured the independence of Scotland from the Saxons.

Dark Ages battles were very much rough-and-tumble infantry affairs with little or no tactical finesse. A commander was considered to have real ability if he occupied the high ground and secured both his flanks, both of which would be second nature to a modern commander.

An Unbeatable Offa

Militarily speaking, the eighth century was Mercia's property. Mercia's central position (see Figure 3-1) gave it what later strategists call *interior lines* (the ability to transfer troops from one frontier to another without leaving their own soil). This enabled the Mercian kings to throw their weight about in no uncertain manner.

Aethelbald of Mercia successfully invaded Wessex in 733 and Northumbria in 744. His cousin Offa won a violent internal struggle for the Mercian throne and, in a comparatively short reign ending in 769, made his mark not only on British but also on European history, being hailed as 'brother' by the Emperor Charlemagne and 'King of the English' by the Pope. He campaigned against everyone until of the old heptarchy only Wessex remained outside his direct rule.

Offa is best remembered for leaving his mark on the landscape in a way that no one since the Romans had done (see Chapter 2). His principal enemies were the Britons in Wales, who frequently raided across the border. To stop this Offa mobilised his subjects and set them to building a huge ditch and bank, topped by a fence, stretching all the way along the frontier from the Severn estuary to that of the Dee (roughly along the line of the modern border between England and Wales). Watchtowers equipped with beacons provided warning of an impending raid and the local communities mobilised to meet it. Most raids were for cattle, and even successful raiders were unable to drive them over the ditch. This ditch became known as Offa's Dyke and much of it remains visible to this day.

Shipping in the Viking Menace

Things had been looking rosy for the Saxons – they'd ousted the Britons from what was to become England (and the Saxons gradually became known as the English, too) and had carved the country up into several kingdoms. But that was not to last – in 789 the first Viking raid on England took place on the coast of Dorset. In 793 Vikings sacked the monastery on Lindisfarne, an island off the Northumbrian coast. The following year they raided the Scottish coast and the year after it was the turn of Ireland. Soon, raids were coming in thick and fast all round the coast of Britain, and the Vikings were establishing themselves on the Scottish islands. In 851 they sacked London and Canterbury, although on this occasion the raiders were caught and defeated. The year after marked the first Viking settlements in England.

Viking was originally a Norse word describing a journey with lots of fighting, rape, and pillage along the way, although now it has become synonymous with those who took part in these activities. The Vikings came from all over Scandinavia. They were fine seamen and navigators who made voyages to Iceland, Greenland, and even to the North American coast. They also travelled deep into Russia along its great rivers. They made wonderfully intricate carvings and fine wooden buildings. But mostly we remember the Vikings as ferocious raiders and formidable warriors who employed shock and terror as psychological weapons.

In addition to the more usual weapons of sword and spear, the Vikings brought the terrible one- or two-handed fighting axe to the battlefields of Britain. As if that was not enough, they held a particular type of warrior, the *berserker*, in high esteem. Whether it was the joy of battle or simple blood lust, the berserker fought like a madman, hacking and killing regardless of his own wounds, until he either dropped dead or no one was left to kill. People avoided berserkers on the rampage if at all possible, even if they did add a new word to everyone's English dictionary.

One element making the Vikings so dangerous was an understanding of strategic principles that had not been seen in Britain since Roman times. For example, when attacking a specific kingdom in force, they sometimes did so from different directions, forcing the defenders to split their resources.

Some Vikings settled in territory they had overrun, others enjoyed the annual cycle of raiding. Such was their energy that even when they were defeated they kept coming back again and again. By 866 the Vikings, or Danes as they had become commonly known, had taken York and within eight years they had been able to conquer the kingdoms of Northumbria, Mercia, and East Anglia. Everywhere north of Watling Street, running from London to Shrewsbury, was now known as the *Danelaw,* after the new owners.

In recent years some historians have attempted to rehabilitate the grizzly reputation of the Vikings by describing them as economic tourists seeking investment opportunities. It's a point of view, but names like Eric Bloodaxe and Sven the Skullsplitter give us more than a hint about their business methods.

The Saxons Fight Back: Alfred and Aethelstan

The Vikings' unfortunate victims came to believe that no one could get rid of them and to begin with, they were right. But in 871 a warrior named Alfred and his brother, Aethelred, King of Wessex, decisively defeated a Danish invasion at the Battle of Ashdown, in Berkshire. Aethelred died shortly after and Alfred succeeded to the crown. He was well aware that the Danes were determined to destroy Wessex and in 878 the Danes were back in force under their king, Guthrum.

Most modern Britons remember Alfred as the king who burned his hostess's cakes. Yet he was the only English king ever to have been called 'the Great'. He was a scholar and a law giver, a good administrator, an astute soldier, and the man who gave England a navy capable of tackling the Danes at sea. Maybe we shouldn't be surprised that he never devoted much time to cookery!

After Ashdown, things went very badly for Alfred. The Danes forced him into hiding (where he burned the cakes), but he ran an effective guerrilla campaign gathering his strength all the time, and then fell on the Danes at Edington (in Wiltshire), inflicting so convincing a defeat that Guthrum asked for terms and promised to leave Wessex alone. Alfred didn't trust the Danes and continued to build up his navy. He also established an early warning system based on beacons and set up local militias known as the *fyrd* that could be assembled quickly in an emergency. In 886, following renewed Danish raids, Alfred drove the Danes out of London and gained territory north of the Thames.

In 893 the Danes raided again, this time hoping to split Alfred's forces with a seaborne landing on the south coast and an invasion from the north. The Saxons quickly blockaded the first landing, although some of the Danes managed to escape. Alfred and his son Edward the Elder defeated both invasion forces in fighting that ranged across southern and western England.

Their grand plan may have been in tatters, but the Danes were unwilling to give up. In 895 they sailed up the river Lea, a tributary of the Thames east of London, in large numbers. Alfred responded by building two forts at the mouth of the river, which he blocked with a heavy boom. Trapped, the Danes had to abandon their ships and scuttle back to the Danelaw on foot.

In Alfred's reign, the Saxons probably adopted some of the Danes' methods of warfare, including fighting with axes from behind interlocked shields.

Alfred died in 899, but Edward, his son and successor, continued his work. In 903, having repulsed a fresh Danish raid, Edward advanced deep into the Danelaw itself, inflicting one defeat after another. For years an almost permanent state of war existed, with the Saxons steadily gaining the upper hand.

Edward's son Aethelstan did even better than his father. He recovered Mercia, threw the Danes out of York (their principal stronghold in the north), reconquered Northumbria, and campaigned successfully in Scotland and Wales, receiving the homage of their rulers. In 937 the resentful King Constantine III of Scotland attempted to halt Aethelstan's runaway progress, but his army took a fearful hiding at the Battle of Brunanburgh (see the following section).

The Battle of Brunanburgh, 937

Aethelstan's English (as the Saxons were now becoming known) army fought the Battle of Brunanburgh against Constantine III of Scotland's allied army of Welsh, Norse/Irish, Danes, and Scots. The precise site of the Battle of Brunanburgh remains the subject of scholarly argument, but Bromborough on the Wirral shore of the Mersey (in northwest England) is a strong candidate.

A Viking named Olaf Guthfrithson commanded Constantine III's army, said to be 18,000 men strong (massive for this time – see the sidebar 'Sizing up a Dark Ages army'). Aethelstan waited until he had assembled an army of comparable size, including a mounted element, before marching to meet the alliance. For this period, these are very large armies indeed and represent maximum effort on the part of those involved.

Sizing up a Dark Ages army

When reading contemporary accounts of battles during the Dark Ages, we should regard with a degree of suspicion statistics relating to the size of armies and casualties suffered and inflicted. The scribes who wrote these accounts simply recorded what they had been told, and if the king who was the scribe's boss inflated the size of his own army, readers would realise what an important fellow he was. Likewise, if he inflated the size of the enemy he had just beaten, this told people what a grand general he was. Reducing the scale of his casualties and raising those of the enemy produced a similar result. It was wonderful public relations . . . but not the truth.

Knocking off a nought or even two off any numbers of warriors may bring us closer to reality. Large armies could not be maintained in the field for long because they could not be fed; if a supply system existed at all, it was unable to keep pace with demand. And as for living off the land, the small, scattered population of Britain was producing just sufficient food for itself, with perhaps a small surplus. Commanders therefore raised armies just large enough for the job in hand, and then disbanded them when the task was over.

The English held a strong position from which they beat off repeated assaults. Then, at a critical moment, Aethelstan launched a counter-attack, shattering Guthfrithson's army and putting it to flight. A panic-stricken rout followed as the English mounted companies inflicted terrible slaughter during a prolonged pursuit. Among those killed by the English were five kings, seven earls, and Constantine's son. We don't know the number of English casualties, but it was trivial by comparison. The alliance collapsed at once and those who survived the battle made their way home as best they could. Constantine decided that he had had enough of politics and vanished into a monastery.

Brunanburgh is one of the most important battles in English history. After Aethelstan's victory here, England not only became a recognisable political entity for the first time but also the dominant power in the British Isles. Aethelstan's legacy was 60 years of more or less uninterrupted peace in which the country prospered and learning and the arts began to flourish.

Turning Back the Tide: Ethelred and Canute

In 978 a 10-year-old boy, Ethelred, ascended the English throne. Ethelred was unlucky in inheriting the crown so young and at a time when the Vikings had resumed raiding. In 991 the Danes narrowly won a battle at Maldon in Essex. Worried stiff, Ethelred paid them to go away. It was an act of incredible stupidity, and his subjects contemptuously described the payment as *Danegeld*. Every year the Danes came back, caused trouble, and demanded more Danegeld – and every year the price went up.

In 1002 Ethelred really flipped. He had several thousand Danes of both sexes and all ages massacred at Oxford in the belief that it would give the rest something to think about. It did. Svein Forkbeard, King of Denmark, launched a series of reprisal raids, chopping up the Archbishop of Canterbury in the process. Ethelred paid him an extortionate amount of Danegeld and he went away, though not for very long. In 1013 Svein returned, demanding the English throne itself. The Danes of the Danelaw (see the section 'Shipping in the Viking Menace' earlier in this chapter) joined him and he would probably have gained the throne had he not died the following year.

Ethelred, who had taken to his heels, made a half-hearted attempt at a comeback but died in 1016. Ethelred and Svein's sons, Edmund Ironside and Canute respectively, continued the struggle. Edmund defeated Canute on a number of occasions, but Canute then defeated him at Ashingdon, also in 1016. The two met and reached an agreement whereby Canute ruled the north of the country while Edmund ruled the south. Edmund's death shortly after left a lingering suspicion that Canute had murdered him.

Canute was accepted as King of England (by his marriage to Ethelred's former wife), and then removed every possible rival claimant to the throne by murdering them, making it quite clear that he was not a man to cross in any way. The Welsh and Scots submitted to him and he expanded his Scandinavian holdings to include Norway and parts of Sweden. Canute proved to be a good, strong king who gave England 20 years of peace and prosperity. On his death in 1035 arguments between Canute's sons from his two marriages, both of whom ruled briefly before dying, blurred the succession for a while. In 1042 the throne passed to Edward the Confessor, but waiting in the wings were the ruthless and ambitious family of Wessex aristocrats, the House of Godwin. When Edward died, very big trouble awaited, and you can read all about that in Chapter 4.

Modern Britons remember Canute for inventing the float-away throne. The story goes that some of his courtiers were real creeps who told him he was so powerful he could turn back the tide if he wanted. He dragged them down to the shore and of course the tide disobeyed him and came in as usual. The courtiers then had to explain themselves, which can't have been easy. There may just be an element of truth in the story, because what it says is that he didn't suffer fools gladly.

Chapter 4

The Hard Knight's Day: The Norman Conquest and Medieval Period

*T*he medieval period (broadly the eleventh to fifteenth centuries) saw plenty of military action both in Britain and involving British (mostly English) armies abroad. At this time, no unified country of Britain existed – the English, Scots, Welsh, and Irish looked after their own affairs and squabbled among themselves as well as with each other.

The year 1066 marked a turning point in the fortunes of the British Isles. Most modern Britons know that in that year William, Duke of Normandy, won a battle near Hastings and had himself crowned King of England. This momentous date is generally considered to introduce the medieval period to Britain, and for most of this period the armoured knight and the castle dominated warfare. But with the introduction of the longbow (and later gunpowder) the influence of the knights began to decline sharply by the fifteenth century.

The battles detailed in this chapter were fought by armies with the following troop types:

✔ **Heavy cavalry**: that's knights to you and me. In this period, heavy cavalry was the tank of the battlefield; they could charge through anything and outfight anyone . . . well almost (read on for details!). Knights charged around wearing full chainmail then plate armour (plates of metal), with brightly decorated shields and horse trapping (incorporating heraldic devices).

✔ **Spearmen:** the bulk of most armies at this time consisted of spearmen, with some body armour and shields. The Scots went one better and increased the length of their spears to around 3 or 4 metres (known as *pikes*); these were good for keeping heavy cavalry at bay.

✔ **Archers:** English and Welsh armies were fond of archers. Bows could shoot an arrow about 185 metres (200 yards) at this time. Some archers were armed with crossbows, which shot powerful short *bolts* with great accuracy.

1066: The Disputed Throne

When the English king Edward the Confessor died on 5 January 1066, no fixed procedures were in place to decide who should succeed him on the throne.

The *Witan* (a supreme council of wise men) had to make the decision, and they had four candidates to choose from:

✔ **Edgar the Aetheling** (the closest blood claimant to Edward): A sickly and unpromising fourteen-year-old.

✔ **Harold Godwinson** (the most powerful noble in England, a good soldier and a gifted politician): He claimed that Edward had named him his successor on his deathbed, although no witnesses were there.

✔ **William** (Duke of Normandy, over the sea in France): He claimed that the pro-Norman Edward had named him as his successor.

✔ **Harald Hardrada** (King of Norway): No one took his claim seriously – although he was a powerful warrior king.

The Witan chose Harold Godwinson, who promptly had himself crowned in Westminster Abbey.

Normally, the Archbishop of Canterbury conducted the ceremony of crowning a new king, but as the Pope had not approved Harold's appointment, the Archbishop of York placed the crown on his head.

Big trouble was now inevitable. William, with the Pope's blessing, now began assembling a large army and building an invasion fleet with which to claim what he believed to be his rightful inheritance. Harald Hardrada did likewise.

The Battle of Stamford Bridge, 25 September 1066

Harald Hardrada reached England first with an army of over 8000 Norwegians and English supporters of the treacherous Tostig, Harold of England's estranged brother. Harold marched north from London with his bodyguard of well-armed professional soldiers, known as *huscarls*, and raised the *fyrd* (an armed local militia, less powerful than the huscarls) along the way, until he was in command of an army of approximately 7000 men.

At this time the English and Norwegians didn't make use of heavy cavalry (knights); both armies fought almost exclusively on foot, with massive two-handed axes and spears, and one-handed swords.

The invaders had already defeated an English force under the northern earls Edwin and Morcar and were confidently lounging about in their camp at Stamford Bridge, on the river Derwent, while the surrender of the city of York was negotiated. The sudden approach of Harold's army on 25 September took them completely by surprise. A group of Norwegians intending to delay the English approach to the bridge was wiped out, but on the bridge itself a single Norwegian, a giant of a man, barred the passage to all comers until he was killed. The English then swarmed across and Harold deployed them in three groups plus a reserve. The Norwegians seem to have been very slow sorting themselves out.

Both sides fought in a similar manner, forming a shield wall in which shields were locked together while the deadly two-handed war axes, spears, and swords did their work. If a shield wall was broken, the resulting slaughter made defeat inevitable. And that's precisely what happened at Stamford Bridge.

The Norwegian shield wall broke under English pressure, and the Norwegian army started to collapse. The Norwegians' ship guard came panting up, hoping to retrieve the day, but were cut to pieces in their turn. During the bloody fighting, Harald Hardrada and Tostig were both killed, along with so many of their men that while their invasion fleet had numbered 300 ships, only 24 were needed to transport the survivors away.

Harold's troops had little rest after the battle against Harald Hardrada, and his army took plenty of casualties in the hard fighting of the shield wall (see the preceding section). Word quickly arrived that William's army had landed at Pevensey, on the south coast, on 28 September. Harold reacted quickly. Such was the speed of his march south that it suggests that part, at least, of his army was mounted. On reaching London he would have been well advised to wait until he had received reinforcements before proceeding, but the news was that the Normans were harrying his people in Kent and Sussex and, unwisely, he decided he must go to their assistance immediately. He marched southeast and near Hastings found a good defensive position along a ridge. Here he decided to give battle behind the traditional English shield wall.

The Battle of Hastings, 14 October 1066

On the morning of 14 October the English army consisted of 2000 huscarls and some 5500 fyrd, a total of 7500 infantry. Opposite them was the Norman army, which included 2000 mounted knights and 5000 infantry. Even when their strength is added together, the total of the two armies amounts to no more than the size of a crowd at a lower-division football match on a Saturday afternoon, yet on this day they fought a battle that seemed to be about possession of a kingdom forming only part of a small island, but is now acknowledged to have been one of the most decisive in world history.

For the Normans, the mounted, armoured knight was their battle winner; for the English, the key weapon was the terrible two-handed axe that would cleave a horse's neck with ease or smash its way through an enemy's helmet or chainmail armour. Hastings saw the two differing methods clash, but which prevailed – the horseman or the axeman?

The first Norman attacks were thrown back with serious losses. The Breton troops forming William's left wing broke, but rallied and turned on a portion of the English army that had rashly pursued them, destroying it. At about this time a report that William had been killed brought the Norman army to the verge of disintegration. Only by removing his helmet and galloping along the line was William able to restore order. A series of mounted attacks against the shield wall met incredibly stubborn resistance and failed with mounting losses. Then, a feigned retreat drew out another portion of the English army, which was also destroyed. Yet, despite the thinning of its ranks, the shield wall held.

William tried one last, desperate measure, alternating periods of high-angle fire by his archers with further mounted attacks. Today, we would call this a combination of firepower and shock action. It worked.

After eight hours of savage fighting the shield wall had become so thin that the Norman horsemen were able to batter their way through by sheer weight of numbers. Harold and his brothers Leofwine and Gyrth were killed in the melee around their standards. The English were pushed off the ridge and into the forest behind, but it was a retreat and not a rout. In a ravine subsequently known as the Malfosse, the rallied huscarls trapped and slaughtered to a man a large party of Norman knights who rashly attempted pursuit in the twilight.

The famous story goes that Harold died when an arrow struck him in the eye. Some historians even argue that the *Bayeux Tapestry* (a lengthy piece of medieval needlework portraying the battle) shows this happening. The truth is that the stitching gives the incorrect impression that the arrow is entering a Saxon's eye, but there is no suggestion that the man is Harold, whose death is recorded in a nearby section of the tapestry.

Each side is believed to have sustained in excess of 2000 killed. As this was a war of conquest, the losses worried the Normans less than you may expect. After all, when the final share-out happened, that left more land for the surviving nobles.

William takes the crown

After burying his dead, William marched west. Having just fought the toughest battle of his life, his was conscious of the small size of his army and used terror to over-awe any potential opposition, burning and looting his way across southern England. He swung north, crossed the Thames, and near Berkhamsted met the two most senior surviving English nobles, the Earls Edwin and Morcar, accompanied by Edgar the Aetheling. They offered William the crown. Expressing surprise and pleasure, he accepted and his coronation took place on Christmas Day in Westminster Abbey, London. As was their custom when the crown was placed on a new king's head, the English gave vent to a mighty shout. Nervous, outnumbered and fearing a rising, the Norman soldiers waded into the crowd, killing large numbers, and setting the nearest houses ablaze. Only William's personal intervention saw order restored.

Fighting over Medieval England

England didn't immediately fall under Norman rule after the Battle of Hastings; the next few years saw some heavy fighting to establish who ruled the roost.

Here's a summary of what happened next:

- Edwin, Morcar, and Edgar the Aetheling all turned against William because he was handing out too much land to his chums: 1067–1068.

- The sons of the late King Harold arrived with an Irish army: 1068.

- The Kings of Scotland and Denmark supported the English resistance: 1069–1071.

The result was that William had to spend much of the next five years fighting to hang on to what he thought was now his. To start with, he had to put down risings in Kent and the West Country. Then, a major rebellion saw the 3000-strong garrison of York massacred. William responded to this with utter ruthlessness, burning towns, villages, and crops, slaughtering livestock, and killing entire populations in what became known as *The Harrying of the North*. It was never forgotten under Norman rule, and never forgiven.

One by one, William disposed of his opponents, but even then places remained where the Norman rule meant nothing. These were areas where geography placed the mounted knight or man-at-arms at a disadvantage, namely mountainous terrain, close forest, or swampland: The Normans did not attempt to invade Wales, and they made precious little progress in the Lake District. (But see the later section, 'Looking north . . . and west', for what happened later.)

In the marshy fenlands of East Anglia, a brilliant guerrilla leader named Hereward opposed the Normans, snapping up their isolated detachments, ambushing their patrols, strolling about their camps in disguise, and generally making life uncomfortable for them. Hereward became an English folk hero and was called 'the Wake' by his countrymen because his watchfulness enabled him to outsmart his opponents at every turn. Despite enormous efforts to catch him, the Normans made no progress at all. As far as recorded history goes, Hereward simply disappears. Some legends suggest that he made his peace with William, others that he was treacherously murdered.

Here a castle, there a castle

If the medieval period conjures up one image, it has to be a castle, introduced by the Normans and built throughout the era. Intended as a noble's home, a stronghold, and a symbol of the noble's power over his land and people, castles began popping up all over the place in the years after the Norman invasion, and continued being refined and built throughout the medieval period.

Early (Norman) castles were known as motte and bailey castles; the *motte* was a man-made, high, flat-topped conical mound on which was built a stockade consisting of tall wooden stakes bound together. This was the principal defensive feature of the castle. The *bailey* was the surrounding area, ditched and ramparted, which housed the garrison's living quarters, stables, and storehouses.

Motte and bailey castles were only built as temporary measures. As quickly as possible, the Normans began constructing permanent fortresses in stone. In these, the *keep*, an enormous tower incorporating living accommodation, a chapel, and storerooms, was the most important feature. The White Tower in the Tower of London is a perfect example. A bailey, consisting of a large, well-defended gatehouse and a series of square towers joined by a high wall named the curtain, was next to be built. The whole was then surrounded by a dry ditch or wet moat, crossed by a drawbridge. Experience revealed that the angles of the square towers were vulnerable to siege catapults, so round towers that provided a deflective surface replaced them.

Castles could be captured by:

- ✔ *Escalade,* which meant climbing long ladders and fighting your way onto the battlements; siege towers did the same, but the defenders could overturn them or set them on fire. Both were unpopular unless your soldiers had a head for heights!

- ✔ **Mining** beneath the defences in order to bring down a tower or section of wall until it collapsed.

- ✔ **Battering the walls** with siege catapults and battering rams in the hope that they would fall down, enabling you to fight your way into the defences.

- ✔ **Starving the garrison out,** which meant a protracted and very boring siege.

- ✔ **Trickery or treachery,** which was more fun and less dangerous.

Castles continued in use throughout the medieval period, although the introduction of gunpowder made them far less powerful. All those tall, straight walls were easy targets for cannon fire, and the rise of gunpowder is dealt with in Chapter 5.

The days of knights

William and his successors governed by means of what has become known as the *feudal system*, in which the king owned all the land and parcelled it out among his most trusted barons. In return, both they and certain towns paid taxes and provided the king with troops to fight his wars. At the bottom of the pile were the wretched English serfs, who paid their rent in cash, kind, or physical labour – and not only to the barons, but also to the Church. For this they received, in theory at least, legal protection.

The knight was one of the most important elements in the feudal system. Knighthood was the lowest strata of chivalry. Everyone above (barons, earls, dukes, and so on), was automatically a knight, although they had to prove themselves before they received the accolade confirming their status (*winning their spurs* was the term used to describe this confirmation). Knights were supposed to spend the previous night in a vigil before an altar and swear to uphold the laws of chivalry, which meant living a Christian life as well as protecting women, orphans, and the less fortunate. Some did, but the entire reason for the knight's existence was to act as a heavy on the king's behalf, which of course made him a bit of a lout.

When the knight wasn't training to fight or actually fighting, he and lots of fellow louts got together and fought for fun at tournaments – that event so well loved in Hollywood's movies. They would *joust*, that is, knock each other off their horses with lances, or batter each other silly with whalebone swords in a popular event known as the *melee*, which was a sort of last-man-standing contest. During the melee, the knight's personal servants, called *varlets*, would keep a careful eye on their master and, if he got floored, go in at considerable risk to themselves and drag him out.

In real war, the knight's weapons included the lance, the one- and two-handed sword, the battleaxe, and the dagger. Bishops were allowed to join in, but as priests they were not permitted to shed blood, so they armed themselves with maces, which were useful for knocking holes in heads. For protection, at the time of Hastings, the knight wore a conical helmet and chainmail armour. By degrees, the shape of the helmet changed until finally it incorporated a visor, and steel plates were progressively added until the knight sallied forth wearing a an entire suit of plate armour, so heavy that if he fell over he was unable to rise without assistance. Again, at Hastings the knight also carried a kite-shaped shield for additional protection; in a shortened form, this was used for much of the period, but was dispensed with altogether when good-quality plate armour became universal in the mid-fifteenth century. The knight's personal coat of arms was displayed on the shield and a cloth sur-coat worn over his armour – a useful means of identifying who was who when all warriors were clad entirely in metal!

Looking north . . . and west

Not everyone – and certainly not those living in Wales, Scotland, and Ireland at the time – felt that William's conquest had much to do with them. But it did. In due course it was to affect them all, and although at the time it seemed of little interest to anyone who wasn't directly involved, it actually planted the seed of a nation that would one day become one of the world's great powers.

The curious thing was that William, now known as the Conqueror, still thought of himself as the Duke of Normandy who also happened to be king of part of an offshore island. The same was true of most of his successors.

Knight-spotting

Today, the effigies of knights in full armour can be found on table tombs in ancient churches and cathedrals across the British Isles. Some seem to lie comfortably. Others have their arms and legs crossed, which means that they died _unshriven_ (without confessing their sins), almost certainly in battle.

True, the Conqueror marched into Scotland in 1072 and compelled the Scottish King, Malcolm Canmore, to do homage to him, but that was simply to show that he was now the biggest kid on the block. He left the Welsh largely alone, although some Normans established themselves in Pembrokeshire, which is still known as 'Little England beyond Wales'. The Irish, too, were left alone for the next hundred years. Then, in 1170, a tough customer called Strongbow, whose real name was Richard de Clare, Earl of Pembroke, landed with an Anglo-Norman army and began taking over the place.

Not all of the early Norman kings spent much time in England. Even Richard the Lion Heart hardly visited the place at all. They were more concerned with enlarging their dominions in France (William and his successors held land on the continent as well as in England). They even took a fancy to wearing the French crown as well.

During these years most of the wars involving British armies were family squabbles about who was going to sit on the throne next, with a variation provided by barons rebelling against the king of the day for reasons of their own. Battles were organised brawls on a large scale. They added little to military science, although returning Crusaders (who fought in religious wars in the Middle East during the eleventh, twelfth and thirteenth centuries) brought with them a much wider knowledge of fortification.

The lack of medieval British military evolution changed when Edward I ascended the throne in 1272. Edward was the warrior king _par excellence_. He fought the French, he fought the Welsh (and conquered them in his War of 1277), and he led his armies north of the border so often that he became known as the Hammer of the Scots. The most significant development of the time was the introduction of the fearsome longbow into the English armies (see the sidebar 'The longbow'). During the Hundred Years' War (see the section 'Fighting the French: A National Sport' later in this chapter), the longbow won great battles and made the English archer the most formidable infantry-man in Europe.

The longbow

One of the deadliest, and certainly the most democratic, weapon of the Middle Ages, the longbow was made from the wood of specially selected yew trees. It was between five and six feet in length and, unlike other bows, was drawn to the ear and not the chest, thereby generating tremendous power. It had a range in excess of 185 metres (200 yards) and was capable of penetrating an oak door or nailing a knight's leg to his horse.

Originally developed in Wales, English armies first successfully used the longbow against the Scots and then, with spectacular results, against the French. Weekly practice with the longbow became compulsory. Marksmen became capable of putting an arrow through a helmet's visor, although in a general engagement the ability to shoot up to a dozen arrows a minute produced fearsome arrow storms in which several thousand arrows were in the air at once. When plate armour was introduced, special arrows with narrow, well-tempered heads were produced to penetrate it. Only the development of cannon put an end to the archer's domination of the battlefield. So great was the archer's impact on English life that it is evident today in many occupational surnames, such as Bowyer, a man who made bows; Stringer, a maker of bowstrings; Arrowsmith, a blacksmith specialising in the production of arrow heads; Fletcher, a man who added the feathered fights to arrow shafts; and, of course, Archer and Bowman.

And why was it democratic? Because for the first time it enabled the ordinary English soldier to hand out a real beating to a heavily armoured aristocratic opponent, and you can't get much more democratic than that!

The Scottish Wars of Independence

All through the medieval period, Scotland was a separate country from England, with its own rulers and its own law. England, needless to say, wasn't very keen on this state of affairs and mounted several campaigns to take control in Scotland.

Plenty of Scots didn't like the idea of being ruled by an English king. Prominent among them was Sir William Wallace, who led a popular rising, with some success, until he was defeated at the Battle of Falkirk in 1298. He was subsequently captured and executed.

Mel Gibson's movie *Braveheart* (1995) provided a most imaginative version of William Wallace's career, complete with a blue face in the imagined style of the ancient Britons (see Chapter 2). In fact Sir William was a knight and therefore a gent in contemporary eyes – and gents simply did not paint their faces blue!

The Battle of Bannockburn, 14 June 1314

William Wallace's death did not discourage the Scots. In 1306 another Scottish noble rebelled, named Robert the Bruce. Over a period of years he gradually eliminated the English presence in Scotland until by 1314 it was restricted to the fortresses of Stirling, Dunbar, and Berwick. Edward II assembled an army and set off to raise Robert the Bruce's siege of Stirling Castle.

No one would describe Edward II as a chip off the old block (his dad was Edward I – see the earlier section 'Looking north . . . and west'). He was a poor commander and his favourites had far more influence over him than was appropriate. Robert the Bruce, on the other hand, was a canny fighter: in advance of the Battle of Bannockburn, an English knight, Sir Henry de Bohun, spotted Bruce and, hoping to impress his boss, charged at the Scot with his lance. Bruce easily avoided the charge, then brained de Bohun with his battleaxe as he galloped past.

On 14 June Bruce, with some 500 cavalry and 9000 infantry, drew up his army in preparation for an English attack. Edward's cavalry, about 1000 strong, was advancing ahead of his infantry, and he launched them against the squares of Scottish pikemen. This masked the fire of his own archers and the attack failed. The archers were then moved out onto the right flank, from which they opened a galling fire. Bruce ordered his cavalry to charge them and, unsupported, they were ridden down. The Scottish squares then advanced into the heart of the English infantry, which was disordered by the repulse of its cavalry. On sighting Scottish reinforcements approaching the field, Edward's army broke and fled. English losses included 22 barons, 68 knights, and about 1000 infantry, plus an uncounted number killed or captured during the pursuit. The Scots lost two knights and approximately 500 infantrymen.

Continuing Anglo-Scottish hostilities

Although fighting spluttered on until 1328, Scottish independence had become a fact and the Peace of Northampton duly recognised it. Despite this, a Scottish army invaded England in 1332, only for Edward III to defeat it at the Battle of Halidon Hill the following year. During this, Edward developed the method of covering the flanks of his men-at-arms with archers, tactics that soon result in English infantry being considered the most formidable in Europe. After the battle Edward was content to remain on the defensive as far as Scotland was concerned. Besides, he was more interested in getting on with the Hundred Years' War (see the next section).

Fighting the French: A National Sport

A trend started in the medieval period that continued on and off until the early nineteenth century – fighting the French. These battles took place on French soil – although at this time, England owned quite a lot of this land anyway.

Although war against France dragged on throughout the medieval period, the most famous series of battles were fought as part of the Hundred Years' War (1337–1457; yes, it did run for more than 100 years!), a prolonged struggle about who was going to be King of France (as in whether he'd be a Frenchman or an Englishman). The battles featured in this section were all part of that on-going campaign.

Medieval wars against the French weren't 'British' wars as such. The *auld alliance* between France and Scotland saw the two nations mutually support each other in their wars against England. If the English were fighting in France, the Scots would try to kick up a ruckus to divert English resources northwards, and vice versa.

The Battle of Crecy, 26 August 1346

After raiding into French territory, Edward III, commanding an army consisting of 5500 archers, 1000 Welsh infantry, and 2500 knights and men-at-arms, was retreating towards Flanders, pursued by a much larger army commanded by the French King, Philip IV. Philip had at his disposal no fewer than 6000 professional and mercenary infantry, including a large contingent of Genoese crossbowmen, 10,000 knights and men-at-arms, and about 14,000 feudal militia.

Edward selected a good defensive position at the top of a gentle slope, with his right resting on the village of Crecy-en-Ponthieu and his left on the village of Wadicourt. His divided his army into three divisions, the right commanded by the young Black Prince (Edward's son), the left by the Earls of Arundel and Northampton, and the reserve, some way to the rear, under his personal orders. The centre of each division consisted of dismounted knights and men-at-arms, flanked by archers echeloned forward so that they could shoot obliquely across the battlefield. This sharing of dangers between the two types of soldier reflected a growing sense of nationality and mutual trust that came to be reflected in civil life. In contrast, continental armies tended to despise their infantry.

Although most of his army was still strung out along many miles of road, Philip decided to attack at once. He ordered his Geneoese crossbowmen forward, but they objected on the grounds that their bowstrings were still wet from recent rain and needed to dry out. Stung by accusations of cowardice, they advanced towards the ominously silent English line, performing a silly dance that involved whooping and waving of arms. We can only assume these antics were intended to bolster their own morale and convey how superior they felt to their apparently primitive opponents. At 150 yards from the line they loosed their first volley, but because of their slack bowstrings it fell short. The English had no such disadvantage, for when it was raining they kept their bowstrings beneath their helmets and only strung their bows when going into action. Now, while the Genoese were cranking up for a second shot, words of command were heard in the English ranks and suddenly the air filled with hissing death as thousands of arrow shafts slashed into the Genoese, felling them by the score and skewering arms and legs. As the crossbowmen began to withdraw in confusion, the first of the French mounted divisions entered the fray, cutting them down as they charged forward. In return, the Genoese emptied several French saddles with their crossbows, much to the amusement of the English.

Suddenly, the French knights found themselves on a killing ground. Knights and horses went down, hindering those behind. Maddened by pain and uncontrollable, wounded horses lashed out at all around them, causing confusion. Pressing bravely on through the arrow storm, the French ignored the archers, the very men who were causing them grief, and made for the dismounted knights and men-at-arms as alone being worthy of their steel. A furious fight raged until the French were either killed or in retreat.

The battle lasted for five hours and during that time 15 such attacks were mounted on the English position. Between these attacks, the agile Welsh infantry fighting for the English sallied forth to bring down and despatch lumbering unhorsed French knights. At the end of it all, the King of Bohemia (an ally of France), the Counts of Alençon and Blois, all the army's principal officers, and 1500 members of the French nobility lay dead. Altogether, French and Genoese killed alone came to approximately 10,000. Edward's losses came to two knights and 100 others killed. Crecy signalled the beginning of the end of the mounted knight's undisputed domination of the battlefield.

The Battle of Poitiers, 19 September 1356

The French aristocrats thought hard about the reasons for their defeat at Crecy (see the previous section). Could the English archers have been responsible? Such an idea was just not socially acceptable. Surely, they said to each other, it was because the English knights fought on foot. Next time, they reasoned, we'll do the same, but just as a precaution we'll wear armour that's been specially strengthened against arrows, even if it is a lot heavier.

Next time came ten years later, when King John of France, leading an army of 3000 crossbowmen and 17,500 knights and men-at-arms, succeeded in bringing the Black Prince's army, consisting of 2000 archers and 4000 men-at-arms, to battle four miles south of Poitiers.

The position chosen by the Black Prince (Edward III's son) resembled that at Crecy in some ways in that it lay along the edge of a plateau and possessed secure flanks. For his part, John decided to employ his knights in four dismounted divisions to attack the English position in succession. Flanking fire from the archers shot the first division to tatters. The second also sustained casualties, but reached the English line and was repulsed only with difficulty. On seeing this, most of the third division fled, although some men rallied on the fourth division, which King John commanded in person.

A pause ensued, during which the archers went out to recover as many arrows as possible, but even then their officers' opinion was that they only had sufficient ammunition for a few minutes' serious fighting. When it became clear that John was about to launch what he hoped would be the decisive attack with his fourth division, the Black Prince demonstrated his ability as a commander. Using the cover of a hill to screen them from view, he sent a detachment of men-at-arms and archers round to a position on the right from which they could fall on the enemy's flank and rear. He then had the horses brought forward and ordered his knights and men-at-arms to mount.

The French had now begun to labour up the slope. Once more the arrow storm lashed them. As they began to puff and pant, a signal was received that the flanking party was in position. The Prince immediately ordered everyone, archers included, to make a headlong charge down the hill. A fierce struggle ensued as they smashed into the French, but the latter broke and fled as soon as the flanking party began attacking their rear. Tired, breathless men burdened with heavy armour were easily overtaken by lightly equipped archers, many of whom returned with four, five, or six noble prisoners whom they could ransom for large sums. A good businessman, the Black Prince bought them all at a discount, collecting the full price later. English casualties amounted to over 1000 killed and wounded. The French loss included 2500 killed, rather more wounded, and 2000 taken prisoner, including King John.

The Battle of Agincourt, 25 October 1415

The third of the longbow's major victories began when a small English army under King Henry V was brought to battle by an army under Charles d'Albret, Constable of France, which outnumbered it fivefold. Henry had 4950 archers and 750 knights and men-at-arms at his disposal, a total of 5700 men. D'Albret could muster 3000 crossbowmen, 7000 mounted and 15,000 dismounted knights and men-at-arms, a total of 25,000 men plus a few guns.

Henry chose his fighting position at the point where the space between two woods narrowed to 850 metres (940 yards). As usual, his dismounted men-at-arms were deployed in blocks with the archers on their flanks. Those archers in the centre of the line formed two wedges, fronted by stakes that were driven into the ground. To the north, d'Albret's army occupied a frontage of 1000 metres (1200 yards). On each flank was a detachment of mounted knights. The centre consisted of three divisions, the first two composed of dismounted knights and men-at-arms, the third of mounted knights. Somehow, during the deployment, the crossbowmen and guns found themselves *behind* the first division, where they could give no support whatever.

The battle began when the archers in the trees on both flanks began sniping at the mounted detachment accompanying the first division. Kicking and plunging in their pain, horses bolted through the dismounted men-at-arms, who were having to tramp across the mud of ploughed fields in plate armour that was even heavier than that worn at Poitiers. Worse still, their original frontage of 1000 metres was now compressed to 850 metres. Such was the crush that some were unable to use their weapons. At close range, marksmen shot many of them through the visor. They struggled bravely on to close with the English men-at-arms. The archers, knowing that their comrades were too few to handle the situation, swarmed out to batter the exhausted French with clubs, swords, and axes. If a knight went down, he was either despatched with a dagger thrust or suffocated when more of his fellows fell on top of him. It was little better than mass butchery, with the arrival of the French second division only adding to the ghastly piles of slain.

It had taken just 30 minutes to destroy two-thirds of d'Albret's army. Henry sent a herald across to the remaining third division, telling them that they would receive no mercy unless they cleared off promptly. They took his advice. English losses included the Duke of York, smothered in his armour, 400 killed, and about 800 wounded. The French lost 8000 killed, including d'Albret, three dukes, 90 assorted noblemen, and 1560 knights, plus 2000 captured.

The English archers won more victories, but things never went quite so well for them again. France was too big, and its population too large, for the English to hold their gains. Thanks to Joan of Arc in the mid-fifteenth century, the English failed to take Orleans, and as the French sense of nationhood began to grow they began to lose ground. Always comparatively few in number, by the 1450s English archers found themselves outranged by well-handled French guns and their reputation for invincibility ended. Besides, there was now plenty of work for them to do at home – the Wars of the Roses were just about to come into bloom (see the next section).

Roses Are Red, Roses Are White

The Wars of the Roses were fought between two lines of descent stemming from Edward III (for more on this, see Sean Lang's *British History For Dummies*, published by Wiley). As might be expected, the wars were about who was going to sit on the throne of England. The Wars of the Roses lasted from 1455 until 1485, although only six weeks' actual fighting took place in all that time. They have been described as bloody, and so they were to the extent that one bunch of nobles was trying to exterminate another, and their supporters as well. In these circumstances, treachery became a highly prized social skill. Ordinary folk stayed well out of the way if they could.

Table 4-1 shows the most important figures for both sides in the war.

Table 4-1	Who's Who in the Wars of the Roses
Lancaster	**York**
Henry VI – who lost France and then his sanity.	Richard, Duke of York – killed by Margaret after the Battle of Wakefield.
Henry's wife Margaret of Anjou – who wore the royal trousers in his house.	Edward IV – illegitimate if the story about his dad being a French archer was true!
Henry and Margaret's son Edward, Prince of Wales – who was killed after the battle of Tewksbury.	Edward's sons the Princes in the Tower – who would therefore have had no claim on the throne either.
Henry Tudor – soon to become Henry VII (more on him later).	Richard III, Edward's brother – forever cast by Tudor propagandist Will Shakespeare as the wicked uncle.

Which rose was which? The story is that the original row took place in a rose garden, where those present were required to show their allegiance by plucking a red or white rose. The Lancastrians favoured the red and the Yorkists the white. Never confuse the two if you visit northern England!

The wars produced the bloodiest battle ever to take place on English soil, fought in a blizzard at Towton in Yorkshire on 29 March 1461. Snow blinded the Lancastrian archers, whose arrows fell short. They were collected by the Yorkists, who opened a continuous galling fire that provoked the Lancastrians into attacking in a six-hour melee, which was only decided in favour of the Yorkists when their reinforcements fell on the Lancastrians' flank. Probable casualty figures are 8000 Yorkists and 10,000 Lancastrians, of whom not less than one-third were killed.

Officially, the last battle of the Wars of the Roses was Bosworth Field (22 August 1485), fought between Richard III and Henry Tudor, the Lancastrian claimant to the throne. Richard, the last native-born Englishman to wear the crown, was killed during the fighting. Henry Tudor (now Henry VII) was of Welsh descent. In outlook he was more a modern than a medieval monarch. To show that he meant business, he quickly passed an act forbidding what was left of the nobility from keeping bodies of armed, uniformed retainers.

The Middle Ages were over. The archer had made the armoured knight obsolete, the gun had done likewise to the archer, and in due course it would see off the castle as well. New weapons would mean new ways of fighting and new types of soldier, too – and Part II shows you just what happened.

Part II
The Arrival of Gunpowder

In this part . . .

Guns and gunpowder spelled the end of the feudal era. They placed the knight on the same footing as the ordinary soldier and were capable of knocking holes in his castle walls. While guns and muskets continued to improve slowly, it took the better part of two centuries before the application of the new technology was complete. During this period, it might take all day to up draw up a line of battle, and by then it was time to go to bed.

While the Tudors were on the throne, the English tended to make more use of gunpowder at sea, but this changed in the middle of the seventeenth century when they had a civil war that dragged in the Welsh, Scots, and Irish as well. One of the war's results was the founding of a regular army. Towards the end of the seventeenth century infantry tactics became much more straightforward as a result of a very simple invention – the bayonet.

Chapter 5

With Pike and Shot: Renaissance Warfare

. . . .

In This Chapter

▶ Introducing gunpowder and guns

▶ Changing infantry tactics

▶ Revolutionary (and revolving) cavalry tactics

▶ Fighting at Flodden and against the Armada

. . . .

Gunpowder changed forever the way men thought about war. No longer were the rich and powerful able to protect themselves with expensive custom-made armour, and no longer did the strong man have an advantage over his weaker opponent. In every sense gunpowder earned its reputation as the Great Leveller. It hastened the demise of the feudal system and was responsible for the formation of professional armies for the first time since the days of Rome (see Part I for earlier warfare).

After the Wars of the Roses (see Chapter 4), England wanted a period of settled government, which the Tudors provided and passed on. Compared to what had gone before, comparatively little military activity took place in Britain between the late fifteenth and mid-seventeenth centuries. In general, the period was characterised by the need to come to terms with new technology and apply it successfully to the battlefield.

This chapter mostly deals with the development of the following types of soldier during this period (each is covered in more detail elsewhere in this chapter):

- ✔ **Infantry:** Archers, pikemen, arquebusiers, musketeers, and, early in the period, billmen and halberdiers.

- ✔ **Cavalry:** The last (and best armoured) of the medieval knights, alongside pistol-armed horsemen.

- ✔ **Artillery:** Guns came into their own at this time, in various shapes and sizes.

Such were the complexities of the gunpowder revolution that forming a battle line became a very slow-motion affair in which artillery, pikemen, musketeers, and cavalry all had to be deployed to their best advantage, so the importance of the professional soldier increased by leaps and bounds..

Introducing Gunpowder Artillery

No one really knows who introduced gunpowder to Europe (from Asia) in a useable form – although the Mongols, who employed more tricks than a cartload of monkeys, used 'thunderous noises and flashes of fire' against the Hungarians in 1241. However, it certainly wasn't until the end of the medieval period (c1500) that gunpowder really took off as a military tool in Europe. Prior to that, guns were considered noisy novelties rather than battle winners in their own right.

Two individuals are usually put forward as the fathers of European gunpowder, both of whom were men of the cloth. The first was a British friar named Roger Bacon, who lived between 1214 and 1294. His hobby was alchemy and he recorded his discoveries in code, probably to protect himself from the wrath of the Church. When his code was cracked in comparatively recent times it revealed the first known recipe for gunpowder. Just the same, it is hard to believe that Roger received a flash of inspiration one morning and managed to mix sulphur, saltpetre, and charcoal together in the right proportions. Maybe it was an accident, maybe it was the result of long research, or maybe someone else had put him on the right track. The second candidate was a mysterious German monk called Berthold Schwarz ('Bert Black' to non-German speakers) who lived in Flanders a little later. We don't know just how Berthold discovered the propellant capacity of the black powder. He did, however, manufacture what was recognisably a gun in 1313 and sent another one to England the following year. An illustrated manuscript of 1326 shows one similar to these, calling it a *Vasi* or *Pot de Fer*. It does indeed resemble a vase from which a large arrow is being shot while a man applies a red-hot iron to the touch-hole.

Early guns were almost as dangerous to their users as they were to the enemy. One of the most famous accidents resulted in the death of King James II of Scotland while he was besieging Roxburgh Castle in 1460. The chronicler of the event obviously wasn't too keen on guns, and he wouldn't have won prizes for his spelling:

> *While this prince, more curious nor became the Majestie of any Kinge, did stand near-hand where the Artytterie was discharged, his thigh-bone was dung in two by a piece of miss-framed gune that brake in the shuting, by which he was stricken to the ground and died hastily.*

Henry VIII was enthusiastic about artillery and was one of the gun makers' best customers. Whatever their type, his guns all had names like *Wales, Cornwall,* and *Lancaster*, and a matched set of 12 were named after Christ's 12 apostles. In England, Sussex gun makers were considered to be among the best and their handiwork was put to good use against the Spanish Armada (see the later section, 'Testing Out the New Ideas').

Getting to grips with different types of gun

Many of the earliest guns were *breech loaders,* the shot and powder being loaded into the rear of the barrel. A major disadvantage of this was a back-blast of flame and gas, reducing the gun's efficiency the longer it remained in action. Because of this, large-calibre siege guns were built as *muzzle loaders,* the powder and shot being loaded in through the front of the barrel in that order. Over time, muzzle loaders became the more commonplace of the two and were to remain so until the later nineteenth century.

Gunners were very practical people and were well aware that engaging targets in the interior of a town or castle or over the crest of a hill required a weapon capable of high-angle fire. This led to the introduction of the short-barrelled *mortar* in the sixteenth century, being joined in the seventeenth century by another high-angle weapon, the *howitzer*. The difference between the two was that while the mortar's elevation was fixed and variations in range were obtained by adjusting the powder propellant charge, the howitzer's charge was fixed and its elevation could be altered. Mortars and howitzers used explosive shells. These were extremely expensive to produce and consisted of a hollow sphere, the two halves of which were cast separately and then welded together. The shell was then filled with powder through a small hole into which a fuse was inserted. The burning fuse remained visible throughout the shell's flight and was a useful guide to accuracy.

By 1600 the number of guns in service was rising dramatically. At this stage they were classified by size and given names such as culverin and cannon (see the following section, 'What's your gun called?'). It wasn't until later, in the eighteenth Century, that more standardised gun classifications emerged, such as by the weight of the shot fired.

Ammunition developed slowly and in accordance with needs as they were perceived. Stone or iron balls were fine for battering holes in walls or putting down a rank or two of the enemy, but not a lot of use as a man killer at short range. The answer to this was *langridge*, a term for old bits of scrap iron, broken glass, and stones that spread out when fired and mowed down everything in its path, like a gigantic shotgun. This was later refined into *grape shot* (consisting of musket balls in a bag or net) and *case* or *cannister shot* (where a thin metal container replaced the bag).

What's your gun called?

Ordnance is the name given to anything that flings, shoots, or fires anything else. It persists to this day in the title of one of the Ministry of Defence's most senior officers, the Master General of the Ordnance.

When the earliest guns were introduced they were classified by name rather than size and type. Some were named after mythical beasts or birds and some had names the explanation for which has long been lost. Table 5-1 lists some of the most common in use between the late fifteenth and seventeenth centuries, with their *calibre* (the internal width of the gun's barrel) and the weight of shot they fired; it's difficult to conceive of a system in greater need of standardisation!

Table 5-1	The Most Common Guns	
Name	*Calibre*	*Weight of shot*
Double cannon	8 inches (20 centimetres)	64 pounds (29 kilograms)
Demi-cannon	6.25 inches (16 centimetres)	33 pounds (15 kilograms)
Culverins	5.25 inches (13.25 centimetres)	17 pounds (8 kilograms)
Demi-culverins	4.5 inches (11.5 centimetres)	10 pounds (4 kilograms)
Saker	3.75 inches (9.5 centimetres)	6 pounds (2.5 kilograms)
Minyon	3.25 inches (8.25 centimetres)	4 pounds (2 kilograms)
Faucon	2.75 inches (7 centimetres)	2 pounds (1 kilogram)
Fauconet	2.25 inches (5.75 centimetres)	1 pound (0.5 kilogram)

Hiring in guns, gunners, and ammunition

Any good businessperson takes advantage of a gap in the market. When guns first appeared, their use in sieges and with field armies immediately presented an opportunity to make big money. Guns were extremely expensive and exchequers were reluctant to burden themselves with the cost of buying them, plus ammunition and gunpowder, and hiring specialists to fire and look after them, as well as teams of oxen or horses to get them to where they were needed. Realising this, smart entrepreneurs bought guns and everything that went with them on their own account, and hired them out at a whacking profit to sovereigns who were on the point of making war on someone.

The obvious disadvantage of this system was that if there was the slightest chance of the entrepreneur's investment falling into the enemy's hands, the last his customer would see of his rented guns was them disappearing over the horizon, albeit at the pace of the oxen towing them. What was more, contractors hired their guns to anyone who could pay, presenting a real threat to the state if they were leased to its internal enemies. Once this blinding flash of the obvious became apparent, the day of the independent contractor came to an end and possession of guns became a royal prerogative.

Henry VIII also established the first regular force of artillerymen in England by installing a paid Master Gunner and 12 Gunners at the Tower of London. This idea was later extended to all the principal towns and royal castles.

Upgrading the Infantry

At the end of the fifteenth century infantrymen were of several types – the archer, the billman, the halberdier, and the pikeman. The last three wore helmet, breast and back plates, and flexible thigh armour called *tassets*.

Most armies through this period had pikemen. However, the billman, the halberdier, and the archer were of less use on the Renaissance battlefield. The *bill* was a pole weapon with an edged blade at the top – watch a hedge-cutter at work and you see how easily a bill could sever a limb! The halberd was another pole weapon incorporating a spear head, an axe head, and a hook for yanking an enemy out of his ranks by the neck. Its end is simple to explain – it was too short to be as useful as a pike, and was not effective against firearms – and by the end of the sixteenth century its use was largely ceremonial. The demise of the longbow is more difficult to explain, and is covered in the very next section.

Waving goodbye to the longbow . . .

Though their days as a battle winner on their own had gone (the great victories of the longbow are discussed in Chapter 4), archers continued to form a major element of any English force, although they were gradually replaced by firearms.

Defenders of the longbow could claim, with some justice, that it had a much higher rate of fire and better accuracy than the new infantry firearms (see the following section for more on these), which remained the case as late as the middle of the nineteenth century. The arrow, however, was less effective against plate armour than it had been against chain mail, whereas the kinetic energy stored in a musket ball, which was far larger and heavier than a modern small-arms round, enabled it to penetrate plate with ease and knock over a man or a horse with its impact.

Firearms were expensive and the longbow remained in use, in declining numbers, for much of the sixteenth century. By 1595, however, its day was done and in that year the trained bands of archers, which formed a national reserve, received a Royal Ordinance instructing them to arm themselves with firearms.

... And saying hello to the arquebus

The introduction of a personal firearm, the *arquebus*, contributed to the demise of archers and halberdiers. This new weapon – resembling a cross between a musket and an old-fashioned pistol with a curved stock – started to be used in British armies around in the middle of the sixteenth century.

The arquebus was originally fired from a rest, but later versions were held against the chest and gripped with both hands, which seems as good a way as any to crack a rib or two. From the arquebus evolved the musket, weighing in at a hefty 11 kilograms (25 pounds), which most definitely required a firing rest. The method of firing the arquebus and the musket changed over time:

1. Early versions were fired by means of a slow match (a *matchlock*) (late fifteenth century).

2. Matchlocks gave way to *wheel-lock* mechanisms, incorporating a toothed wheel activated by a trigger (mid-sixteenth century).

3. Wheel-locks gave way to *flintlock* mechanisms, striking sparks into the priming pan when the trigger was activated (late sixteenth century).

Musketeers fought in ten-deep ranks. When the front rank fired their weapons they turned about and moved to the rear, and then went through the complex business of reloading as they made their way forward to become the front rank again. On their own, musketeers were terribly vulnerable to attack by cavalry, so infantry regiments were organised with a central block of pikemen and a wing of musketeers on either flank. If they were attacked, the musketeers sheltered under the long pikes. The Spanish perfected this type of integrated unit, known as *tercios*, and they were copied all over Europe. In the British Isles they were referred to as 'pike and shot', which sounds more like the name of a good pub.

Early in the seventeenth century the great Swedish warrior king Gustavus Adolphus introduced not only an improved musket weighing just 5 kilograms (11 pounds), which could be fired from the shoulder without a rest, but also one-piece cartridges incorporating powder charge and ball that reduced loading time and therefore increased the rate of fire. The proportion of musketeers to pikemen in a regiment increased and the musketeers' ranks reduced from ten to seven. Armour also started to be abandoned, as its use against muskets was limited.

Riding Around in Circles: Cavalry

Faced with a *tercio* (see the previous section, '. . . And saying hello to the arquebus'), heavily armoured knights had a real problem, being simultaneously vulnerable to the fire of musketeers (which could pierce their plate armour) and kept beyond striking distance by massed pikes. The lance became an encumbrance and was discarded by the English at the end of the sixteenth century, and by the Scots 50 years later; the pistol seemed to offer a solution to horsemen.

Troopers were each equipped with two or three pistols and delivered their attacks at walking pace in ten-deep formations. The front rank discharged its pistols at point-blank range, then wheeled to the rear to reload and move forward by rotation, just like musketeers (see the previous section). This type of cavalry manoeuvre was known as the *caracole*. Only when gaps appeared in the enemy ranks did the troopers attempt to charge in with their swords.

When, some time during the late sixteenth or early seventeenth centuries, the pistol had been accepted as the principal cavalry weapon, an idiotic situation developed. Opposing cavalry units performed the *caracole* against each other, banging away at men and horses to little purpose beyond performing like a carousel ride. Naturally, the cavalry's contribution during the sixteenth and early seventeenth centuries was rarely decisive.

Tumbling walls: Fortifications

The medieval walls of castles and cities were far more vulnerable to cannon fire than they had been to the old stone-throwing siege engines, and they were rarely suitable for defence by artillery. As we see in Chapters 6 and 7, in the seventeenth century fortifications went underground and relied on artillery for their defence.

Henry VIII proved himself to be a little ahead of his time (the sixteenth century) by building a series of 19 coast defence forts from Gravesend on the Thames around the south coast to Pendennis in Cornwall. These forts were revolutionary because they were designed primarily with all-round defence by artillery in mind. The best examples consisted of a circular central keep with small semi-circular bastions attached, surrounding the same number of much larger, inter-connected semi-circular bastions. Each of these elements provided a gun platform with the powder magazines under cover. A wide ditch ringed the fort with a bare *glacis* (a gentle slope) beyond. Many remain in an excellent state of preservation today.

Gustavus Adolphus rationalised Renaissance cavalry tactics (see the previous section for his development of infantrymen). He returned to the principle that one of the cavalry's most important functions was *shock action* (charging into the enemy mass to engage in hand-to-hand combat). His cavalry attacked in four ranks at a fast trot, later reduced to three. Having fired their pistols, the two leading ranks closed at once with the sword, followed by the remainder, who reserved their fire for the subsequent melee. The effect of this on the recipients, long used to the formalities of the *caracole*, was devastating.

Like the infantry, the cavalry abandoned much of its armour as superfluous. A few regiments, designated *cuirassiers*, retained a version of full armour as late as the 1640s, but by then most cavalrymen had reduced their protection to an open, lobster-tailed helmet, and breast and back plates only.

Testing Out the New Ideas

Little action took place between British armies and continental European ones during this era. The English lost Calais, their last remaining possession in mainland France, and Elizabeth I sent volunteers to fight alongside the Protestant Dutch in their struggle against Spain in the continental Wars of Religion. The aims of the Tudor monarchs throughout the sixteenth century were to provide strong central government, internal security, and continuity; despite this, violent religious disturbances occurred during the Reformation and a rebellion took place in Ulster during the last years of Elizabeth I's reign.

With the possible exception of artillery, England's virtual withdrawal from direct continental involvement meant that the country fell steadily behind in military methods, a process that continued well into the seventeenth century. Coupled with this, new weapons and tactics were not universally popular – many soldiers hated the new weapons and did not understand how they could be applied to battlefield tactics.

The Battle of Flodden, 1513

In 1513 King James IV of Scotland invaded England with a 25,000-strong army and 17 guns (remember, at this time the two countries were still very much separate). The Earl of Surrey met him with 20,000 men and 22 light guns. Surrey manoeuvred the Scots out of a strong position on Flodden Edge (in northeast England) by interposing his troops between them and the Scottish border. In the circumstances, James had little alternative but to mount an attack.

Flodden began with an artillery duel. The English served their guns the better and the Scots had the worst of the exchange. This was a bad beginning, but worse was to follow. The Scottish left wing defeated its opposite numbers, but was cut to pieces by the English cavalry when the Scots paused to plunder the dead. The Scottish centre and right wing also advanced to engage in a general melee. The right wing was defeated and as a result the Scottish centre was surrounded.

In close-quarter fighting, the English had a distinct advantage as they had recently adopted the halberd (see the section, 'Upgrading the Infantry' earlier in this chapter for more on this). The Scots, on the other hand, retained their traditional pikes, which were ineffective against the halberd.

The majority of Scots fighting stubbornly around their king were killed, as was King James himself, eight Scottish earls, and thirteen Scottish barons. Almost every one of Scotland's noble families sustained the loss of one or more of its members. Total Scottish casualties amounted to 10,000 soldiers and all their artillery. Surrey's army had 4000 men killed. The pipe lament *Flowers of the Forest* was composed to commemorate Scotland's national tragedy, and remains in use with some Scottish regiments to this day.

The Spanish Armada, 1588

Philip II of Spain, angered by the 'piratical' activities of such English sea captains as Francis Drake as well as Elizabeth's support for the Dutch protestants, assembled a huge invasion force to convey an army of Spanish veterans from the Low Countries to England. The Spanish Armada (fleet) contained some 90 fighting ships and a large number of transports, against which the English could oppose approximately 50 warships.

Although it was a naval battle, the defeat of the Spanish Armada was significant in that the English admirals and captains had long been of the opinion that their warships should fight as floating gun platforms, whereas the Spaniards continued to regard theirs as transport for boarding parties. Against this, if the Armada had managed to ferry the Duke of Parma's veterans from the Low Countries to England, it is unlikely that, with the best will in the world, the English levies hastily assembled at Tilbury would have been able to stand against them for long.

Chapter 6

Hearties versus Gloomies: The Civil Wars

King Charles I was a walking disaster. Everything he touched – foreign expeditions, attempts to interest the Presbyterian Scots in bishops, trying to raise taxes without parliamentary approval, and even attempting to arrest Members of Parliament – went horribly wrong. He was a master of indecision, failing to make up his mind and then changing it when he did, usually without telling anyone else.

To be fair to Charles, in the times in which he reigned (1625–1649) the word compromise meant very little. Charles thought he ruled by *Divine Right* (meaning he was appointed by God) and could do what he wanted, whereas Parliament (elected representatives of the people) thought that he should seek its approval. Charles's Queen, Henrietta Maria, was French and this produced deep suspicion among England's Puritans and Presbyterians, who held a majority in Parliament, that Charles was preparing the way for a return of Catholicism. People felt very deeply about such matters and, since they could not reach agreement, the issues had to be resolved by force. The actions that followed in the mid-seventeenth century became known as the English Civil Wars.

For more on the build-up to the Civil Wars, seek out a copy of Sean Lang's *British History For Dummies* and Philip Wilkinson's *The British Monarchy For Dummies* (both published by Wiley).

Although everyone knows these campaigns as the English Civil Wars, British Civil Wars would be more accurate. Soldiers from England, Wales, Scotland, and Ireland all took part, as whoever sat on the English throne was powerful enough to influence affairs across the British Isles.

Battles in the English Civil War were fought by the following types of soldier:

- **Musketeers:** Along with pikemen, musketeers formed the basis of infantry units. They wore little or no armour, and were equipped with slow-loading, heavy muskets, with an effective range of about 45 metres (50 yards).

- **Pikemen:** Carrying long spears, their main role was to use these weapons to protect their fellow musketeers from cavalry attack. Pikemen usually wore some armour, and worked alongside the musketeers (see Chapter 5 for more on this battle formation).

- **Cavalrymen:** Armed with swords and pistols, Civil War cavalry could choose to fire or charge. Some were heavily armoured (known as *cuirassiers*), and others, known as *dragoons*, acted as mounted infantry who rode to the battlefield but fought on foot muskets.

- **Artillery:** As detailed in Chapter 5, many calibres and types of gun existed, and were used both on the battlefield and in sieges.

Figure 6-1 shows typical infantrymen from this period.

Figure 6-1:
A musketeer and pikeman from the English Civil War.

Those who fought for Charles became known as *Cavaliers*, while their Parliamentarian opponents were called *Roundheads*. According to tradition, Cavaliers were jolly fellows who grew their hair long, and were natty dressers who sang and drank a lot, and chased wenches. Roundheads cut their hair shorter (hence the name), dressed soberly, disliked merriment of any kind, and got a real boost from singing psalms. In fact, men from both armies looked and behaved in a similar manner, but they still hated each other's guts.

The First Civil War

In 1642 King Charles I and Parliament both raised armies to resolve their grievances by force. Opinion as to who was in the right was strongly divided, setting neighbour against neighbour and splitting families down the middle. As with any civil war involving an element of religion, the struggle was to be bitter, unforgiving, and at times merciless.

The armies that marched to war in 1642 consisted largely of amateurs, led by a few veterans of the continental wars of religion who knew their business (for more on these continental wars, see Sean Lang's *European History For Dummies*, published by Wiley).

The army of Parliament was led by the Earl of Essex. Parliament's army was larger than the Royalist force, but the king was fortunate in having Prince Rupert of the Rhine, one of the outstanding cavalry leaders of his day, among his commanders.

Setting the Civil War in swing

The first battle of the war took place at Edgehill, Warwickshire, on 23 October 1642. Prince Rupert (naturally fighting on his uncle's side) chased the Parliamentary cavalry off the field and pursued it out of sight. In his absence Essex put in a sharp counter-attack, but Rupert's eventual return to the field forced Essex's army to withdraw and fall back on London.

The royal army followed up as far as Turnham Green on the outskirts of London, only to find that Essex had been reinforced by the London *Trained Bands* (a standing militia) and now possessed far more than his original strength. If a general engagement had been fought, Charles would probably have won and entered his somewhat subdued capital. As it was, he dithered magnificently and after a brief skirmish decided to withdraw to Oxford, which became his headquarters.

1643 also went badly for Parliament, although a Puritan farmer and Member of Parliament from Huntingdon, Oliver Cromwell, defeated a force of Royalist cavalry at Grantham (Lincolnshire) in March. Charles also sustained a reverse at Gloucester, but by now Parliament was becoming desperate:

✔ In Yorkshire, Royalists carried all before them.

✔ In the West Country, Royalists under Sir Ralph Hopton trounced Sir William Waller's Roundheads at Stratton in May, fought a hard battle against them at Lansdowne near Bath on 5 July, and defeated them at Roundway Down, Devizes, on 13 July.

✔ In the midlands, Rupert won a victory at Chalgrove Field near Oxford on 18 June and took Bristol on 26 July.

In August, Parliament empowered local authorities to raise troops by conscription, only for the Royalists to follow suit.

The Scots had played no part in the war before 1643, but a now-desperate Parliament was prepared to offer them anything to enlist their support. On 25 September it concluded a Solemn League and Covenant with them, promising not only to protect Presbyterianism in Scotland but also to impose it through-out England and Wales. In return, the Scots began assembling a large army under the veteran Alexander Leslie, Earl of Leven, ready to participate for Parliament in the next year's campaigning.

Civil War sieges

By 1643, the King controlled northern and western England and Wales, while Parliament controlled the English midlands and southeast. Inevitably, these areas contained pockets that were sympathetic to their respective enemies, and within those pockets were castles and fortified manor houses that each side had to neutralise. As well as operations by the field armies, the war involved numerous siege operations.

In general, the medieval castles withstood their ordeal by gunfire for longer than had been expected. The general rule was that if cannon blasted a breach in the walls through which a storming party could enter, the garrison was invited to surrender. It was not dishonourable to accept such an offer if the castle was no longer considered defensible. In such circumstances the garrison may or may not be permitted to march out with honour. If the offer was rejected, the garrison could expect the worst. In places where a castle's natural position rendered it less

vulnerable to gunfire, starving the defenders into submission was sometimes the only option. In one instance the people in the garrison were so weak that they were unable to dismantle the barricades that they had erected in the gatehouse and the besiegers had to do it for them.

When Parliament captured a castle or fortified manor it was usually *slighted* to prevent its being defended again. This meant throwing down the battlements into the moat, ripping the massive gates off their hinges in the gatehouse, removing the lead from roofs, and selling internal timber. If that was not enough, gunpowder was used to blow down the more important towers and sometimes half the keep as well. The process led to the English countryside being dotted with picturesque ruins, for which we blame Cromwell for more than his fair share. This in turn resulted in the Edwardian music hall song *I'm One of the Ruins Cromwell Knocked About a Bit*, usually sung by ladies of a certain age.

The siege of Lathom House

The most famous siege of all was that of Lathom House in Lancashire, held for the king by the redoubtable Charlotte de Tremouille, Countess of Derby, in the absence of her husband. The Countess felt that 3000 men would be required to man the defences properly, yet the Earl, departing to raise troops for the King's cause in the Isle of Man, left her with just 300 and a few small guns. The siege lasted from May 1643 until June 1644. It was conducted on behalf of Parliament by a Colonel Alexander Rigby, a lawyer and Member of Parliament for Wigan who held a deep-seated grudge against the entire Stanley family, of which the Earl was head. One of his preacher cronies described Lathom House as Babylon and the Countess as the Scarlet Woman herself. That would simply have amused her, for she was the toughest of cookies and more than a match for Rigby in every way.

For months, the siege amounted to nothing more than a distant blockade. That didn't work because the local people had been tenants of the Stanleys for centuries and kept the garrison supplied with food. Early in 1644 Sir Thomas Fairfax, Parliament's commander in the north, began to take an interest and the siege was taken in hand seriously. Guns began battering the walls, but because the house lay in a hollow their balls only struck the upper courses and were unable to bring down any section. By no means a gifted soldier, Rigby had sited his guns poorly. This was a major omission for which he would pay dearly.

The Countess's men were perpetually short of powder and what they had was reserved for the estate's gamekeepers, who were the best shots and regularly picked off any Roundhead foolish enough to venture within range of the walls. When the powder began to run out, the garrison made a sortie and obtained more from the besiegers' gun positions. Further sorties succeeded in *spiking* (disabling) the enemy guns by hammering nails into their touch-holes, inflicting casualties, and taking prisoners. Morale inside the walls was sky-high. Outside it was nearly at rock bottom. Then, Rigby had an idea. He had a mortar (see Chapter 5 for more on these guns) brought up from Cheshire at great expense, hoping that its shells would set the timber-framed buildings in the house's interior ablaze. The mortar succeeded in firing a few shots, causing a certain amount of damage. However, a meticulously planned sortie from the house captured it and the mortar was gleefully dragged inside the walls on a sledge. Disheartened, the besiegers began deserting.

In May, Rigby learned that Prince Rupert and the Earl of Derby had entered Lancashire from the south. Abandoning the siege, he marched to Bolton, where Rupert caught up with him. After the Roundheads had rashly killed several prisoners in cold blood in front of the royal army, the prince gave orders that no quarter was to be given when the town was stormed. Needless to say Rigby, as slimy a politician as any, survived. Disguising himself as a Royalist, he galloped through the streets and on to safety, shouting joyously, 'The town is ours!' Rupert sent no fewer than 23 captured Colours to Lathom House, where they were hung in triumph. He went on to capture Liverpool and, accompanied by the Earl, reached Lathom on 13 June. The Earl and Countess left for the Isle of Man and Rupert marched on into Yorkshire.

After a Parliamentarian victory at Marston Moor, a second siege began at Lathom House in August 1644. The garrison held out until December the following year. After the king's defeat at Naseby in June 1645, hopes of relief began to fade. In December, Charles advised the defenders of Lathom to seek the best terms they could get. They were offered the honours of war, which would have enabled them to march out with their Colours, arms, and personal possessions. This was too much for the mean-spirited Rigby, who was fully aware that those in the house were on the verge of starvation, and he withdraw the offer. He demanded unconditional surrender, which was accepted. The garrison left with their lives, what they were wearing, and nothing else.

Campaigning in 1644

The intervention of the Scots army (see the previous section) proved decisive in northern England. It altered the entire strategic situation and resulted in the joint Scottish and Parliamentary army besieging the Royalist commander, the Duke of Newcastle, in York. Prince Rupert marched to his assistance through the Pennines. Fairfax, Parliament's commander in the north, abandoned the siege and marched to Long Marston, west of the city, where he received reinforcements. This enabled Newcastle and Rupert to join forces. The scene was now set for the Battle of Marston Moor.

The Battle of Marston Moor, 2 July 1644

Marston Moor was the largest engagement of the first Civil War, fought just outside York. Rupert's army consisted of 11,000 infantry and 6500 cavalry, a total of 17,500 men, and 16 guns. The Scottish/Parliamentary army, jointly commanded by Fairfax and the Earls of Manchester and Leven, possessed 18,000 infantry and 9000 cavalry, a total of 27,000 men, and 25 guns. Rupert was unwise to offer battle when so seriously outnumbered, but it was not in his nature to refuse it.

The Royalist cavalry was contained by counter-attacks on both flanks. In the centre, a general advance by the Parliamentary allies overwhelmed the Royalist infantry after a bitter struggle. One of the best regiments in the king's service, Newcastle's Whitecoats, came close to routing their opposite numbers but were surrounded. Too proud to accept quarter, they went down fighting, only 30 of them being taken alive.

Estimates place the Royalist and allied killed at 3000 and 2000 respectively, but desertions were heavy on both sides. Rupert was left with only 6000 men to withdraw into Lancashire. When York surrendered to the Parliamentarians on 16 July, the Royalist presence in the north was reduced to a handful of isolated garrisons.

Swings and roundabouts

Aside from Marston Moor (see the previous section), the Royalists sustained a defeat at Nantwich in Cheshire. But on 6 June, the King defeated Waller at Cropredy Bridge, near Oxford. He then turned southwest, trapping Essex at Lostwithiel in Cornwall. Essex managed to escape with his cavalry, but his infantry surrendered on 2 September, handing over all their artillery.

The following month, Manchester, Waller, and Cromwell managed to concentrate their forces to produce a 22,000-strong Parliamentary army. On 22 October they confronted the king, who had only 10,000 men at his disposal, at the Second Battle of Newbury. The Roundheads failed to coordinate their attacks properly and the surprising result was a drawn battle, enabling Charles to fall back on his base at Oxford. For some reason, Manchester declined to pursue him.

The New Model Army

For all that he was a most unpleasant individual, Oliver Cromwell was undoubtedly the best commander that either side possessed in the Civil War. He began by commanding the troops raised by the Eastern Association of six East Anglian counties. He trained and disciplined his men thoroughly and always exercised tight tactical control over them in action, so that after a successful charge his cavalry did not carry out an uncontrolled pursuit, as Prince Rupert's did so often. This meant that they were available for the next phase of the fighting, which usually decided the battle. Such was their reputation that they became known as the *Ironsides*.

In January 1645 Cromwell urged Parliament to adopt what he called 'a frame for the whole militia'. What he proposed, in fact, was a standing army to be raised by conscription and paid for by taxation. The army consisted of 12 infantry regiments containing about 14,000 men, 11 cavalry regiments with 6600 men, and 1000 dragoons.

The last were infantrymen who rode to battle but fought on foot, their name being taken from the *dragon*, a French version of the musket with which they were equipped. Cromwell expanded the artillery and made some progress towards standardising its guns. Training methods were loosely based on those of the Ironsides. As constituted, the New Model Army overcame the local militias' reluctance to serve beyond their home territories. In addition, the army was to receive a uniform, the colour of which was russet (a shade of red).

Cromwell's ideas were passed by Parliament and reinforced in April 1645 by a measure styled the *Self-Denying Ordinance*, requiring Members of Parliament to relinquish their military commands. Sir Thomas Fairfax succeeded Essex as Captain General of the Army and Cromwell obtained a dispensation allowing him to continue serving as Lieutenant General.

For their part, the Scots had begun to look uneasily over their shoulders, for in Scotland James Graham, Marquis of Montrose, had raised several of the Highland clans on behalf of the King and on 1 September he inflicted a defeat on government troops at Tippermuir.

Reaching a conclusion: 1645–1646

In Scotland, Montrose inflicted one defeat after another on his Parliamentarian opponents, beginning with Inverlochy (2 February), then Auldearn (9 May), Alford (2 July), and finally Kilsyth (15 August). He had now secured most of Scotland for the king.

In England, Charles succeeded in taking Leicester after sustaining severe casualties that he could ill afford. He was still operating in the Midlands when a Parliamentary army commanded by Fairfax and Cromwell surprised him at Naseby, and the decisive battle of the war was fought there on 14 June.

The Battle of Naseby, 14 June 1645

At Naseby, Charles possessed 4000 infantry and 5000 cavalry, a total of 9000, and 12 guns. Fairfax and Cromwell had 7000 infantry and 6000 cavalry, a total of 13,000, and 13 guns.

Both armies were drawn up with their infantry in the centre and their cavalry on the flanks, with a small reserve behind. In addition, the Parliamentarians deployed a regiment of dragoons (see the sidebar, 'The New Model Army' earlier in this chapter) along the hedges to the west of the battlefield, covering the approach to their position. The battle began with successful cavalry charges by the right wings of both armies, but while Prince Rupert's Cavaliers pursued their opponents as far as the Parliamentary wagon lines, Cromwell exercised tight control. After he had driven off Langdale's Northern Horse he led his second line in an attack on Lord Astley's Royalist infantry in the centre, which, despite its inferior numbers, was pushing back the Parliamentary centre. At this point Charles could have launched his reserve and Langdale's rallied cavalry in a decisive counter-attack that would have smashed into Cromwell's flank. Unfortunately, one of his supporters, believing that the battle was lost, attempted to lead the king away. In the ensuing confusion the moment passed. The Parliamentarian dragoons mounted their horses and joined in the attack on the Royalist infantry, most of whom, heavily outnumbered and beset on three sides, surrendered. One regiment, Rupert's Bluecoats, declined to do so and fought to the bitter end; the rest of the royal army broke and fled.

Surrendering to the Scots: Charles calls it a day

The few troops remaining to the king in the south and west of England were unable to stem the tide of Parliamentary victory. One after another, the king's strongholds surrendered. In Scotland, a Parliamentary force commanded by General David Leslie destroyed Montrose's Royalist army at Philiphaugh on 13 September 1645. The last Royalist field force in England was defeated at Stow-on-the-Wold in 21 March 1646.

Charles gave himself up to a Scottish force, and the Scots sold him to Parliament for £400,000. Parliament, which owed its soldiers several months' pay, told the New Model Army to disband. The army not only refused to do so, but made it clear that it was running things from now on.

Meanwhile, Charles bargained with the Scots, with Parliament, and with the army. He promised this, that, and the other, then changed his mind until everyone was thoroughly confused. To make matters worse, he escaped from London to the Isle of Wight. It was just his luck that the island's governor was Parliament's man. The Governor imprisoned the king in Carisbrooke Castle, and that made the Scots very angry indeed, as they believed that they had been on the point of being granted everything they wanted from Charles.

The Second Civil War

By 1648, after the army had forcibly taken charge of the country, many people had had enough of the army's way of doing things.

Risings occurred in Kent and Essex, which Fairfax put down, while Cromwell dealt with similar troubles in south Wales. In July, the Duke of Hamilton crossed the border with a Scottish army and was joined by northern Royalists. He was now at the head of some 24,000 men, although they were poorly equipped and lacked guns. On 17 August they were strung out along many miles of road when Cromwell, with 6000 infantry and 3000 cavalry, drove into their flank. Only a small number of Hamilton's troops were involved and Cromwell forced them back into Preston, in Lancashire.

The rest of the Royalist army disintegrated, with the major portion trying to escape to the south. On 19 August Cromwell brought its infantry to battle near Warrington, which then was part of Lancashire, and forced them to surrender. Hamilton and his cavalry got as far south as Uttoxeter, in the West Midlands, before Cromwell's men rounded them up.

The army was now determined to be rid of Charles. On 6 December it prevented over 100 Members of Parliament with known moderate opinions from entering Parliament. Those members whom they did permit to sit became known as the *Rump*. The Rump convened a court trying Charles for making war on his own people, and therefore for treason. He refused to recognise the court and, predictably, Parliament found him guilty and sentenced him to death. During these proceedings his courage and dignity provoked much sympathy. Charles I was beheaded on 30 January 1649. A Commonwealth replaced the monarchy and, on Cromwell's instructions, the crown itself was smashed to pieces and destroyed.

The Third Civil War

The Scots, disgusted by the king's execution (see the preceding section), opened negotiations with his exiled son (who was to become Charles II), who agreed to abide by the Solemn League and Covenant (the section 'Setting the Civil War in swing' earlier in this chapter has more on this). He was invited to Scotland and crowned King of Scotland on 1 January 1651.

Cromwell, fully aware of what was going on, had already crossed the border in July 1650 and was marching on Edinburgh. His opponent, the veteran David Leslie, manoeuvred cleverly and employed a 'scorched earth' policy that forced the Roundheads to rely on the fleet for their supplies. Disease, hunger, and exhaustion reduced Cromwell's strength by half, leaving him with just 11,000 men to face Leslie's 20,000. Cromwell withdrew through Musselburgh and then to Dunbar, where Leslie boxed him in against the coast. Cromwell seriously considered embarking the army on his ships and was prepared to sacrifice his artillery, horses, and baggage if necessary.

Leslie believed that such an evacuation was inevitable. At this point, the Elders of the Kirk, a group so grim that by comparison the English Puritans looked like a song-and-dance troupe, started nagging him. On 2 September they persuaded Leslie to descend from the strong position he held on Doon Hill during the night to attack Cromwell's army the following morning. In fairness, he would not have done so unless he thought he could win. In the meantime, Cromwell had detected a weakness on the Scottish right and it was against this weakness that he directed a major attack at first light, while his artillery was concentrated against the enemy left. Only a splutter of musketry met Cromwell's attack and he simply rolled up Leslie's line. Cromwell's men killed some 3000 of the Scots and captured 10,000, together with all their guns. Cromwell claimed that his own casualties amounted to just 30 killed, a figure that even the gullible may have found hard to digest. Dissent arose among the Scots, but Cromwell was unable to take advantage of it as he was ill. It was not until the middle of the next year that major hostilities resumed.

The Battle of Worcester, 3 September 1651

Charles II crossed the border from Scotland with the intention of marching on London in the hope of gaining his throne, but attracted little support. Cromwell followed him, and Charles turned to give battle at Worcester. His army, which included 6000 Scots, consisted of 8000 infantry, 4000 cavalry, and some guns. Cromwell produced 18,000 infantry, 9000 cavalry, and some guns.

The Parliamentary army began by attacking across the rivers Severn and Teme on bridges of boats built by its engineers. Charles's army beat them back and opened an attack on the enemy centre. He was making some progress when Cromwell returned and broke the Royalists' cavalry, then drove their infantry into the city, where most of them surrendered. Royalist losses amounted to 3000 killed and up to 7000 captured, along with all their artillery. Few of the Scots succeeded in making it back to their own country. Charles became a fugitive for six weeks before escaping to the continent. Cromwell's casualties almost certainly came to more than the 300 he admitted to.

Worcester was the last battle of the Civil Wars, although some Royalist strongholds held out until 1652. It was not, however, the last battle that the New Model Army fought.

The Irish Campaign, 1649–1652

Fighting took place in Ireland between English Royalists, a Catholic Confederacy, the Anglo-Irish gentry, and the native Irish. To restore order and establish the Commonwealth's authority, Cromwell crossed to Ireland in September 1649. Such was the climate that neither Royalists nor Catholics expected much in the way of mercy, and Royalist Catholics none at all. Most had taken refuge in fortified towns, but their ancient walls offered little defence against Cromwell's New Model Army with its wide experience of siegecraft. Drogheda fell in September 1649, Wexford in October 1649, and Clonmel in May 1650. At every captured fortress the defenders and many others were ruthlessly massacred. After the fall of Clonmel, Cromwell returned to England, leaving his subordinates to carry on with the reign of terror. The last Royalist stronghold in Galway surrendered in May 1652. In some parts of Ireland the very name of Cromwell is still hated.

Campaigning for the Commonwealth

During the Franco-Spanish War of 1653–1659, Cromwell's Commonwealth sided with the French. In 1658 six Cromwellian regiments formed part of an Anglo-French army that besieged Dunkirk. On 3 June French forces defeated a strong Spanish relief force, including 2000 English Royalists under the Duke of York (later James II), four miles east of the town in what became known as the Battle of the Dunes. Anglo-French losses amounted to 400 killed and wounded. The Spaniards lost 1000 killed and 5000 captured. Dunkirk surrendered 10 days later, followed by other Spanish fortresses in Flanders. King Louis XIV of France was so pleased with the result that he ceded Dunkirk to Cromwell (Charles II, permanently short of money, sold it back to Louis in 1662).

Chapter 7

Founding a Regular Army: The Late Seventeenth Century

C romwell's death in 1658 and Parliament's invitation to Charles II to return to the throne in 1660 meant the end of the New Model Army. You couldn't get much more anti-monarchy than those chaps, and inviting the king back meant the return of a monarchy.

However, the end of the Civil Wars didn't mean the end of the need for a standing army. All the major continental powers now possessed their own standing armies, and in the changed circumstances of the times, Britain could not do without one. This chapter covers the earliest days of Britain's first regular army, from 1660 to 1695.

The formation of the Regular Army saw the use of the following troop types in the late seventeenth century:

- ✔ **Infantry:** Most infantrymen (or regiments of foot) were musket armed, although a few pikes remained. New types of infantrymen emerged in this period – fusiliers and grenadiers (see the section 'Introducing new types of soldier', later in this chapter, for more on them).

- ✔ **Cavalry:** Regiments of horse were armed with swords and pistols, and regiments of dragoons fought as mounted infantrymen.

- ✔ **Artillery:** Guns were used both on the battlefield and in sieges.

For more on how the army looked, see the section 'Dressing for battle', later in this chapter.

The Changing Army

Raising the new army from scratch presented difficulties. Designed to be a volunteer, long-service army, the numbers required to raise new regiments meant that they had to be recruited by persuasion. That was no easy task. Even regular soldiers dislike being shot in the best of causes, so why should a civilian expose himself to death, wounds, hard living, tough discipline, brutal punishments, and poor pay? He may receive bed, board, and clothing, but was that enough? Some men did indeed enlist because the life appealed to them. The rest were petty criminals whom the magistrates told to join as an alternative to prison, men trying to escape their debts, husbands escaping their wives, and those down on their luck or starving because they were unable to find employment. If a recruit could read and write, he was lucky because he was well on the way to becoming a corporal.

In the days before permanent barracks were built, the army often quartered its men in inns. The civilian population detested soldiers, regarding them as useless, drunken, licentious brutes. As no police existed at the time, the government often used the army to put down riots and disturbances. The curious thing is that having been forced by circumstances to become soldiers, and knowing that their countrymen despised them, the recruits began to value each other on their merits, came to rely on their colleagues, and so recovered their self-respect. The regiment became their home and family. This was the beginning of something that remains peculiar to the British and some Commonwealth armies, namely regimental spirit. We may want to remember the Duke of Wellington's comment (a century or so after the formation of the regular army) on his troops:

> *They are the scum of the earth – it really is remarkable what fine fellows we have made of them!*

Raising a regiment: The proprietary system

When Parliament raised a new regiment, it gave a prominent individual such as a peer or a significant landowner authority to carry this out, voting him a sum of money for the task. He also received the sums that the regiment's first officers paid for their commissions (see the next section), as well as government money handed over to him and his successors in subsequent years for the regiment's maintenance. The regiment was, in practical terms, this man's property. He was its colonel and was responsible for running it (including its complex financial deals such as pay, uniform allowance, purchase of horses, and recruiting costs).

This *proprietary system* was open to abuse, as the colonel was allowed to pocket whatever he could save from the regiment's running expenses. He perhaps claimed allowances for soldiers listed on the muster roll who did not exist, or did a deal with a contractor to supply inferior-quality goods such as uniforms. By no means all colonels were crooked, but for some raising a regiment was a licence to print money.

Colonels rarely served with their regiments; lieutenant colonels commanded them in the colonel's absence. Although each regiment had an official number, during the early days of the Regular Army period people generally knew it by its colonel's name.

Buying a commission

Most officers purchased their *commissions* (a commission is a document signed by the sovereign authorising the individual name to serve as an officer in one of the armed services), as they did every step of promotion up to lieutenant colonel. An officer serving with one regiment could purchase promotion when a vacancy appeared in another, and he transferred across. Guards regiments were considered an elite, the rest of the army's cavalry and infantry being referred to as *line* regiments. Commissions in the guards cost twice as much as those in line regiments because those holding them were of a social standing acceptable to the monarch. Commissions in the cavalry cost more than those in the infantry because their holders were drawn from a stratum of society that could afford country pursuits based on the horse, not always affordable to others; indeed, many cavalry officers went to war mounted on their own horses. The government set a tariff for commissions, but in reality prices were much higher. When he retired or left the army, the officer sold his commission. If he was lucky it had appreciated in value and he used the money to buy a pension.

The system of commission by purchase is difficult to defend, but in truth it worked very well. Most officers came from a stratum of society used to making decisions and giving orders, and were quite capable of courageous leadership if the circumstances demanded it – although the odd idiot or bad egg did put in an appearance. Not every officer bought his commission, however. In some regiments, promising *non-commissioned officers* (NCOs; that is, corporals and sergeants) were granted commissions as adjutants, quartermasters, and paymasters.

On active service, vacancy and merit played a part in obtaining promotion. After a particularly successful action, some NCOs and even private soldiers received a battlefield commission. Officers of the Royal Artillery and Royal Engineers, having received specialist training, did not need to purchase their commissions, but as their promotion was by seniority a lieutenant may have reached middle age before he attained his captaincy.

Introducing new types of soldier

Evolving military technology led to new types of soldier appearing in the army. Gunpowder offered more possibilities than merely being the propellant in guns and muskets – it could be used in a *grenade*, too. When thrown into the enemy's ranks, these hand-held bombs caused casualties among those closest to them. Of course, no one wanted a grenade exploding too close to their own troops and for that reason the new *grenadiers* (who threw the bombs) were only selected from the tallest men, as they were able to throw further. Because the tricorne hat worn by most of the line infantry interfered with the natural swing of the arm when throwing a grenade, grenadiers wore a headdress similar to a bishop's mitre, with the front embroidered to a regimental pattern (shown in Figure 7-1).

Another new type of solider was the *fusilier,* who got their name because they were armed with an improved type of musket, called a *fusil*. Their original purpose was to provide an escort for the Royal Artillery's guns. This meant not only defending the guns against the enemy, but also preventing the civilian drivers from making off with the horses when things seemed to be taking a turn for the worst (the ancient practice of hiring teams of horses to pull the guns was to continue throughout this period). The first fusilier regiment was The Royal Fusiliers (City of London Regiment), 7th Foot, raised in 1685. They wore similar caps to the grenadiers.

One event changed the nature of the infantryman's war in the seventeenth century more than any other. French soldiers invented the *bayonet* by accident and of necessity during the 1640 siege of Bayonne. Pikemen were in short supply and, to defend themselves at close quarters, musketeers cut the heads off pikes and stuck them in the muzzles of their muskets, which they otherwise only used as clubs. This *plug bayonet* had the obvious disadvantage that the musket could not be fired when it was in use, so the *ring bayonet*, which fitted over the musket's muzzle, followed quickly, and the *socket bayonet*, which clipped on to permanent fittings on the musket barrel, succeeded it in turn. As a result of this invention, the musketeer became his own pikeman and the pikeman proper disappeared from the battlefield.

Dressing for battle

All soldiers in the Regular Army wore a uniform, unlike in earlier times. A uniform provided a useful means of identification in battle that had not existed in any clear form previously, and it added to an individual unit's *esprit de corps* (pride in your regiment). The national colour chosen for English armies was scarlet and the cut of a soldier's coat was not very different from a civilian's.

For most practical purposes, the army discarded the remaining vestiges of armour after the Civil Wars (see Chapter 6). Many cavalry regiments still wore iron skull caps under their tricorne hats and heavy cavalry continued to wear the breastplate for a while, the reason in both cases being to protect the wearer against sword cuts. Figure 7-1 shows a typical infantryman, grenadier, and cavalryman of the late seventeenth century.

Figure 7-1: English infantryman, grenadier, and cavalry-man in the late seventeenth and early eighteenth centuries.

Regiments recognised each other by the facing colour of their cuffs and, later, turned-back coat tails and lapels. As a general rule, Royal regiments had blue facings, English regiments white, Scottish regiments yellow, and Welsh regiments green, but many exceptions existed. Royal regiments wore blue breeches, and the rest wore white. Until 1716 the Royal Artillery wore scarlet, but after that date its uniforms were blue with scarlet facings. Engineers wore scarlet for the excellent reason that they were too valuable to lose, and to an enemy sniper this colour made them indistinguishable from their infantry working parties.

The First Regiments

The longest-serving armed unit in Britain is the Yeoman of the Guard, which Henry VII formed in 1485 as a personal bodyguard. Next comes the Honourable Artillery Company, directly descended from The Fraternity of the Guild of St George, which Henry VIII incorporated in 1537. These, however, are not regular units, and even some of those that are actually predate the formation of the Regular Army in 1660.

The first regiments actually to be embodied in the army were:

- ✔ **The Buffs (The Royal East Kent Regiment) or 3rd Foot, 1572**. Originally raised by Elizabeth I as 'The Hollands Regiment'. Still serving with the Dutch when Charles II declared war on Holland in 1665, and refused to fight against England, so was absorbed into the British army.

- ✔ **The Royal Scots or 1st Foot, 1633**. Claimed descent from a Roman legion serving in Scotland, hence its nickname of 'Pontius Pilate's Bodyguard'. During the Crimean War this assertion led to a punch-up with a French infantry regiment that claimed descent from the legion that had been on duty at the Crucifixion. The Royal Scots' continuous existence began under Charles I in 1633. It subsequently served the King of France before transferring back to the British service.

- ✔ **The Coldstream or 2nd Foot Guards, 1650**. Originally Monck's Regiment in the New Model Army. Disliked being second to the Grenadier Guards and deliberately adopted the motto *Nulli Secundus* (second to none).

- ✔ **The Life Guards, 1660**. Served as Charles II's escort while he was in exile.

- ✔ **The Grenadier or 1st Foot Guards, 1660**. Originally known as 'The Royal Regiment of Guards'. Accompanied Charles II in exile.

- ✔ **The Royal Horse Guards, 1661**. Began life as a Parliamentary regiment.

- ✔ **The Queen's Royal Regiment (West Surrey) or 2nd Foot, 1661**.

- ✔ **The King's Own Royal Regiment (Lancaster) or 4th Foot, 1680**.

- ✔ **The Scots Guards or 3rd Foot Guards, 1685**. Originally formed about 1639.

More infantry regiments formed between 1685 and 1689, more in 1701, and other at intervals up to 1800. Seven regiments of horse and six of dragoons became established between 1681 and 1689.

In theory, an infantry regiment had a nominal strength of 1200 and contained ten companies. Two companies, known as the *flank companies*, differed from the rest. One was the Grenadier Company, containing the biggest and strongest men in the regiment (who also lobbed grenades at their enemies – described in the section 'Introducing new types of soldier' earlier in this chapter), and the other was the Light Company, whose men were employed as *skirmishers* (usually marksmen who picked off the enemy's officers and kept the enemy's skirmishers at a distance). On active service, these companies were often temporarily removed from the regiment to form Grenadier or Light regiments. Orders were given within a company by:

- ✔ A captain
- ✔ A lieutenant
- ✔ An ensign or second lieutenant
- ✔ Two sergeants and three corporals

Regiments of horse consisted of six troops, each with a nominal strength of 100 men. The troop's leaders were:

- ✔ A captain
- ✔ A lieutenant
- ✔ A cornet
- ✔ A quartermaster-sergeant and three sergeants or corporals-of-horse.

Colours

An infantry regiment possessed two *Colours* (regimental flags), the Sovereign's and the Regimental Colour; this holds true even today. Before going on campaign, a regiment trooped its Colours along the ranks, allowing soldiers to recognise them amid the noise, confusion, and dense smoke of a real battle. In action Colours were deployed in the centre of the regiment's line and formed a rallying point in critical circumstances.

The Colours enshrined the regiment's honour, spirit, and traditions, and men guarded them to the death if the situation warranted it. The capture of an enemy Colour was a signal feat of arms.

Cavalry regiments carry a single standard or swallow-tailed guidon of smaller dimensions than the infantry Colours. The Royal Regiment of Artillery has never possessed Colours, but attaches a similar importance to its guns.

Battle honours and honour titles

Battle honours started to be awarded to regiments that have distinguished themselves in specific battles or campaigns, and this tradition continues in the modern British army. Honours are not awarded for defeats, no matter how gallantly a regiment may have fought, nor in civil wars. The honour consists of a name and sometimes a date, and is embroidered on a regiment's Colours.

The first battle honour, Tangier, 1662–80, was awarded to The Grenadier Guards, The Coldstream Guards, The Royal Dragoons (The Royals, 1st Dragoons), The Royal Scots, and The Queen's Regiment. This was for the defence of Tangier, which formed part of Portuguese princess Catherine de Braganza's dowry when she married Charles II.

Preparing for War: Logistics, Ballistics, and Fortification

The introduction of a Regular Army, and the increasing professionalism and organisation of the troops, required the military support services and infrastructure to catch up:

- ✔ **Logistics** (the science of supply) involves everything an army eats, wears, and uses, and requires considerable forethought. At this period logistic science was in its infancy, but the need was apparent for conveniently sited supply depots and *magazines* (weapon, gunpowder, and ammunition storage). Logistics went hand in hand with accountability, which meant that from the outset an item of equipment such as a musket had to be signed for every time it changed hands. This made the last signatory responsible for the item, ensuring that he took care of it and preventing its loss or sale to interested outsiders. This started the ball rolling on a bureaucracy that, as discussed in Chapter 13 on the Crimean War, got completely out of hand and resulted in severe hardship for the fighting troops.

- ✔ **Ballistics** (the study of how guns and their ammunition perform) was still at a comparatively early stage. The army had much to learn, but it already knew a great deal about such things as trajectories, fuse setting, and probable casualties inflicted at a given range. Heavy guns always played a major role in sieges, but the army was now giving serious thought to lighter weapons with increased mobility that field armies used together in batteries. Infantry battalions were already issued with two small guns apiece, manned at first by their own men but later by members of the Royal Artillery.

- ✔ **Fortification** underwent a radical change. Medieval castles were no match for sustained gunfire, and Henry VIII's old forts still left dead ground for the enemy to exploit (see Chapter 5). The same was not true of wedge-shaped *bastions*, which provided mutual support covering every angle of approach; from these bastions evolved the *star system* of fortification (so called because the overall design of a fortress consisting of bastions linked by curtain walls resembled a star). Most of these defences were sunk into the earth, with only the fighting parapets and gun embrasures visible above ground. From their outer edges the permanent defences consisted of a sloped glacis, counterscarp, ditch, scarp, and ramparts. To an outside observer, even the parapets were difficult to spot as a deep layer of earth covered them to cushion the impact of cannon balls and so reduce the danger from flying stone splinters.

Vauban forts: The best of the best

The master of the star system fortification was a French officer, Sebastien le Prestre du Vauban, who became the French army's Director of Engineering. Vauban's approach was precise and mathematical. Given the number and type of guns employed in a siege, together with the construction of the fortress, he calculated with reasonable accuracy how long the defences may be capable of holding out. Comparatively few Vauban-style fortresses were built in the British Isles, but British engineer officers had to be familiar with them as they had to deal with them in Europe. The new complexities of fortification and siegecraft led to the establishment of permanent bodies of military engineers, whose work also included bridge and road building.

To launch an assault on such a fortress without adequate preparation was to invite crippling casualties; mining offered an alternative if the ditch was dry, but this involved tunnelling through the foundations of the counterscarp, then under the ditch, and finally through the thickness of the scarp. The only method likely to guarantee success was to concentrate artillery fire against a weak spot in the defences; these batteries were dug in 550 metres (600 yards) from the walls, and connected by a trench that became known as the First Parallel. From this zigzag *saps* (smaller trenches) were pushed out and the guns brought forward to establish a Second Parallel 250 metres (300 yards) from the defences. This was repeated until a Third Parallel existed within musket shot of the defences. When the defences had been battered into silence and a breach in the walls effected, the garrison surrendered, or the attacker launched an assault.

Getting Some Action!

The Regular Army's first campaign took place in North Africa, defending Tangier against the Moors until possession of the town was relinquished in 1684.

The Battle of Sedgemoor, 6 July 1685

The following year the Duke of Monmouth (the illegitimate son of Charles II) landed in the English West Country to raise the standard of rebellion against his unpopular uncle, James II, who had become king in February 1685 after Charles II's death. Government troops destroyed the Duke's small army, consisting mainly of countrymen armed with little better than scythes, at

Sedgemoor on 6 July 1685. The Duke rashly attempted a night approach march with his raw levies, but this failed to achieve the hoped-for surprise. The outcome of the battle was predictable. Nevertheless, the battle demonstrated the efficiency of well-drilled infantry armed with muskets and is interesting for the presence of a Regular Army officer named John Churchill, who later became Duke of Marlborough (for more on him, see the very next chapter).

The Battle of the Boyne, 1 July 1690

In 1688, William of Orange, a staunch Protestant married to James II's daughter Mary, landed in Devon with Dutch troops to overthrow the pro-Catholic King of England, James II (for more on this, see Sean Lang's *British History For Dummies*, published by Wiley). No fighting took place, the army simply joining William's cause. When James escaped to France, Parliament adjudged him to have abdicated and conferred the crown jointly on William and Mary. Then James thought better of leaving and attempted to recover his throne, landing in Ireland in 1689 with some French troops. He managed to put together 18,000 infantry and 5000 cavalry, most of whom were Irish Catholics, and six guns. James was withdrawing towards Dublin when, on 1 July 1690, William's army forced a battle at the crossing of the river Boyne. William had 35,000 men at his disposal: 26,500 infantry, 8000 cavalry, and 50 guns. As well as English and Dutch, his army included Irish Protestants and French Huguenots. English regular regiments present included 11 cavalry or dragoon regiments and 12 infantry regiments.

William launched a frontal attack across the river, simultaneously sending a force upstream to fall on James's left flank. William's attack met fierce opposition, but as soon as pressure from the flanking force made itself felt, James's army began to disintegrate. For such an important battle, casualties were remarkably light on both sides: William had 2000 men killed or wounded, while James suffered 1500 casualties.

James took off for France again and died in exile, although his family and supporters, named *Jacobites* (the posh Latin name for James or Jimmy is Jacobus), continued to be a real pain in the neck for the British monarchy in the next half-century (see Chapter 9).

Under William's rule, British troops took part in the long-forgotten War of the League of Augsburg (1689–1697). They fought in several equally forgotten battles, some of which were very bloody indeed, but the only one deemed worthy of a Battle Honour was Namur, 1695.

Part III
Wars of Succession, Independence, and Revolution

THE 1ST DUKE OF MARLBOROUGH COMMEMORATES HIS VICTORY AT BLENHEIM

"Remember, 'Blenheim' is 'ei', not 'ie'."

In this part . . .

For over a century, the United Kingdom was at war with France almost continuously. Some of the wars were about who was going to sit on which throne where, and some were about who was going to dominate territories in North America and India. Rebellions were also put down closer to home. The British Army was heavily involved when 13 of the American colonies rebelled, winning most of the battles in what many people on both sides felt was an unnecessary civil war. During the French Revolutionary and Napoleonic Wars Britain was involved in yet more fighting in various parts of the world, notably Spain and Portugal, and played a major part in the final defeat of Napoleon at Waterloo.

This period saw the British Army begin to forge traditions that have lasted to the present day, fighting under such gifted commanders as Marlborough, Amherst, Wolfe, and Wellington.

Chapter 8

O'er the Hills and Far Away: Marlborough Country and Beyond

. . . .

In This Chapter

▶ The War of Spanish Succession, 1701–1714

▶ The War of Austrian Succession, 1740–1748

▶ The Seven Years' War, 1756–1763

▶ Fighting in India, the Americas, and Gibraltar

. . . .

*T*he keystone of British foreign policy in Europe in the eighteenth century was to preserve a balance of power, which required preventing too much power passing into the hands of any one European royal family. This meant that the cause of most of the wars fought during the century was dynastic. Later in the century, rival British and French interests overseas meant that fighting took part in many parts of the world (see the section 'Same Old Enemy, Brand New Venues' later in this chapter for more on these campaigns), leading some historians to describe this conflict as the first of the world wars.

Although primarily a sea power, Britain committed its army to these wars to fight alongside its allies. After a virtual absence from the European continent of two-and-a-half centuries, the British soldier quickly re-established his reputation as a tough opponent, stubborn to the point of immobility in defence and very difficult to stop when he attacked.

This was the era of the red-coated, tricorne hat-wearing soldier, arrayed on the battlefield in neat lines and columns. There had been a regular army for just a few decades by the start of the eighteenth century (see Chapter 7); soldiers were little changed from those outlined in the previous chapter, and the uniforms they fought in were similar; and some advances were made in cavalry warfare – see the sidebar 'New cavalry developments' for more information.

One of the best-remembered recruiting songs of the period, still sung today, was 'O'er the Hills and Far Away' – just the thing to attract young men who wanted to go places and do things. Parliament liked the song too, because it had never forgotten that the New Model Army once booted its members, honourable and otherwise, out into the street (see Chapter 6) . . . so it liked to keep the troops fully occupied abroad. Figure 8-1 shows the location of the main battles featured in this chapter.

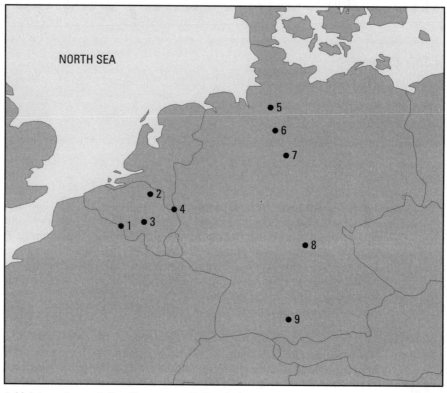

Figure 8-1:
Major
British
battles in
eighteenth-
century
Europe.

1. Malplaquet	4. Ramilles	7. Emsdorf
2. Oudenarde	5. Minden	8. Dettingen
3. Fontenoy	6. Warburg	9. Blenheim

New cavalry developments

In 1746 Parliament began to convert the old regiments of horse into dragoons. Dragoons received less pay, rode less expensive horses, and were generally cheaper to maintain. Naturally, this was not a popular move for those directly involved, so as a sop to their wounded pride they were allowed to call themselves *Dragoon Guards*. Obviously, spin doctoring is not the newest of the black arts.

In 1756 an entirely new form of cavalry soldier began to make his appearance. One troop from each of the existing regiments received specialised training in scouting, reconnaissance, obstacle clearing, and fighting in rough or close country, as well as the usual cavalry roles. Individual soldiers were expected to use their initiative, a novel concept at the time. Designated *Light Dragoons*, they raided the coast of France with the help of the Royal Navy in 1758. French dockyards and marine arsenals were destroyed and raids were made on inland towns. Such was the uproar that French troops had to be withdrawn from the fighting in Germany to reassure the population. As a result, four Light Dragoon regiments were raised, numbered 15th to 18th.

The War of Spanish Succession, 1701–1714

It didn't matter to Britain who clambered aboard the Spanish throne . . . as long as it wasn't Louis XIV of France. The Dutch, Austrians, Prussians, and several German states agreed, so they formed a Grand Alliance and war was on. In 1704 British *marines* (soldiers for sea-service as they were known officially) captured Gibraltar and held it against all comers, and in 1708 they also captured the island of Minorca. These successes in Spanish territory, however welcome, paled into insignificance compared to the victories that Marlborough was winning elsewhere with his Allied armies.

In the War of Spanish Succession, the army's leader was John Churchill, Duke of Marlborough, one of the great captains of any army throughout history. Marlborough was a rare combination of strategist, tactician, and logistician, a commander who insisted that one of his officers' most important duties was the welfare of their men, a general so interested in the daily details of his soldiers' lives that they gave him the affectionate nickname of Corporal John. The British generals who commanded in the later wars of the eighteenth century were not of quite the same calibre as the Duke of Marlborough, but some of them produced quite extraordinary results; others were merely competent; and one, Lord George Sackville, later Lord George Germaine, should have been shot (more on him in 'The Battle of Minden, 1 August 1759' later in this chapter and in Chapter 9).

The Battle of Blenheim, 13 August 1704

A stalemate on the Danube front (one of the areas where the Grand Alliance was facing off against the French and their Bavarian allies) and the need to break the Franco-Bavarian siege of Vienna started the build-up to this famous battle.

Marlborough's British troops marched from the Low Countries all the way to Bavaria to play their part. Thanks to Marlborough's planning, replacement shoes and other supplies had been purchased in advance and were collected along the route. When the allied army of Prince Eugene of Savoy joined Marlborough's, this forced the Franco-Bavarian army under Marshal Count Camille de Tallard to react and give battle.

The Allied army under the joint command of Marlborough and Eugene consisted of 65 infantry battalions and 160 cavalry squadrons – a total of 52,000 men, of whom 10,000 were British. Tallard's Franco-Bavarian army consisted of 79 infantry battalions and 140 cavalry squadrons – a total of 56,000 men and 90 guns. The river Danube on the right and a range of wooded hills on the left protected Tallard's position. Most of his infantry was positioned in three villages along his front:

- Blenheim on the right
- Oberglau on the centre left
- Lutzingen on the left

Marlborough noted that only lightly supported cavalry held the Franco-Bavarian centre between Blenheim and Oberglau, and that a large area of undefended water meadows lay between the enemy lines and the Nebel stream, a tributary of the Danube. He therefore decided to keep the enemy garrisons of the villages fully occupied while his principal thrust tore open Tallard's centre. The Allies' early-morning approach to the battlefield achieved a complete tactical surprise, although it could not fully exploited as Eugene's imperial troops had further to march than Marlborough's wing of the combined army, which contained the British contingent. At 12.30 p.m. Marlborough and Eugene attacked simultaneously.

Lord Cutts's British battalions failed to break through Blenheim's defences, but caused the French such concern that the local commander committed his army's entire infantry reserve to that village, without bothering to mention it to Tallard. The result was that no fewer than 27 infantry battalions were crammed uselessly into the village and the much smaller British force was able to contain them. At Oberglau the Allied attack met determined resistance, but Marlborough brought up reinforcements and here, too, contained the garrison. On the right, Eugene's troops also pinned down the garrison of Lutzingen. Meanwhile, British troops were fording the Nebel and forming up in the fields beyond.

Tallard, suddenly aware of the danger, ordered his cavalry to charge the British. For a while the outcome remained in doubt. Then Marlborough personally brought up a brigade of *cuirassiers* (heavy cavalrymen protected by breast and back plates) that Eugene had made available. This threw back the French counter-attack and by 5.30 p.m. the Allies had broken through the French centre. The Bavarians left the field, with Eugene snapping at their heels. At 11 p.m. the garrison of Blenheim surrendered. Tallard, together with Marshal de Marsin and several more generals, was captured. The victory was complete, but it cost the Allies 12,000 killed and wounded. Franco-Bavarian losses included 20,000 killed and wounded, 14,000 captured, 6000 desertions, and 60 guns taken. As a result of the battle the Allies raised the siege of Vienna and overran Bavaria.

The Battle of Ramillies, 22 May 1706

The Allied victory at Blenheim (see the previous section) so enraged Louis XIV that he wanted nothing better than the chance to restore the prestige of the French army. He ordered Marshal Duke François de Villeroi, commander of his troops in the Spanish Netherlands, to bring Marlborough to battle. That was generous of him, because Marlborough had been trying to bring Villeroi to battle for some time, without success!

The two armies converged near Namur, in modern-day Belgium. Marlborough's Allied army possessed 74 infantry battalions and 123 cavalry squadrons, a total of 62,000 men and 120 guns. Villeroi's strength amounted to 70 infantry battalions and 132 cavalry squadrons, a total of 60,000 men, and 70 guns.

Marlborough began the battle with an aggressive *feint* (diversionary attack) against the French left. It looked serious enough to Villeroi, who reinforced his apparently threatened flank with infantry from his centre. On the Allied left, however, the French cavalry seemed to be gaining the upper hand until Marlborough brought up additional squadrons from his centre and right and drove them off the field. The Allied cavalry then swung right to roll up the French line, while an infantry assault stormed its way into the village of Ramillies in the centre of Villeroi's position. What was left of the French army was forced to conduct a disorderly retreat.

Marlborough's casualties included 1000 killed and 3600 wounded. French losses came to 8000 killed and wounded, 7000 captured, and 50 guns. The Allies took a further 14,000 prisoners as one French fortress after another surrendered to Marlborough as he overran the Spanish Netherlands. Villeroi got the sack.

The Battle of Oudenarde, 11 July 1708

After Ramillies (see the preceding section), Marshal Duke Louis Joseph de Vendôme took charge of the French forces, and proved himself an aggressive commander. In 1708, however, the young Duke of Burgundy was given nominal command of the French Army of Flanders, although he left Vendôme to exercise operational command. Vendôme outmanoeuvred Marlborough during the early days of July, but Burgundy lost his nerve and ordered Vendôme not to give battle. A right royal row ensued and the troops were aware of it. Meanwhile, Marlborough was joined by his ally Eugene. Thanks to the bickering in the French camp, the Allies were able to make an unopposed crossing of the river Scheldt. They converged on Oudenarde, where the French had concentrated, and made a plan of attack similar to that used at Blenheim (see 'The Battle of Blenheim, 13 August 1704', earlier in this chapter).

The Allied army consisted of 85 infantry battalions and 150 cavalry squadrons, a total of 80,000 men. The French had 90 infantry battalions and 170 cavalry squadrons. The Allies were unable to put their 'Blenheim plan' into action because Vendôme, having finally knocked some sense into Burgundy's head, launched an attack of his own. The battle was marked by heavy, continuous fighting rather than tactical skill. By dusk the Allies had driven in both of Vendôme's flanks, ensuring victory, and it looked as though this double envelopment would trap the French centre. However, many of the French managed to escape during the night.

The Allies lost 2000 killed and 5000 wounded, while French losses included 4000 killed, 2000 wounded, 9000 captured, and 3000 desertions. Marlborough's victory restored the strategic initiative to the Allies and the capture of the French city of Lille followed later in the year.

The Battle of Malplaquet, 11 September 1709

Much of 1709 was spent in inconclusive manoeuvring, but in September the Allies laid siege to Mons, and Marshal the Duke Claude de Villars (commanding the nearest French army) advanced to relieve the town. He entrenched his troops at the nearby village of Malplaquet, knowing this would provoke Marlborough into attacking him. Having left some 20,000 men in the siege lines, the Allies advanced on Malplaquet, where they fought Villars's force on 11 September.

In total, the Allies possessed 128 infantry battalions and 253 cavalry squadrons, a total of 110,000 men (of whom 90,000 were engaged at Malplaquet), and 100 guns. Villars had 96 infantry battalions and 180 cavalry squadrons, a total of 80,000 men, and 60 guns. The Allied plan was for Eugene to mount a holding attack on the French left while part of Marlborough's troops mounted a similar attack on the enemy right. Marlborough's intention was to smash through the French centre once Villars had committed all his reserves.

Amid bitter fighting, Eugene was wounded but refused to leave the field. Villars was wounded so badly while leading a counter-attack that command passed to Boufflers (his second-in-command). When Marlborough's hammer-blow attack broke through the French centre during the afternoon, Boufflers promptly counter-attacked with his last reserves and re-established the line. Marlborough and Eugene committed their remaining reserves and once again penetrated the enemy's centre. Boufflers, lacking the resources to mount another counter-attack, initiated a withdrawal that his troops executed in good order.

Allied casualties included 6500 killed and 14,000 wounded. The French lost 4500 killed, 8000 wounded, and 10 guns captured. Everyone was horrified by these figures. Marlborough had political enemies at home and they used the losses against him to such good effect that Queen Anne removed him from active duty in 1711.

Handing out the spoils of war

The War of Spanish Succession spluttered on until the Treaty of Utrecht, signed in 1713, provided a basis for ending hostilities. Nearly everyone got prizes. Britain got Newfoundland and part of Canada. Its allies got large slices of Europe, mainly at Spain's expense. Spain got a king it could live with . . . and France got nothing.

The War of Austrian Succession, 1740–1748

When Maria Theresa ascended the throne of Imperial Austria in 1740, a number of European rulers challenged her right to it. Others with differing views put their oar in until, once again, the real issue in dispute was whether France was to become the dominant power in the continent. Naturally, Britain allied itself with those who weren't too keen on that idea, including Holland, Hanover, Hesse, and various German states.

The Battle of Dettingen, 27 June 1743

The Allied army attempted to separate the French from their Bavarian allies, but was forced to retreat when the French got across its lines of communications with Flanders. These lines needed to be reopened before any further action could be taken. On 27 June 1743 the Army was marching west along the north bank of the river Main only to find a French army, last seen on the south bank of the river, blocking its path at the village of Dettingen. French artillery also began firing on the Allied column from across the river.

King George II of England commanded the Allied army, accompanied by his second son, William Augustus, Duke of Cumberland. He had under his command some 40,000 British, Hanoverian, and Hessian troops. His opponent was Marshal the Duke Adrien de Noailles, with 30,000 troops under his command.

Most of the British troops at Dettingen had not been on active service since Marlborough's day (see 'The War of Spanish Succession, 1701–1714', earlier in this chapter) and were not fully trained.

Both armies deployed with one flank on the river and the other on the Spessart hills to the north, the bulk of their cavalry being drawn up beside the river Main. Noailles, thinking that it would be terrific fun to capture the British king, sent a force along the south bank to cross the river at Aschaffenburg, behind the Allied army, hoping to trap it. George despatched the British and Hanoverian Foot Guards to contain the move, which came to nothing. The battle itself was a confused, untidy affair. George's horse bolted, but he got it under control and dismounted beside an infantry regiment, commenting that he could trust his own legs not to run away with him. The French cavalry, led by the Maison du Roi regiment, mounted a charge but were driven back after what seems to have been a fiercely contested mêlée. In this, Cornet Richards of the Britain's 8th Horse (later 7th Dragoon Guards) was surrounded and received no fewer than 30 wounds defending the regiment's Standard. George II later presented him with this Standard, an award considered to be the equivalent of the modern Victoria Cross. Dragoon Thomas Brown exposed himself to terrible danger but succeeded in rescuing the Standard of the 3rd Dragoons (later 3rd Hussars), for which the king knighted him (for more on the importance of Standards, see Chapter 7).

Lieutenant Colonel Sir Andrew Agnew of Lochawe gave strict orders to his regiment, the 21st Foot (Royal Scots Fusiliers), that they were not to fire until they saw the whites of the enemy's eyes. At one stage during the fighting it looked as though they were about to be attacked by a French cavalry regiment. The 21st Foot gave a few volleys and then went for it with their bayonets, killing many of the enemy and chasing the rest off the field. For infantry to attack cavalry in this way was unheard of and stood the accepted rules on their head (or so the French probably said when they drew breath).

Then the turn of the French infantry came. The British regiments formed the first line of the Allied infantry. Some regiments fired their opening volleys at extreme range and wasted them. Others waited until the range had closed to within 90 metres (100 yards) then let fly, inflicting heavy losses. For some reason, possibly the previous repulse of its cavalry, something like panic swept through the French ranks. Led by one of France's poshest regiments, the Gardes Françaises, the infantry and cavalry alike headed through Dettingen and over the boat bridges by which they had crossed from the south bank. One of these capsized, pitching those on it into the river, in which many drowned.

The battle was over. Some 2500 of George's soldiers were killed or wounded. The French lost 5000 killed, wounded, and drowned. The French withdrew across the Rhine and the Allied army continued on its way to Flanders.

Dettingen was the last occasion in history when a king led British troops into battle. Among the officers present were George Augustus Elliott, the future defender of Gibraltar during its epic siege (see the section, 'Defending Gibraltar', at the end of this chapter); Lieutenant James Wolfe, who captured Quebec (more on this in 'The French and Indian War, 1753–1763', later in this chapter); and Lieutenant Jeffrey Amherst, who rose to the rank of Field Marshal and was largely responsible for ejecting the French from Canada (see 'The French and Indian War, 1753–1763', later in this chapter).

The Battle of Fontenoy, 11 May 1745

In spring 1745 the priority for the Duke of Cumberland, commanding the Allied army, was to relieve the besieged fortress of Tournai. To achieve this he first had to defeat a French army commanded by Marshal Count Maurice de Saxe, accompanied by King Louis XV. Cumberland's British-Hanoverian-Dutch-Austrian army (and that's quite some combo!) consisted of 56 infantry battalions, 87 cavalry squadrons, and 80 guns. Saxe commanded 66 infantry battalions, 129 cavalry squadrons, and 70 guns.

Saxe had serious doubts about his troops' ability to stand against the British in the open, so he selected a strong defensive position. His right rested on the little town of Antoing on the Scheldt, from which his line ran along a low ridge to Fontenoy, and then along another low ridge to the dense Barri wood. Antoing and Fontenoy were both heavily fortified. In addition, three redoubts reinforced the line connecting the two. Two further redoubts were positioned on the left flank. One of these, at the corner of Barri wood, was named the Eu Redoubt, after the regiment holding it. Cumberland's plan was for the right wing of his army, led by British regiments, to attack the French line between Fontenoy and Barri wood, while the left wing, led by the Dutch, attacked between Fontenoy and Antoing. At the last moment the British spotted the Eu Redoubt, and as it was clearly capable of firing into the flank of the British advance, it had to be taken. Cumberland detailed one Hanoverian and three British battalions for the job, under a Colonel Ingoldsby of the 1st Foot Guards. Unfortunately, apart from asking for some artillery support, Ingoldsby refused to move. To make matters worse, the Dutch attempts failed to take Fontenoy. This meant that the British advance would now come under fire from both flanks. Nevertheless, Cumberland decided that it should go ahead.

The regiments (see the sidebar 'Fontenoy: Who was there?' for which) mounted the gentle slope of the ridge, taking casualties from the flank as they did so. As they breasted the rise, they came face to face with the enemy's Gardes Françaises and the Gardes Suisses. In the aftermath of Dettingen, the British infantry had concentrated on delivering precise, close-quarter volleys. During an exchange of fire, both French Garde regiments sustained serious casualties and fell back in disorder. The advance continued into the heart of the French position, where each British regiment formed a *square* (the recognised defence against horsemen) in anticipation of a counter-attack by cavalry. Saxe brought up eight infantry battalions from his second line, but they were dealt with in a similar manner to the Garde regiments. The British then formed a single large, hollow square and this blasted every cavalry attack that came within range, emptying saddles by the score.

At this stage, Cumberland may have won a victory if he had ordered the British cavalry to counter-charge. He could not, because he had come further forward than an army commander should and was trapped inside the square. When he was at last able to send an officer out with orders to bring up the cavalry, the horsemen found their way blocked by crowds of fleeing Dutchmen, whose own attacks had failed dismally.

Fontenoy: Who was there?

As the brave infantry action at Fontenoy holds a special place in their history, it's worth looking at which regiments took part:

✔ **First Line:** 1st Foot Guards (1/Grenadier Guards), 2nd Foot Guards (1/Coldstream Guards), 3rd Foot Guards (1/Scots Guards), 1st Foot (1/Royal Scots), 21st Foot (1/Royal Scots Fusiliers), 31st Foot (1/East Surrey Regiment), 8th Foot (1/The King's (Liverpool) Regiment), 25th Foot (1/The King's Own Scottish Borderers), 33rd Foot (1/The Duke of Wellington's (West Riding) Regiment), 20th Foot (1/Lancashire Fusiliers).

✔ **Second Line:** 3rd Foot (1/The Buffs (East Kent Regiment)), 23rd Foot (1/Royal Welsh Fusiliers), 32nd Foot (1/The Duke of Cornwall's Light Infantry), 11th Foot (1/The Devonshire Regiment), 28th Foot (1/The Gloucestershire Regiment), 34th Foot (1/The Border Regiment), 20th Foot (1/The Lancashire Fusiliers), and Hanoverians.

Go ahead and shoot! See if I care!

One story about the Battle of Fontenoy concerns who asked whom to fire first. It has a basis in fact. The most generally accepted version is that when the British and French Guards were on the point of engaging each other, Lord John Hay, commanding the 1st Foot Guards' Grenadier or King's Company, stepped forward with a flask in his hand. Raising his hat, he drank his enemies' health and called across to them: 'We are the English Guards and we hope you will stand till we come up to you and not swim the Scheldt as you did the Main at Dettingen!' Turning round, he continued: 'Men of the King's Company, these are the French Guards and I hope you are going to beat them today!' His men answered with a cheer. The French officers raised their hats and bowed in a spirit of equal sarcasm. The French volley did little damage, but the British reply bowled over much of the French line. Those still on their feet, imagining that they were about to be charged with bayonets, took to their heels. Another version has it that what Hay actually said was along the lines of: 'Gentlemen of France, perhaps you would care to fire first?'

Saxe now prepared to destroy the incredibly stubborn British square. He brought up four guns loaded with grapeshot and fired at close quarters, blowing holes in the British ranks. The Irish Brigade, consisting of Irish emigrants serving the French king, came up on the right flank of the square, and the rallied Garde, together with other regiments that had just seen off the Dutch, came up on the left. The Irish lost their brigade commander and a third of their strength, and their comrades on the other flank made no progress either. Saxe threw in his last reserve, the cavalry of the Maison du Roi, and Cumberland ordered the diminishing British square to retire, which it did in good order. The British cavalry, free at last from the crowds of Dutch fugitives, came forward and provided a screen for the infantry regiments as they formed up and marched off.

Conservative estimates put the number of casualties sustained by each side as well in excess of 7000. In addition, numerous desertions occurred from the Allied army. At one stage senior French officers believed that they had lost the battle. Saxe commented in his despatch, 'We have won a victory, but may I never see such another.' He went on to capture Tournai and other fortresses in the Austrian Netherlands, while George II withdrew the British from the Continent to deal with the rebellion in Scotland (see Chapter 9).

The Seven Years' War, 1756–1763

The War of Austrian Succession (see the previous section) ended in a draw, with most nations finishing up exactly where they began. The peace that followed was only a lull, however, as Frederick the Great of Prussia had designs on Austrian territory, resulting in a general European war. British concerns included the safety of Hanover and stopping the French from winning a dominant position in Europe.

Losing Minorca, 1756

In April 1756 a French army of 15,000 men under Marshal Duke Louis de Richelieu sailed to Minorca and laid siege to the ancient and ruinous Fort St Philip, near the capital, Port Mahon. A 3000-strong garrison including the 4th Foot (1/The King's Own Royal Regiment (Lancaster)), the 24th Foot (1/South Wales Borderers) and the 34th Foot (1/The Border Regiment) defended the fort. In command was tough, vigorous, 84-year-old General Blakeney, who put up a spirited defence.

Minorca provided an excellent naval base in the Mediterranean and the British were loath to lose it. On 19 May a Royal Naval task force with reinforcements aboard appeared off the island. The following day it had the worst of an encounter with the French fleet and sailed away. The British naval commander, Admiral John Byng, was court-martialled for failing in his duty, convicted, and shot. Many felt that the punishment was unduly harsh. Even the French had some sympathy for him.

Fort St Philip could expect no further help. The garrison's strength had now been reduced to 1500 troops. It resisted for 70 days and even during the final French assault, which was only partially successful, the defenders inflicted 2000 casualties on the enemy. Recognising that further resistance was pointless, Blakeney asked for terms of surrender. Richelieu, a chivalrous opponent, granted the garrison the full honours of war, including the right to embark for home.

The Battle of Minden, 1 August 1759

In the summer of 1759 a Franco-Saxon army under Marshal the Marquis Louis de Contades successfully manoeuvred itself into a position between an Allied army under Duke Ferdinand of Brunswick and the Hanoverian territory that the Allies were supposed to defend. Ostensibly, Contades had simply to march out of Minden and on into Hanover, while for Brunswick the priority was to reopen communications with friendly territory. Contades had 80 infantry battalions and 61 cavalry squadrons, a total of 54,000 men, and 170 guns under his command, while Brunswick's British-Hanoverian-Hessian-Prussian army possessed 46 infantry battalions and 61 cavalry squadrons, a total of 42,500 men, and 187 guns.

Brunswick appreciated that Contades's position at Minden was too strong to attack, but he believed that by offering the French the bait of a 10,000-strong detachment at the grimly named village of Todtenhausen ('Houses of the dead') two miles downstream from Minden, he could fall on their flank if they fell for the ruse. They did, and a spy brought details of their plans to him.

By 1 a.m. on 1 August Brunswick knew that the French were on the march to snap up what seemed to be easy prey. His army was already camped in eight columns, the order in which it would make its approach march to the intended battlefield. Grumbling, the troops were turned out of their blankets and moved off through the windy, rain-lashed darkness. At first light, about 4.30 a.m., they were approaching Minden Heath. They could see Todtenhausen shrouded in the smoke of battle, but the howling gale whipped away the sound of the guns. As they got nearer, the details of Contades's deployment became apparent. His right rested on the Weser and his left in some marshland. Contrary to the accepted custom of the day, his cavalry was massed in the centre and his infantry on the wings, almost certainly because the centre of the battlefield offered firmer going for the horsemen.

Brunswick's No 3 Column, commanded by Lieutenant General August von Spoercken and deployed in two lines, contained both battalions of the Hanoverian Guard Regiment, Hardenburg's Hanoverian regiment, and six British regiments. These six regiments were later known as the 'Unsurpassable Six'. They were the 12th Foot (1/The Suffolk Regiment), 37th Foot (1/The Hampshire Regiment), 23rd Foot (1/Royal Welch Fusiliers), 20th Foot (1/Lancashire Fusiliers), 51st Foot (1/The King's Own Yorkshire Light Infantry), 25th Foot (1/The King's Own Scottish Borderers); to this day, they still commemorate Minden Day (see the sidebar 'Minden roses').

Shortly after 6 a.m. one of Brunswick's aides reached von Spoerken with orders to advance *at* the sound of the drum. This lost something in translation and the order was understood to mean advance *to* the sound of the drum. The troops were set in motion, drums beating and Colours flying. The problem was that they were heading straight for the mass of French cavalry – and charging cavalry usually rode over marching infantry and slaughtered them (infantry instead formed a square, presenting an impenetrable hedge of bayonets to the horsemen). It was obvious that a terrible mistake had been made. More aides galloped after the column, which halted briefly with an exchange of words that haven't survived, and, the drums rolling, it was off again. The regiments continued to march on across the heath, ignoring the cannon shot that ploughed through their ranks, as well as the long-range musketry of two French infantry regiments. The Duke of Fitzjames, commanding the French cavalry, could hardly believe his eyes. He launched his first line in a charge when the scarlet-coated infantry were just over 90 metres (100 yards) away. Two factors influenced what happened next:

- The British and Hanoverian infantry had recently been trained to aim their fire directly at a specific man or horse rather than at the enemy's line.

- Deprived of sleep, wet through, and missing their breakfast, the British and Hanoverians were in the filthiest of tempers and simply wanted to get at someone.

Not until the thundering squadrons were 9 metres (10 yards) away did the leading British brigade let fly. The French seemed to ride into a glass wall and their regiments dissolved into a tangle of dead and wounded troopers and screaming, kicking horses in their death agony. The second line of French cavalry charged and met an identical fate. So did the third line. The British and Hanoverians resumed their advance and the opposing Saxon infantry who then confronted them withdrew after a sharp fire fight.

By now, Contades had abandoned any idea of taking Todtenhausen and was withdrawing the wreckage of his army, not simply into Minden but right through it. Dumbfounded, he could only remark:

> *I have seen what I never thought to be possible – a single line of infantry break through three lines of cavalry rank in order of battle and tumble them to ruin.*

French losses amounted to 7086 killed, wounded, and taken prisoner, plus 43 guns captured. The Allies lost 2762 killed and wounded, of whom 1330 were British. Of the six British regiments under von Spoercken's command, losses in three were 60 per cent, in one 40 per cent, and in two 20 per cent.

Minden roses

The Unsurpassable Six and their modern successors have always celebrated 1 August as Minden Day. Wherever the regiments are based, they hold a parade in which officers and men alike wear roses in their caps. The custom goes back so far that no one knows who started it. It was said to commemorate the roses that the regiments picked on their way to the battle, and generation after generation of soldiers have accepted this as fact, until it has become an article of faith.

But hang on a minute – didn't the approach march take place in darkness, driving rain, and a high wind? Yes, and no one would want to pick flowers in such circumstances. Are there any roses on Minden heath? Yes, a few wild dog roses, small and not worth picking, let alone putting in your hat. Is the whole story a myth then? Not necessarily. As the troops closed in on Minden, they could have found roses in domestic and ornamental gardens. And after a day like they'd had, you can't blame the lads for sticking them in their hats after a job well – really well – done.

One man could have turned a decisive victory into the utter rout of the French army – Lord George Sackville, commander of the British and Hanoverian cavalry. From the moment of the first French charge, Brunswick had sent aide after aide to him, ordering him into action. Irked by Brunswick's failure to consult him earlier, he was in a fouler mood than most and determined to be bloody minded. He insisted on obtaining clarification of minor details and refused to move, even when the French army was streaming into Minden in disorder. It was perfectly clear to his own officers what was required, but when his second-in-command, the Marquis of Granby, began leading squadrons in the right direction, Sackville pulled him up sharply. It was a disgraceful episode and every trooper felt the shame of it. By the end of the day Sackville had been placed under open arrest. He was sent home, court-martialled, cashiered, and declared unfit to serve the king in any military capacity whatever.

The Battle of Emsdorf, 14 July 1760

In 1760 the Duke of Brunswick's Allied army faced an even larger French army than the one it defeated at Minden the year before (see the preceding section). Brunswick decided to mount a raid against the French rear depot at Marburg, using six battalions of Hanoverian and Hessian infantry, some German irregulars, and the newly raised British 15th Light Dragoons (later 15th Hussars), under the command of the Erbprinz of Hesse-Kassel (see the sidebar 'New cavalry developments', earlier in this chapter, for more on this new type of cavalryman). The enemy troops in the area of the depot included five infantry battalions and a regiment of Hungarian *hussars* (light cavalry), commanded by Maréchal de Camp Glaubitz.

The Erbprinz achieved complete surprise. When Glaubitz attempted to fall back towards Marburg he found the 15th Light Dragoons blocking his path at Emsdorf. He swung south through some woodland, abandoning his guns. When he emerged from the woods he again found the 15th waiting for him, and they took a number of his men prisoner when the regiment charged. Again Glaubitz took to the woods, and once again the Light Dragoons charged him when he emerged. This time the British sustained serious casualties, but once more Glaubitz headed south under cover of the trees. Finally, when he emerged for the third time only to find the 15th waiting for him yet again, he surrendered to the regiment's senior officer, Major Erskine.

During the entire engagement, the French sustained 2600 casualties, including 1665 men whom the Light Dragoons captured. In addition, the French lost five guns and nine Colours, mainly to one British regiment. The 15th lost 125 men and 168 horses killed or wounded, plus 6 soldiers dead of heat stroke.

The Battle of Warburg, 31 July 1760

At Warburg, a village on the Diemel river 20 miles northwest of Kassel, the Duke of Brunswick fought his principal opponent, Lieutenant General Le Chevalier du Muy. Brunswick had 24,000 men at his disposal, while du Muy had 21,500 (both forces being only part of the overall armies available to either side).

The French, marching in the direction of Hanover, found their way forward blocked by the advance guard of Brunswick's army, so du Muy took up a defensive position along a ridge. After Brunswick's men stormed a dominant feature on his left, du Muy's line began to crumble. At this point the British cavalry, led by the Marquis of Granby, charged the French cavalry on du Muy's right wing and drove it right off the field, thereby restoring the honour so tarnished by Lord Sackville at Minden the previous year (see the earlier section, 'The Battle of Minden, 1 August 1759', for more on this). Routed, the French army began streaming towards the distant Rhine. Casualties on both sides were comparatively light: 1200 killed and wounded in the Allied army, and 1500 in the French, plus 12 guns captured.

The Marquis of Granby took the welfare of his men very seriously. Out of his own pocket he established inns for those of his NCOs who were disabled at Warburg, setting the men up for life. He named these inns 'The Marquis of Granby', and the signs of those that survive today still show the Marquis, bald headed and galloping straight for the ranks of the French at Warburg.

Same Old Enemy, Brand New Venues

Over many years, Britain and France developed overseas interests both for economic reasons and for settlement as colonies. Inevitably as the two countries were at war so often, hostilities spread. For more on the general scope of British interests overseas, see Sean Lang's *British History For Dummies*, published by Wiley.

The principal areas affected by war between Britain and France in the eighteenth century were the West Indies, North America, and India. In this sense, the Seven Years' War is regarded by many as the first of the global wars.

Possessing the West Indies

Possession of the West Indies was critical to the economies of the major European powers, because the islands produced sugar in the large quantities required for the newly fashionable drinks of tea, coffee, and chocolate, as well as spices that had previously been obtainable only in the Far East. These commodities produced enormous profits that national exchequers came to rely on. When the nations eventually concluded peace treaties, they willingly gave up huge areas of land in exchange for the return of comparatively small islands.

The principal players in the Caribbean were Britain, France, and Spain, but the Dutch and even the Prussians had smaller fingers in the pie. The key to the entire theatre of war was the British Royal Navy, which dominated the seas and landed the army just where it was needed to deprive other people of their islands.

In 1762 British Admiral George Rodney commenced an offensive against French and Spanish possessions in the West Indies. The surrender of Grenada, St Lucia, and St Vincent followed Martinique's surrender on 12 February. On 20 June a 10,000-strong British force, including no fewer than 22 infantry regiments and supporting artillery, landed on Cuba. Commanded by George Keppel, Duke of Albemarle, it laid siege to Havana. The 56th Foot (2/The Essex Regiment) stormed the principal fortification, Moro Castle, on 30 July and the town surrendered shortly after. Included in the surrender were 12 warships and approximately £5 million in cash and merchandise, an immense sum at the time.

The French and Indian War, 1754–1763

In North America, the French held Canada in the north and New Orleans in the south. Their strategic object was to join the two with forts and settlements along the Mississippi and Ohio rivers and in so doing stop the westward expansion of the British colonies lying along the east coast of the continent. The British were determined to prevent this. Both sides recruited native American allies, although the French were more successful in doing so.

In 1754 the French built Fort Duquesne on the site of present-day Pittsburgh. They then attacked and took the British Fort Necessity, near Uniontown, Pennsylvania, which Lieutenant Colonel George Washington and a detachment of Virginia militia had held. The British reaction was that they must throw out the French and establish a dominant British presence in the Ohio basin.

Braddock's disaster

On 9 July 1755 Major General Edward Braddock was advancing through a forest near the Monongahela river to attack Fort Duquesne with 1400 regulars and 450 colonial volunteers, when a force of 900 native Americans with French officers ambushed him on a track. The native Americans, invisible among the trees, fired into the rigid British line, and the British returned useless volleys at their unseen opponents until Braddock died and half his men were down, at which point the survivors fled. George Washington, then just a colonel, rallied them and led them back to Virginia.

Most of Braddock's command consisted of the 44th Foot (1/The Essex Regiment) and the 48th Foot (1/The Northamptonshire Regiment), which had only recently arrived in America and contained a high proportion of raw recruits. They stood their ground longer than expected, but it was apparent that the tactics of the European battlefield were quite unsuited to close country (leading to new developments, outlined in the next section).

Raising new regiments: Rifles and Rangers

Not long after Braddock's defeat (see the preceding section), the British army raised the 60th Royal American Regiment, four battalions strong, at Governor's Island, New York, with the object of combining the qualities of the scout with the discipline of the trained soldier. The new regiment's commanding officer was Swiss, Colonel Henry Bouquet, and at first most of the men were either German immigrants or Germans recruited in Europe. Most of them had some experience of hunting and shooting in their day-to-day lives.

The 60th Royal American Regiment was drilled in *open order* (not shoulder to shoulder, but with spaces between the ranks and files), both in *quick time* (about 140 paces per minute) and *double time* (running); taught to load and fire quickly in the standing, kneeling, and lying positions; instructed in swimming, survival, self-sufficiency, and elementary field fortification; and generally required to use their personal initiative. Their training included a period of several weeks spent in the woods during which, save for a small ration of flour, the men relied entirely on whatever game or fish they could shoot or catch. The success in action of this, the army's first light infantry regiment, was such that it earned a permanent place in the establishment, becoming known in due course as The King's Royal Rifle Corps.

Captain Robert Rogers, a native of Massachusetts, raised an irregular unit of New Hampshire colonists. Having lived the life of a frontiersman in his youth, Rogers had an ingrained knowledge of woodcraft as well as an understanding of Indians and their ways. His unit was known simply as Rogers' Rangers. It specialised in the art of providing advance and rear guards, intelligence gathering, deep penetration patrols, raiding, and sabotage. Today it would be classed as an elite special forces unit and was the first such to serve with the British army. It earned itself a tremendous reputation, but was disbanded when the war ended in 1763. It was hardly a surprise that when the United States army decided to form its own commando units during the Second World War it chose to call them Rangers.

The success of Bouquet and Rogers's methods led to the widespread adoption of their light infantry tactics by British regiments in North America. With this came a style of dress more suited to the environment:

- ✔ The brim of the tricorne hat was let down.
- ✔ The coat was shortened by removing the turnback skirts.
- ✔ The long gaiters were reduced to short leggings.

Hair was cut short and instead of tramping through the forest with a knapsack full of pipeclay and hair-dressing, the soldier now carried extra ammunition and rations. A hatchet was added to his equipment and the barrel of his musket was browned to eliminate reflected light. Fighting in close country took place in open order, while in more open terrain a two-deep firing line replaced the three-deep formation used in Europe.

Wolfe's war in the wilderness

Britain and France fought over several thousand sparsely inhabited square kilometres in which the best routes were rivers and lakes. Canada could, of course, be entered from the sea via the St Lawrence river, but the principal route from the British colonies was north up the Hudson valley, then across Lakes George and Champlain and down the Richelieu river. In May 1756 Louis, Marquis de Montcalm, arrived in Canada and became the French commander-in-chief. In July, the Earl of Loudon became the British commander in North America. After some inconclusive manoeuvring, both sides went into winter quarters.

1757 and 1758 saw the action in North America hotting up:

- In June 1757, Loudon launched an unsuccessful expedition against the French fortress of Louisbourg on Cape Breton Island.

- In August 1757, Montcalm, with 4000 regulars and 1000 Indians, laid siege to Fort William Henry on Lake George. The garrison held out until it could no longer defend the fort and the French granted it the honours of war when it surrendered. As the British marched away, accompanied by their families, the Indians set upon them, resenting being deprived of their traditional reward, namely the confiscation of a defeated enemy's scalps. The massacre continued until Montcalm brought up his French troops to put a stop to it.

- In December 1757, General Ralph Abercrombie replaced Loudon, who had failed to produce results.

- In February 1758, General Jeffrey Amherst reached Halifax, Nova Scotia, with reinforcements. In May, the British launched a second expedition against Louisbourg, involving 9000 regulars and 500 colonials. The fortress, along with 12 warships, surrendered on 27 July after heavy fighting in which Brigadier General James Wolfe distinguished himself.

- In July 1758, a major failure at Fort Ticonderoga on Lake Champlain balanced out this major success. Here, Montcalm had incorporated a ridge in front of the fort into the defences, erecting an abatis of felled trees chained together at the top of the slope. Abercrombie, commanding 6000 regulars and the same number of colonials, could think of nothing more constructive than repeated frontal assaults that piled up 1600 casualties. He was forced to withdraw and Amherst succeeded him in September.

✔ In November 1758, the pendulum swung in favour of the British once more. Brigadier General John Forbes, commanding a force that included a battalion of the Royal Americans under Henry Bouquet and a Virginia regiment under Colonel George Washington, fought its way past the scene of Braddock's disaster and advanced on Fort Duquesne. Without bothering to dispute the issue, the French blew up the fort and withdrew. The British repaired it and renamed it Fort Pitt.

Because of the Royal Navy's command of the sea, the French's situation had become serious. The British decided on a three-pronged advance in 1759:

✔ The capture of Fort Niagara to isolate Upper Canada from the St Lawrence. Brigadier General John Pridaux accomplished this with 2000 regulars. The fort fell after a short siege in which Pridaux was killed.

✔ The capture of Forts Ticonderoga and Crown Point, opening the Champlain valley route to the St Lawrence. Amherst, with 11,000 regulars and colonials, took personal charge of the operations against Fort Ticonderoga, which fell on 26 July. He took Crown Point on 31 July and it became his headquarters during the winter.

✔ Penetration of the St Lawrence from the sea and an amphibious assault on Quebec. In the most dramatic events of the campaign, Major General Wolfe's army arrived at the St Lawrence river from Louisbourg in June 1759 and established itself on the Isle of Orleans, downstream from Quebec. Wolfe's major problem was that steep cliffs covered every approach to the fortress; he decided to use a diagonal path up the cliffs west of the city, and during the night of 12/13 September Wolfe's troops scaled this and deployed on the level Plains of Abraham above it. Montcalm led the French army out of the defences to give battle. Each side had approximately 4500 men in line. The French fired an ineffective volley, but the much superior British musketry quickly worsted them, the first volleys not being delivered until the two sides were only 35 metres (40 yards) apart. Having sustained some 600 killed and wounded in a matter of minutes, the French began streaming back into the city. The British loss amounted to 58 killed and 600 wounded. Wolfe and Montcalm both received mortal wounds during the battle. Quebec surrendered on 18 September.

Menaced by three converging British armies, the Marquis de Vaudreuil, Governor of Canada, surrendered Montreal, his last stronghold, on 8 September 1760. Under the terms of the Treaty of Paris, France gave up all claims to territory in North America (save for New Orleans) in exchange for the return of the West Indian islands of Martinique and Guadaloupe.

Getting curried away: War in India

British involvement in India began in 1600, when Queen Elizabeth I granted a charter to a group of businessmen calling themselves The Company of Merchants of London Trading into the East Indies. This evolved into the Honourable East India Company (shortened to John Company or the Company), which virtually became a sovereign state with the right to declare war on non-Christian nations should it so wish. Business with the Indian sub-continent was highly profitable, but the Company was not the only one with fingers in the pie. Its rivals were the Portuguese, the Dutch, and, of course, the French. Friction and occasional fighting between the Europeans was more usual than between the traders and the locals, who were achieving more and more autonomy as the once-powerful Mogul Empire slid into decline.

The Company raised its own troops to protect its *factories* (the term used for its trading centres) against its rivals and native princes hostile to its interests, and supported those with whom it was on good terms. The Company's growing holdings in land and increased influence in Indian affairs meant that it had to raise still more troops until it possessed three armies, located in Bengal, Madras, and Bombay, to say nothing of its own navy.

British officers in the Honourable East India Company commanded the native troops, the service appealing to them partly because they did not have to purchase their commissions (see Chapter 7 for more on this), and partly because of the good lifestyle that they could have at little cost in India. The Company also raised European regiments. The men who joined them were a hard lot, often with good reason to exile themselves for life, but they received better pay than the Regular Army could offer and they lived well.

The rise of Robert Clive

Robert Clive arrived in India to work as one of the Company's clerks. He hated it so much that he tried to blow his brains out with a pistol. The pistol misfired, which was fortunate for future British interests in India. In 1743 Clive was in Madras when the French took the city. He escaped and, disgusted with the Company's lackadaisical attitude to military matters, obtained a commission in its army with the object of shaking things up. Clive was capable of inspiring great loyalty. At one point, during the siege of Arcot (see below), his *sepoys* (Indian soldiers) said that they would give their rice ration to the Europeans, whose health had begun to break down, and subsist on the thin gruel that came from its straining, but Clive would not permit it.

In July 1751 a French puppet ruler named Chanda Sahib laid siege to the British garrison of Trinchinopoly. Clive, with only 200 Europeans and 300 sepoys, sought to draw Chanda off by occupying his fort at Arcot. He succeeded. Chanda came steaming up with 10,000 followers. The fort was in such a ramshackle state that most people wouldn't have bothered about it, but Chanda took its loss personally because it happened to be in his capital. He was unable to make any impression on the defences, although after two months he had reduced the garrison to 120 Europeans and 200 sepoys, and little food remained. Chanda asked for a meeting with Clive under a flag of truce, and told Clive to give up or he would put everyone in the fort to the sword. Clive made a number of very pointed personal comments about Chanda and his father, as well as stating bluntly that if he thought that the ragbag of scruffs he called an army was capable of storming a breach that British soldiers held he had better do some serious thinking. No records exists of Chanda's reply, but probability suggests the local equivalent of: 'Right, you've asked for it!'

Chanda led his attack with a herd of elephants with iron plates strapped to their heads to batter down the gates. Iron plates or not, elephants presented a large target and thick though their hides may have been, they disliked the pain inflicting by musket balls whacking into them. Out of control, the elephants turned and bolted through the mob behind, trampling some and scattering the rest. Chanda's next assault was by raft across the fort's moat. Clive personally directed a gun and, using grapeshot (see Chapter 5 for more on types of artillery shot), quickly cleared the raft. Having sustained 400 casualties, Chanda's army disbanded itself. The fort's defenders lost six men. British prestige throughout India soared, while that of the French took a nose-dive.

Five years later, British interests took a severe knock. Suraj-ud-Daula, the Nawab of Bengal, took exception to the growth of the Company's power on his doorstep. In June 1756 he captured Calcutta, which the Company had founded as the focal point of its activities. A number of European captives died in unpleasant circumstances after being incarcerated in what became known as the notorious Black Hole of Calcutta (a dungeon). An expedition commanded jointly by Clive and Admiral Charles Watson (probably a Company officer) left from Madras. This included the 39th Foot (1/The Dorsetshire Regiment), the first British regiment to serve in India and the first in a long line of British regiments that the Company hired to strengthen its own armies. The expedition recaptured Calcutta on 2 January 1757.

In March, Clive captured the French post at Chandernagore, enabling him to march inland against Suraj-ud-Daula without fearing for his lines of communication. The two armies met at Plassey, a village on the Bhagirathi river, on 23 June. Clive had 2100 sepoys, 800 Europeans including part of the 39th Foot, and 10 guns. The Nawab had 53,000 men, including a small French contingent, and 53 guns. Clive's troops concentrated in and around a grove of trees. The Nawab's almost encircled them. Apparently, it wasn't going to be much of a contest. This, however, was India, and nothing was quite what it seemed; if it had been, Clive was unlikely to have offered battle in such circumstances. He knew, for example, that most of Suraj's commanders were conspiring against the Nawab. He was also in regular correspondence with the most important of them, Mir Jafar, who urged Clive to attack. The battle began with an exchange of artillery fire, the British faring the better. Then a tropical rainstorm broke over the battlefield. Clive ordered his gunners to keep their powder dry. The Nawab's gunners failed to do this, the result being that their guns were useless when the storm passed. A cavalry charge mounted against the British position was blown to pieces. Clive, observing a definite lack of enthusiasm in the opposing ranks, ordered a general advance. He repulsed an infantry counter-attack at the same time as Mir Jafar pointedly kept his troops inactive. The Nawab's army then began shredding away from the field until nothing remained of it save the French element, which continued to fight to the last.

Clive's troops sustained the loss of five killed and 45 wounded, while the Nawab's army had 500 killed and wounded plus five guns captured. Suraj was murdered soon after and Mir Jafar succeeded him. The battle, one of the most important in Indian history, effectively gave Bengal to the Company.

The French fight back

In 1758 French reinforcements under Baron Thomas Lally reached Pondicherry, the principal French base in India. An energetic commander, Lally besieged and captured the British Fort St David to his south and in December laid siege to Madras. The following month a British relief force defeated his army at Masulipatam and forced him to abandon the siege. A year later, at the Battle of Wandiwash, Lally sustained a further defeat at the hands of General Sir Eyre Coote. He withdrew to Pondicherry, where the British besieged him and he surrendered in January 1761.

Although the Treaty of Paris restored Pondicherry to the French in 1763, the Compagnie des Indes was dissolved in 1769. As Dutch and Portuguese operations had already been severely restricted, British interests in India no longer had any major European challengers.

Defending Gibraltar

The defence of Gibraltar against the French and Spanish between the years 1779 and 1783 is among the greatest epics of British military history. Commanding the garrison was Lieutenant General George Augustus Eliott. His strength never amounted to more than 7500 men, drawn from five British and eight Hanoverian infantry battalions, plus artillerymen and engineers (several artillery developments sprang up from this campaign – see the sidebar 'Gibraltar's red-hot action'). The Spanish opened the siege with 16 infantry battalions and 12 cavalry squadrons, a total of 14,000 men and 150 guns. In June 1782 the French arrived with 35 infantry battalions and 16 cavalry squadrons, bringing the total number of besiegers to 40,000, with artillery in proportion. The siege last for three years, seven months, and twelve days. It cost the garrison 333 killed, 911 wounded, and 536 dead from disease. French and Spanish losses amounted to an estimated 5000 killed and wounded.

Year after year, the garrison stood off attacks by land and sea, its morale maintained by Eliott's leadership and determination as well the Royal Navy's breaking of the enemy blockade on three occasions to bring in vital supplies. At one time, when no fewer than 6000 shells were landing in the town each day, Eliott led a dramatic sortie that smashed up the enemy's siege lines and spiked its guns.

Gibraltar's red-hot action

The siege of Gibraltar was remarkable for a number of developments in the field of artillery:

✔ Lieutenant G.F. Koehler, Eliott's aide-de-camp and assistant engineer, developed a depression carriage enabling guns to fire at targets well below the line of sight possessed by a conventional carriage.

✔ Captain Mercier of the 39th (1/Dorsetshire) Regiment solved the difficulty of firing as far as the besiegers' lines, usually 1500 to 1800 metres (1700 to 2000 yards) distant, by the suggestion of firing the 14-centimetre (5.5-inch) explosive shell normally used in mortars from 24-pounder guns of the same calibre. He fitted the shells with calculated fuses so that they exploded directly above the heads of the enemy working parties.

✔ Lieutenant Henry Shrapnel, Royal Artillery, followed on from Mercier's idea in 1784 by developing the type of ammunition that still bears his name, by filling a fused hollow shell with spherical shot and a bursting charge.

✔ The gunners' *pièce de résistance*, however, was *red-hot shot* (literally, cannonballs heated to a red-hot temperature), developed as a defence against the enemy's heavily protected floating batteries (themselves designed to beat the garrison into submission at close quarters). Red-hot shot was first used in action on 13 September 1782. By noon the next day, having absorbed 8300 of the glowing projectiles, all ten floating batteries had either blown up or burned to the waterline. After that, the siege amounted to nothing more than a mere blockade.

Chapter 9

Risings and Rebellions: Jacobites and Americans

The Stuart kings never quite understood why people didn't want them back on the throne of Great Britain. Perhaps they should have read Sean Lang's *British History For Dummies* (published by Wiley) which explains the whole situation – if they had, lots of innocent people would have been saved a great deal of grief. The American colonists, on the other hand, had a sound case for their call to arms against the crown, but if both sides hadn't been pig-headedly stubborn, perhaps they would not have engaged in a shooting war with their mother country. This chapter gets to grips with the military action that followed the political wrangling in Scotland and America.

The propaganda put out by the Jacobite losers in one case and the American victors in the other tends to obscure the fact that the Jacobite Risings and the War of Independence were actually civil wars, fought between the British government and aggrieved British citizens in Scotland and America.

With the notable exception of a few new units detailed in this chapter, British soldiers of this period were little changed in appearance from those described in Chapter 8. However, the infantry fought the American War of Independence in a slightly smarter version of their earlier uniform. This was a coat cut away above the knees and gaiters, now black rather than white, that reached to just below the knee. A bearskin had replaced the mitre cap worn by grenadiers and fusiliers.

One Day My Prince Will Come, 1708

In 1701 Parliament passed the *Act of Settlement*, which said that if Anne, the second daughter of the exiled James II, died childless after she ascended the throne, the crown was to pass to Sophia, Princess of Hanover, a granddaughter of James I, and that all future sovereigns were to be Protestants. Anne succeeded William III in 1702, a year after James II died. Five years later Parliament passed the Act of Union, where England and Scotland became one country, and Great Britain was born.

James II's son, James Edward, wasn't within a sniff of the crown and became known as the Old Pretender (to the throne). Someone told him that the Act of Union had made most Scots very angry indeed (although in fact it hadn't) and in 1708 he arrived in Scotland, expecting a spontaneous uprising in his favour. No uprising occurred, nor did crowds cheer, bands play, or flags wave. Even the French troops he'd had promised to him didn't turn up because a storm had scattered their ships. No one seemed to care that he was in Scotland, so he went back to France.

Here Comes James – Again! The 'Fifteen'

Despite the failure of James Edward to stir up trouble (see the previous section), some of Scotland's most powerful families thought themselves wise to keep a foot in both camps (Anne's and James Edward's). Some individuals also enjoyed plotting for its own sake. When they drank the Loyal Toast to the British monarch after dinner, some folks passed their glasses over a finger bowl and thereby drink the health of 'the king over the water', James Edward. When Anne died in 1714, George, Sophia's eldest son, arrived from Hanover and became George I of England. He didn't speak English, he didn't like England, and he wasn't a popular figure. The moment seemed right for the cloak-and-dagger crowd to put their plans into action, starting the 1715 Jacobite Rebellion.

The principal instigators of the 1715 Rebellion were the Earl of Mar in Scotland and the Earl of Derwentwater, egged on by a rascally Member of Parliament named Thomas Foster, in the north of England. They seemed to think that because people didn't like George from Germany they were bound to like James Edward from France. Their thinking wasn't logical, but plenty of waverers existed to back the idea if the Jacobites experienced a success or two.

In Scotland, Mar managed to raise a 7000-strong army consisting mainly of Highlanders armed with muskets, Lochaber axes, swords, and shields, and famed for their ferocious charges. On 13 September, at Sheriffmuir, east of

Dunblane, Mar met John, Duke of Argyll, commanding a government army consisting of 2200 infantry and 960 dragoons. The right wings of both armies put their respective opponents to flight and then returned to the field. Both sides spent the rest of the day glaring at each other from a distance of 350 metres (400 yards). Casualties had been light: Mar lost 250 killed and wounded, while Argyll lost 350. Technically it was a drawn battle, but Mar needed a clear-cut victory to win further support and his army simply dissolved.

In England, the rebel army also included a contingent of Highlanders and a number of Jacobite landowners joined in, dragging their unwilling tenants with them. Foster persuaded everyone to let him command, and he led them south through Lancashire, where the support he promised simply did not materialise. His intentions were to capture the port of Liverpool, and then join an entirely imaginary army of Welsh Jacobites that he thought would come swarming out of the hills. The reality of the situation fell far below his ambitions. On 13 November the energetic Major General Wills, who had 2500 men at his disposal including five regiments of dragoons, brought Foster up short at Preston. Wills boxed in the rebels in the town centre, although they beat off his attacks. The following morning, nevertheless, Foster surrendered. Of his 3000-strong army, 42 had been killed or wounded and 1468 were taken prisoner. The rest had escaped through a gap in the government cordon during the night, and were on their way home. That was the end of the rebellion in England.

James Edward reached Scotland in December. By then the rebellion was all but over. As the last of his Highland supporters dispersed, he returned to France on 5 February 1716. For those of his supporters captured in arms the penalties were, depending on rank, the headsman's axe, the hangman's noose, transportation for life, or, if they were lucky, a spell in prison.

¡Hola! Spain's (Mini) Invasion of Scotland, 1719

In 1719 the Spanish government, annoyed by the Royal Navy's continual balking of its plans in the Mediterranean, decided to send an expedition to Scotland in support of James Edward. The weather seemed to be on King George's side and a gale scattered the Spanish ships. Some got through to the western Scottish isles, however, and in due course landed their troops, amounting to approximately one battalion, on the west coast of the mainland. Some Jacobite support was forthcoming from the local clans, but not a lot. Commanded by George, Earl of Marischal, they began marching inland along the narrow and desolate pass of Glenshiel.

On 10 June the Jacobites learned that a government force, commanded by General Wightman, was moving towards them from the opposite direction. The Jacobites immediately deployed in an extremely strong position across the pass. Whiteman's regiments closed up during the afternoon and launched a series of attacks. These proved too much for the Highlanders, who simply disappeared. This left the Spaniards, alone and under fire from four mortars, to face Wightman by themselves. Their position was hopeless and they surrendered next day.

The Jacobites Return . . . And This Time They're Bonnie: The 'Forty-Five'

For many years the Jacobite cause seemed lost. Then in July 1745, Charles Edward, James Edward's son, decided to make one last, all-out attempt to recover the crown while Britain was heavily involved in the War of Austrian Succession (see Chapter 8 for more on this war). Cloak-and-dagger folk prepared the ground well, and when Charles raised his standard at Glenfinnan, no fewer than 2000 clansmen rallied to it. Ominously, rather more, whose support for the Stuarts had cost them blood and treasure in the past, stayed away.

Charles would become known as the Young Pretender, but for the moment his Highlanders called him Bonnie Prince Charlie. In later years, writers such as Sir Walter Scott and Robert Louis Stephenson would deeply romanticise the lost cause of the Forty-Five Rebellion; however in reality, Charlie was half Polish, spoke with an Italian accent, drank heavily, womanised, and was over-refined to the point that he wouldn't touch butter if breadcrumbs were mixed with it. He didn't wear Highland dress until someone told him that it was good public relations. In fact, he didn't like Scotland at all, Gaelic was gibberish to him, and he tended to look down on the Highlanders who were willing to fight and die for him. His one lasting achievement is to appear, year after year, on the lid of Scottish biscuit tins.

The Battle of Prestonpans, 21 September 1745

Having appointed Lord George Murray as his military commander, Charles began marching on Edinburgh. On 17 September Charles took the city without difficulty and held an expensive party to celebrate. Meanwhile, Lieutenant General Sir John Cope, commanding a 2000-strong government army including two regiments of dragoons and six guns, had deployed at Prestonpans, six miles east of Edinburgh. During the night of 20/21 September, Murray led the Jacobite army right around Cope's position. Dawn found it deployed just 180 metres (200 yards) from the government army's left flank. Cope's troops just had time to change front when the Highlanders charged. A ragged volley failed to stop them. It took only ten minutes of savage hand-to-hand fighting to destroy Cope's army, which sustained 1800 casualties, including 1500 prisoners, and lost all its guns. Jacobite losses amounted to 30 killed and 80 wounded.

The outcome of the battle attracted sufficient recruits to the Young Pretender's cause for him to cross the border with an army of 4500 infantry and 400 cavalry. He took Carlisle and Manchester and then marched on to Derby, which he reached on 4 December. All seemed to be going his way, but concern was growing that no support was forthcoming from English sympathisers. The Duke of Cumberland was coordinating the response to the Jacobite invasion, and Jacobite intelligence sources suggested that proceeding further into England would risk two strong government armies crushing the rebellion between them. After some debate, Charles reluctantly fell back into Scotland.

The Battle of Falkirk, 17 January 1746

Cumberland followed Charles closely until his advance guard got a bloody nose near Penrith. The encounter, which took place on Clifton Moor, was the last battle fought on English soil. Now back in Scotland, Charles laid siege to Stirling Castle, a task for which he was ill equipped. Meanwhile, a government army under Lieutenant General Henry Hawley recaptured Edinburgh and was advancing to break the siege. Murray deployed his Jacobites on the moorland above Falkirk and on 17 January 1746 Hawley's troops began emerging from the town to engage them. They had barely formed up when the Highlanders launched a devastating charge that swept away most of Hawley's line. Murray's forces killed or wounded about 350 of Hawley's men and captured 600, and the government army lost all its guns and baggage. The Jacobite army's casualties were negligible.

Hawley went insane with rage. For starters, he smashed his own sword against Falkirk's market cross. Then he hanged 31 dragoons who rejoined their regiments after the battle on the idiotic charge of 'deserting to the rebels'. Finally, when the Jacobites began releasing their prisoners, he had 32 returned infantrymen shot for cowardice. Forever after, he went by the nickname of the Hangman. The irony was that on 1 February the Jacobites abandoned the siege voluntarily and retreated into the Highlands.

The Battle of Culloden, 15 April 1746

Shortly after the government humiliation at Falkirk, Cumberland arrived to take command in Scotland, and followed up the Jacobite withdrawal. He trained his men rigorously in techniques of bayonet fighting designed to meet the Highlanders' style of fighting with *broadsword* (a sword with a wide blade for cutting rather than thrusting) and *targe* (a light shield).

On 15 April the Jacobite army was in position on Culloden Moor, five miles east of Inverness. It was 5400 strong and consisted of 21 small (mainly Highlander) infantry battalions, 400 cavalry, and 12 guns. Cumberland's army lay within striking distance to the east. It was 9000 strong and consisted of 15 regular infantry battalions, four regiments of dragoons, a number of Scottish volunteer units, and 16 guns. During the night the Jacobites tried to mount a surprise attack on Cumberland's camp. Already on the verge of starvation and now utterly weary, they lost their way and had to return to their starting point. Cumberland's army, fed and rested, followed up and deployed for battle as it approached Culloden.

For 30 minutes Cumberland's artillery hammered the Jacobite line. The ordeal was too much for the patience of some clans. They launched piece-meal charges that the government army easily defeated; a few men broke through the first line of infantry, only for the second line to despatch them. A double envelopment by the government cavalry completed the destruction of Charles's army, which they pursued to within one mile of Inverness. Cumberland's men killed about 1000 of the rebels and captured 558, together with all their guns. Government losses amounted to 50 killed and 239 wounded.

Cumberland's savage treatment of his prisoners and the brutal repressive measures he imposed afterwards earned him the title of the Butcher, but he had won a decisive victory that destroyed Stuart ambitions forever. Some people still regard the battle as a Scottish defeat. In fact, more Scots were fighting for King George on 16 April than for Prince Charlie, whose army also included French and Irish elements.

Subsequent political measures destroyed the old clan structure. Relieved of their responsibilities, the lairds (landowners) preferred sheep and deer to populate their glens rather than people, who provided less profit. As a result of these evictions, called the *Highland Clearances*, Highlanders in their thousands emigrated to the New World or went to live in the cities. They also provided a ready recruiting ground for some of the finest regiments in the British army (see the sidebar, 'The Highland regiments').

The Highland regiments

The first regiment composed of Highlanders was the 42nd (originally 43rd) Foot, also entitled The Royal Highland Regiment but more commonly known as The Black Watch. The term Black refers to the dark government tartan, and Watch simply describes the role it was originally intended to perform: policing the glens. The regiment proved to be so efficient that it quickly found itself serving as conventional line infantry in numerous theatres of war. Raised in 1739, several more Highland regiments followed it about this time, but the army disbanded these a few years later. More Highland regiments became part of the Regular Army's establishment in the 1770s and more again in the 1790s.

The advantage for a Highlander joining a Highland regiment was that, apart from the scarlet coat, he wore traditional dress (in his regiment's tartan, of course) and, at the time and for many years after, he and his comrades could converse in their native Gaelic. Reminders of the old days of clan warfare remain. For example, the pipes can rouse Highlanders to berserk fury before an attack so that they become almost impossible to stop.

During their early years, the failure of others to recognise the sensibilities of Highland culture, let alone the fact that Highlanders simply would not tolerate flogging as a punishment, led to no fewer than 16 incidences of mutiny. Despite this, Highlanders and Sassenachs (to Highlanders, everyone south of the Highlands) settled down quickly together and proved to be a formidable combination. Nowhere in the British army is the power of tradition stronger than in the Highland regiments. During both World Wars, men from all over the Commonwealth and the United States travelled to Great Britain with the sole object of joining the Highland regiment in which their father, grandfather, or even great-grandfather once served.

The American War of Independence, 1775–1783

People don't rebel without good reason. In America the reason was not an attempt to seize the British throne, but anger at the taxation that the British government imposed on the American colonists. Rubbing salt into the tax-related wound, the colonists had no representatives in Parliament and therefore had no say in the matter. Their slogan, therefore, was 'No taxation without representation'. It was a fair point – hadn't a civil war taken place in England about such things a century earlier (see Chapter 6)?

For sheer stubborn stupidity, George III's government took some beating. It viewed most colonists as Puritans, no-hopers, bond-servants, or criminals transported for the common good, and considered that they had no business asking for seats in Parliament. For their part, the colonists' more extreme political leaders decided that if that was how the government felt, then they would form their own government and become independent of Britain. What the situation boiled down to was a handful of obstinate people on both sides who weren't prepared to compromise. A fight became inevitable.

The war that followed was a civil war. Most of the colonists considered themselves to be English, Scots, Welsh, or Irish. Fighting their own kind was not what they wanted, unless they were forced into it. Taken as a whole:

- One third of the colonists wanted complete independence from Britain.
- One third wished to retain ties with the Old Country.
- One third just wanted to get on with their lives in peace.

In the New England colonies in the northeast, a higher proportion of people wanted independence; in the southern colonies the reverse applied. And the French Canadians, who were doing better under British administration than they had when France had ruled them, were all for preserving the status quo. War hardens attitudes and communities, neighbours, and families were forced to decide whether they were revolutionaries or loyalists (see the sidebar, 'The loyalists'), and that was a tragedy.

The Battles of Lexington, Concord, and Bunker Hill, 1775

The first shot of the American War of Independence was fired on 19 April 1775. General Thomas Gage, the British Governor of Massachusetts, received word that the colonists were stockpiling munitions at the town of Concord. He despatched 700 men from the Boston garrison to seize these. On Lexington Common they found a company of militiamen barring their path. Someone fired a shot, the troops opened fire, and the militiamen scattered, leaving eight of their number dead and ten wounded. When they got to Concord, Gage's men found that colonists had removed some of the munitions, but the Governor's troops destroyed the rest. The march back to Boston was a nightmare. Colonists sniped continually at Gage's column and some men had to carry the wounded, which slowed its progress. If reinforcements had not arrived from Boston the future of the troops would have been doubtful. As it was, British casualties for the day amounted to 73 killed and 174 wounded, while the colonists lost 93 killed, wounded, and missing.

Some 15,000 rebels drawn from several New England colonies besieged Boston. On 15 June, Congress appointed George Washington as commander of its new revolutionary army (with the rank of major general) and gave instructions for the fortification of Bunker Hill overlooking Boston harbour (for some reason the work actually took place on the lower Breed's Hill). Meanwhile, Gage had secured reinforcements to bring his garrison up to 7000. With the reinforcements came three generals who would each play a significant role as the war continued: John Burgoyne, William Howe, and Henry Clinton.

At dawn on the morning of 17 June, Gage reacted to the American fortifications on Breed's Hill. The warships in the harbour bombarded the rebel position and Howe crossed the bay with 2200 men. Incredibly, the 1200 rebels holding the position stood off two attacks, although they all but exhausted their ammunition supply doing so. A third assault carried the position at the point of the bayonet. Howe's troops sustained over 1000 casualties, while the rebels lost 140 killed, 271 wounded, and 30 captured.

Although Gage claimed a costly success, the battle did not change the overall situation. The number of rebels surrounding Boston grew month by month until by March 1776 there were no fewer than 26,000 of them. In addition, they had emplaced some captured British heavy guns. Howe, now commanding in place of Gage, recognised that remaining in Boston would solve nothing and on 17 March he evacuated the city and sailed for Halifax, on the Canadian coast.

The loyalists

Many people in the colonies took up arms to maintain the link with Great Britain. Loyalists formed numerous units and these served alongside the regular regiments, usually with a stiffening of regular soldiers.

Most loyalist troops dressed in green to indicate their status. The best known of these units was the British Legion, consisting of both cavalry and infantry elements. Lieutenant Colonel Banastre Tarleton was its commander, a British regular officer who became the most outstanding cavalry leader of the war, winning one engagement after another until the Legion suffered a serious reverse at Cowpens in 1781. Tarleton gave his name to the smart, fur-crested helmet that light dragoon regiments and the Royal Horse Artillery later wore. A cruel streak marred his brilliance and led his enemies to name him 'Bloody' Tarleton, a nickname conferred for an incident in which he was, ironically, innocent.

After the war most loyalists left the United States for Canada, Newfoundland, or Nova Scotia. Among them was Flora MacDonald, who helped Prince Charles Edward Stuart escape from Scotland following his defeat at Culloden (see the section 'The Jacobites Return . . . And This Time They're Bonnie: The 'Forty-Five', earlier in this chapter).

Rebel failures in Canada

American General Richard Montgomery, with 1000 men, managed to penetrate Canadian territory by way of the Richlieu river in the autumn of 1775 and occupied Montreal on 13 November. Simultaneously, Benedict Arnold set out with a similar number of Americans to the St Lawrence river, which he reached after a gruelling march through Maine reduced his strength to 600 men. On 3 December Montgomery joined him and took command at his camp near Quebec, bringing with him 300 men from Montreal. On 31 December they launched a foolish assault on the formidable defences of Quebec in a driving snowstorm. The 1800-strong garrison, commanded by Sir Guy Carleton, the British Governor General of Canada, experienced no difficulty in repelling the attack. His men killed Montgomery and wounded Arnold, also killing or wounding almost 100 of the attackers and capturing 300.

Arnold and the rebel survivors remained in the vicinity until May 1776, then fell back on Montreal when General Burgoyne arrived with British and German reinforcements. General John Sullivan was now commanding the rebel forces in Canada, and he planned a counter-stroke that he hoped would restore the initiative to him. In June he despatched General John Thomas with 2000 men to attack Trois-Rivières; Thomas's troops lost their way and blundered into Burgoyne's entire army. Predictably, the British army dispersed the rebel force. Sullivan hastily abandoned Montreal and withdrew first to Crown Point and then to Ticonderoga.

In a perceptive letter Arnold had already written to Sullivan, he commented that there was nothing to be gained for the rebel cause in upper or lower Canada, and that they had better return to their own country before it was too late.

New York, New York

British General Howe had 32,000 men at his disposal, including regiments hired from the ruler of Hesse (in modern-day Germany). This was a propaganda gift to the rebels, who could not only claim that the London government was quite prepared to use foreigners against its own people, but also invoke foreign assistance of their own whenever they wanted. In fact, Kings Louis XVI of France and Charles III of Spain, still smarting from the losses they endured during the Seven Years' War (see Chapter 8), were gibbering with delight at Britain's transatlantic problems and had already authorised the despatch of munitions to the American colonists.

Howe believed that a major defeat would destroy the rebels' will to fight. His transports arrived off New York on 2 July 1776. Two days later Congress made its formal Declaration of Independence (for more on this, see Steve Wiegand's *US History For Dummies*, published by Wiley). There could be no going back for either side now.

Washington predicted that New York would be Howe's objective and posted some 7000 men under Major General Israel Putnam on Long Island, retaining a similar number himself in Manhattan. Howe landed 20,000 men on Long Island and on 27 August expertly turned the American left, forcing Putnam to abandon his position with the loss of 200 killed and 1000 captured. Howe lost 400 men killed or wounded. Washington evacuated Long Island during the night of 29–30 August and abandoned New York on 12 September (the city remained in British hands for the rest of the war). Howe followed up by:

- Manoeuvring Washington off Harlem Heights on 16 September
- Defeating Washington at White Plains on 28 October
- Storming Fort Washington, overlooking the Hudson, on 16 November, taking 2800 Americans prisoner

The rebels abandoned Fort Lee, on the opposite shore, on 18 November, along with much war material. Washington commenced a retreat across New Jersey and into Pennsylvania. On 12 December Congress fled from Philadelphia to Baltimore, conferring dictatorial powers on Washington, whose army stood at just 3000 men. Now was the moment for Howe to finish the business, but he lacked the killer instinct and instead dispersed his troops into winter quarters throughout New Jersey.

The revolutionary flame was on the verge of flickering out, but in a few short days Washington fanned it back to life. He realised that a combination of Christmas and complacency rendered the British vulnerable to a counter-stroke. On Christmas night 1776, under cover of a blizzard, Washington crossed the Delaware with 2400 men and overran the Hessian post at Trenton. Of the 1400-strong garrison, his men killed 30 and captured 1000, along with a large quantity of military stores. Two Americans froze to death and five were wounded. By 2 January 1777 the British area commander, Lord William Cornwallis, had closed in on Trenton with 5000 men. A further 2500 men, based at Princeton, some 12 miles away, were ordered to join him with a view to mounting an attack on the Americans next day. That night, Washington left his camp fires burning and slipped round Cornwallis on a little-used track. He now possessed 1600 regulars and 3600 militia. On 3 January he inflicted a defeat on the Princeton reinforcements and captured yet more stores. He then made a rapid march to Morristown before Cornwallis could react. This placed him in a position to menace the communications of British garrisons in central and western New Jersey, resulting in their withdrawal.

Making plans with Johnny and George

'Gentleman Johnny' Burgoyne was a fair soldier, an absentee Member of the House of Commons, a poet, a playwright, a successful gambler, a sportsman, and a compulsive party goer. The best parties were in London, so he left Canada on winter leave. He judged, correctly, that the heart of the revolution lay in the New England colonies and formulated a plan to isolate the rebels there by a triple thrust converging on Albany in the Hudson valley. First, Howe's army would strike north up the river from New York, then a force under Colonel Barry St Leger would advance along the Mohawk to its confluence with the Hudson, and finally his own army would enter the Hudson valley by the traditional route from the north. In London, he discussed his ideas with Lord George Germain (who, as Lord George Sackville, had brought such disgrace on the cavalry at Minden – see Chapter 8) and been declared unfit to serve the Crown in any military capacity. Since then, Germain had become a close friend of King George III and been appointed Secretary of State for the Colonies in Lord North's government. It beggars belief, but Germain now had more say in how the war should be run than anyone else. He accepted Burgoyne's plan, then made a hideous blunder by informing Howe of the details while leaving it to his discretion whether he played his part in it or not. As it happened, Howe's plans for 1777 involved an advance against Philadelphia with a view to forcing Washington into a decisive battle. He was, in any event, senior to Burgoyne and fully intended to exercise the discretion Germain had given him. Unaware of the strategic time bomb ticking away beneath his feet, Burgoyne returned to Canada and prepared to take the offensive.

The Saratoga Campaign, June–October 1777

Burgoyne began moving south from Canada in June 1777. He defeated the American forces holding the Lake Champlain sector, but his advance was slowed down by felled trees, enabling the Americans to concentrate troops from all over New England. On 3 August he received the shattering news that Howe was not cooperating (see the previous section for their planning problems). At this point, Burgoyne could have abandoned his advance and consolidated his gains, but he chose not to.

On 16 August the rebels ambushed a column of Brunswick mercenaries, sent to secure supplies at Bennington, and over 900 men were killed, wounded, or captured. Again, Burgoyne could have retreated, but he pressed stubbornly on. In the middle of September he found further progress halted by an entrenched position near Saratoga, held by 7000 Americans under Major General Horatio Gates. On 19 September Burgoyne mounted an unsuccessful attack, known as the Battle of Freeman's Farm, sustaining 600 casualties to the Americans' 300.

Meanwhile, Clinton had marched up the Hudson with more British troops, taking Forts Clinton and Montgomery on 6 October. He then returned to

New York, hoping that this diversion had been helpful to Burgoyne. It hadn't, because Gates now had 9000 men under his command. When Burgoyne launched a second attack on 7 October (the Battle of Bemis Heights) he simply sustained another 600 casualties to the Americans' 150. The American strength continued to grow, until it outnumbered Burgoyne's remaining 5700 men by three to one, and Burgoyne surrendered.

To the Americans, victories at Saratoga served as a balance to Howe's successes in Pennsylvania, but they went much further than that. France not only recognised the United States of America but also declared war on Great Britain in 1778, to be followed by Spain in 1779, and Holland in 1780. In the long term, an American victory was assured and Saratoga can therefore be seen as the war's major turning point.

Fighting at Philly

Howe believed that capturing Philadelphia, the seat of Congress, while simultaneously destroying Washington's army, would make the revolution collapse. On 23 July 1777 he sailed from New York with 18,000 men, bound for Chesapeake Bay. Landing at Elkton, he set off for Philadelphia, defeating Washington at the Battle of Brandywine on 11 September. Ten days later, a British night attack routed the brigade of Brigadier General Anthony Wayne at Paoli. The Congressmen fled first to Lancaster and then to York, once more conferring dictatorial powers on Washington (see the section 'New York, New York', earlier in this chapter) in the hope that he would keep them safe. On 26 September, Howe entered Philadelphia, but having been reinforced to a strength of 13,000, Washington attempted to attack the main British encampment at Germantown on 4 October. His plan was too complex and his senior commanders blundered in their attempted execution of it, incurring 700 casualties and losing 400 prisoners.

After Germantown, Washington's army, now much reduced, spent a miserable, freezing winter at Valley Forge. While Howe had repeatedly proved to be the better tactician, his lack of killer instinct permitted the American army to survive its ordeal. It also cost Howe his job and Clinton came forward to replace him. Meanwhile, a German calling himself General Baron Augustus von Steuben was licking the Americans into shape. He was neither a general nor a baron, and probably not a 'von' either, but he was quite correct in saying that if the Americans wanted to start beating British regulars in the open field, they needed to become as disciplined and fully trained.

In June 1778, following the outbreak of war between Great Britain and France, Clinton began marching overland to New York. Washington, with 13,000 men, followed closely. On 28 June an attempt to intercept Clinton's withdrawal at Monmouth came to naught when Major General Charles Lee mishandled the American advance guard. The result was a hard-fought action that proved the worth of Steuben's training methods, but failed to stop Clinton's army reaching New York. Lee was court-martialled and dismissed from the service.

Georgia on my mind, 1779–1781

So far, the war in the southern colonies had consisted of guerrilla activities by rebel or loyalist groups. At the end of December 1778, however, British regular troops defeated the local rebel militia and occupied Savannah, Georgia. In September 1779, the French Admiral D'Estaing arrived off the port with 4000 French troops. Having joined forces with the local rebel commander, he laid siege to the town. Unwilling to expose his ship to autumn gales, he insisted on assaulting the British lines on 9 October. A deserter warned the 3500-strong British garrison, commanded by Brigadier General Augustine Prevost, and they threw the attackers back, having inflicted 800 casualties in exchange for 150 of their own. D'Estaing embarked his troops and sailed off while his American allies returned to Charleston, South Carolina.

The British were planning no major operations against the northern colonies, but it seemed as though they could bring the southern colonies under control. The main actions of this campaign were:

✔ Clinton's 14,000 British troops laid siege to Charleston. Bombarded by land and sea, General Benjamin Lincoln's garrison held out until 12 May 1780, then surrendered. Clinton, in no mood to be generous, granted only partial honours of war. Included in the surrender were 5400 prisoners, four frigates, 400 guns, and a huge quantity of small arms and ammunition. It was the worst American disaster of the war and it looked very much as though South Carolina as well as Georgia could be recovered for the Crown.

✔ Clinton returned to New York, leaving Cornwallis with 8000 men to pacify the area. Unfortunately, Cornwallis didn't believe in the modern hearts-and-minds method of winning over the population. It wasn't enough for him that people should stop being rebels, they had to join in the fight against other rebels, and that was too much to ask. He was also heavy handed in the matter of confiscations, especially of slaves. This stimulated guerrilla activity, and the brutal methods that Tarleton's loyalist British Legion employed to obtain results infuriated the population.

✔ Gates, commanding the American forces in the south, assembled an army of 3000 men, mainly militia, and marched into South Carolina. On 16 August Cornwallis with 2400 regulars and loyalists met him at Camden and routed him, inflicting losses of 900 killed and 1000 captured.

✔ Rebel militia virtually wiped out an 1100-strong loyalist unit commanded by Colonel Patrick Ferguson at King's Mountain, North Carolina, on 7 October. Apart from Ferguson, everyone present was American born. Worse was to follow, for Brigadier General Daniel Morgan worsted Tarleton at Cowpens, South Carolina, on 17 January 1781, killing 110 and capturing 830 from Tarleton's total strength of 1100. Morgan, commanding approximately the same number, lost only 12 killed and 61 wounded. The news that Tarleton's hated Legion was beaten at last provided a greater boost to American morale than the size of the engagement suggests.

- ✔ Major General Nathanael Greene replaced Gates as the American commander in the south after the Battle of Camden. He assembled a 4400-strong army, consisting mainly of militia and partially trained regulars, and advanced into North Carolina. At Guilford Court House, he established a defensive position in depth on Cornwallis's projected route to Wilmington, where the British hoped to replenish their supplies. On 15 March, Cornwallis attacked the position with just 1900 men. As much of the battlefield consisted of woodland, Greene's troops were unable to support each other and the British were able to fight their way through each of the defences in turn, at the cost of 500 killed, wounded, and missing. Greene broke off the action and withdrew, having sustained 1300 casualties and lost four guns.

- ✔ Greene realised that while he could replace his casualties, his opponents could not. As he advanced into South Carolina, local British commanders beat him at Hobkirk's Hill on 19 April, Fort Ninety-Six on 19 June, and Eutaw Springs on 8 September 1781.

The overall result of this campaign was that the British had to withdraw isolated garrisons, so that by the end of September only Charleston and Savannah remained in British hands south of Virginia. Cornwallis, having decided that he could no longer hold the Carolinas and Georgia, marched north into Virginia. It was to prove a fateful decision (the following section explains why).

Turning the world upside down

Cornwallis marched into Virginia because he thought that he could gain supplies and reinforcements there. That could only be at Clinton's expense, but back in London, Lord George Germain thoroughly approved of the strategy, so that was that (see the section 'Making plans with Johnny and George' earlier in this chapter for more on Germain's role).

On 4 August, in response to orders from Clinton, Cornwallis occupied Yorktown, on the tip of the Virginia peninsula. This proved to be the deciding moment of the war.

By land and sea, Washington and his French allies closed in. Cornwallis believed that Clinton would keep him supplied and despatch reinforcements should the need arise, but at the critical moment the Royal Navy temporarily lost its command of the sea at the Second Battle of the Capes, 5–9 September. By the end of the month, 9500 Americans and 7500 French regulars were besieging Yorktown.

Cornwallis made the mistake of withdrawing inside his inner defences in the hope that Clinton would come to his assistance. This meant that the entire defended area was now within range of the allies' siege artillery. On 14 October Cornwallis lost two important redoubts. He pushed new batteries forward and beat off an American counter-attack two days later. A storm forced Cornwallis to abandon the idea of evacuating at least some of his troops across the York river to Gloucester. In addition to his other worries, ammunition was running low and smallpox had broken out among his troops. Realising that defeat was now inevitable, he asked Washington for terms. Remembering the humiliating terms imposed on the American garrison of Charleston, the rebels decreed that when the British marched out, their bands would not be permitted to play a French or American march. With wry humour equal to the occasion, the bandmasters chose 'The World Turned Upside Down', a popular song that ironically had formed part of one of Gentleman Johnny Burgoyne's comic operas.

Neither side undertook any more major military operations in North America after the fall of Yorktown. Everyone was sick of the war and simply wanted to get out of it on the best terms possible.

Britain lost 13 colonies in North America, but its merchants did better business with the former colonists than they had done before. The Americans found that they had exchanged one set of politicians for another, but at least they could vote for or against the new lot. Congress was stony broke, despite having disbanded its army.

Chapter 10

Revolting Frenchmen, The Grand Old Duke, and Boney: The French Revolutionary and Napoleonic Wars

To the surprise and horror of Europe's ruling establishment, the down-trodden French common folk rose against their king in 1789. The other European powers, however, saw the French Revolution as a threat to the existing order of things, and some governments took steps to restore the *ancien régime* by force. By degrees, the revolution passed into the hands of extremists who revelled in slaughtering their real or imagined opponents. The execution of King Louis XVI and Queen Marie Antoinette was the last straw for many; Great Britain would probably have declared war on France if the French had not declared war on the British first, in 1793. For more on the causes and impact of the French Revolution, see Sean Lang's *European History For Dummies* (published by Wiley).

The British army was committed to a mismanaged and mercifully short-lived campaign in the Low Countries. The French responded by attempting to invade Wales and providing armed assistance for a rebellion in Ireland. After this, British concern about the security of India prompted a major expedition to Egypt, and as the war became global they despatched smaller expeditions elsewhere. And this is just the prelude to the real showdown with Napoleon, covered in Chapter 11.

Militia and yeomanry regiments

French enthusiasm for spreading revolutionary values throughout Europe resulted in an overhaul and expansion of the British home defence forces. *Militia* regiments, usually raised by county, were recruited by ballot, although any individual so chosen could pay a substitute to take his place. On mobilisation, militiamen were liable to serve for a period of five years. Those willing to transfer to the regular army were formed into drafts and received postings to regiments overseas. Militia drafts regularly reinforced Wellington's army during the Peninsula

War and were generally considered to raise the overall quality of that army. Gaps in the militia ranks left by outgoing drafts were filled from *fencible* regiments, another type of reserve unit with a limited liability for home defence only. England, Wales, Ireland, and the Isle of Man all had militia. Scotland had none, but formed the largest number of fencible units. Well-to-do individuals formed volunteer cavalry regiments known as *yeomanry*, most of which had a county basis; yeomen had to provide their own mounts and at least some of their own equipment.

The British army at this time had entered a period of evolution. Dragoons had long since abandoned the mounted infantry role and fought purely as heavy cavalry, not mounted infantrymen. In 1800, further uniform changes took place: Infantry wore a *coatee* (a short, close-fitting coat) and a stovepipe shako or headdress, although fusiliers continued to wear the bearskin; rifle regiments wore green uniforms, and light cavalry wore blue. Militia and yeomanry regiments started to appear (see the sidebar of the same name). The army also formed the Royal Horse Artillery, equipped with light horse-drawn guns to support the cavalry, in 1793; it wore a uniform similar to that of the light dragoons and quickly became regarded as an elite.

Campaigning with the Grand Old Duke of York: The Low Countries, 1793–1795

British Prime Minister Pitt ordered a British army under command of the Duke of York to capture Dunkirk. His army consisted of 6500 British, 13,000 Hanoverians, 8000 Hessians, and 15,000 Dutch, but he had to withdraw to Ostend when the French defeated his Austrian allies further south. In fact, the Austrians preferred to employ their troops elsewhere and left the Duke in the lurch altogether. Pitt reinforced him with another 10,000 men under Lord Moira, and York withdrew into Holland. On 15 September 1794, though heavily outnumbered by the French, York fought a battle at Boxtel, an engagement that may have been totally forgotten if it had not given the future Duke of Wellington his baptism of fire. The then Lieutenant Colonel Arthur Wesley (the name Wellesley came later, as did the Wellington title; read more about him in Chapter 11) completely smashed up an attacking French column with disciplined, close-range volley firing by the 33rd Foot, the regiment that would later bear his name.

The Duke of York never had a chance of inflicting a decisive defeat on the French. Worse still, his army was totally unequipped to spend a winter in the open. His men dropped like flies from disease, exposure, and starvation, which forced him to withdraw into Germany in February 1795. In April, leaving part of the artillery and all the cavalry to support the Hanoverians, the survivors embarked for home. The French had been responsible for only a small percentage of the fatalities the British sustained.

The disastrous campaign in the Low Countries made a deep impression on the Duke of York, appointed Commander-in-Chief of the British army on his return. The army's rank-and-file strength had expanded steadily from 40,000 in 1793 to 125,000 just two years later. This led to a proportional demand for officers. In this context, many who offered themselves lacked any form of qualification or instinct for their duties, and some of those in receipt of commissions were actually infants. The most notable example of the fashion was that snappy dresser George 'Beau' Brummel, who resigned his commission when his regiment was ordered to Manchester, commenting that he could not be expected to serve abroad. The Duke, an efficient administrator, swept away this sort of nonsense and greatly improved the administration that served the army so badly. In 1801 he founded the Royal Military College, training regimental and staff officers. Another of his introductions was the Royal Wagon Train, a forerunner of the modern Royal Logistic Corps, which did away with the tiresome business of hiring civilian drivers.

Everyone knows the nursery rhyme, 'The Grand Old Duke of York'. The trouble is, the Duke may have been grand but he wasn't old (he was 30, actually), he had more than 10,000 men, and as he was campaigning in the Low Countries, hills were in short supply. What the rhyme says, really, is that the poor chap wasn't getting anywhere fast, and that was true enough. When the American War of Independence ended (see Chapter 9), the British government let the army run down, just as it did and would do after every war. Not only a manpower shortage existed, everything the army needed was in short supply, and too many office-based bunglers were building empires for themselves.

The Battle of Fishguard, February 1797

Whenever possible, the French liked to make trouble for the British at home. In 1796 a 13,000-strong invasion force commanded by General Hoche hoped to effect a landing in Bantry Bay, Ireland, to stir up trouble with the help of anti-British Irish folk. Some of Hoche's ships arrived but bad weather prevented a landing. Of the rest, five were lost in storms, six were captured, and the rest went home.

The following year the French decided to mount an expedition to Wales. In command was an American named William Tate. Originally of Irish extraction, Tate had served as a rebel artilleryman during the American War of Independence; his qualifications for the job in hand seemed to be the ability to speak English and a dislike of the British. His troops, known as the 2nd Legion de Francs, consisted of some 1200 gaol sweepings, deserters, and former rebels against the Revolution. It seems probable that General Hoche considered Tate and his troops very expendable indeed, judging from his orders: After being put ashore near the Bristol Channel, they were to burn Bristol, capture Chester and Liverpool, destroy port facilities and fill in docks as they went, and raise the country in rebellion. Obviously, they would have no shortage of things to do.

The wonder is that what happened next has not become a musical or an ice show. Unable to agree with the ships' captains on a suitable landing place in the Bristol Channel, Tate agreed to put his command ashore somewhere in Cardigan Bay. In fact, the troops landed on a rocky headland close to Fishguard on 22 February 1797. The locals spotted them and raised the alarm. Some French troops went out to forage and quickly became drunk on wine the local people had salvaged from the wreck of a Portuguese ship. Others were shot while trying to steal from farms. A Welsh woman tipped one down a well, but he survived, and a fierce lady cobbler named Jemima Nicholas rounded 12 up with a pitchfork. Meanwhile, the Lord Lieutenant of Pembrokeshire, Lord Cawdor, was assembling a counter-invasion force. While the troops were gathering, a number of Welsh women in their traditional scarlet cloaks and black steeple hats apparently lined up to give a distant impression of infantrymen. The story may well contain an element of truth. Lord Cawdor's army finally numbered 43 men of his own Pembroke Yeomanry, 100 Cardigan militia, 93 Pembroke volunteers, 191 Fishguard Fencibles, a 148-strong naval party with two 9-pounder cannon, and some attached officers, giving a grand total of 575, or approximately half of the invaders' strength. However, Tate and his officers were in no mood to fight; in the circumstances, surrender seemed the most comfortable option. Tate initiated a courteous correspondence with Lord Cawdor, as a result of which the invaders grounded arms and marched off under escort.

So ended the last 'invasion' of the British mainland. As if the whole business had not been bizarre enough, the battle honour Fishguard was subsequently awarded to the Pembroke Yeomanry although they had fought no battle.

The Great Irish Rebellion of 1798

Planned and executed by the Society of United Irishmen, the events of 1798 are a rare example of Protestants and Catholics working together for what they believed to be the good of Ireland. The Protestant Ascendancy wanted more power for the toothless Parliament in Dublin, and the Catholics (in the majority in Ireland) wanted the full rights and privileges enjoyed by other Irish citizens. The inspiration for this rising was the French Revolution and its architects were Wolfe Tone and Napper Tandy. They agreed the date for the rebellion as 24 May and ingeniously set the time to coincide with the passing of mail coaches through the towns and villages, so creating an ever-enlarging ripple across the countryside. For more on the political situation, see Mike Cronin's *Irish History For Dummies* (published by Wiley).

The rebellion's fortunes were mixed. In some areas the local British garrisons experienced no difficulty in containing the outbreak, in others they had to fall back. In general, the rebels lacked discipline and direction; some took time off to settle old scores and the old religious rivalries surfaced before long. Throughout May and on into June, British regular troops, yeomanry, and militia brought one area after another back under government control, sometimes with little mercy being shown to those involved in the uprising.

The rebellion was at its strongest in County Wexford, where the rebels held the towns of Wexford and Enniscorthy in strength. Commanded by Lieutenant General Gerard Lake, some 10,000 troops fought a pitched battle against 16,000 rebels at Vinegar Hill, near Enniscorthy, on 12 June. They routed the rebels, who lost approximately 4000 men killed or wounded, and the back of the rebellion was broken. Folklore sometimes presents the battle as an Anglo-Irish contest, but most of Lake's troops were Irish yeomanry and militia regiments.

Too late in the day, the French awoke to what was happening. On 22 August approximately 1000 French troops under General Joseph Humbert landed at Killala Bay in County Mayo. Having been joined by a large number of Irish rebels, Humbert inflicted a defeat on Lake at Castlebar. The engagement was notable on two counts:

- Most of the Irish element in both armies took to their heels at the first cannon shot.

- A lone Highland sentry, positioned at the top of a flight of steps in the town, fought with such ferocity that the bodies of his French assailants surrounded him when he was finally killed.

Humbert must have known his was a fool's errand, but he gamely continued to march in the direction of Dublin, hoping that more rebels would join him. In fact, the reverse applied. The new Viceroy of Ireland, Lord Cornwallis, carefully coordinated the movement of his own and Lake's armies until they finally cornered Humbert near the village of Ballinamuck on 8 September. Humbert fought for a token half hour, then surrendered. Cornwallis's forces killed several hundred rebels, mostly during the pursuit, and captured 90.

The London government, severely shaken by the rebellion and angered by the Irish Establishment's inability to keep order, passed the Act of Union in 1800. This merged the Kingdom of Ireland with the Kingdom of Great Britain and allowed Ireland to send elected members to the Westminster Parliament, governing the country from London rather than Dublin.

Chasing the French out of Egypt, 1801

On 12 April 1798 General Napoleon Bonaparte, commander of France's 40,000-strong Army of the Orient, sailed from Toulon for Egypt. He intended to occupy Egypt as a stepping stone to India, thereby ruining British trade in the Middle and Far East. Although Napoleon's land campaign in Egypt went well, the British Admiral Nelson ruined his strategic aim by destroying the French fleet at the Battle of the Nile on 1 August 1798. This left the French army completely stranded.

Egypt was a province of the Ottoman Empire and to secure its possession, Bonaparte made a fruitless foray into Palestine. On returning to Egypt his troops repulsed a Turkish landing from British ships at Aboukir on 25 July 1799. On 23 August he abandoned his troops and returned to France aboard a fast frigate.

Britain wanted the French out of Egypt altogether, so in 1801 a combined British–Turkish force of 18,000 men assembled at Rhodes under the command of General Sir Ralph Abercrombie. Setting sail for Egypt, it made an opposed landing from ships' boats on 8 March. The landing should have been made before dawn, but it was full daylight when the troops were committed. A hail of round shot, shells, grape, and musketry met them. The French smashed and sunk several boats, and cavalry who waded into the sea attacked the occupants of others. More than a few of the British took a ducking. A sergeant had to hold one tiny Guards officer's head above the water to prevent him from drowning. Despite this, Abercrombie's troops reached the shore in increasing numbers and drove off the French. Thrown back into Alexandria, the French counter-attacked on 21 March. The 28th Foot (1/The Gloucestershire Regiment), occupying an incomplete *redoubt* (fortification) in the sand dunes, found themselves engaged in a furious fire-fight with a French grenadier regiment that called itself the Invincibles; more French grenadiers were closing in behind the 28th. The order was given for the regiment's rear rank to face about, and for a while each rank fought its own battle against superior numbers. In due course, the Invincibles pulled back, leaving the 28th to go to the assistance of their neighbours, the Black Watch, who were also surrounded. The battle ended with the repulse of a major cavalry charge that failed to reach the British line. British casualties amounted to 1376 killed and wounded, including Sir Ralph Abercrombie, who sustained a mortal wound. French losses were estimated at 3000. In recognition of their remarkable feat, the 28th were awarded the distinction of wearing the number 28 on the back of their headdress, signifying the regiment's ability to fight in two directions at once. In due course, a small sphinx badge replaced this.

Without the need for serious fighting, Cairo and Alexandria both passed into allied hands. Disheartened and isolated from their homeland, the 26,000 French troops remaining in Egypt surrendered and received a free passage home in September 1801.

Fighting France Here, There, and Everywhere

The Peace of Amiens, signed on 27 March 1802, ended hostilities between Great Britain and France, but only for a while. It was simply half-time (well, nearly) in a war lasting 22 years (see Chapter 11 for the war's conclusion). In May 1803 it was time to start fighting again. In both halves of this protracted war, British troops were involved in operations that most Britons have now all but forgotten about. This is a good place to give brief details:

- **Holland, 1799.** When Holland became part of the French sphere of influence, it was of paramount importance to stop the Dutch fleet falling into the hands of the French. In August 1799 the Duke of York returned to Holland at the head of 27,000 British troops as part of a combined operation to secure the Dutch warships at the island of Texel, which surrendered to a British naval squadron. Joined by two Russian divisions, the Duke fought several engagements with the French and then, having secured his objective, signed a convention with them in October. Under the terms of this the allies withdrew from Holland, the British repatriated French and Dutch prisoners, and the Dutch fleet remained in British hands.

- **Copenhagen, 1801 and 1807.** On 2 April 1801 the 49th Foot (1/Royal Berkshire Regiment) and the Rifle Brigade served as marines during the naval battle in which Nelson destroyed the Danish fleet. In 1807 a larger British force successfully besieged Copenhagen to prevent the Danish fleet falling into French hands. A division under the command of the future Duke of Wellington beat off a Danish relief force.

- **Malta, 1798–1800.** In 1798 the Maltese rose against the French force that was occupying the island. British troops served alongside the Maltese until the French surrendered on 5 September 1800. This marked the beginning of a long association of the British armed services with Malta that ended only in comparatively recent years.

✔ **India, 1803.** Napoleon liked to sneer that Wellington was a 'sepoy general' because of his service in India. That was not only unfair to the sepoys, who were trained, disciplined, professional soldiers with fine fighting qualities, but also a very serious underestimation of Wellington's abilities as a commander. One wonders how the French Emperor would have coped with the situation confronting the then Major General Sir Arthur Wellesley at Assaye on 23 September 1803.

Assaye was a village in Berar located between the confluence of the Juah and Kaitna rivers, approximately 250 miles northeast of Bombay. Wellesley had only 4520 British and Indian troops at his disposal, including 2170 infantry, 1200 cavalry, and a small number of guns. His British troops included the 19th Light Dragoons, the 74th Highlanders (2/Highland Light Infantry), and the 78th Highlanders (2/Seaforth Highlanders). His object was to destroy the Mahratta field army in the Deccan, which may seem overambitious considering that that army, commanded by Dowlut Rao Scindia and the Rajah of Berar, consisted of 30,000 cavalry, 17,000 infantry (including 10,500 regulars), and 190 guns. French instructors had trained it and a German officer named Pohlmann commanded its infantry. Initially, both armies confronted each other across the Kaitna. Wellesley observed that two villages faced each other on opposite banks of the river, some way beyond the Mahratta left, and correctly deduced that a ford connected them. Using broken ground for concealment, he led his troops across and then deployed to face the enemy with his right protected by the Juah and his left by the Kaitna. This forced the Mahrattas to turn towards him, but because the front narrowed as the two rivers flowed towards each other, they were only able to deploy a fraction of their strength. Incredibly, it was the British who took the initiative. Despite local checks it took them only three hours to drive the Mahratta army off the field with the loss of 6000 killed or wounded and 98 guns captured. British casualties amounted to 428 killed and 1156 wounded or missing, about one-third of their strength. Following a further defeat at Laswari, Scindia sued for peace.

In later years, Wellington described Assaye as his greatest victory, and proportionately the bloodiest action he ever witnessed.

✔ **Naples, 1806.** Having crowned himself Emperor of the French in 1804, Napoleon Bonaparte began seeing to it that his relatives were nicely settled on other people's thrones. The throne of Naples he gave to his brother Joseph. In 1806 a 5000-strong British force under General Sir John Stuart landed in Naples with the intention of helping guerrillas fighting in support of the deposed King Ferdinand IV. General Jean Reynier, commanding 6440 men, opposed Stuart near the village of Maida. The disciplined volleys of the British line blew the French attack columns apart and the French sustained further casualties as they broke and fled. Stuart's losses amounted to 387 killed and wounded. French casualties included 1785 killed or wounded plus a large number of prisoners. As the anticipated guerrilla support was not forthcoming, Stuart withdrew his force to Sicily. Maida Vale in London takes its name from the battle.

✔ **The West Indies, 1794–1810.** The slaves on former French colonies (handed to the British at the peace of Amiens) thought that the revolutionary slogan of Liberty, Equality, and Brotherhood applied to them, too. Understandably, they reacted badly when they learned it didn't. In Haiti they reacted with such extreme violence that a large British force was despatched in the hope that it would restore some sort of order, as they didn't want mayhem spreading to Jamaica and the rest of their islands, as this would destabilise the whole region. In the event, the British only achieved partial success. During the French Revolutionary and Napoleonic Wars estimates claim that no fewer than 100,000 British soldiers lost their lives in the West Indies, the majority dying from tropical diseases.

✔ **The South Atlantic, 1806–1807.** Operations against Spain's South American territories proved less than fruitful (Spain being allied to France at this time). In June 1806 a small British force made an unauthorised landing at Buenos Aires, but the local militia forced it to surrender. The following year General Joseph Whitelocke mounted a much larger expedition from the United Kingdom. It occupied Montevideo, in modern Uruguay, in July 1807, then descended on Buenos Aires. A popular uprising followed in which the British troops, unused to street fighting, were confronted by barricades and heavy firing from the rooftops, and were finally forced to surrender. There was no point in pursuing these adventures further, as Spain's colonies were on the point of rebelling against their mother country anyway.

Chapter 11

Wellington Boots the French Out: The Peninsula to Waterloo

*T*he British naval hero Nelson won a great victory against the French and Spanish at sea in the Battle of Trafalgar in 1805. This removed the threat of invasion from France, and Britain could concentrate on counter-measures to Napoleon's domination of Europe. At first these consisted simply of an economic blockade, but in retaliation Napoleon prohibited the import of British goods into Europe. Apart from smuggling, neutral Portugal offered the only through route open to British commerce. This incurred Napoleon's wrath and in 1807 resulted in a French invasion of Portugal. By the conclusion of this campaign, Napoleon had not only been defeated in the Peninsula but in the rest of Europe as well and the French monarchy had been restored. Despite this Napoleon returned to try his luck once more, only to meet his final defeat at Waterloo, one of the most famous battles in British military history. Sandwiched between these two events, America took up arms against Britain once again (see Chapter 9 for preceding events). So this chapter covers a rather hectic few years!

British soldiers fighting in the Napoleonic Wars fought as described in Chapter 10. Figure 11-1 shows the uniforms of some common fighting troops.

One aspect of warfare that changed over the Napoleonic Wars was the reintroduction of armour. The French army's *cuirassier* cavalry regiments wore polished steel helmets and breast and back plates; French *carabinier* cavalry regiments enjoyed much the same sort of protection, but in brass. This type of heavy cavalry, consisting of big men armed with long, straight swords, mounted on big horses, were very formidable opponents. French dragoons and Chevaux-Legers Lancers also wore helmets. In the British service, only the Household Cavalry, dragoons, and the dragoon guard cavalry regiments wore helmets (the exception being the Royal Scots Greys, who wore bearskins).

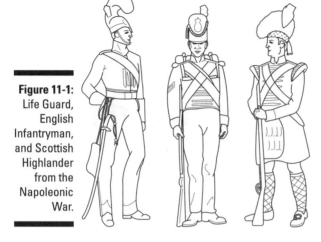

Figure 11-1:
Life Guard, English Infantryman, and Scottish Highlander from the Napoleonic War.

The Peninsular War, 1808–1814

In March 1808 Napoleon invaded Spain and imposed his brother Joseph as king. That was one of the most serious mistakes of his career. The Spanish, being a proud people, were having none of it. The whole of the Iberian peninsula rose in violent rebellion against the French and a merciless guerrilla war isolated the French garrisons. On 19 July a 20,000-strong French army, outnumbered and surrounded, capitulated at Baylen. Shortly after, the British government, which had been supplying the guerrillas with money and weapons, decided to commit troops to the war, which would last until 1814. Figure 11-2 shows the location of the major actions of this war, which the French would refer to as the *Spanish Ulcer* because of the drain it placed on their resources.

The British force sent to Portugal was approximately 16,000 strong and commanded by Lieutenant General Sir Arthur Wellesley, who had been told to hand over command when senior officers arrived. After landing at Mondego Bay on 1 August 1808, 2000 Portuguese joined him and he brushed aside a French covering force at Rolica. As the combined army continued its march on Lisbon, the French army of Portugal confronted it on 21 August at Vimeiro, 32 miles northwest of the capital. Marshal Andoche Junot commanded the French, 13,000 strong, and he launched a series of attacks that the British line shot to pieces. Having lost 3000 killed, wounded, and captured, as well as 13 guns taken, the French withdrew. Allied losses included 160 killed and 505 wounded.

Sir John Moore

Born in Glasgow in 1761, Moore served with the 51st Foot (1/King's Own Yorkshire Light Infantry) during the American War of Independence and became a strong advocate of light infantry tactics. He was seriously wounded at Alexandria in 1801, and shortly before the Peninsular War he established a special training camp for a brigade consisting of the 43rd and 52nd Foot (1/ and 2/Oxfordshire and Buckinghamshire Light Infantry) and the 95th Rifles (1/The Rifle Brigade). William Napier, the historian of the campaign, wrote that, as the brigade expanded into the crack Light Division, they had no equals as soldiers, thanks to Moore's methods. Certainly the sharp-shooting 95th, with their Baker rifles, earned a reputation for sending French regiments to bed all but officerless. In addition to his being one of the army's ablest generals, Moore's soldiers liked as well as respected him and genuinely mourned him when he was killed at Corunna.

Figure 11-2:
The major
battles
of the
Peninsular
War.

It was most unfortunate that Wellesley's superiors, Generals Sir Harry Burrard and Sir Hew Dalrymple, arrived shortly after the battle. Junot asked for terms. Burrard and Dalrymple were only too pleased to supply them. Junot's army would not only be returned to France in British ships, it could take all its plunder and loot with it! Junot may well have choked over his wine in disbelief, but he certainly wasn't going to argue. The folks back home in Britain didn't see it all in quite the same overgenerous light. A court of inquiry recalled Burrard, Dalrymple, and Wellesley to explain themselves. It exonerated Wellesley of all blame, but in the meantime Lieutenant General Sir John Moore (see the sidebar about him) took command of the army in Portugal.

The Battle of Corunna, 16 January 1808

In September 1808, with the promise of support from no fewer than 125,000 Spanish irregulars, Moore advanced into northern Spain to sever the French lines of communication between France and Madrid. For a while all went well, although the Spanish provided very little practical assistance. Meanwhile Napoleon came forward to take personal control of the situation. By 4 December he had taken Madrid. He then swung northwest to threaten Moore with overwhelming numbers. Moore received warning of Napoleon's approach. He ordered his two light brigades to make for the port of Vigo, while the rest of the army commenced an epic 250-mile retreat to Corunna over the wild, snow-covered Cantabrian mountains. Rations were in seriously short supply and the troops faced immense physical demands. For much of the time, Moore remained one step ahead of his pursuers. Napoleon, having heard that Austria was preparing to renew hostilities, departed for France on 1 January 1809, complacent in the belief that the war in Spain was over. Marshal Nicolas Soult took up the pursuit of Moore's army, which began entering Corunna on 11 January. Embarkation and the destruction of stores commenced at once.

By 16 January enough of Soult's troops had arrived for him to launch an assault. By then, the British cavalry and the greater part of the artillery were safely aboard their ships. The ensuing battle was fought between Moore's remaining 15,000 infantry and Soult's 20,000 force of all arms. Some of the fiercest fighting took place on a low ridge above the village of Elvina, where the French attacked, counter-attacks driving them back through the village. During the evening the British beat off the last French attacks. Soult sustained 2000 casualties. The British sustained half that number, including Moore himself, who was mortally wounded; by 8 a.m. on 17 January the last of the British troops were aboard. Napoleon may have thought that the Corunna evacuation marked the end of the Peninsular War. In fact, it had barely started.

The Battle of Talavera, 27 July 1809

In their eagerness to crush Moore (see the preceding section) the French had unconsciously given Portugal time to reorganise and retrain its army under British officers and NCOs. Sir Arthur Wellesley returned to the Peninsula in

April 1809 and assumed overall command; in May he outmanoeuvred Soult and forced him to withdraw, abandoning artillery and baggage as he did so. Wellesley next planned an advance on Madrid in conjunction with a Spanish army commanded by General Gregorio de la Cuesta, giving him a total strength of 54,000, including some 33,000 totally unreliable Spanish who promised much and delivered nothing.

On 27 July a 46,000-strong French army commanded by Joseph Bonaparte and Marshal Claude Victor attacked the Allies' position at Talavera, 70 miles southwest of Madrid. The Spanish, snugly entrenched, fired one nervous volley then took to their heels, spreading tales of defeat and disaster far and wide. Eventually, their own cavalry rounded up all but 6000 of them and escorted them back, although they played little or no part in the fighting. During two days of hard fighting the French attacked the British line again and again, only to be counter-attacked and thrown back each time. Neither side gained a clear-cut tactical victory, but Wellesley claimed strategic success as the French fell back towards Madrid. The French lost 761 killed, 6391 wounded, 206 missing, and 20 guns captured. British casualties amounted to 801 killed, 3915 wounded, and 645 missing. The Spanish claimed to have sustained 1207 casualties, but as they hadn't done any real fighting the figure possibly relates to fugitives still on the run. Wellesley vowed never again to conduct joint operations with the Spanish.

Shortly after, a captured courier told the British that Soult and others were already marching south to cut Wellesley's communications with Portugal. Reacting quickly, Wellesley had his troops concentrated on Portuguese soil by the end of August. On 26 August he was elevated to the peerage, becoming Viscount Wellington of Talavera and of Wellington.

The Battles of Torres Vedras and Busaco, 27 September 1810

Save in the Peninsula, the year 1810 found Britain abandoned by all its continental allies, so Wellington (formerly known as Wellesley) remained on the defensive. He built three deep defensive belts, known as the Lines of Torres Vedras, stretching from the river Tagus to the Atlantic ocean. Having made them impenetrable to an attacker, Wellington stripped the country bare for many miles in front of the lines so that his opponents would not be able to feed themselves without an immense logistical effort.

While the lines were being constructed, Wellington continued to menace the French with his field army, now 50,000 strong (including 24,000 Portuguese). On 27 September 1810, while withdrawing to the lines, he fought a holding action at Busaco against Marshal Andre Massena's 60,000-strong French army. The French failed to scout properly, and their attacking columns suffered serious losses and were repulsed after heavy fighting. The British and

Portuguese sustained 1250 casualties, the French 4600. Wellington completed his withdrawal into the Lines of Torres Vedras. Massena examined the fortifications, realised that he could neither storm them nor maintain his army in front of them, then withdrew.

The Battle of Fuentes de Onoro, 5 May 1811

Wellington's strategic aim for the 1811 campaign was to capture the frontier fortresses of Almeida, Cuidad Rodrigo, and Badajoz, to secure his base in Portugal. At the end of April he laid siege to Almeida, but on 2 May he learned that Massena's army, resupplied and reinforced, was on its way to break the siege. Its route would take it through the straggling village of Fuentes de Onoro on the little river Dos Casas, and Wellington took up a defensive position on a ridge to the west of the stream. The two armies were in contact on 3 May, but no major action took place for two days. By then Messena's 46,000 troops seriously outnumbered the 21,450 British and 2500 Portuguese that Wellington had available.

Massena tried to turn the Allied right, but the stubborn withdrawal of the British infantry squares and cavalry, in which each covered the movements of the other by bounds, brought the French advance to a halt. Massena then launched a series of infantry attacks that saw the village of Fuentes de Onoro change hands several times. At around noon he flung a fresh 18 battalions into the fight, forcing the British and Portuguese defenders out. Wellington personally ordered the 74th Highlanders (2/Highland Light Infantry) and 88th Foot (1/Connaught Rangers) to retake the village. Out of battle, the wild Irishmen of the 88th were often in trouble with the authorities, but in action any general was delighted to have them under his command. Now, in a bayonet charge that combined Highland ferocity with hair-raising Irish yells, the French were winkled from house after house, hounded down alleyways, and chased along streets as though the fiends of hell were after them. As if this were not bad enough, the 71st Highlanders (1/Highland Light Infantry) and 79th Highlanders (1/Queen's Own Cameron Highlanders) followed through the attack until not a live unwounded Frenchman remained in the village. This virtually ended the battle, for although Massena mounted a fresh attack there was no heart in it and fighting petered out. Given the nature of the fighting, casualties were remarkably light: Wellington lost 1545 killed and wounded while Massena lost 2192.

The result of the battle was far closer than Wellington would have liked, causing him to comment later on what it might have been had Napoleon commanded the enemy in person:

If Boney had been there, we should have been beaten.

Just the same, Massena had failed to win and fell back on Ciudad Rodrigo. Unable to relieve Almeida, he instructed its governor to blow up the fortifications, destroy his stores, and fight his way out, which he did. Shortly after, Massena was removed from his command and saw little further active service.

One incident during the battle of Fuentes de Onoro involved two guns under the command of Captain Norman Ramsey, Royal Horse Artillery. Cut off in the fighting, Ramsey *limbered up* (mounted to a horse-drawn vehicle) the guns and charged through the surrounding horde of French cavalry, many of whom were galloping alongside the mounted gunners, exchanging sabre cuts with them. Together, horses, limbers, and guns weighed several tons travelling at speed, so it would have required an act of supreme courage or stupidity on the part of any Frenchman to stand in their way. Ramsey broke clear and a counter-charge by the 14th Light Dragoons drove his pursuers off.

The Battle of Albuera, 16 May 1811

Some 120 miles to the south of Cuidad Rodrigo (see the preceding section), Sir William Beresford had laid siege to Badajoz. On 12 May he was informed that Soult was advancing to relieve the fortress. Leaving a covering force in the siege lines, Beresford marched to the dusty little town of Albuera, which lay in Soult's path. There, a Spanish contingent under a general named Joachim Blake joined him, giving Beresford a total of 35,000 men: 7000 British, 13,300 Portuguese, and 14,700 Spanish. He deployed along a ridge to the south of the village, fronted by a stream named the Chicapierna that became the Albuera in front of the village.

Beresford's numbers should have given him a decisive advantage from the outset. Soult, however, had carried out a detailed reconnaissance and spotted a potentially fatal weakness in the Allied deployment. On 16 May he sent a substantial number of his troops straight down the road to Albuera, acting as though they were the vanguard of a major attack. While Beresford's attention was occupied with this, Soult swung off the road and, under cover of a wooded hill, marched the rest of his army westwards, crossed the Chicapierna, and was suddenly present in overwhelming strength on Beresford's right flank. Here's what followed:

> ✔ **Blake's Spanish contingent held the line.** For Beresford, the moment was one of acute apprehension, for no one knew whether the Spanish would fight or not. Under his personal direction the line changed front to meet the attack, while Major General the Hon William Stewart's British 2nd Division began moving forwards to come into line beside them. Stewart's leading brigade, commanded by Sir John Colborne, came up on the Spanish right, its regiments angled against the flank of the French column. The brigade fired two volleys, little realising that within minutes three out of every four of its men would be lying dead or

seriously wounded. Torrential rain driven by high winds, interspersed with lashing hail storms, descended on the battlefield.

✔ **Colborne's brigade was about to charge the French with bayonets when disaster struck.** Lieutenant General Marie Latour-Maubourg, commanding the French cavalry, had watched Colborne's regiments going into action and decided to take advantage of the fact that they were still not only deployed in line and therefore terribly vulnerable to his horsemen, but also apparently unaware of his presence due to the weather. Latour-Maubourg immediately ordered his own right-hand brigade, consisting of Polish lancers and French hussars, to charge them. The galloping horsemen simply rode over and trampled the British infantry into the mud in rapid succession. Regiments dissolved into small groups fighting back to back for survival against the thrusting lances and slashing sabres. The Colour parties (see Chapter 7) became the centre of desperate struggles. Lieutenant Matthew Latham, holding the King's Colour of the Buffs, his nose and cheek slashed off and his sword arm hanging by a thread, continued to clutch the Colour with his left hand while his enemies barged each other out of the way in their efforts to seize the prize. At length, trampled and speared repeatedly, they knocked Latham off his feet but he still retained his hold on the precious silk. Then, as his enemies were forced to defend themselves against a counter-charge by the British 4th Dragoons (later 4th Hussars), he used the last of his strength to tear the Colour from its staff and stuff it into his jacket for safekeeping.

✔ **Colborne's fourth regiment, the 2/31st Foot (later the East Surrey Regiment) had just enough time to form *square* (a defence against cavalry attack).** As the lancers and hussars bore down, a blast of musketry emptied a number of their saddles and galloped on in search of easier prey. Beresford and his staff seemed ideal victims, but proved not to be. Beresford, a man of great physical strength, seized a lance that had been thrust at him, grabbed its owner by the throat and flung him over his saddle. Closing round the general, his staff cut their way out. Then, almost as suddenly as they had come, the French cavalry had gone.

✔ **A second French infantry column began to advance up the slope alongside the first.** All that stood in their path was the 2/31st's little square, just 418 men strong; matters began to look very bleak for Beresford. Stewart, however, was already hurrying his second brigade forwards and this came immediately into action. A murderous duel of attrition followed. No one was sure how long it lasted. The men loaded and fired mechanically, though their ranks were ripped through by French musketry and cannon fire. As men dropped, so their comrades closed in to the left or right on the Colours. If the Colours went down, someone lifted and raised them again. Each regiment's line became shorter and shorter while the gaps between it and its neighbours grew wider. Stewart was hit twice, and the second brigade's commander, Major General Daniel Hoghton, sustained several minor wounds then fell dead with three musket balls in his body. Lieutenant Colonel William

Inglis of the 57th took his place. Inglis was a seasoned campaigner who had fought in the American War of Independence, in the West Indies, and in the Peninsula since 1809. Knowing that his men could not maintain the present rate of attrition for much longer, he rode along the ranks giving encouragement, but his horse was killed under him and a four-ounce grapeshot in the neck felled him. Propping himself up on one elbow, he fiercely exhorted his regiment: 'Die hard, Fifty-Seventh! Die hard!' From this battle onwards, until the regiment's independent history ended a century and a half later, it was known as the Diehards.

✔ **Inglis's men of the 57th evidently thought he was dying, and in anger, their rate of fire became faster and their aim meaner.** Captain Ralph Fawcett, a 23-year-old veteran of several battles, refused to be carried to the rear when he received a mortal wound. Instead, he had himself placed on a little hillock just behind the line, from which he continued to encourage his men. Ensign Jackson carried the King's Colour, ripped by seventeen bullets and its staff broken, and he, having been hit for the third time, handed it on to Ensign Veitch while he had his wounds dressed. On Jackson's return Veitch refused to hand the Colour back and was himself seriously wounded shortly after.

✔ **The third of Stewart's brigades, Colonel the Hon Alexander Abercrombie's, began coming into line.** Now approximately 3,000 British infantry faced 8,000 French. The British muskets did the greater damage, because many of the French, packed tight in their columns, were unable to use their weapons. On the other hand, the fact that the French artillery took such a terrible toll of the British ranks placed the odds firmly on the side of the enemy. The Spanish were a spent force, Stewart's division was fighting itself to destruction, and the ammunition supply was failing. Beresford, deeply depressed, believed that he had lost the battle. His only concern at that moment was to save as much as he could of his army. He gave orders for the King's German Legion to abandon Albuera village and for his Portuguese division to cover the line of retreat.

✔ **As the British prepared to retreat, the insubordination of one of Beresford's staff proved to be his salvation.** 26-year-old Colonel Henry Hardinge disagreed with his chief's gloomy assessment and galloped across to Major General Sir Lowry Cole, who had positioned his 4th Division in reserve behind the British cavalry. He urged Cole to mount an immediate counter-attack. Cole was reluctant to do so without a direct order from Beresford, but gave way when one of his brigade commanders, Lieutenant Colonel Sir William Myers, pointed out that the French were clearly about to launch their final assault on the ridge. Cole was determined not to make same mistake that had given the French cavalry their golden opportunity earlier. He formed his British and Portuguese light companies in column on his right flank, then in line came the two Portuguese regiments of Brigadier General Harvey's brigade, then Myers's British brigade.

- ✔ **Observing the British advance, Latour-Maubourg launched four regiments at Harvey's brigade.** Horses went crashing and riders tumbling from the British and Portuguese firing until the French galloped back whence they had come. Harvey then formed a protective shoulder with which to cover the counter-attack itself, which Myers's brigade made. Cole's 1/7th and 2/7th (later Royal) Fusiliers deployed obliquely within 180 metres (200 yards) of the huge French infantry columns, who turned every possible musket and gun on the advancing British brigade. Myers was killed, Cole and commanding officers of the three regiments went down seriously wounded, and great gaps were blown in the ranks. The ranks closed and still the Fusiliers came on. French officers, including Soult himself, desperately tried to get the mass of their columns into ordered ranks that could reply effectively to the British volleys. They failed and their troops, who had scented victory only minutes earlier, became unsettled.

- ✔ **Soult, having lost about 8,000 men, had no alternative but to withdraw across the river and into the trees.** During his withdrawal the British recovered five of the six captured guns, as well as the Buffs' Regimental Colour. Many of the 500 prisoners that the French had taken escaped. Losses of German and Portuguese (both British allies) amounted to approximately 600 men. The Spaniards lost 1368. British casualties exceeded 4000.

Of Beresford's British regiments, he sent the 29th home to recover their strength and they did not fight again during the war. It would be two years before the Buffs and the 57th fought another battle, while the survivors of the 2/7th and 2/48th merged with their 1st battalions. Beresford returned temporarily to the siege of Badajoz, although neither it nor Cuidad Rodrigo fell until the following year (see the next section).

Although the bloodbath of Albuera did not produce long-term results, the battle is extremely important to any student of British military history because no finer example exists of that intangible quality, regimental spirit, at work. Men simply did not desert their embattled companies, nor companies their regiments, nor regiments their neighbours, for reasons of comradeship and pride and the shame that they would have to face afterwards if they ran. Soult knew that something indefinable had been at work, but he wasn't quite able to put his finger on it. 'There is no beating these troops,' he wrote after the battle. 'I always thought they were bad soldiers – now I am sure of it. I had turned their right, pierced their centre and everywhere victory was mine – but they did not know how to run!'

The storming of Ciudad Rodrigo and Badajoz, 19 January and 7 April 1812

Wellington wished to carry the Peninsular War deeper into Spain, and needed to take the fortresses of Ciudad Rodrigo and Badajoz to do so. His troops hated sieges, which involved the hard labour of digging trenches and then manning them in all sorts of weather. After this, the breaches smashed in the enemy's fortifications had to be stormed, and that was always a desperate and bloody business. A group of volunteers known as the *Forlorn Hope* usually led such attacks. The task was suicidal, but no shortage of volunteers for it ever existed, as the reward for survivors was generally promotion.

The British stormed Ciudad Rodrigo on 19 January 1812 and Badajoz on 7 April. In both cases the French garrison employed every means known to military science to prevent storming of the breaches. These included *cheveux-de-frise*, which were balks of timber with protruding sword and bayonet blades, and concealed mines capable of blowing groups of attackers to kingdom come. Cannon firing grape swept the approach to the breaches, as did intense musketry. In addition, the garrison flung blocks of masonry and incendiary material onto the attackers.

The storming of Ciudad Rodrigo cost the life of General 'Black Bob' Crawford, commander of the famous Light Division, and 561 men were killed or wounded. That of Badajoz cost 3000 casualties, including five generals wounded. The attackers underwent a horrible ordeal and once inside the town they discovered large stocks of alcohol that they used to deaden the reality of their experience. Soon they became a dangerous, drunken mob, beyond the control of their officers. They embarked on an orgy of terror, debauchery, and wanton destruction that left a lasting stain on the British army's reputation.

The Battle of Salamanca, 22 July 1812

After Ciudad Rodrigo and Badajoz fell (see the preceding section), Wellington, now an Earl, led the Allied army into central Spain. His strength now amounted to 3254 cavalry, 47,449 infantry, and 60 guns. After three weeks of manoeuvring, Marshal Marmont's French Army of Portugal, consisting of 3400 cavalry, 46,000 infantry, and 78 guns, provoked battle close to the city of Salamanca, a town on the river Tormes, 100 miles northwest of Madrid.

Marmont, dangerously overconfident despite the fact that he was unable to see the entire battlefield, drew the wrong conclusion from dust clouds in the Allied rear, which he interpreted as a sign that Wellington was withdrawing. He instituted a move bypassing the Allied right flank in the hope that he was heading off his opponents. Wellington quickly sensed his intention and, seeing a chance to inflict a serious defeat, redeployed his troops, and as each division of the French flanking force came up the British routed it in detail. Marmont was seriously wounded, as was his successor, General Jean Bonnet, and for 20 minutes the French were without a commander. General Bertrand Clausel restored order and launched a dangerous counter-attack into the angle of the Allied line, but Wellington had already reinforced this and his troops contained the attack.

Following this failure the French army broke. Its defeat would have been even more severe if a Spanish force holding the bridge at Alba de Tormes, lying directly on the French line of retreat, had not decided to abandon its positions. The Allies sustained 5200 casualties. The French lost 14,000 men, including 7000 prisoners, plus 20 guns. As a result of the battle of Salamanca the French temporarily abandoned Madrid and raised the siege of Cadiz, the seat of the Spanish government.

General Maximilien Foy, one of Marmont's divisional commanders, generously commented that Wellington's conduct of the battle placed him in the same rank as Marlborough (for more on this great commander, see Chapter 8); for his achievements in 1812 the Prince of Wales (then British Regent) elevated him in the peerage to the rank of marquis.

The Battle of Vittoria, 21 June 1813

The near destruction of Napoleon's Grande Armée in the snows of Russia put paid to any hope of holding Spain. During the spring of 1813, the French combined the armies of the South, Centre, and Portugal and began withdrawing northwards towards France; their combined strength amounted to 7000 cavalry, 43,000 infantry, and 153 guns, but camp followers who had attached themselves to the French in Spain, and also many wagons containing loot from all over the country, handicapped the columns. Wellington's strength now included 8317 cavalry, 27,372 British, 27,569 Portuguese, and 6800 Spanish infantry, as well as 90 guns. During the winter his troops had rested, reorganised, and re-equipped.

Wellington caught up with the retreating French at Vittoria, a town south of the Zaborra river, 40 miles southeast of Bilbao, and launched an attack on 21 June. Mutually supporting assault columns, assisted by the enemy's failure to destroy the bridges over the Zaborra, pressed the armies of the South and Centre steadily back towards Vittoria. An Allied flanking move did not produce all the results Wellington wanted, although it did tie down the French

Army of Portugal north of the town. When the French broke, only those on foot or horseback were able to escape. Their guns and other wheeled vehicles became locked in an inextricable tangle in and around the streets.

Allied losses came to 740 killed, 4174 wounded, and 266 missing. French casualties included 756 killed, 4414 wounded, and 2829 missing, plus the loss of 151 guns, 415 ammunition wagons, and huge quantities of stores. The British drove the French, who lacked artillery and transport, back through the Pyrenees and into France. The battle earned Wellington his field marshal's baton. It also encouraged Austria to rejoin the Allies, which now included Russia and Prussia, in the struggle against Napoleon. Having taken the fortress of San Sebastian, Wellington advanced into France. He successfully besieged Bayonne and defeated Soult at Orthez in February 1814. He took Bordeaux early in March. Soult retired to Toulouse and Wellington again defeated him on the hills outside that city on 10 April. Two days later Wellington received word that the Austrians, Prussians, and Russians had entered Paris and that Napoleon had abdicated on 6 April. For now, the Napoleonic Wars were on hold – but see the later section 'Catching the 1815 to Waterloo' for Napoleon's return.

The War of 1812

In 1812, the United States declared war on Great Britain in defence of free trade and sailor's rights. It was perfectly true that the Royal Navy's warships had been behaving in an extremely high-handed manner, stopping American merchant vessels and taking seamen off to make up their own crews, to say nothing of the damage that the British blockade of European ports caused to American businesses, but the real motive was the conquest of Canada, and no better time for it existed, now that the United Kingdom was fully committed to the war in Spain and Portugal (see the preceding section).

Although this war is referred to as 'The War of 1812', it was actually fought between 1812 and 1815. The action was fought on two fronts – the northern theatre and the Atlantic front, as well as at sea.

The northern theatre

During the first two years of the war, operations in the north were of a comparatively minor nature and in overall terms tended to favour the British; action in the northern theatre took place on the Niagara front and the St Lawrence sector.

Actions in 1813

After some initial British successes on the Niagara front and an unenthusiastic showing by the American militia, the British attacked an American position on Queenston Heights on 13 October; the Americans sustained 250 killed or wounded and 700 captured. The British lost their commander, General Sir Isaac Brock, and 13 more killed, as well as 96 wounded.

In the spring of 1813 matters began to improve a little for the Americans:

- Brigadier General Zebulon Pike, with 1600 men under his command, seized and burned York, as Toronto was then known.

- Under pressure from an American army at the end of May, British forts along the Canadian border were abandoned, bringing the entire Canadian bank under American control.

- Brigadier General Jacob J. Brown's small American garrison decisively repulsed an amphibious raid against Sackett's Harbor on 29 May, mounted by Lieutenant General Sir George Prevost, the British Commander-in-Chief North America.

American success proved to be an illusion. At Stony Creek on the night of 5 June, 2000 Americans, incompetently commanded by Brigadier Generals William Winder and John Chandler, were routed by a 700-strong British force under the command of Brigadier General John Vincent. The Americans had not even bothered to post sentries when their opponents came howling out of the darkness with bayonets fixed, and they lost all their artillery and baggage. Other American forces started to evacuate their forts, and during the night of 18/19 December Lieutenant General Gordon Drummond's men took the American-held Fort Niagara by a sudden attack. Drummond's deputy, Major General Phineas Riall, then advanced along the south bank of the Niagara, brushing aside opposition from the local militia, and burned Lewiston, Black Rock Navy Yard, and Buffalo in reprisal for earlier burnings in Canada.

If the year ended badly for the Americans on the Niagara front, the news from the St Lawrence sector was just as bad: A complex plan for the capture of Montreal was formulated involving American Brigadier James Wilkinson with 8000 men and Brigadier Wade Hampton with a further 4000 men. The combined force was to capture Montreal, despite the fact that the British garrison outnumbered them and overlooking the small matter of the city's extensive fortifications. Hampton quickly came to grief. On 25 October British and Canadian troops confronted him in close country near the Chateaugay river; led by Colonel George Macdonnel, the British and Canadian force only had 1500 men, but by having bugle calls blown all round the Americans created the impression of a much stronger force. Hampton tried frontal and flank attacks, but when these failed he meekly withdrew to Plattsburg, having sustained no more than a handful of casualties. A small British force of 800 regulars and Indians under Colonel J.W. Morrison harassed Wilkinson's journey down the St Lawrence river and on 11 November, near Cornwall, Wilkinson

landed 2000 regulars under Brigadier General John Boyd to deal with the
threat. When the two forces encountered each other at Chrysler's Farm, the
Americans came into action piecemeal and the British drove them back to
their boats, inflicting the loss of 249 killed or wounded and 100 captured.
Next day, discovering Hampton's retreat, Wilkinson abandoned the entire
operation and went into winter quarters at French Mills on the Salmon river.

Action in 1814

The 1814 campaign began with Wilkinson renewing his advance into Canada
from Plattsburg and Sackett's Harbor. He had 4000 men under his command and
promised 'to return victorious or not at all'. A wiser general would have kept
quiet on the subject, because at Le Colle Mill, a small border fort held by only
600 men, he received a sharp check and immediately returned to Plattsburg.
Naturally, his superiors dismissed him on the spot. His successor was Major
General Jacob Brown, who had earlier conducted the successful defence of
Sackett's Harbor (see the preceding section).

Brown was an unusually efficient New York militia officer with the ability to
get the best out of his men. He did not approve of the present war, but that
did not prevent him from performing his duty to the best of his ability. His
second-in-command and commander of his 1st Brigade was Brigadier General
Winfield Scott, a regular officer whom the British had captured at Queenston
Heights and then exchanged. He was also present at Chrysler's Farm, where
he was mortified by the performance of the American regulars. A firm believer
in the lessons to be taken from military history, he was well aware that in
the present circumstances only strict discipline and constant training would
produce the required results. His men were regular soldiers, but as there was
a shortage of blue cloth, they wore grey uniforms normally issued to the
American militia.

The Battle of Chippewa, 5 July 1814

British naval blockades had so ruined the commerce of the New England states
that there was serious talk of them withdrawing from the Union. President
Madison agreed to enter into peace talks with Great Britain, but sent word to
Brown that an unqualified American success would strengthen the hand of
his negotiators. Brown's orders were to cross the Niagara, capture Fort Erie,
and advance to the Chippewa river. If he won a victory he was to exploit this
by continuing his advance and capturing Forts George and Niagara.

Brown crossed the river on the night of 2/3 July and gained an unexpected
success. The British officer commanding Fort Erie, Major Thomas Buck,
despatched a warning that the Americans had landed. And with that he
considered his duty done, placing so broad an interpretation on the words
'invasion in force' that he simply handed over the fort. News of the American
landing reached British General Phineas Riall at Fort George at about 8.30 a.m.
on 3 July. He immediately mobilised his troops and directed them to the
Chippewa. By the morning of 5 July he had assembled approximately 2400
men and six guns. His snipers already had the American camp under fire and

his engineers were replacing the decking on the Chippewa bridge. As yet unaware that Fort Erie had capitulated, he decided to advance across the river and drive the Americans back to their boats.

During the afternoon Riall crossed the Chippewa bridge and deployed in an area of cleared forest that became known as The Plain. Shortly after, Scott's brigade reached the area from the south, wheeled smartly left, and formed their line of battle opposite. At first Riall had taken the grey-uniformed regiments to be militia, but observing their drill and steady bearing, he remarked, 'Why, these are regulars!' The respective artillery of the two sides was already in action, but Riall pushed the 1st and the 100th forward in anticipation of their firing two volleys and then charging with the bayonet. This was a mistake, as the two regiments masked the fire of his guns. Scott, on the other hand, told his artillerymen to ignore the British guns and concentrate their fire on the red-coated infantry.

The Americans fired the first volley at 90 metres' (100 yards') range. It caused casualties, but the British closed in to within 45 metres (50 yards) before replying. Far from letting the British intimidate them, Scott's men stood their ground. A murderous fire fight ensued, lasting some 20 to 30 minutes. The British sustained the heavier loss because of American artillery fire. The battle reached resolution when four more guns reinforced Scott. Riall, recognising that his regiments could not withstand the increased punishment for much longer, ordered a withdrawal across the Chippewa. The Americans followed up, but heavy artillery fire from across the river halted them and they withdrew to their camp.

A recent detailed analysis of the casualties sustained puts the total killed on both sides, including Indians, at about 200. Riall had 321 men wounded and Scott 219. Chippewa was an undeniable American victory, the part played by Scott's brigade being commemorated in the grey dress uniform worn by the officer cadets at West Point Military Academy.

The Battle of Lundy's Lane, 25 July 1814

After a period of inconclusive manoeuvring following Chippewa (see the previous section), Brown resumed his advance, and opposing him, Drummond arrived to control British forces. Drummond's force met Brown's at Lundy's Lane, where British artillery, including rockets and field guns, was emplaced on a small hill dominating a wide belt of open farmland to the south.

By the evening of 25 July the American advance guard was within sight of the British position. Scott was in the lead and he sent Brown a message to the effect that he was about to attack the British. Scott was as overconfident as Riall had been at Chippewa (see the previous section):

✔ He swung three of the 1st Brigade's regiments off the road to the left and deployed parallel to the British line.

✔ He detailed his fourth regiment to guard his right flank beyond the road. Immediately, cannon and rocket fire tore his main body apart.

✔ He could have withdrawn, but chose not to, commenting first that by standing fast he would overawe his opponents (yes, really!); and second that if the rest of the Americans came up they would despair if they saw him pulling back!

✔ He ordered his men to open fire at extreme range. That did little or no damage, so at about 6 p.m. he ordered them to shorten the range by advancing 90 metres (100 yards). This simply made matters worse, because the Canadian Glengarry Light Infantry, uniformed in green like rifle regiments, began to engage the Americans from the left, assisted by three companies of the Royal Scots that Drummond had sent forward. Shortly after, the Americans ran out of ammunition.

Dusk turned to darkness and the British guns had ceased firing. By now, the three American regiments had sustained casualties amounting to 60 per cent of their strength, but on the right flank their 25th Infantry had an unexpected success. It advanced towards the British lines and become involved in skirmishes with Canadian militia. Riall was hit in one of these clashes and the Americans took him prisoner. Brown himself now arrived on the battlefield, together with his 2nd and 3rd Brigades. He decided to take advantage of the darkness and mount an attack on the British gun line. In this Drummond's failure to set advance lookouts, despite the near presence of the enemy, aided him. The gamble worked. After firing a volley the Americans charged up the hill and into the gun position with the bayonet. They killed some of the gunners and captured others, but more made off with the rammers, sponges, buckets, handspikes, and horse teams without which possession of the guns meant little. Drummond launched a series of counter-attacks aimed at recovering the guns. These failed, largely because the clutter of limbers and wagons parked in Lundy's Lane broke them up.

The fighting took place in pitch darkness that prevented recognition of uniforms, and even the common language of the combatants added to the confusion. In murderously close exchanges of fire, most of the senior officers on both sides sustained wounds. British and American soldiers alike unexpectedly found themselves playing the role of captive or captor. The Americans shoved their prisoners through the church door and the prisoners promptly escaped by climbing through a window at the far end of the building.

At 11 p.m. Scott led his men in an attack against what he believed to be the British flank. The fire of three regiments, the Royal Scots, the 103rd, and the 104th, raked his column's ranks until it withdrew. By now, only 100 or so men remained in the American ranks and they were openly muttering about Scott's judgement. Recognising that he had forfeited his men's confidence, he made his way across the American rear to the 25th Infantry, where a musket ball through the shoulder incapacitated him.

By 11.30 p.m. firing gradually died away. Brown believed that the British had gone and that he had won a victory. Knowledge that his division's losses had been crippling, combined with exhaustion and a painful wound, led to his accepting a suggestion that his troops should withdraw to their camp for food and rest. In fact, the British regiments were lying down just a few hundred metres into the darkness and at first light they formed up. By 7 a.m. they were in possession of the deserted battlefield. By 10 a.m. it was apparent that the Americans did not wish to renew the contest. During the afternoon, they broke camp and began retreating to Fort Erie.

Lundy's Lane was the most bitterly contested battle of the war. British casualties from all causes were probably in the region of 800. Brown reported the loss of 173 killed, 571 wounded, and 117 missing, a total of 861. Drummond followed up the American withdrawal to Fort Erie. In September he decided to abandon the siege, and at the end of November Brown's replacement, Major General Izard, blew up Fort Erie's entrenchments and took his troops back across the river. Elsewhere, General Prevost launched an invasion of New York state with 10,000 men, but was unable to advance beyond Plattsburg when the British lost control of Lake Champlain. The war in the north was over in all but name.

The Atlantic front

The British planned a series of amphibious operations against major population centres in the belief that they would expose the Washington administration's fundamental inability to deal with an enemy who could strike wherever and whenever it liked. Neither for the first nor the last time, the British Army became a missile fired by the Royal Navy.

The wide expanse of Chesapeake Bay was strategically the most important stretch of water on the American east coast, providing as it did access to the northern and southern states, while its feeder rivers reached deep into the surrounding hinterland. A British squadron under Rear Admiral Sir George Cockburn ranged the length and breadth of the bay, destroying anything that may be the slightest use to the American war effort. Cockburn was never able to land more than 400 seamen and marines, but the arrival of four regiments of Peninsula veterans under Major General Robert Ross provided the means to strike a heavy blow. The two men planned a combined operation in which the object was nothing less than the capture and temporary occupation of Washington itself:

   ✔ **Ross's troops landed at Benedict on the Patuxent river on 19 August 1814.** Apart from two 3-pdrs, Ross lacked artillery and decided to rely on Congreve rockets, one of which each infantryman could carry if other transport wasn't available. Ross was in a hurry and this told on his men, who had been cooped up on the troop-decks of their transports for weeks. When speed was required, they adopted a pace known as the *Moore*

Quickstep, which consisted of three steps trotting followed by three steps marching. This, coupled with broiling heat, caused exhausted stragglers to fall out along the way.

✔ **On 21 August the column reached Nottingham.** The day after, Ross feinted towards Fort Washington on the Potomac river, then changed direction again, and by evening was in Upper Marlborough. The march to Old Fields on 23 March was a short one and many of the stragglers caught up. By now, the regiments were back in trim and covering the ground as rapidly as they had in Spain.

✔ **On 24 August they headed towards Bladensburg, where they could cross the East River and enter Washington from the northeast.** At Bladensburg, their advance guard discovered some 6500 American militi-amen and some guns drawn up across the river. The American artillery stopped an attempt to rush the bridge, but the British found that the river was fordable and quickly established themselves on the far bank.

Rockets started to fly past the American militiamen's ears, twisting, turning, and exploding unpredictably in mid-air. This was too much for the militiamen, who fled; the only armed Americans remaining on the field were some 500 sailors, marines, and regular soldiers, who made a gallant stand until they were overwhelmed. The Battle of Bladensburg cost Ross 64 killed and 185 wounded. American casualties amounted to 26 killed, 51 wounded, and 100 taken prisoner.

✔ **Later on 24 August, Ross's troops entered Washington** and the following day, as a reprisal for the destruction of York, burned the uncompleted Capitol, the President's Palace on Pennsylvania Avenue, and every public building except the post office. The only private house they burned was one from which snipers had killed a British soldier, wounded three more, and shot Ross's horse under him. The Washington Navy Yard, containing a recently completed frigate and a sloop, was already ablaze when the British arrived. Ross pointedly ignored Cockburn's orders that he should 'destroy and lay waste' the city. The private citizens, having been reassured that neither they nor their property were in any danger, readily agreed to look after those of the British wounded who were too ill to be moved. That evening the landing force marched back the way it had come and on 30 August was aboard its ships once more.

✔ **On 1 September it seemed as though the British were coming back.** As a diversion to Ross's operation, a naval force was proceeding up the Potomac. It consisted of two frigates and several smaller warships under the command of Captain James Gordon, RN, who became the model for C.S. Forester's naval hero, Horatio Hornblower. On reaching Alexandria, downstream from Washington city, Gordon confiscated a huge quantity of merchandise and, with 21 prizes of various sizes, returned down river to the bay, having fought his way past several American batteries in the process.

The next objective for a raid was the port of Baltimore, lying at the head of Chesapeake Bay. The direct approach to Baltimore lay up the Patapsco river, but a line of sunken blockships and Fort McHenry, protected from close-range bombardment by a wide stretch of shoal water, denied access to the harbour itself. However, by landing at North Point at the mouth of the Patapsco, Ross believed that his troops could reach Baltimore, 16 miles distant. The landing took place early on 12 September. The troops marched steadily up the peninsula until, at its narrowest point, a force of 3200 militiamen halted them at Gadfly Wood. In a sharp fight, the British dislodged the militia at some cost. Among the British casualties was Ross himself, shot dead by a sniper as the battle began. His successor, Colonel Arthur Brooke, continued the advance until he was within sight of Baltimore's defences, then camped for the night.

Detailed examination the next day revealed that the Americans had constructed a formidable line of redoubts and defences that fairly bristled with bayonets. In fact, no fewer than 13,000 militiamen were present in and around Baltimore, and there was no doubt that they would fight well from behind fixed defences. Brooke was aware that his troops – angered by the death of Ross – were in fighting mood and would certainly storm the entrenchments, although the cost would be high. That could not be justified in a campaign of amphibious raiding. Admiral Sir Alexander Cochrane, now commanding in the bay, agreed. During the night, the troops disengaged silently and marched back to North Point, where they embarked.

From 5 a.m. on 13 September until 7 a.m. the following day, Fort McHenry was under continuous bombardment. Because of the shoal water only shallow-draught warships were involved, and even they could only engage at maximum range. Over 400 shells and rockets exploded inside the fort, while hundreds more cannon balls, their force diminished by distance, smacked into the masonry walls. So stoutly was the fort constructed that little damage was done. Conversely, while the Americans stuck to their guns, their return fire barely touched the warships. Watching the bombardment from aboard one of the larger ships was a successful Washington lawyer named Francis Scott Key. Something of a poet in his spare time, he recorded the event in verse, noting proudly that despite all the uproar, the American flag continued to fly over the fort. Key finished his poem in a Baltimore tavern. The local newspaper published it under the title of 'The Bombardment of Fort McHenry', but it soon became known as 'The Star-Spangled Banner'. It was then set to a tune called 'Anacreon in Heaven', which a Mr John Stafford Smith composed specially for the Anacreontic Society of London, whose principal activity seems to have been drunken singing. The combined poem and music became the American national anthem, although it did not receive official recognition as such until 1931.

Fighting beyond the bitter end: New Orleans, 1815

On Christmas Eve 1814 the British and American negotiators agreed the terms of a peace treaty. Everything was to be as it was before the first shot was fired, which made the whole war absolutely pointless. In future, the Royal Navy would not impress American seamen (with the defeat of France the need to do so had vanished), while the Americans would stop trying to conquer Canada and expand westwards (the logical direction). Unfortunately, it took weeks for the news of the treaty to reach everyone, and in that time fighting carried on.

Cochrane's fleet left Chesapeake Bay for Jamaica, where it received further troop reinforcements with which to capture New Orleans. On the night of 23/24 December the American commander in New Orleans, Major General Andrew Jackson (a future President), launched an attack on the British camp, supported by two small warships, the *Carolina* and the *Louisiana*. The British beat the attack off with some loss, although the presence of American warships on the river had come as a most unpleasant surprise. Packenham acquired some ships' guns to fight back with, and when the *Carolina* next appeared the British set the ship ablaze with red-hot shot. The *Louisiana* continued upstream. Packenham decided to mount a general assault on Jackson's defences on 8 January 1815. Obviously, before this went in, the position on the right bank had to be captured. He detailed one regiment for the task, but it was delayed. Recklessly overconfident, Packenham decided to attack regardless of the uncleared position opposite. He exposed his men to a murderous crossfire that killed or wounded 2100 of them, and he paid for his mistake with his life. The irony was that the attack on the right bank succeeded brilliantly, but only after the main assault had failed. The overall American loss in this, a battle fought after the war had ended, amounted to seven killed and 70 wounded. The landing force withdrew and, perhaps wisely, Jackson did not attempt pursuit.

Catching the 1815 to Waterloo

When the French King Louis XVIII assumed the throne of his ancestors after Napoleon's earlier defeat (see the section 'The Battle of Vittoria, 21 June 1813', earlier in this chapter), he behaved as though the French Revolution had never taken place. It was careless of him and his subjects didn't like it. Of course, Napoleon Bonaparte, in exile on the island of Elba, had agents in France who kept their master fully informed. Napoleon reached the conclusion that the time was right for a comeback and escaped, landing in France on 1 March 1815. The army and a large section of the population welcomed him. By 20 March Napoleon was once again Emperor of the French.

As the great powers of Europe had already declared Napoleon to be an outlaw, they began to mobilise for an invasion of France. Napoleon also mobilised his resources, directing his attention first to the two Allied armies in Belgium, the one Prussian under Field Marshal Prince Blucher, and the other a collection of different nationalities under the Duke of Wellington.

Wellington's army was over 80,000 strong at the start of the campaign. Only about a third of its strength was British. Most of his magnificent Peninsular infantry had been shipped across the Atlantic to fight the Americans (see the preceding section), and many of those present lacked experience and were very young. He still possessed British cavalry and artillery units who had served in Spain, as well as the excellent regiments of the *King's German Legion*, consisting of exiles from Hanover and other states, which had been on the brink of disbandment. Just how well the rest of the army would fight was an open question. It consisted of contingents from the recently reconstituted armies of Hanover, Brunswick, and Nassau, with a large contribution from the Netherlands including elements of dubious loyalty who had actually fought for Napoleon the previous year. Wellington's second-in-command was the young Prince of Orange. In theory, the army was organised in corps, but that was not how it would fight.

Wellington and Blucher were well aware that when Napoleon was confronted by two armies in the past, he used two-thirds of his strength to defeat one enemy army while the remaining third fought a holding action against the other. Then, having driven the first off the field, he concentrated against the second and destroyed it. The Allied commanders therefore decided on the ultimate object of combining their strength and defeating Napoleon in a single battle. Of the two principal protagonists, commentators generally consider Wellington to have been at the peak of his abilities. The view is that Napoleon, on the other hand, passed that point some years earlier. In addition, he was suffering from piles and cystitis and was in generally poor health.

The Battles of Ligny and Quatre Bras, 16 June 1815

On 15 June Napoleon seized Charleroi. Wellington's army concentrated around Brussels, with Blucher's Prussians some miles to the east. Both began marching south that night, Wellington to Quatre Bras crossroads and Blucher to the village of Ligny.

Napoleon ordered Marshal Ney, with the left wing of the French Army of the North, approximately 22,000 men strong, to eject Wellington from Quatre Bras while the remainder of his army tackled the Prussians:

- ✔ At Quatre Bras on 16 June Ney seemed to be somewhat in awe of Wellington and did not press his early assault when only 7800 Allied troops had reached the position. By the end of the day, Wellington had 31,000 men under his immediate command and Ney's chance of seizing the crossroads had vanished. After dark, Wellington commenced an orderly withdrawal to the position he had selected at Mont St Jean, south of the village of Waterloo, having learned that the Prussians had received a mauling at Ligny and were retreating. At Quatre Bras, both sides incurred over 4000 casualties.

- ✔ At Ligny the inexperienced Prussians had fought doggedly until Napoleon's Imperial Guard broke their centre during the evening. As Blucher was injured, General Count August von Gneisenau assumed temporary command. He decided to withdraw northwards, as this enabled him to remain in contact with Wellington. When Blucher recovered sufficiently to resume command, he sent a message to Wellington to the effect that he would join him at Waterloo.

The following morning Napoleon decided that he would concentrate against Wellington and sent Marshal Emmanuel de Grouchy in pursuit of the Prussians with 33,000 men. The following day Grouchy managed to engage the Prussian rearguard, but by then the rest of Blucher's army was converging on Waterloo. Wellington carried out his withdrawal to Mont St Jean shielded by British cavalry and Royal Horse Artillery.

The Battle of Waterloo, 18 June 1815

After the battle of Quatre Bras (see the previous section), Napoleon and Wellington were on a collision course to fight a major engagement. The main events of the battle, one of the most decisive in history, took place within a remarkably small area, two-and-a-half miles wide by a mile deep. The battlefield consisted of a shallow valley. Wellington's army occupied the gentle ridge to the north, while the French positioned themselves to the south. The centre of the Allied position was the point where the track crossed the Brussels–Charleroi highway. Some distance ahead of the Allied centre-right was the chateau of Hougoumont, which Wellington decided he would defend. Likewise, he would also hold La Haye Sainte Farm, situated beside the main road ahead of the Allied centre. Wellington deployed his artillery obliquely along his front with the intention of breaking up attacks. Napoleon established a *grand battery* (artillery) to the east of the highway, with the object of engaging the Allied centre.

Wellington's Allied army consisted of 50,000 infantry,12,500 cavalry, and 156 guns, a total of approximately 68,100. The French Army of the North, excluding those with Grouchy (who was facing off some distance away against the Prussians), included 49,000 infantry, 15,750 cavalry, and 246 guns, a total of approximately 72,000.

The torrential rain that fell during the night of 17/18 June created so much mud that it delayed the start of the battle by several hours. When, at last, the ground began to dry out from the previous night's rain, Napoleon decided to take the initiative. He believed that Wellington was extremely sensitive about his right flank, and that an attack by General Reille's II Corps would force Wellington to reinforce it by drawing in units from his centre. Once they had weakened the centre in this way, General Drouot d'Erlon's I Corps would smash through it to the east of the Brussels–Charleroi road. This alone, Napoleon believed, would be sufficient to cause the disintegration of the Allied army. The battle that followed can be broken down into a series of key events:

- **The struggle for Hougoumont.** Altogether some 3500 men, including British guardsmen, King's German Legion, Nassauers, Hanoverians, and Brunswickers, played a part in the defence of the chateau of Hougoumont during the day, under the overall command of Lieutenant Colonel James MacDonnell. Between 11.30 a.m. and 6 p.m. the French made no fewer than seven determined attempts to capture the position. It was soon apparent that Wellington had no intention of weakening his centre, yet the French commander Reille persisted in committing infantry that were sorely needed elsewhere, almost certainly on the instruction of the Emperor's brother, Jerome Bonaparte, who was actually one of Reille's subordinate divisional commanders.

  During one attack, a huge axe-wielding French lieutenant named Legros of the 1st Legère forced his way through the chateau's north gate with 30 or 40 men, and charged into the northern courtyard. The British closed the gate by main force and killed all of the intruders, save for an unarmed drummer boy. Reille brought up a howitzer battery that shelled the buildings until they were ablaze, yet guardsmen kept firing until the floors they were standing on were on the verge of collapsing. When the British sent back an urgent request for ammunition to the ridge, an extremely brave private of the Royal Wagon Train delivered it, disregarding both the French shellfire and the terrible danger posed by the burning building to drive his ammunition wagon to the north gate, where his horses were killed. Historians have never properly established his name, but believe it to be either Brewer or Brewster. At the end of the day, Hougoumont was a ruin, but it was still in Allied hands.

- **D'Erlon's attack fails.** Between 1.30 and 2 p.m. d'Erlon's 16,000-strong corps crossed the valley and began mounting the gentle slope to the left-centre of the Allied position. A Dutch–Belgian brigade, already decimated by artillery fire, broke and fled, but British troops filled the gap.

They halted the French attack and a furious fire fight ensued. The deadlock broke when the British Household and Union cavalry brigades charged obliquely into the flank of the huge French infantry column, slashing and lopping until the whole mass disintegrated and fled down the slope, leaving large numbers of dead, wounded, and prisoners behind.

And now the British cavalry repeated the mistake they had made so often in the Peninsula. Flushed with victory, they charged on, sabering at will, until they reached Napoleon's grand battery, where they began cutting down the gunners. In this area, the mud was almost axle deep and the exhausted horses found the going difficult. A sudden counter-attack by French cuirassiers and lancers smashed into the British, emptying many saddles. The British turned for home, but their tired mounts were unable to outdistance the enemy, who speared many men through the back. The French pursuers rallied and withdrew once they were within range of the British line, having destroyed the better part of the two brigades.

✔ **The French cavalry are destroyed.** Napoleon, feeling unwell, handed over tactical control of the battle to Ney. The advance guards of two Prussian corps were closing in from the east and to counter them Napoleon had already directed General Count Lobau's IV Corps, amounting to one-third of his available infantry excluding the Guard, to the village of Plancenoit. In the meantime, the grand battery opened fire on the Allied army.

Ney observed what appeared to be a concerted movement to the Allied rear among the Allies on the ridge. Wellington had ordered his infantry to retire behind the crest of the ridge, which offered them some protection from the French artillery. Combined with this, empty ammunition wagons, wounded men, and columns of French prisoners under escort were all moving rearwards at the same time. Ney misinterpreted this as a sign that Wellington was withdrawing from Mont St John, and so Ney launched a mass attack with his cavalry.

The Allied infantry formed square to defend against the cavalry. British gunners fired into the approaching mass until the last possible moment, then ran for cover into the nearest squares. The French surged round the squares, but were unable to penetrate the hedges of bayonets. They fell in droves before the steady Allied volley firing. One survivor recalled that the sound of musket balls striking *cuirasses* (breast plates) was like hail hitting a window. When the French were thoroughly disorganised, the Allied cavalry drove them back off the ridge. At this point, the gunners returned to their guns and fired into the retreating enemy. The French repeated these attacks time and again with the same result, but in between them the Allied squares had to endure the fire of the grand battery – a stern test even for veteran infantry. Most of those present were inexperienced, but they stuck the fight out just the same. So severe were some Allied regiments' casualties that the site of their squares was marked by their dead, lying in ranks as they had fallen. Even so, by 5.30 p.m. the magnificent French cavalry had almost ceased to exist.

✔ **La Haye Sainte Falls.** On his return to the field, Napoleon still believed that he had time to beat Wellington before turning on the Prussians, whom his Young Guard had successfully counter-attacked at Planceoit. He ordered Ney to take La Haye Sainte, whatever the cost. A few thousand men from d'Erlon's rallied corps advanced on the farm. At that moment the King's German Legion's reinforced 2nd Light Battalion, which had defended its position brilliantly throughout the day, ran out of ammunition. Requests for more ammunition repeatedly went unanswered, for the simple reason that the Germans were armed with the Baker rifle and only larger-calibre Brown Bess musket ammunition was readily to hand. As the last shots spluttered out, the French swarmed into the farm. Those few of the garrison who could escaped to the ridge.

At this point the 23-year-old Prince of Orange, more used to the company of ladies of a certain age than the battlefield, ordered two King's German Legion battalions to recapture the farm, despite being warned that a unit of cuirassiers was nearby. Obediently, the two battalions advanced and were cut to pieces in the open. Seeing this, some Allied infantry withdrew of their own accord, one Netherlands cavalry brigade refused to come forward, and a Hanoverian hussar regiment galloped off the field to spread alarm and despondency in Brussels. There was now a yawning gap in the centre of the Allied line. Luckily, Ney had nothing left with which to exploit the situation. Napoleon, absorbed with renewed pressure from the Prussians, declined at first to release any more troops from the elite Imperial Guard. By the time he finally agreed to Ney's request, Wellington had closed the gap with troops drawn from elsewhere on his line.

✔ **The French Guard is beaten.** Shortly after 7.30 p.m. Napoleon committed his Middle Guard to an assault on the Allied right-centre. The weary infantrymen of d'Erlon's and Reille's corps began cheering wildly, for whenever the Emperor committed his Guard it was to deliver the *coup de grace* to a beaten enemy. Equally heartening was the news that the rising thunder of cannon fire to the east marked the approach of Grouchy. It was a lie, but the two things together raised the French anticipation of victory. The Middle Guard advanced up the slope between La Haye Sainte and Hougoumont, picking its way over the debris of the failed cavalry attacks. They lost men to British artillery fire, but marched on without pause. They passed through the now abandoned line of guns and emerged from the smoke expecting to see their enemies break and run, as they always had. Instead, all they saw was a small group of mounted officers watching them impassively from just beyond the crest. Invisible to them but lying in a sunken lane was Major General Peregrine Maitland's 1st Brigade, consisting entirely of British Guardsmen.

Suddenly, long scarlet ranks rose from the earth. In one terrible minute of precise, close-range volley firing, 300 of the Middle Guard's *chasseurs* (light infantry) were killed or wounded. Others tried to fire back over the heads of their comrades, to no avail. Then, with a cheer, the British came on with bayonet. The entire French column broke and fled. Maitland halted the pursuit when his men were level with Hougoumont and returned to the ridge.

To Maitland's left was Major General Sir Colin Halkett's 5th Brigade. Two of its regiments, the 30th (1/The East Lancashire Regiment) and 73rd (2/The Black Watch), had suffered severely during the earlier French cavalry attacks. Halkett pushed his two remaining regiments, the 33rd (1/The Duke of Wellington's Regiment) and the 69th (2/The Welch Regiment), forward to cover the left of Maitland's advance, but suddenly grenadiers of the Middle Guard confronted them. A volley stopped the French for the moment, but their accompanying horse artillery began firing into the British line, which Halkett ordered back to the crest. The two regiments became intermingled during the withdrawal and lost control when Halkett was wounded. The French came on without much enthusiasm and by the time they reached the crest, Major Kelly of Wellington's staff had restored order in the two British regiments. The French Grenadiers were already having the worst of a fire fight when a Dutch horse artillery battery began firing into their right flank. They, too, broke and ran.

A third French column, consisting of more chasseurs, advanced against Major General Sir Frederick Adams's 3rd (Light) Brigade, positioned to the right of Maitland's brigade. On the right of Adams's line was the 52nd (2/Oxfordshire and Buckinghamshire Light Infantry), commanded by Colonel Sir John Colborne. With Adams's approval, Colborne waited until the French had reached the crest, then wheeled the 52nd out of the line until it was parallel with the left flank of the French column and opened fire. The chasseurs halted, formed a line facing him, and a ferocious fire fight ensued. During the next four minutes, 150 men of the 52nd were killed or wounded, but the French loss was greater. As the range closed, Colborne gave the order to charge. Cheering, his men went for the chasseurs, who broke and fled wildly in the direction of La Haye Sainte. Reforming, the 52nd continued to advance across the slope, eliminating the last elements of resistance.

The watching French army had seen the Middle Guard disappear into the fog of powder smoke. It had heard the rattle of musketry rise to a decisive roar – and then the unbelievable had happened. In ones and twos, then in groups, then in hundreds, the running figures of guardsmen appeared. As realisation of what had happened dawned, a terrible cry of despair spread along the front: *'La Garde recule!'* If the Guard had been beaten, what chance did anyone else have?

✔ **The Prussians arrive.** Everything began to happen very quickly. One Prussian corps came up on Wellington's left after an exchange of not particularly friendly fire, and another finally broke through the French line at Plancenoit. On the ridge, Wellington gave the signal for his whole line to advance. Within 15 minutes of the Guard's defeat, the entire French army was fleeing in complete disorder. While the Prussians carried out a ruthless pursuit, Wellington and Blucher met at an inn, suitably named La Belle Alliance.

'*Quelle affair!*' commented the elderly Prussian field marshal; as well he may, for within a comparatively small area lay 47,000 dead, dying, or wounded men and no fewer than 25,000 horses. Wellington's army sustained the loss of 15,100 killed and wounded, of whom 9999 were British. Prussian losses amounted to approximately 7000 men. The French Army of the North lost 25,000 killed and wounded, 8000 prisoners, and 220 guns captured.

Napoleon abdicated on 22 June, and on 15 July he surrendered to the British. On 7 August he sailed aboard HMS *Northumberland* for lifelong exile on the island of St Helena, deep in the South Atlantic. Waterloo was the last major action of the French Revolutionary and Napoleonic Wars that ravaged Europe for 22 years.

Part IV

Nineteenth-Century Wars

The 5th Wave
By Rich Tennant

"We're primarily a spice company. Recently, our most popular spice has been gunpowder."

In this part . . .

Benefiting as they did from the Industrial Revolution and command of the sea, it was natural that British merchants should seek outlets for their goods in every part of the world. Conflict with local vested interests frequently led to the army's involvement, mainly in India, and Great Britain acquired an empire almost by accident. British soldiers fought on every one of the world's continents, frequently against the odds, and were rarely worsted in the hundreds of battles, large and small, that they fought. Britain also battled against Imperial Russia in the Crimea, and two wars against the Boers in southern Africa, losing one and winning the other.

This was an era of rapid technological change that included the introduction of breech-loading rifles and artillery, machine guns, railways, and the electric telegraph, all of which the army learned to use to its best advantage. It also saw the far-reaching reforms that created the famous county regiments that served with great distinction in two World Wars and beyond.

Chapter 12

Britain's Little Wars: Imperial Expansion

With Napoleon safely out of the way for good (see Chapter 11), the British government immediately demobilised tens of thousands of soldiers. Those who remained in the army after 1815 had changes to contend with, as outlined in the section 'The Changing Face of the Army'. By way of contrast, soldiers posted to India had a comfortable life. In barracks they employed Indian servants for every conceivable task. Life for British private soldiers in India was good and they lived like gentlemen. But life abroad wasn't always rosy, as you can read in the section 'Have Guns, Will Travel, 1815–1852', later in this chapter.

After the Napoleonic Wars, the army introduced new uniforms that may have looked nice but were horribly impractical. Coats were cut uncomfortably tight and a taller, wide-crowned, top-heavy shako – difficult to keep on if the wearer moved – replaced the smart Waterloo version. In due course a version of the stovepipe shako with peaks fore and aft, known as the *Albert pot*, replaced it. Sometimes concessions to the climate were made on foreign service by providing white shako covers, but in other respects the troops continued to swelter in the uniforms they wore in Europe. One change that not everyone involved welcomed was the conversion of the light dragoon regiments to hussars or lancers. The process began prior to Waterloo and continued for the next 40 years.

The Changing Face of the Army

Although officers' and sergeants' *messes* (in which members ate separately from the troops when not engaged in operations) existed prior to the Napoleonic Wars, they had now become, and remain, an essential element in regimental life. A regiment's Colours are housed in the officers' mess during peacetime. In both messes, portraits and paintings of events in the regiment's history hang from the walls and items of silverware, usually purchased by subscription or presented by retiring members, are displayed on special occasions. These items, collected over a regiment's lifetime, vary from elaborate centrepieces to cups used as trophies in the field of sport or military activity. Each mess has its own traditions, which are passed on from generation to generation.

The Royal Military College, Sandhurst, founded in 1812, was descended from the slightly older Royal Military Cadet College, Great Marlow, as was the Staff College, Camberley. Sandhurst's function was to educate young potential infantry and cavalry officers in the basics of their profession. It became possible for the army's Commander-in-Chief to grant commissions without purchase (see Chapter 7) to cadets who had successfully graduated from Sandhurst, or to young men whose fathers had distinguished themselves in the service. Royal Artillery and Engineer cadet officers were educated at the Royal Military Academy, Woolwich. With one short break during the Second World War, both institutions ran in parallel until they amalgamated in 1947 to become the Royal Military Academy, Sandhurst. Young officers bound for the Honourable East India Company's service received their training at the company's own academy, situated at Addiscombe.

Have Guns, Will Travel, 1815–1852

As the late Field Marshal Lord Carver commented in his book *The Seven Ages of the British Army* (Weidenfeld & Nicolson, 1984), in the years between Waterloo and the death of the Duke of Wellington in 1852, no significant campaigns took place. On the other hand, much happened in widely separated areas of the world involving the British army or the Honourable East India Company's army as well as the Royal Navy. Some of these events were policing or punitive actions, or even tidying up messy situations, but they were necessary and sometimes had to be repeated later in the century. Generally speaking, the number of troops involved was not large. Describing these actions from west to east gives some idea of their geographic scope.

South Africa

No fewer than eight Frontier or Kaffir Wars took place, lasting until March 1853. The British fought these against Xhosa tribesmen who perennially raided settled European territory. Friction also occurred between the British and the Boers, who were of Dutch origin and were the original white settlers in South Africa. During the Great Trek of 1835–1840, thousands of Boers journeyed north out of British-controlled territory to found their own states, later known as the Orange Free State and the Transvaal (but they came back to haunt the British later – see Chapter 16).

Aden

Situated at the southern tip of Arabia, Aden is strategically positioned on the route to India via the Mediterranean and across the Sinai peninsula to the Red Sea. Aden is unbearably hot, yet its inhabitants built their city in the airless crater of an extinct volcano. Their business at the beginning of the nineteenth century was slaving and piracy, so they were not pleased when their Sultan agreed to lease the harbour to the Honourable East India Company in 1838. They fired on a company ship, provoking a military operation the following year. After the British bombarded the harbour defences into silence, a landing party took possession of the town. Aden became a useful coaling station for the Royal Navy and for merchant vessels on passage to the Far East.

Persia (Iran)

Persia believed that it had a legitimate claim to the Heart region of Afghanistan and in 1836 carried out an invasion and occupation of the province. British policy was to preserve Afghanistan as a buffer state between India and continued Russian expansion in Central Asia. Under heavy diplomatic pressure from Britain, the Persians withdrew.

In 1856 the Persians returned and refused to budge. In December an Honourable East India Company task force landed at Bushire on the Persian Gulf and stormed the fort of Reshire. Reinforcements under Sir Henry Havelock reached Bushire the following month, bringing the strength of the task force up to about 4500 men under the overall command of Sir James Outram. On 27 January a 6900-strong Persian army attacked Outram at Koosh-ab, but the British decisively routed it, leaving over 700 dead on the field. British losses amounted to 10 killed and 62 wounded.

During this action the Poona Horse captured a standard that was topped by a silver hand, bearing a date equivalent to AD 1066. The device still forms the centre of the regimental badge worn by the post-Indian Independence Poona Horse. The British regiments entitled to the Battle Honour Koosh-ab were the 64th (1/North Staffordshire Regiment) and the 2nd Bombay European Regiment, an Honourable East India Company unit that was later absorbed into the British army as the 106th (2/Durham Light Infantry).

After the battle Outram took an amphibious expedition up the Euphrates, but the Persians were unwilling to fight and in April renounced their claim to Heart permanently.

Ceylon (Sri Lanka)

Ceylon (captured from the Dutch during the French Revolutionary Wars) proved to be a very difficult place to govern, partly because the interior was extremely unhealthy and partly because the Sinhalese inhabitants didn't want to be governed by anyone in particular, not even their own people. An attempt to place a British candidate on the throne in 1803 led to the massacre of an entire column. By 1815 it was apparent that the reigning monarch, Sri Wikrama, was a tyrant who would be torn limb from limb by his subjects, if they could only get their hands on him. Lieutenant General Sir Robert Brownrigg led several columns to Kandy, Sri Wikrama's capital in the centre of the island, without losing a man. The British then shipped Sri Wikrama off to India for the good of his health and reached an agreement with the grateful Kandyan chiefs granting sovereignty of the entire island to the British.

A dissatisfied minority of Sinhalese rebelled against this agreement in 1817. Reinforcements arriving from India suppressed the rebellion. The British response was to issue pardons and only execute two of the ringleaders. After this, the British put in place a system of indirect rule, similar to that employed in India, with the indigenous chieftains in each province retaining considerable authority. The resulting peace, quiet, and prosperity must have puzzled those who had grown up in a climate of pandemonium.

Burma

The First Burma War began in 1824 when Burmese troops entered Cachar, a British protectorate. In addition, a 30,000-strong Burmese army under General Maha Bandula entered the Arakan coastal region and threatened the port of Chittagong.

Burmese failure to exploit their early successes led the British to adopt a defensive policy in these regions, while employing an indirect approach to break into the enemy's heartland through the back door. An expeditionary force, 5000 strong, assembled in the Andaman Islands under Brigadier General Sir Archibald Campbell and on 10 May landed at Rangoon, which was virtually undefended. Campbell's troops were soon surrounded and under attack, as well as being ravaged by disease as the monsoon season continued. Maha Bandula, caught wrong-footed, arrived with his army in August, having made forced marches all the way from the Arakan. During the autumn, Campbell also received reinforcements, including a rocket battery. On 1 December the British repulsed a major assault on their positions, and a fortnight later Campbell broke out and began advancing up the Irrawaddy river towards Ava, the Burmese capital, located near modern Mandalay. On 2 April 1825 Bandula made a stand at Danubyu. A British counter-attack routed his troops and a rocket killed Bandula himself. Campbell continued his advance, but halted for the monsoon season at Prome and entrenched his camp. The Burmese, now under the command of Maha Nemyo, closed in around the camp. On 30 November they launched a major assault. In three days of fierce fighting, with gunboats on the river supporting Campbell's troops, the British destroyed the Burmese army and killed Nemyo. Campbell resumed the advance until his troops reached Pagan, 70 miles short of Ava, on 9 February 1826. Here, Burmese envoys requested terms, which the British granted. Burma surrendered Assam, the Arakan, and the Tenasserim coast, and agreed to pay a large indemnity.

Burma: Take two

The Second Burma War began in March 1852. Pagan, the Burmese king, disliked the British. He breached the terms of the treaty agreed with Campbell, harassed British businesses and shipping, and pointedly ignored a warning that his actions must stop.

A 9000-strong expeditionary force under Lieutenant General Henry Godwin took Ragoon and, with close naval cooperation, advanced up the Irrawaddy. The Burmese army retired northwards, but the British defeated it after a hard fight at Pegu on 3 June, when the Burmese made a stand. Hostilities ceased during the rainy season, but on 9 October the British occupied Prome. In December the Honourable East India Company annexed the province of Pegu, which meant most of southern Burma and Rangoon as well. This area later became known as Lower Burma. The British told Pagan to accept this or expect the destruction of his kingdom if he resisted. He wasn't really in a position to comment, as his half-brother, Mindon Min, had just overthrown him. Mindon didn't say yes and he didn't say no, but he had no wish to be on bad terms with his new neighbours so he accepted the British offer.

Burma: Take three

Mindon Min's surrender (see the previous section) wasn't quite the end of the story in Burma. Mindon's son Thibaw did his best to dilute British influence by encouraging diplomatic contact with France and Italy, interfering with the British teak trade, and finally, in 1885, imposing a huge fine on the Bombay-Burma Trading Corporation. This was too much. Lord Dalhousie, the Viceroy of India, sent him an ultimatum demanding protection of British interests. On 7 November Thibaw ordered his subjects to drive the British into the sea. The British response was immediate. Some 9000 troops under Major General Harry Prendergast sailed up the Irrawaddy in 55 steamers, brushing aside opposition as they went. On 26 November, as the flotilla approached Ava, Thibaw offered to surrender. He told his army to stop fighting and became a prisoner. On 28 November Prendergast entered Mandalay. In 1886 the British formally annexed Upper Burma. From start to finish the Third Burma War lasted just two weeks.

China

In 1833 the Honourable East India Company's monopoly on trade with China expired. That meant that British merchants attempting to do business with China had to rely on the Westminster government to protect their interests. And to import anything at all into China meant paying 'squeeze' to a number of officials, and that absorbed any profit margin. The exception was opium, which India grew in large quantities. As an estimated minimum of 16 million Chinese were addicted to the drug, the demand for it was high and constant. The Imperial Chinese government, aware of the damage it was doing, tried to prohibit the trade. Its methods were high-handed in the extreme:

 ✔ Confiscating and destroying British merchandise

 ✔ Opening fire on British warships while they were evacuating British refugees from Canton

Lord Palmerston, the British Prime Minister, demanded reparations and a permanent base from which to conduct trade. The Chinese refused point blank. Action didn't stop there.

The First Opium War

In 1840 Palmerston despatched a punitive amphibious expedition to the area, including 4000 British and Indian troops under Major General Sir Hugh Gough. It was soon apparent that the Chinese were neither equipped nor trained for a modern war. During an early naval battle they attacked the British squadron with 13 war *junks* (oriental ships). After the British had blown up the Chinese admiral's junk with a rocket, 10 more surrendered and the rest made off. This set the tone for the rest of the First Opium War:

 ✔ In February 1841 the British stormed the Borgue Forts at the entrance to the Pearl River. The expedition then moved up river and attacked Canton on 24 May. The Chinese government offered to pay £600,000 in reparation. This was not enough for Palmerston and the war continued. During further coastal operations the British bombarded and captured Amoy on 26 August, followed by Ningpo on 13 October.

 ✔ In 1842 the focus of operations shifted to the Yangtze river. The expedition took Shanghai on 19 June and on 21 July stormed the city of Chinkiang. British casualties amounted to 34 killed, 107 wounded, and three missing.

Chinese losses were horrific, but what sickened Gough and his soldiers most was the sight of women and children being killed by their own people rather than allowing them to be taken alive by the 'foreign devils'. The troops were withdrawn at the earliest possible moment. Hostilities ended on 17 August when the Chinese Emperor's government sued for peace. Under the terms of the Treaty of Nanking, China paid an indemnity of £5 million, ceded Hong Kong to Great Britain, and opened the ports of Amoy, Foochow, Ningpo, and Shanghai. The war's principal lesson was that China was simply incapable of defending itself, and of this the Great Powers were to take full advantage.

The Second Opium War

It was an unfortunate trait of the Imperial Chinese government that after a while it no longer felt bound by the treaties it signed. In October 1856 local officials seized the British ship *Arrow* in Canton. That was enough to start the Second Opium War. The British bombarded Chinese ports and occupied Canton. When an Anglo-French force captured the Taku forts at the mouth of the Pei-ho river in May 1858, the Chinese agreed to negotiate. Under the Treaty of Tientsin, China reached an agreement with Great Britain, France, the United States, and Russia to open more ports to international trade, receive diplomatic legations in Peking, legalise the import of opium, and establish a customs service under foreign supervision.

The only problem was that the Chinese government had not the slightest intention of abiding by the treaty. It became clear that its terms would have to be enforced. A squadron of British gunboats tried to fight its way past the Taku Forts on 25 June 1859, but the Chinese sharply rebuffed it, so that it lost four gunboats and 434 men from a landing party. The rumour was that since the Royal Navy's earlier visit a Russian military engineer who was still sore at his country's defeat in the Crimean War (see Chapter 13) had considerably strengthened the forts. Whatever the truth, the allies could not leave the matter as it was. On 30 July 1860 a joint amphibious expedition, including 11,000 British and Indian troops under Lieutenant General Sir James Hope Grant and 6700 French under Lieutenant General Cousin-Montauban, landed on the coast to the north of the Pei-ho's mouth and marched overland to attack the forts from the rear. Four forts were involved, a Small and a Large North Fort, and a Small and a Large South Fort, the larger forts being closest to the river's mouth. The expedition decided to attack the Small North Fort first.

Shortly after first light on 21 August the British and French storming parties surged forward. The obstacles in their path were formidable. They consisted of, in turn, a deep dry ditch, an open space obstructed by an *abatis* consisting of trees felled in the direction of the attackers, then a wide flooded ditch, a 20-feet-wide belt of *panjis* (sharpened bamboo stakes), a second flooded ditch, and another belt of *panjis* leading up to the 15-feet-high walls of the fort. Swamps restricted the advance to a narrow frontage. Despite this, the attackers somehow overcame every difficulty, spurred on by national rivalry. Ensign John Chaplin of the 67th (2/Hampshire Regiment) narrowly won the race to plant a national flag on the fort's central tower. The 500-strong Chinese garrison put up a hard fight, but only 100 of its men survived. Across the river, the Chinese abandoned the Small South Fort immediately. The commander of the Large North Fort blustered a bit, then surrendered to the French. The Large South Fort, now isolated, surrendered next day. The allies captured over 600 guns of various types in the two South Forts alone.

The allies advanced up river to Tientsin, marched on Peking, and twice defeated a Chinese field army that tried to bar their passage. At this point the Chinese government indicated its willingness to negotiate, but then behaved with astounding stupidity. It made hostages of the allied negotiators in the hope of preventing a further advance. Grant ignored the threats and, having closed in on the capital, was about to storm it when the Chinese submitted to every one of the Allied demands, including the surrender of Kowloon on the mainland opposite Hong Kong, the payment of a large indemnity, and ratification of the various treaties that had been signed. When the Chinese returned some of the hostages, the Allies discovered that the Chinese had tortured the remainder to death. In reprisal, Grant burned to the ground the Yuen-Ming-Yuen, a group of palaces set in beautiful gardens. For the next 40 years, the Chinese Imperial government avoided further conflict with the Western powers.

New Zealand

A degree of friction always existed between the indigenous Maori population and British settlers. It intensified as expansion of settlements produced a clash of cultures and began to threaten the Maori way of life. This boiled over into two Maori Wars, the first lasting from 1845 to 1847 and the second from 1860 to 1870. These involved British regular infantry regiments and local units. These were wars of sudden ambush and sniping, fought out amid the luxurious vegetation of the New Zealand bush. In the end, both sides recognised that nothing was to be gained by further fighting and reached a workable compromise enabling them to live together.

The Maoris can be ranked among the British army's most formidable opponents, for a number of reasons. They tattooed their heads and other parts of their bodies to produce a fearsome appearance. They used firearms, but thoroughly enjoyed hand-to-hand fighting, in which they used spears, stone or wooden axes, and clubs. What the average British soldier found very difficult to deal with was that the Maori women took part in the fighting alongside their menfolk. It went completely against the British soldier's nature to kill women.

The other aspect of warfare peculiar to the Maoris was the concept of the *pa*, a base surrounded by earthworks and stoutly constructed stockades from which attacks were launched. The interior was a complex of inter-connected trenches, rifle pits, and underground chambers. The secondary purpose of the pa was to inflict unacceptable casualties on an attacker, but if a situation was reached in which it was no longer considered defensible, its abandonment was not disastrous as the Maoris simply built another one somewhere else.

India

Expansion by Imperial Russia across Central Asia convinced the British government that Russia's ultimate aim was the acquisition of India. The Russians were quite happy to encourage this belief by discreet means, in the knowledge that with a major part of Great Britain's strength committed to the defence of India, it couldn't intervene in Europe. This, as shown in Chapter 13, was not altogether true, but the British government was always reluctant to weaken the garrison of India without good reason.

Britain and Russia's involvement over India is known as the *Great Game*. It played out with conspiracies, murders, spies, double agents, and political officers in the wild mountainous terrain of India's northwest Frontier and Afghanistan. The Great Game was the Victorian equivalent of the twentieth-century's Cold War.

The First Afghan War

Maintaining a pro-British ruler on the throne of Afghanistan was vital to Britain in the Great Game, securing India's 'back door'. In 1835 Dost Mohammed succeeded to the crown, but three years later he was having problems with his Russian-backed Persian neighbours to the west and with the Sikhs to the south. He asked Lord Auckland, the Governor General of India, to assist. Auckland refused brusquely, so Dost Mohammed turned to the Russians, who quickly sorted things out with the Persians. Auckland, believing that this was simply a prelude to Russian troops appearing on the Indian border, reached the conclusion that Dost Mohammed had to go.

It seems not to have occurred to Lord Auckland to attempt to resolve the Russian involvement in Afghanistan through the normal diplomatic channels between London and St Petersburg. Instead, in a decision bordering on imbecility, he despatched a 21,000-strong army under General Sir John Keane into Afghanistan in 1839, occupying Kandahar in April, storming the fortress of Ghazni in July, and capturing Kabul on 7 August. Dost Mohammed became a prisoner and was sent to India. A British nominee, Shah Shuja, replaced him and Keane returned to India, leaving a garrison in Kabul to support two British diplomats, Sir William Macnaghton and Sir Alexander Burns.

Dost Mohammed was a popular king, and in November his son, Akbar Khan, led a major uprising. His men murdered Macnaghton and Burns and surrounded the British garrison. Major General William Elphinstone commanded the garrison, but he was elderly and ill, and worse still, he was a ditherer. He dithered to the point that Akbar Khan was all but telling him what to do. He agreed that his garrison should not only leave Kabul but quit Afghanistan altogether, under safe conduct. This action amounted to nothing less than a shameful capitulation.

In his decision to leave, Elphinstone faced three difficulties from the outset:

- ✔ His march was being made in the dead of winter.

- ✔ His column contained 4500 soldiers and 12,000 camp followers, including many of the *sepoys'* (Indian soldiers') families.

- ✔ His army marched heavy. An officer's kit, including heavy furniture and everything else necessary for his comfort in the field, required several baggage animals or carts. Add to that numerous servants, contractors of every kind, and drivers for the hundreds of animals needed to transport everything.

In effect, Elphinstone signed everyone's death warrant. No sooner had the column left Kabul than Akbar Khan's tribesmen fell on it, killing at will. Day by day the column struggled on, leaving a trail of dead and dying in its wake. Only the British 44th (1/The Essex Regiment) and the Bengal Horse Artillery retained the ability to fight back, but at Gandamak in the Jagduluk Pass tribesmen surrounded their remnant. With no hope in sight, the 44th removed their Colours from their staffs and Captain Souter wore them as a sash to prevent their being recognised. They made a final stand, fighting back to back, but the end was inevitable. Although Souter was wounded, the tribesmen spared his life since they took the richly embroidered 'sash' to indicate a man of great importance who made a valuable hostage. They also spared the lives of three or four wounded privates, perhaps with a degree of admiration. Elphinstone was also spared but died a prisoner. In less than a week since leaving Kabul the entire column had been wiped out.

Only one European, Dr William Brydon, and a bare handful of Indians got through to the fort of Jellalabad, held under the command of Brigadier General Robert Sale. Sale conducted an energetic defence of the fort, making regular sorties that cost his besiegers dear. On 16 April 1842, an avenging army under General Sir George Pollock relieved Jellalabad.

Pollock fought his way to Kabul, first taking the heights on either side of the road to draw the teeth from any planned Afghan ambush. The skeletons of Elphinstone's doomed column lined the road itself. The British reached Kabul in September. They released the prisoners and the arrival of the Kandahar garrison, which had also withstood a siege, reinforced the army. As the disaster of the previous year had seriously damaged British prestige, Pollock needed to emphasise to everyone interested that this sort of treachery simply did not pay. He blew up Kabul's grand bazaar and citadel, and then withdrew to India, being sniped at along the way.

Meanwhile, the unfortunate Shah Shuja was assassinated in March 1842. The British allowed Dost Mohammed to return to the throne. Many people must have wondered what the fighting had all been about. As for Lord Auckland, Lord Ellenborough replaced him, and was to provoke the next war in the area (see the following section).

The conquest of Scinde

Scinde lay in the northwestern corner of the Indian subcontinent in what today is Pakistan. Together, the demands and threats made by Lords Auckland and Ellenborough provoked such anger that on 15 February 1843 an 8000-strong mob attacked the British Residency, which a handful of men defended led by a promising young officer named James Outram.

General Sir Charles Napier, a 61-year-old veteran of the Peninsular War (see Chapter 11), quickly put together a 2600-strong relief force, including 500 men of the 22nd (1/The Cheshire Regiment), and set off immediately. On 17 February they encountered the 20,000-strong army assembled by the Amirs of Scinde at Meeanee. Believing that a defensive stance would unsettle his native regiments, Napier attacked at once, personally leading his troops in action with a musket and bayonet. The Amirs sustained a crushing defeat, losing some 5000 killed or wounded and several guns, while Napier's losses amounted to only 256 killed or wounded. Napier then mounted his British troops two to a camel and made a forced march across a belt of desert in extreme heat, won a second battle at Hyderabad, and relieved the Residency. By August he had pacified the area and the British annexed Scinde.

Reputedly Napier advised the Governor General that the campaign was over in a famous Latin cryptogram *Peccavi* ('I have sinned' – that's right, 'Scinde'). Historians have cast some doubt on this, but it remains a good story.

The First Sikh War

The continued expansion of the Honourable East India Company's rule over Indian states led to a feeling that the Punjab would be next, a view that events in Scinde reinforced (refer to the previous section). Despite this, the Elphinstone debacle in Afghanistan suggested that the possibility existed of beating the British (refer to the section 'The First Afghan War' earlier in this chapter), and a pre-emptive strike would probably guarantee Sikh independence.

A martial race, the Sikhs possessed a uniformed, disciplined, and trained army. It was an army that happily fought with *tulwar* (a curved sword) and shield at close quarters when its muskets had been fired. It gave the British regiments their toughest contests since the Napoleonic Wars and on several occasions it came close to breaking the Honourable East India Company's native infantry regiments.

On 11 December 1843, a 20,000-strong Sikh army under Lal Singh crossed the river Sutlej into British territory. General Sir Hugh Gough marched to meet them with 11,000 men. The two armies met at Mudki, 30 miles south of Ferozshah, on 18 December. Gough had little more than half his opponent's infantry, but he had a distinct advantage in artillery, 42 guns against 22. On its own, that would not have won the battle. Gough was a firm believer that in India one attacked, whatever the odds, and that was what he did. After a hard fight the Sikhs withdrew to Ferozshah, having sustained approximately 3000 casualties and lost 15 of their guns. British losses amounted to 215 killed and 655 wounded. Both armies had received reinforcements by the time Gough reached Ferozshah on 21 December. Lal Singh now possessed 35,000 men (including 25,000 regulars) and 88 guns, and his army had dug itself into strong entrenchments. Gough had almost 18,000 men and 65 guns. He attacked in failing light during the later afternoon and the Sikhs repulsed his men with serious casualties. Gough attacked again the following morning and captured the entrenchments. Shortly after, a fresh Sikh army under Tej Singh, 30,000 strong with 70 guns, reached the battlefield and attempted to recapture the position. At this point, the British artillery ran out of ammunition and an officer, crazed by sunstroke, ordered the cavalry to withdraw to Ferozshah, which they did, followed by the horse artillery. Victory lay within Tej Singh's grasp but, crediting Gough with greater subtlety than he actually possessed, Tej Singh interpreted this as an aggressive move against his own flank and beat a hasty retreat across the Sutlej. Gough's casualties amounted to 694 killed and 1721 wounded. The Sikhs lost 4500 killed and wounded, plus 78 guns.

In January 1846 the Sikhs attempted to recover their fortunes by pushing a force of 15,000 men and 67 guns under Ranjur Singh across the Sutlej to ravage British territory in the Ludhiana area. On 28 January Major General Sir Harry Smith, with 12,000 British and Indian troops and 32 guns, caught up with Ranjur Singh at the village of Aliwal. Smith launched a textbook attack in which he employed infantry, cavalry, and artillery to their best advantage and they cooperated with one another. They routed the Sikhs, who lost over 3000 men killed, wounded, and drowned as they fled across the river, plus all their artillery, stores, and supplies. Commentators have described Aliwal as 'the battle without a mistake', a viewed shared only by the victors and those with no interest in the outcome.

Still not discouraged, Tej Singh crossed the river again in February with 20,000 men and 70 guns. They established a strongly fortified position near the village of Sobraon, below the confluence of the Sutlej and Beas rivers. After reconnaissance established the strength of the position, Gough closed up to the Sikhs with 15,000 British and Indian troops, plus 100 guns including a siege train. On 10 February, after a two-hour bombardment in which the heavy guns expended most of their ammunition, the British attack went in, driving the Sikhs from their entrenchments after a brief but fierce fight. Some 3000 Sikhs died in the fighting or drowned in the Sutlej, while the British wounded 7000 and captured 67 guns. British losses amounted to 164 killed and 2119 wounded. Gough pursued the beaten Sikh army across the river and on to Lahore, the capital of the Punjab. There, on 11 March, the parties signed a treaty making the Punjab a British protectorate.

The Second Sikh War

Many Sikhs didn't like living in a British protectorate, and in their minds, a rematch was on the cards. On 20 April 1848 Sikhs provoked an incident in which they killed two British officers and the Second Sikh War started.

This time Gough moved first. On 9 November, he crossed the Sutlej with 20,000 men and advanced to meet the Sikh army forming under Sher Singh before it could be reinforced. On 22 November an inconclusive cavalry action took place at Ramnugur, where the Sikhs prevented a crossing of the Chenab river. It was not until the new year that Gough was able to bring on a general engagement with Sher Singh. This took place at Chilianwallah, in Lajore province south of Jhelum, on 13 January 1849. By then Sher Singh's army had grown to 40,000 men and 62 guns. Gough allowed himself to be provoked into fighting in fading afternoon light and launched an attack without adequate reconnaissance or artillery preparation.

That the British guns played a lesser part than they should have done at Chilianwallah was the fault of a cavalry commander, Brigadier General Pope, an officer grown so old in the Honourable East India Company's service that he required the assistance of two soldiers to mount his horse. Pope was informed that his line was drifting to its left and beginning to mask the British guns. He should have given the order 'Threes – right!', which would have resulted in his regiments taking ground to their right, so clearing the gunners' line of sight. Inexplicably, the order he actually gave was 'Threes – about!' Obediently, the two Indian regiments in the centre turned out, followed by the two British regiments on the flanks. Now, everyone was going the wrong way. Interested, the Sikh cavalry followed. This led to an increase in pace, to which the Sikhs conformed. Soon, both sides were going faster and faster until the British and Indian regiments had gained enough of a lead to turn about. The Sikhs overran several guns, then caught up and killed Pope and a few of the slower riders, before returning to their own lines with many a merry tale to tell. A brutal infantry combat in dense jungle resolved the battle. Casualties on both sides were severe and Gough withdrew. British losses came to 2746 killed and wounded, while the Sikhs lost 3894, although the British could not be said to have defeated them.

Gough's handling of the battle, and particularly his apparent willingness to accept heavy casualties, attracted such serious criticism both in India and at home that his superiors decided to replace him with General Sir Charles Napier, the victor of the campaign in Scinde. Before that happened, however, Gough again caught up with Sher Singh at Gujerat, 68 miles north of Lahore. Although Gough's artillery was the stronger (90 guns as opposed to 60), Sher Singh's 60,000 men, including a contingent of Afghans from Dost Mohammed (see the section 'The First Afghan War', earlier in this chapter), heavily out-numbered Gough's 25,000 infantry. Despite this, Gough had learned the lessons of Chilianwallah, and on 21 February his artillery began the battle with a two-and-a-half hour bombardment of the enemy position. This was so effective that when his infantry assault went in the Sikhs broke and fled, having sustained over 2000 casualties. The British captured all the Sikh guns and Gough's cavalry pursued the Afghans through the Khyber Pass as far as Fort Jumrud. British losses amounted to only 92 killed and 682 wounded.

Sher Singh's defeat decided the war. The British annexed the Punjab, and this, together with Scinde, formed the line of the northwest frontier, which saw almost continuous military activity for the next century. This time, the Sikhs accepted the outcome of the war and subsequently became staunch allies of the British.

Chapter 13

Helping Turkey Fight the Bear: The Crimean War

One day in 1853 there was a terrific punch-up in the Church of the Holy Sepulchre in Bethlehem. It was between Roman Catholic and Greek Orthodox monks, and it was all about who was responsible for keys and who was allowed to place a silver star in the sanctuary. As a result, several of the Orthodox brethren received fatal injuries. The Turkish police, no doubt as puzzled as everyone else by the sight of holy men battering each other sense-less, were unwilling to intervene in so sensitive an area, and simply stood by. Tsar Nicholas I of Russia, nominal protector of the Orthodox Christians within the crumbling Ottoman Empire, was delighted to have an excuse to start a war. His objective was to secure access to the Mediterranean through the Bosphorus and the Dardanelles, and if that meant destroying the Ottoman Empire in the process, so be it. He sent the Sultan an insulting series of demands that no self-respecting ruler could accept, then invaded Romania, which was a Turkish province at the time.

Napoleon III of France was anxious to be seen as a major figure in interna-tional affairs, and sided with Turkey. The British government didn't have much time for Napoleon, whom it regarded as a slightly seedy adventurer, but its traditional policy had been to support Turkey as a check to Russian expansion, and it certainly had no intention of permitting a Russian presence to alter the naval balance in the Mediterranean. It was, in effect, playing an extension of the Great Game (find more on this in Chapter 12). British and French naval squadrons arrived off Constantinople. On 4 November, suitably encouraged, the Sultan declared war on Russia, followed on 28 March 1854 by Britain and France, now allies. They decided to teach the Tsar a lesson by destroying the Russian naval base of Sevastopol, on the south coast of the Crimea. The Allies assembled a 50,000-strong expeditionary force for the purpose. The British contingent consisted of one cavalry and five infantry divisions. The Crimean War had begun.

Armies with the following types of soldier fought the Crimean War:

- ✔ **Infantrymen:** Infantry still fought in close formations (as they had done during the Napoleonic Wars) in the Crimea, the exception being light infantry regiments who adopted a more flexible, open fashion. The new Enfield rifle gave British regiments a distinct advantage over their opponents.

- ✔ **Heavy cavalry:** Dragoons and dragoon guards were employed for shock action intended to shatter the enemy's formation. The mounted infantry role had long since been abandoned by the British heavy cavalry regiments.

- ✔ **Light cavalry:** Hussars and lancers were employed in scouting, reconnaissance, and forming screens during advance or retreat, but were still capable of shock action.

Very clever – They call it technology, you know!

The advent of railways meant that troops could move from one place to another faster and in greater numbers than ever before; larger armies could take the field and trains could deliver everything they needed. Likewise, the steamer had an advantage over the sailing ship in that it did not depend on wind and tide to anything like the same degree. Consequently, steamers could transport troops to anywhere in the world in a fraction of the time previously needed. The electric telegraph enabled commanders in the field to inform their political masters of the current situation and request reinforcements or supplies as necessary. The telegraph, however, was a mixed blessing, as politicians were now able to badger generals who already had enough to think about, and war correspondents of the expanding popular press were able to file despatches illustrating the shortcomings of the military. The army regarded correspondents as a necessary evil, and tolerated rather than encouraged their presence.

Developments in armaments meant that infantry battles were about to undergo a radical change. *Percussion caps*, eliminating the need to prime a musket's touch hole, were adopted for general use in 1839. Of even greater importance was the invention of a French officer, Captain Claude Minie, who produced an elongated rifle bullet with a hollow base. When fired, the hollow base expanded to fit the grooves of the rifle, eliminating the loss of propellant gases that occurred with the old, loose-fitting balls. This not only increased the range of the weapon by a considerable margin, but also the penetrative power of the round itself. A new Royal Small Arms Factory established at Enfield in Middlesex manufactured this weapon, named the Enfield rifle-musket, which armed the infantry as a whole and not just the rifle regiments. Regiments received the first issues in 1854.

- **Artillerymen:** Field and horse artillery were employed in support of infantry and cavalry operations. Guns fired shot, shell, or canister ammunition as appropriate. Heavy artillery, armed with heavy guns and mortars, was extensively employed during the Siege of Sevastopol.

- **Engineers:** When it came to siege warfare, the engineers, including sappers and miners, were among the most important men in the army, as they were responsible for constructing the attackers' siege works.

The British army had not fought a continental enemy for 40 years. At this stage, it was simply a collection of fine-quality regiments that had never worked together. As field days and reviews were the only occasions when the troops left barracks, some of their commanders had little idea of how much frontage their regiments needed in various situations. Warfare was moving on though – see the sidebar 'Very clever – They call it technology, you know!'.

In the Red Corner: Commanding the British Army

No doubt the British government thought it was doing the right thing by appointing experienced officers to command four of the five infantry divisions. It was just unfortunate that their last experience had taken place during the Napoleonic Wars. Queen Victoria's cousin, the 35-year-old Duke of Cambridge, who had no experience at all but at least was willing to learn, commanded the remaining infantry division.

In command of the British contingent was a very nice old gentleman, Lord Fitzroy Raglan, who had lost an arm at Waterloo. He had served under Wellington and had been his military secretary for 25 years. On Wellington's death he was appointed Master General of the Ordnance. Now aged 67, he had never commanded so much as a company. To compound his difficulties, his staff were virtually untrained in their duties, and his cavalry commanders were little better:

- Lord Lucan, brave but none too quick on the uptake, commanded the cavalry division. This consisted of a *Light Brigade*, with lancer, hussar, and light dragoon regiments, and a *Heavy Brigade*, with dragoon and dragoon guard regiments.

- Lord Cardigan, that most dangerous of animals, the stupid man who thinks himself clever, commanded the Light Brigade. Cardigan shared a deep mutual antipathy with his divisional commander, Lucan.

- Brigadier General the Honourable James Scarlett commanded the Heavy Brigade, and he was refreshingly normal. Lacking practical experience, he was prepared to learn and in time produced excellent results.

The Battle of the Alma, 20 September 1854

On 13 September the Allies landed at the wryly named Calamita Bay on the west coast of the Crimea. They spent several days consolidating their position, then began marching south towards Sevastopol. On 19 September they reached the river Alma. On the high ground beyond the river the grey mass of the Russian army was drawn up, with General Prince Menshikov in command. Menshikov had constructed some earthworks, bristling with guns, that became known as the Great Redoubt, while a smaller earthwork, the Lesser Redoubt, covered another position. Field batteries punctuated the length of his line at intervals and skirmishers lined the bank of the river below. Some 37,000 men were available for the defence of the position. Considerately, Menshikov had built a viewing platform so that the ladies and gentlemen of Sevastopol society could watch the fun.

The battle took place the following day. The Allied plan was that on the right the guns of the fleet would support the French and Turkish attack and, once it had drawn off sufficient strength from the Russian centre, the British would deliver their assault on a two-division frontage. Raglan had 27,000 men available for this. The advance would be made with the 2nd Division on the right and the Light Division on the left, supported respectively by the 3rd and 1st Divisions. The Light Brigade would cover the open left flank. Problems arose during the initial deployment and early stages of the allied advance. The left-hand French division overlapped into the British 2nd Division's area, causing the 2nd to overlap in turn into the Light Division's area. The Light Division advancing obliquely to the right instead of straight ahead compounded the error, with the result that neighbouring regiments from both divisions became intermingled.

After some initial success, heavy fire pinned down the French and Turks. Raglan halted the British advance to await developments, instructing the men to lie down so that the fire of the Russian artillery passed over them. Ninety minutes later, at about 3 p.m., a hysterical French staff officer arrived. He gave a thoroughly overstated account of his countrymen's losses and beseeched the British to commence their own attack. Raglan gave the necessary orders and the long scarlet ranks began approaching the river. The Alma itself varied widely in its depth, so that some men emerged almost dry shod on the far bank, while others had to wade chest deep, and some drowned in unsuspected potholes.

The British advance

The advance up the slope was in the teeth of the enemy's artillery fire. The river crossing had aggravated the earlier deployment confusion, so that in places British officers vainly tried to separate their regiments. To make matters worse, Brigadier General George Buller, commanding the left-hand brigade of the Light Division, seems to have suffered a temporary brainstorm. The Light Brigade was already screening the left flank of the advance, but he ordered the 77th (2/The Middlesex Regiment) to wheel left and form a hard shoulder. If this may be considered odd, what came next stretches credulity to the limit, for he ordered his two remaining regiments to form square, as though cavalry was about to attack them. The fighting Irishmen of the 88th (1/The Connaught Rangers) did so with a very bad grace, but the 19th (1/The Green Howards) ignored the order, realising that it would simply make them a sitting target for the Russian guns, to which they were closest. Instead, they joined Brigadier General Sir William Codrington's brigade, consisting of the 7th (1/Royal Fusiliers), the 33rd (1/The Duke of Wellington's Regiment), and the 23rd (1/Royal Welch Fusiliers). In addition, thanks to the confusion caused by intermingling, a large part of the 95th (2/The Sherwood Foresters) had also attached themselves to the brigade.

On the right of the Light Division's advance, a two-column battalion of the Kazan regiment counter-attacked the 7th. A murderous fire fight ensued in which the new Minie bullet proved its worth (see the sidebar 'Very clever – They call it technology, you know!'), penetrating to the depth of two or even three ranks of the dense Russian formations.

Despite enduring crippling losses, the Russians stood their ground and began to take a steady toll of the Fusiliers. Raked by cannon and musket fire, Codrington's brigade closed in remorselessly on the summit. As the Russian gunners strove to get their weapons away, the 23rd swarmed over the breastwork of the Great Redoubt. Half-eaten picnics, top hats, fans, and other impedimenta belonging to Sevastopol's recently departed gentry littered the area. Codrington's brigade allowed themselves to relax while inspecting this debris. Menshikov, a good soldier, knew very well that attacking troops were at their most vulnerable just after they have taken an objective, and he launched the Vladimir regiment in a counter-attack.

Codrington's men rallied quickly and were shooting away the head of the Vladimir column when a strange incident took place. An apparently desperate staff officer galloped along the line shouting, 'Don't fire! For God's sake don't fire! The column's French!' This was nonsense, of course, but the strange officer then ordered a bugler of the 19th to sound the cease fire. Other buglers along the line took up the call and firing died away. The officer then ordered another bugler to sound retire, which was also taken up. The troops looked round, expecting to see the 1st Division coming up to support them, but the slopes were bare of all but their own casualties. At that moment, the Vladimir opened fire. The British lost the Great Redoubt as the Russians pressed their line sullenly down the slope, exchanging fire as they retreated.

The Guards and Highlanders advance

The reason for the 1st Division's absence (see the preceding section) was that while its commander, the Duke of Cambridge, may have been a nice enough chap, he didn't know what to do. His division contained the Guards and the Highland Brigades, regarded as the best in the army, but he had hesitated until sharply ordered to move off by General Richard Airey, Raglan's principal staff officer. The division crossed the river with the Guards on the right and the Highlanders on the left. Within the Guards Brigade, commanded by Major General H.J.W. Bentinck, the Grenadier Guards were on the right, the Scots Fusilier Guards in the centre, and the Coldstream Guards on the left. While ranks were being dressed after the crossing, Bentinck received a call for urgent assistance from Codrington. Foolishly, he addressed his next order to the Scots Fusilier Guards alone: 'Forward! Forward, Fusiliers! What are you waiting for?' With equal foolishness, the young officers carrying the Colours set off up the slope at a cracking pace, so that the companies on either side began to trail back into an irregular arrowhead.

The Russians were swarming over the breastworks of the recaptured redoubt, pressing the thinning line of the 23rd back down the slope. The British Guardsmen had reached a point just short of the 23rd when the unknown staff officer (see the previous section for his first appearance) put in another appearance, shouting 'Retire! Fusiliers, retire!' Whether he meant the 23rd or the Scots Fusilier Guards remains unknown. The 23rd, having lost more men to the fire of the Vladimir, took it to mean them and withdrew through the ranks of the guardsmen, several of whom were bowled over. It was now the turn of the Scots to receive the Russians' fire. Simultaneously, the regiment's senior officers came to the conclusion that the retire order applied to them, too. The withdrawal was hurried and disorderly.

The Grenadiers and the Coldstream now commenced their advance up the slope. Once more the strange staff officer put in an appearance, shouting warnings to retire and avoid firing on 'the French'. This time, no one paid him the slightest attention. His identity remains a mystery to this day, though the possibility exists that he was a Russian whose task was to cause confusion. The two Guards regiments wheeled inwards against both flanks of the Vladimir's column and opened a tremendous fire at only 90 metres' (100 yards') range. The deadly Minie rounds sent the Russians tumbling by the dozen. The Scots Fusilier Guards, despite having lost 171 men killed or wounded, including 11 officers, completed their rally quickly. They came up to take their place in the centre of the brigade's line and fired devastating volleys into the head of the enemy column. The Vladimir gave ground and slowly the Guards pushed them up the hill. When the Guards had advanced to within 35 metres (40 yards) of the Great Redoubt, they received the order to charge. The French heard their cheer a mile away. They bundled the Vladimir out of the position, although the Russians rallied and continued to fire.

The Highland Brigade, with Major General Sir Colin Campbell in command, forded the Alma upstream of the Guards. Campbell had first seen action as a boy during the Napoleonic Wars. He was a tough, no-nonsense soldier, still vigorous despite his 61 years, and inclined to directness of speech. In Campbell's world, there were only two sorts of people: Scots, and those who were not Scots.

The Duke of Cambridge, having ridden ahead, came across Buller, whose 77th had actually found some Russian infantry to fight out on the left, while the 88th still stood in their square, muttering angrily. It was at that precise moment that Codrington's brigade finally gave way, taking the Scots Fusilier Guards with them. With men dying all around and the apparent failure of the British assault, the inexperienced Duke plaintively asked Buller what he was to do. As tactfully as he could, Buller advised him to continue with his advance. Unconvinced, the Duke trotted over to Campbell, who had just appeared at the head of his brigade, and suggested that a disaster would occur unless the 1st Division was withdrawn. Campbell replied bluntly that a disaster would occur if it *was*. He then outlined his plan for the capture of the eastern shoulder of the Russian position and the Lesser Redoubt. Having agreed to this with considerable misgiving, the Duke, who was far from lacking in courage, joined the Guards Brigade in their assault and was actually one of the first into the Great Redoubt. Campbell *echeloned* (stepped back) his brigade from the right with the 42nd (1/The Black Watch) leading, then the 93rd (2/The Argyll and Sutherland Highlanders), then the 79th (1/The Queen's Own Cameron Highlanders). As his regiments passed, the 88th shouted sarcastic remarks at Buller for leaving them to wait idly by. Campbell told them to stop standing about and get into line alongside the 77th.

The Russians counter-attack

The Russians launched four battalions of the as-yet-uncommitted Sousdal regiment in a counter-attack against the advancing Highlanders' flank. The reason for Campbell's deployment immediately became clear. The first two Russian battalions, hoping to *enfilade* (fire into the flank of) the Black Watch, were themselves enfiladed by the 93rd. The next pair of battalions, accompanied by some cavalry, tried to enfilade the 93rd, but were themselves enfiladed by the 79th. Firing and advancing steadily, the Highlanders were driving the Sousdal before them when Raglan sent up two horse artillery battles to complete its defeat. Seriously alarmed, the Russian artillerymen in the Lesser Redoubt withdrew their weapons and galloped to the rear. As the long line of feathered Highland bonnets appeared above the crest, Prince Menshikov accepted defeat and sanctioned a general withdrawal. Incredibly, Campbell's losses were just 15 killed and 83 wounded.

On the far side of the British sector, the 7th and the Kazan regiment were still firing into each other at close quarters when the 2nd Division worked its way past and the 55th (2/The Border Regiment) came up on the fusiliers' right, then wheeled onto the flank of the Kazan and destroyed it with a series of volleys. Only 35 minutes had passed since the British attack began. Raglan's losses amounted to 362 killed and 1621 wounded. French and Turkish losses probably came to fewer than 500 killed or wounded. Russian casualties included 1800 killed and an estimated 3700 wounded.

Sauntering on to Sevastopol

The allies spent two days clearing the battlefield and then resumed their march on Sevastopol. Menshikov had left a garrison in the fortress and retired into the Crimea's interior with his field army.

The Battle of Balaklava, 25 October 1854

For a short period after the Alma (see the previous section), it would have been possible for the allies to occupy the north side of Sevastopol roadstead, rendering the city vulnerable to direct artillery fire and untenable in the long term. However, the allies felt that they would require supply ports in the immediate future and therefore crossed the Tchernaya river and marched round to the heavily fortified south side, establishing siege lines. Astutely, the French laid claim to the small harbours of Kamiesch and Kazatch. That left the British with the port and harbour of Balaklava, unsuitable as a military harbour and a 11-kilometre (7-mile) trek away. Inevitably, a large portion of the army would have to be employed as carrying parties at any one time.

The Russians were not fools, and indeed anyone with half a head could see that if the British did not hold Balaklava the Allies would be in desperate trouble. That is exactly what Prince Menshikov planned. The area in which he wanted his troops to attack consisted of a plain extending northeast from Kadikoi to the Fedioukine Hills, subdivided into north and south valleys by a shallow ridge named Causeway Heights. Six redoubts had been built along the ridge, manned by Tunisian troops from the Turkish contingent. At the western end of the ridge the camp of the British Cavalry Division provided a link between the siege lines and Balaklava, as well as a base from which patrols could operate along the Tchernaya river. The immediate defence of Balaklava was the responsibility of Major General Sir Colin Campbell's Highland Brigade, but on 25 October the need to provide carrying parties had reduced this to a single regiment, the 93rd. In support was an artillery battery based at Kadikoi and a second battery manned by Royal Marines on the hills above Balaklava to the east of the track.

The thin red line

As dawn broke on 25 October, a cavalry patrol galloped back along the south valley. Its commander informed Lord Lucan that three Russian infantry divisions had crossed the Tchernaya. One was climbing the Fedioukine hills, another was approaching Causeway Heights, and the third was attacking one of the Turkish redoubts. As the patrol commander spoke, the sound of gunfire came from the far end of the ridge. Lucan immediately sent word to Lord Raglan, who ordered the 1st and 4th Division to leave their camps and march immediately to the Balaklava plain. The French, also aware of the problem, had already despatched two infantry brigades and two cavalry regiments to the edge of Sapoune Heights. It was as well that the allied commanders had not underestimated the seriousness of the situation, as the Russian force consisted of 22,000 infantry, 3400 cavalry, and 78 guns.

By 8 a.m. the Russians had driven the Tunisians out of the first four redoubts. Russian lancer and hussar regiments entered the North Valley, while their artillery batteries prepared for action on Causeway Heights. Suddenly, four squadrons detached themselves from the main body of the Russian cavalry and headed directly for Kadikoi. At that moment they could not see the 93rd, who were lying in a fold in the ground to protect themselves from the fire of the guns on Causeway Heights. When the Russians were 800 metres (900 yards) distant, Campbell ordered the 93rd to stand in line, instead of forming square as was the usual defence of infantry against cavalry. Campbell's reasons were:

- ✔ He had every confidence in the new Enfield rifle and wished to maximise his firepower.
- ✔ He had a low opinion of the Russian soldiers' ability.

Tradition immortalises the scarlet, feather-bonneted ranks of the 93rd as 'the thin red line', although the phrase that William Howard Russell, the correspondent of *The Times* who was watching the drama unfold from Sapoune Heights, actually used was 'that thin red streak tipped with steel'. At 550 metres (600 yards) the 93rd fired their first volley. It emptied few saddles, but provided time to reload. They fired a second volley at 300 metres (350 yards). More men and horses went down. The Russians reined in. By now the Highlanders' blood was up. There was murmuring and a stirring in the ranks. Campbell understood his people well. He knew that in another minute there would be no holding them. They would break into a berserk charge and go for the enemy with the bayonet. He brought them up sharply: Ninety-Third! Ninety-Third! Damn all that eagerness! His interjection had the desired result, but he did allow the regiment's grenadier company to move out and fire a third volley at which the Russians turned and rode back over Causeway Heights. All of this has tended to obscure the part played by the Royal Marine gunners in the battery on the hills behind the regiment, who claimed that it was their accurately fused shellfire that made the Russians turn tail.

The charge of the Heavy Brigade

The second act of the battle was about to begin. The Cavalry Division, formed up at the head of the north valley, could see nothing of what had just taken place (see the preceding section for that action). Lord Lucan, the divisional commander, received an outdated order to detach eight squadrons from the Heavy Brigade and send them in the direction of Balaklava 'in support of the Turks'. As the Turks (Tunisians) had already left the field the order made little sense, but as the defence of Balaklava did make sense, Lucan complied. Under the leadership of Brigadier General the Honourable James Scarlett, commander of the Heavy Brigade, the 5th Dragoon Guards started off, with the Royal Scots Greys, the 6th Inniskilling Dragoons, and the 4th Dragoon Guards following. Unknown to the allies, the main mass of the Russian cavalry was already crossing Causeway Heights into the south valley.

The first warning to the Heavies was a long line of lance points breaking the crest to their left. The Russians, who outnumbered the allies by a very wide margin, crossed the summit and halted at a dry ditch. Scarlett wheeled his regiments to their left and dressed their ranks. The Russians, correct in the belief that Scarlett was about to charge, pushed forward their outer wings so as to envelop their opponents. Scarlett ordered the charge with 350 metres (400 yards) to go, uphill, and they started slowly, increasing their pace as they went. With a cheer they smashed five ranks deep into the Russian mass. The Russian greatcoats were too thick to penetrate with swords, so the majority of the British cuts were at their opponents' heads. Against this, the Russian sabres were blunt and inflicted bruises rather than cuts, while the lancers found their unwieldy weapons useless in this type of close combat. Nevertheless, while the British had the best of it for the moment, the Russians heavily outnumbered them and the issue of who would win remained in doubt.

While the Russians' attempt to envelop the Heavy Brigade may have seemed full of menace, it was to prove their undoing. Scarlett brought up an Inniskilling

Dragoon squadron, which smashed into the Russian left wing from behind. Simultaneously, the 4th Dragoon Guards and the Royal Dragoons, brought up by Lord Lucan at the gallop, tore into the opposite flank. The Russian mass heaved, shredding away to the rear, and finally turned to bolt back over the crest into the north valley. For good measure, the Royal Marine battery sent several shells into the packed ranks. After a brief pursuit, Scarlett sounded the recall.

The Russians sustained an estimated 200 casualties, mostly wounded, while the British loss was a mere fraction of this. Feeling justifiably pleased with themselves, the members of the Heavy Brigade rallied and returned to their position at the end of Causeway Heights. Shortly after, the entire Cavalry Division could see the Russian cavalry sorting themselves out behind a battery of guns at the far end of the north valley. The two sides had now set the scene for the third phase of the battle, which involved one of the most famous episodes in British military history.

The charge of the Light Brigade

Lord Raglan observed the entire battlefield laid out beneath him. At the far end of Causeway Heights he could see Russian horse teams hauling away the Allied guns from the captured redoubts. He was acutely conscious that the Duke of Wellington (see Chapter 11) had never lost a gun, so what he saw troubled him. He issued an order for the Cavalry Division to recapture the guns, little understanding that when viewed from a height the contours of a rolling landscape become flattened, and that because of this Lucan could not see what was perfectly obvious to anyone on Sapoune Heights.

The pencilled order that General Airey drafted still exists. It read:

> *Lord Raglan wishes the cavalry to advance rapidly to the front – follow the enemy and try to prevent the enemy carrying away the guns. Troop Horse Artillery may accompany. French cavalry is on your left. Immediate.*

The order was vague in the extreme and to make matters worse the messenger Airey chose to carry it was Captain Lewis Nolan, hot-tempered and barely subordinate, who despised Lucan. Under pressure, Lucan's brain worked slowly, but as the rising ground prevented him seeing what was going on at the far end of Causeway Heights, he did ask Nolan for clarification as to which guns Lord Raglan meant. Nolan insolently flung out his arm in the general direction of the Russians, unable to keep the sarcasm from his voice: 'There, my lord, is your enemy! There are your guns!' The only guns visible were those at the far end of the north valley, and it was quite contrary to tactical usage for cavalry to charge a battery from the front. Lucan could have declined the order until he received definite and unequivocal orders from Raglan himself, but Nolan had unsettled his judgement and he took the captain's words at face value. His brigade commanders, Lord Cardigan and Brigadier General Scarlett, accepted the order philosophically, but knew they were making a death ride.

Within the Light Brigade, the leading rank consisted of the 13th Light Dragoons on the right and the 17th Lancers on the left, the second rank of the 11th Hussars behind the Lancers, and the third rank of the 8th Hussars and the 4th Light Dragoons. When all was ready, Lucan's trumpeter sounded the advance and the Cavalry Division (both Heavies and Lights) entered the North Valley at a fast walk that soon became a trot. It had a run of a mile and a half to make. Unable to believe their eyes, Russian artillerymen ahead and on both flanks loaded their guns and waited for the slaughter to start. Soon the Heavy Brigade, its mounts tired from their earlier exertions (see the preceding section for 'The charge of the Heavy Brigade'), began to fall steadily behind.

What happened next reflected a horribly grim justice. Nolan had decided to ride with the 17th Lancers. He suddenly realised where the attack was heading and desperately tried to change its direction. He galloped ahead, shouting to Lord Cardigan and pointing to the right. At that moment the Light Brigade entered the killing zone. A shell burst near Nolan, sending a splinter of steel into his chest. He gave an unearthly shriek and then his mount carried him back through the ranks.

Artillery fire began to tear the Light Brigade apart. Its pace rose to a canter and soon to a flat-out gallop. Onlookers found themselves unable to take their eyes off the spectacle. 'It is magnificent, but it is not war!' one French general commented. For Lucan, riding between his two brigades, the dreadful trail of dead and maimed men and horses was too much. He sounded the halt. Scarlett brought his regiments to a standstill, then retired them out of range, but the Light Brigade did not hear the call. Their order was now ragged but, driven to insane rage by their losses, the Light Brigade tore through the battery at the end of the valley, spearing or cutting down the Russian gunners, and setting about the already discomfited Russian cavalry standing stationary beyond. Then, when no more could be done, they turned for home, having to fight their way past Cossacks who tried half-heartedly to cut them off. Very few would have got through if it had not been for a brilliant charge by the French 4th Chasseurs d'Afrique along the slopes of the Fedioukine hills.

Lord Cardigan, riding well ahead of the brigade, was first through the battery, and was the first survivor to reach his own lines. Undoubtedly courageous, he saw his duty as being to lead his men into their attack, and that he had done. An appalling snob, he did not see his task extending to hand-to-hand fighting, like a common trooper.

From start to finish, the charge of the Light Brigade had taken just 20 minutes. Of the 678 men who had taken part, 247 were killed, wounded, or were prisoners in Russian hands. In addition, some 500 horses had been killed or were so severely injured that they had to be put down. In practical terms, the Light Brigade had ceased to exist. The courage, discipline, and determination of its members was to pass into legend, but the fact remained that an enormous blunder had been committed. Lucan, as divisional commander, was at fault for not using his discretion and for failing to obtain confirmation of Raglan's intentions. Airey must also take a share of the blame for his ambiguous drafting of the written order, as must Captain Nolan for the manner of its delivery. Cardigan returned home to a hero's welcome.

Allied casualties at Balaklava amounted to 615 and those of the Russians to 627. As soon as the British infantry appeared, the Russians withdrew the way they had come.

The Battle of Inkerman, 5 November 1854

On the morning of 5 November the Russians made a second attempt to break the siege of Sevastopol (the first being Balaklava – see the previous section) with a joint attack by the fortress's garrison and the Russian field army in the Crimea. Most of the fighting took place on Inkerman ridge at the head of Sevastopol harbour. A heavy autumn mist not only helped the Russians to surprise the British picquets, but also prevented them from seeing how few troops opposed them during the early stages of the battle, while for their part the British were unaware that overwhelming odds confronted them. The mist also prevented senior officers on both sides from exercising effective control, so that the fighting resolved itself into a prolonged series of brutal hand-to-hand conflicts, often led by junior officers and NCOs. For this reason, Inkerman became known as 'the soldiers' battle'.

As the mist began to clear, no fewer than 100 Russian guns were visible on Shell Hill, at the northern end of the plateau. These soon began to silence the British field batteries. However, the British hauled two long 18-pounder guns, each requiring teams of 150 men on the drag ropes, up from the siege park. These outranged the Russian batteries and soon began knocking guns and *limbers* (ready-use ammunition trailers) about, as well as blowing up an ammunition wagon.

A British and French counter-attack on Shell Hill, supported by the fire of 50 guns, commenced at about noon. At 1 p.m. the Russians began pulling back and within two hours the whole of Inkerman ridge was once more in Allied hands. The British had lost 635 killed and 1938 wounded, and the French 175 killed and 1568 wounded. Of the 35,000 Russians actually engaged in the fighting on Inkerman ridge, no fewer than one-third became casualties: 4400, including six generals, were killed, and 7559 were wounded.

Bungling Beyond Belief

The autumn gales played havoc with the British encampments and as the weather continued to deteriorate further the troops began to suffer severely. They were still wearing the uniforms in which they landed, which were hopelessly inadequate for a Crimean winter. Nor were their rations adequate and they had no fuel to cook the little food they did receive. The unending cycle of trench duty and carrying parties exhausted them. They lived in leaking tents, slept in damp blankets, and had nowhere to dry their clothes when they were wet. Sentries froze to death overnight in the depths of the winter. Other men died from cholera, dysentery, pneumonia, influenza, and exposure. For those who remained, the burdens were proportionately heavier. The medical services simply could not cope with the droves of men reporting sick. The field hospitals became places to die and the base hospital at Scutari, opposite Constantinople, was almost overwhelmed, until Miss Florence Nightingale and her nurses imposed order on it. The Cavalry Division's remaining horses stood hock deep in frozen mud, gnawing hungrily at each other's manes and tails, and finally died from starvation.

Yet none of this was necessary. Food, fuel, clothing, and fodder aplenty was present in Balaklava, just a few miles away. A ship reached there loaded with left boots and a *lighter* (barge) of brand new greatcoats was left uncovered so that they became soaked and rotted. Ships came in and discharged their cargoes onto the mountains of stores already on the quayside. The trouble was that the army's purchasing, ordnance, supply, transport, and medical services were under the control of incompetent bureaucrats.

William Howard Russell in his despatches to *The Times* reported all of this faithfully, as did other journalists. The general public was furious. People may not have liked the company of soldiers at close quarters, but Mr Russell's earlier reports had made it clear that they had fought like heroes and now the manner of their treatment was a national disgrace. Such was the uproar that it brought the government down. By the spring of 1855 the new government shipped thousands of pack animals from all over the world into the Crimea, ripped the bureaucratic tangle apart, sent navvies to improve the track, built huts to replace the tattered tents, and made a start on a railway. The burden on the troops eased, many returned from hospital, reinforcements arrived, and it became possible to concentrate on the capture of Sevastopol once more.

The Fall of Sevastopol, 8 September 1855

The key to ending the Crimean War was the fall of Sevastopol. The events leading up to this major event were as follows:

- ✔ **17 February:** The Russian field army, under the command of Prince Mikhail Gorchakov, made a half-hearted attempt to break the siege of Sevastopol, but the Turks at Eupatoria repulsed them.

- ✔ **8–18 April:** A major Allied bombardment of the defences took place, causing over 6000 Russian casualties. The Allies did not assault and under the expert direction of the Russian fortress engineer, Colonel Frants Todleben, physical damage was quickly repaired.

- ✔ **May:** A squadron of Royal Navy gunboats penetrated the Sea of Azov, severing sea communications between the Russian interior and the Crimea. As the Sevastopol garrison and the Russian field army received most of their supplies along this route, in the long term this was to have a decisive effect.

- ✔ **17–18 June:** The Russians successfully repulsed Allied attacks on two major fortifications, the Malakoff and the Redan, with heavy casualties. Lord Raglan died 10 days later and General Sir James Simpson succeeded him.

- ✔ **16 August:** Gorchakov made one final attempt to break the siege. Using two corps, he tried to smash his way through the French and Sardinian lines on Traktir ridge, above the Tchernaya river. After a battle lasting five hours, he withdrew, having sustained 3229 killed and over 5000 wounded, as opposed to the total allied loss of 1700.

- ✔ **8 September:** The Allies renewed their assaults on the Malakoff and the Redan. The French took the Malakoff in a model operation, but the British assault failed with heavy loss. However, the loss of the Malakoff and its ability to command the interior of the Redan with gunfire meant Sevastopol was no longer defensible. That night the Russians blew up their remaining fortifications and retired across the harbour. The following day the Allies entered the city and set about destroying the Russian naval base.

Hostilities were still taking place in the Baltic and the Caucasus, but the fall of Sevastopol really ended the war. Under the terms of a peace treaty signed in February 1856, the Allies agreed to evacuate the Crimea and guaranteed Turkish security. Approximately a quarter of a million Russians and the same number of Allies died in the war, the majority from disease; the British also introduced the famous Victoria Cross as a result of this war (see the sidebar of the same name). But what about the monks whose unholy bout of fisticuffs started the whole thing off? Everyone had forgotten about them.

The Victoria Cross

On learning of the many deeds of gallantry and self-sacrifice that her seamen and soldiers performed during the Crimean War, Queen Victoria provided the encouragement for an award for acts of supreme courage. A Royal Warrant created the award, which took her name, on 29 January 1856, applying retrospectively to the Crimean War. Only members of the Royal Navy and the British Army who, in the presence of the enemy, had performed a signal act of valour or devotion to their country were eligible to receive the Victoria Cross. Only the merit of conspicuous bravery could establish a claim for the award, and in this context everyone was equally eligible.

The Victoria Cross was, and still is, made from the metal of cannon captured at Sevastopol. It takes the form of a simple Maltese Cross embossed with a crown surmounted by a lion and the legend 'FOR VALOUR'. In total, only 1356 Victoria Crosses have ever been awarded, of which 295 were posthumous. As its founder intended, its recipients come from every conceivable walk of life, making it the rarest and most democratic gallantry award in the world. Great care is exercised in selecting those considered eligible. Written statements are required from three witnesses to the deed. In circumstances where an entire unit has distinguished itself in a heroic manner, a number of

Victoria Crosses in proportion to its size are awarded, the actual recipients being chosen by ballot among its members. The final decision always rests with the sovereign, who personally presents the award at an investiture.

The terms of the original Royal Warrant have been modified over the years. During the Indian Mutiny (see Chapter 14) the Victoria Cross was granted to civilians working under military command. In 1858 its provisions were extended to include 'circumstances of extreme danger', but reverted to 'in the presence of the enemy' in 1881. In 1867 colonial forces throughout the Empire became eligible. The one exception was the Indian Army, whose supreme award for valour remained for the time being the Indian Order of Merit, instituted by the Honourable East India Company in 1837. At first, no provision was made for posthumous awards, but this changed during the Second Boer War (see Chapter 16) and a number of awards were conferred retrospectively. In 1911 officers and men of the Indian Army became eligible, and in 1920 eligibility was further extended to the newly formed Royal Air Force, as well as matrons, nursing sisters, and nurses serving under military command. Initially, those awarded it could forfeit the award through disgraceful conduct. Only eight such forfeitures took place and King George V abandoned the forfeiture clause.

Chapter 14

Rebels, Rajahs, and a Rani: The Indian Mutiny

. . . .

In This Chapter

▶ Why the Bengal Army mutinied

▶ The Siege of Delhi, 1857

▶ The Reliefs of Lucknow, 1857–1858

▶ Central Indian campaigns, 1858

▶ The end of the East India Company, 1860

. . . .

*T*he Indian Mutiny was the most tragic event of the two centuries of the British presence in India. The mutiny was a large and very dangerous uprising that, under better leadership, may have ended British rule there and then. Indeed, so small was the British garrison of India that without the help of Indian troops, it would have found it almost impossible to put down the mutiny.

A variety of causes existed for the mutiny, and it could have been avoided altogether if the British had paid greater attention to the *sepoys'* (Indian soldiers') grievances. In the end, the governance of India passed from the Honourable East India Company to the British crown, which reformed the Indian army so that such tragic events could never happen again.

The battles detailed in this chapter were fought by armies with the following troop types:

- ✔ **Sepoys:** Native Indian infantry serving with the British East India Company's army.

- ✔ **Sowars:** Native Indian cavalry troopers serving with the Company's army.

- ✔ **Europeans:** The European troops of the British East India Company, these troops differed little from their British Army counterparts save that they were better paid and were a hard lot who generally had good reasons for wanting to spend their lives in virtual exile.

The Mutiny Begins

Early in 1857 something odd began to happen in the villages of Bengal. At night, a runner arrived at a particular village and gave the head man a chapatti. He also told him to bake more chapattis and pass them on to neighbouring villages. Even now, no one knows who started this strange version of the chain letter, let alone what it meant, but the underlying and rather sinister significance was that something wide-ranging and probably violent was about to take place.

Reasons for the outbreak of violence that was the Indian Mutiny include:

- An old Indian prophecy had it that in the centennial year of the Battle of Plassey the British would be driven from India forever.

- The Honourable East India Company was generally averse to becoming involved in local affairs, but some areas existed in which it felt its intervention was necessary, stamping hard on customs to like *thagi* (ritual murder in honour of the goddess Kali) and *satee* (the burning alive of widows on their husbands' funeral pyres), thereby annoying those with vested interests in such matters. Nor did the Company's well-meaning regulations on inheritance and land tenure meet with universal approval.

- Many Hindus saw the well-intentioned activities of Christian missionaries as part of a British plot to violate the caste system and imperil their souls. This feeling overflowed into the Honourable East India Company's Bengal army, which contained a significant proportion of high-caste Hindus and Rajputs, recruited mainly in Oudh. They objected very strongly to a recent regulation requiring them to serve overseas if need be, as according to their faith a sea passage lost them their caste. The sepoys in the Bombay and Madras armies considered this attitude to be right over the top, but the fact remained that it existed.

- Up to the time of the Sikh Wars in the 1840s (see Chapter 12), Bengal sepoys could discuss such problems with their British officer. As memories of that war faded, however, the Company had commissioned a new generation of quite unsuitable British officers who made no bones about the fact that they actually disliked the sepoys. Despite their presence, enough decent officers remained to warn the generals that serious trouble was in the offing. For their part, the generals, grown old in India and knowing that sepoys took pride in their soldiering, refused to countenance any idea that a mutiny was a distinct possibility.

- The Honourable East India Company decided to re-equip its troops with Enfield rifles. A disaffected workman at the Dum Dum arsenal probably started a clever and effective rumour that the grease on the new paper cartridges for these rifles, which the sepoys had to bite open, was a mixture of cow and pig fat. As the Hindus held cows as sacred and the Muslims abominated pigs, this rumour destabilised the entire native element of the Bengal army. The problem was not just that any sepoy handling the

> cartridges would be regarded as unclean and forbidden to sleep with his
> wife until he had been through a ritual purification, they also saw the
> action as a deliberate step along the road to enforced Christianity. The
> average sepoy was terrified, and that terror conditioned all his subse-
> quent actions.

Too late, the authorities listened and promised to redress the last of these
grievances, but some stupid, insensitive officers were determined to force the
issue. Early in 1857 the Company disbanded several regiments that refused to
accept the cartridges. In April, 85 troopers of the 3rd Light Cavalry, serving
with the Meerut garrison, refused to accept the cartridges. They were court
martialled and sentenced to a term of imprisonment with hard labour. The
rest of the Company's native regiments at Meerut now felt driven into a
corner. They considered their only alternatives:

- They could accept the cartridges and risk losing their souls.
- They could refuse the cartridges and face severe punishment.
- They could mutiny and sweep away the system that had placed them in
  such terrible danger.

By now, British shortcomings in the Crimea (see Chapter 13) were common
knowledge and this almost certainly influenced the sepoys' decision to mutiny.
On Sunday 10 May, while the British element of the garrison was at church
parade, the mutiny became a fact when the sepoys cut down British officers,
violated their wives with burning torches until they died, and slaughtered
their children. The native regiments then marched off to Delhi. The march
had a strange, nightmare quality about it: It was smartly done in full uniform
with medals, bands playing the old English country airs to which the ranks
had always swung along, the Colours carried proudly, and the mess silver
safely packed along with the baggage. On reaching Delhi the following day the
garrison promptly joined the mutineers. Once more, the Indians hunted down
and massacred British officers, civilians, women, and children. A handful of
the British managed a hair-raising escape after blowing up the city's arsenal.
The mutineers found a leader in the elderly Bahadur II, King of Delhi, whom
both Hindus and Muslims could accept, proclaiming him Emperor of Hindustan.
Bahadur appointed his eldest son, Mirza Mogul, commander of his new army.

The news spread like wildfire across northern India. In one garrison after
another the Honourable East India Company's native troops mutinied, although
in some places the disaffected regiments were disarmed and dispersed before
they did any damage. One of the worst incidents took place at Cawnpore: For
three weeks in early June 1857, 300 British and loyal Indian soldiers under Sir
Hugh Wheeler held the mutineers at bay from a makeshift entrenchment. Under
offer of safe conduct to Allahabad, which was still in British hands, the British
embarked on the river craft that were to take them to safety. The mutineers
then massacred the men and violated, tortured, and mutilated the women
and children, flinging their bodies down a well.

The Siege of Delhi, 8 June–20 September 1857

General Sir George Anson, Commander-in-Chief India, received orders on 12 May 1857 to besiege Delhi. With commendable speed he put together what became known as the Delhi Field Force. At first it consisted of only the 9th Lancers, the 75th (1/The Gordon Highlanders), two Royal Horse Artillery troops, the 1st and 2nd Bengal Fusiliers (European), the 9th Light Cavalry, and the 4th Irregular Cavalry. Of the two native infantry regiments present, one mutinied and cleared off to Delhi while British disarmed the other. By 17 May, Anson's column was moving, but the strain of events had been too much for the 70 year old and 10 days later he died from cholera. General Sir Henry Barnard succeeded Anson and continued the march. At Baghpat Colonel Archdale Wilson joined Barnard with the remnant of the Meerut garrison, consisting of two squadrons of the 6th Dragoon Guards and part of the 60th Rifles (1/The King's Royal Rifle Corps), some loyal Company cavalry, and seven guns, including five taken from mutineers who had tried to stop the garrison crossing the river Hindon.

A 30,000-strong mutineer army with 30 guns, dug in at Badli-ke-serai, six miles north of Delhi, halted Barnard's progress. True to the British tradition of attacking in India whatever the odds, Barnard's 4000 men sailed into the enemy mass, which broke and fled after a short fight. The advance continued, finally coming to a halt on a long ridge to the northwest of the city walls, too rocky to dig into. To put it at its most optimistic, the situation was unusual. A British force consisting of 600 cavalry, 2300 infantry, and 22 guns, holding a barely tenable position, was 'besieging' 40,000 mutineers with several hundred guns, snug behind seven miles of 7.3-metre (24-feet) high masonry curtain walls, with bastions mounting artillery at regular intervals, the whole fronted by a ditch 6 metres (20 feet) deep and 7.6 metres (25 feet) wide. It was all a matter of perspective. Barnard was too weak to mount any sort of attack. The rebels, on the other hand, attacked repeatedly without success.

On 1 July a large contingent of mutineers from the Bareilly garrison joined the rebels inside the city. One of the newcomers, Bakht Khan, an Indian artillery officer with 40 years' experience, promptly persuaded Bahadur that he was the man to lead the army. Naturally, Mirza Mogul resented being sacked, with the result that mutual suspicion and recrimination became the norm among the rebels' senior commanders.

Barnard died from cholera on 5 July. His successor, General Thomas Reed, was already ill and had to hand over to Archdale Wilson a fortnight later. Wilson proved to be a sensible commander who decided to concentrate on holding his ground until sufficient reinforcements and a siege train arrived. Reinforcements were arriving, in small numbers, but they were barely keeping pace with the daily losses.

KEY PLAYERS

John Nicholson

John Nicholson was one of the most remarkable commanders in British military history. Of commanding stature, austere, humourless, and deeply religious, he possessed a powerful personality that impressed itself on those around him. Once, Nicholson pursued a notorious malefactor into the mountains, caught, fought, and killed him, then displayed the man's head on his desk as a warning to others that they should keep their criminal tendencies under control. Such deeds made him a legend among the wild tribes of the northwest frontier. His method of dealing with local ringleaders of the mutiny was swift, simple, and direct. He tied them with their backs to the muzzles of cannon and blew them apart.

The Sikhs not only respected his strength of purpose and scorn of soft living, but also recognised an individual with the rare gift of leadership. Thousands of Sikhs volunteered to serve under Nicholson, enabling him to press the siege of Delhi vigorously. The troops instinctively called him 'The General'. Nicholson most loyal adherents were a troop of barely governable Multani horsemen. When a sniper's bullet killed Nicholson, they flung themselves on his grave and cried like children. He was 35 at the time of his death and would become known as the Hero of Delhi. His statue remained near the Kashmir Gate until Indian Independence, when it was shipped to Lisburn in Ulster where his family had lived and where his memory is still honoured.

Reinforcing the besiegers

The great infusion of strength and firepower needed came from the Punjab, annexed only nine years earlier. There, Sir John Lawrence, the Chief Commissioner, had reacted very quickly on the outbreak of the mutiny, disarming suspect regiments as well as securing arsenals and important strategic points. One of his commanders, Brigadier-General John Nicholson (see the sidebar on him), possessed immense influence among the local people, and thanks to this he was able to send the Delhi Field Force no fewer than three Punjabi cavalry regiments and seven Punjabi infantry battalions, followed by a heavy siege train and a unit of Punjabi *sappers* (engineers) and miners.

The arrival of Nicholson and his troops doubled the size of the Delhi Field Force. The siege train (including numerous heavy guns and mortars plus hundred of carts carrying 1000 rounds per gun and ample powder, all drawn by plodding elephants and bullocks) occupied no less than 21 kilometres (13 miles) of road and was still some way behind. Bakht Khan, aware of the fact, sent out 6000 men to capture the siege train. Wilson, whose agents informed him of this, sent Nicholson with 2500 men and 16 guns in pursuit. Nicholson caught up with the rebels at Najafghar on 25 August and routed them in an hour-long fight, capturing all their guns and baggage. The morale of the British soared, while that of the mutineers took a nose dive. Now that the constraints of discipline were gone, the mutinous regiments began to fall apart and the rebel army, joined by the city's undesirables, started to mutate into an armed mob. As a professional artilleryman, Bakht Khan knew what the siege guns could do to the ancient city walls and urged an envoy to go to the British on 30 August with a tentative offer of terms. The British sent the envoy packing.

Assaulting Delhi's walls

On 3 and 4 September 1857 the British siege train arrived and began its work against several pre-determined sections of the defences at once. Shattered masonry and dismounted cannon began to tumble into the ditch. Over the next few days, the rebels did everything in their power to storm or silence the batteries, without avail. Archdale Wilson still had barely sufficient resources for one assault:

- ✔ If it succeeded, the mutiny would suffer a serious blow.
- ✔ If it failed, Britain had little future in India.

Nicholson bullied Wilson into making an attack as soon as the British had made practical breaches in the defences. At first light on 14 September an assault by five columns, assisted by a party given the suicidal task of blowing in the Kashmir Gate, started. This boiled down to 5000 men attacking a force of over 30,000, consisting mainly of trained regular soldiers who held a fortified position. Longer odds are difficult to imagine. When the moment came, Numbers 1 and 2 Columns charged forward, running through a blizzard of musketry that shot down the ladder parties immediately. Others snatched up the ladders and men, dead or alive, tumbled down the counter-scarp to the bottom of the ditch. The British discovered that the ladders were too short unless they placed them on the *berm* (a shelf at the top of the slope), which was too narrow to hold them. It took several endless minutes to pile up rubble and the bodies of comrades into heaps on which they could place the ladders, and they had to carry out the work under a rain of masonry blocks from above. However, such was the fury of the attackers, many of whom had slaughtered wives and families to avenge, that no one could stop them. Crawling hand over hand up the debris of the breaches or clambering up the ladders, they swarmed onto the ramparts and in savage fighting pitched the rebels off the walls.

Fighting inside the city

At the Kashmir Gate a small party of Bengal sappers and miners under Lieutenants Duncan Home and Philip Salkeld had the suicidal task of blowing in the gate. Half of them were killed or mortally wounded, but they succeeded. Number 3 Column charged over the smoking wreckage into a square known as the Main Guard, where Numbers 1 and 2 Columns and the reserves joined it. Then the difficult and dangerous process of methodical street fighting began, clearing each house in turn as the advance into the city progressed.

Although those fighting inside the walls were unaware of it, the entire operation was on the brink of disaster. To the west of the city, Major Reid's Number 4 Column was advancing through the heavily fortified suburb of Kishengunj to the Kabul Gate. Nothing went as planned. Reid's promised artillery support did not materialise, and the mutineers routed its raw Kashmiri contingent. More rebels began pouring through the Kabul and Lahore Gates and started to push the column back. Reid was wounded and his successors gave contradictory orders. If the mutineers turned right they would trap three British columns in the city. Major Henry Tombs's troop of Bengal Horse Artillery, which lost 27 of its 48 gunners, and the cavalry just managed to contain the threat. The pressure eased a little when Number 2 Column stormed the Moree Bastion and the Kabul Gate from within, and the arrival of the Guides Infantry and the Baluchi Battalion finally brought the situation under control.

Wilson moved his command post into the city of Delhi during the afternoon. The early success of the assault was clouded by the realisation that although he now controlled a quarter of the city, he had lost a quarter of his fighting strength. In addition, Nicholson had received a mortal wound. For a moment, Wilson toyed with the idea of withdrawing, then decided that to do so courted disaster. After so much bloodshed the infantry were becoming stale, but by now siege artillery had been brought in and this demolished any centre of protracted resistance. The mutineers were already beginning to leave in large numbers and by 20 September Delhi was in British hands.

Hodson's heroism

Most people would consider the capture of Bahadur enough high-risk activity for the time being, but Hodson took out 100 of his men to bring in three Indian princes, all of whom had given active support to the mutineers and connived at their atrocities. They were hiding in the same tomb as Bahadur, and the message Hodson sent in to them was that he was taking them back to Delhi, dead or alive. The huge crowd shouted for the princes to lead them in an attack on the soldiers, but none of the three had any stomach for a fight. They went off in a cart with a 10-strong escort while Hodson and his men faced down the mutineers once more. The troopers used their horses to control the crowd, and finally had the several thousand mutineers penned inside the grounds of the tomb. Hodson told them to throw down their arms. They began to mutter angrily. Hodson repeated his order, sharply. Incredibly, the mutineers obeyed, then shuffled off. So many of them had been at the tomb that it took two hours to collect all the weapons. Hodson and his men then set off after the cart carrying the princes, catching up with it not a minute too soon. A mob intent on rescuing the princes was surrounding it and the escort was in trouble. Hodson, realising that the princes could once again become the chosen figureheads of the mutineers' cause, borrowed a carbine and shot the three of them dead. The British then displayed the princes' corpses for three days at a spot where the mutineers had committed some of the worst atrocities. Naturally, Hodson's action provoked controversy, but it undoubtedly saved lives, both British and Indian.

When the British took the Red Fort in Delhi, Bahadur was hiding with his family in a tomb six miles outside the walls. Major William Hodson was sent to bring him back to the city. Hodson was a natural *beau sabreur* (dashing adventurer), who enjoyed fighting for its own sake and was a noted swordsman. Taking just 50 of his sowars, he told Bahadur that the British would spare his life if he surrendered at once. For two hours Hodson and his little band faced down thousands of demoralised but still armed and dangerous mutineers. Bahadur and his queen then gave themselves up and Hodson escorted them back to Delhi. However, he hadn't quite finished for the day, as the sidebar 'Hodson's heroism' relates.

From start to finish of the siege, the casualties that the Delhi Field Force incurred amounted to 992 killed, 2795 wounded, and 30 missing, a total of 3817, of whom 1677 were Indian soldiers. It is impossible to estimate how many mutineers and their supporters were killed during the siege, but the number was far greater than the British casualties and more were tried and executed after the seizure of the city.

The lesson for the mutineers was that if they could not win at Delhi, they could not win at all. Much hard fighting remained, but after Delhi the fortunes of the mutineers declined steadily.

The Reliefs of Lucknow, 1857–1858

Lucknow was the capital of the former kingdom of Oudh, an area from which the mutineers drew much of their support. It was a typical Indian city of the period, sprawling and labyrinthine. The British Residency was in its own enclosure on a small plateau. On all sides save the north the buildings of the city pressed against or overlooked it.

Sir Henry Lawrence, the Chief Commissioner for Oudh, saw the mutiny coming. He began fortifying the Residency and laying in supplies for a siege during May. News of the Meerut mutiny reached him on 14 May, and shortly after, he received a tip-off that the native element of the Lucknow garrison would mutiny on the evening of 30 May. Lawrence moved the city's European community inside the defences. The warning proved to be accurate, but before the mutineers could reach the Residency the under-strength 32nd (1/The Duke of Cornwall's Light Infantry) and 4/1 Battery Bengal European Artillery chased them out of town. For the moment, these two units and about 300 loyal sepoys constituted the entire garrison.

Defending Lucknow

By 12 June news came that every British outpost in Oudh had fallen. Towards the end of the month, reports said that the Cawnpore garrison had surrendered, although some time elapsed before the defenders of the Residency learned of its horrible fate (see the section 'The Mutiny Begins, 1857' earlier in this chapter). They were, however, becoming increasingly conscious of their own isolation. On 29 June Lawrence learned that a small force of mutineers had reached Chinhut, some 10 miles distant. He led out a sizeable portion of the garrison to deal with them, but to his horror discovered that they numbered 10 times the figure he expected. Having sustained 200 casualties and lost five of its 11 guns, his force withdrew into the Lucknow defences. The Chinhut affair was a disaster, as the British defeat led every mutineer and malcontent for miles around to converge on the city. As many of the larger buildings close to the perimeter were still standing, the enemy's fire could reach everywhere in the defences. At any one time there were reputedly no fewer than 8000 mutineers and their supporters firing into the Residency. Shellfire mortally wounded Lawrence on 2 July and command passed to Colonel J.E.W. Inglis of the 32nd, later promoted to brigadier general.

Inglis pursued a much more aggressive defence than Lawrence had, instituting a series of successful sorties that wrecked the enemy's forward posts. The mutineers resorted to mining under the defences. The garrison's engineers, with the assistance of former tin miners from the 32nd, counter-mined and usually won the brutal subterranean fights that took place in hot, claustrophobic semi-darkness. On 10 August, however, the mutineers did succeed in blowing a gap in the defences. Above ground, most of their comrades showed little inclination to exploit it, and those that did the British quickly shot down.

While the fighting raged, the garrison had other challenges to overcome. Overcrowded living conditions, poor sanitation, intense heat, and the difficulties involved in disposing of human and animal remains all contributed to the spread of diseases such as cholera, dysentery, and smallpox that killed or incapacitated as many people as the mutineers' fire.

Havelock and Outram to the rescue: The First Relief

Details of the rebels' atrocities had become public knowledge in Britain. As women and children were in the Residency, the only politically acceptable course was to despatch a relief column as quickly as possible. In a strictly military context, the loss of the Lucknow Residency would have been of no importance whatever. Reinforcements were on their way to India from the United Kingdom and elsewhere, but they would take time to arrive.

The officer chosen to lead the relief column was Brigadier General Sir Henry Havelock, a Regular Army officer who, having no money of his own, had chosen to serve permanently in India, where living was cheaper. Now aged 62, he may have been considered too old for the task, but he had a wide-ranging experience of active service, including the epic siege of Jellalabad (see Chapter 12). He was entirely reliable and possessed a cool head in action. On 30 June he began assembling his troops at Allahabad on the Ganges, just south of the Oudh frontier. They included the 64th (1/The North Staffordshire Regiment), the 78th (2/Seaforth Highlanders), the 84th (2/York and Lancaster Regiment), an Honourable East India Company regiment, the Madras European Fusiliers (later 1/Royal Dublin Fusiliers), 3/8th Battery Royal Artillery, 20 volunteer cavalry, and an irregular cavalry unit of doubtful value. All the regular units were under strength and only 2000 men were actually available for Havelock's apparently impossible mission.

On 7 July Havelock set out for Cawnpore, knowing that the mutineers had massacred the garrison but believing that the women and children were still alive and held captive. On 11 July, 3500 mutineers barred the column's path at Fetehpur, where the rebels discovered that the new Enfield rifles shot holes in their ranks beyond the reach of their old Brown Bess muskets, the balls from which were simply pattering into the dust. When Havelock gave the order to advance with the bayonet, the mutineers bolted. From start to finish, the 'battle' had lasted a mere 10 minutes. No British casualties resulted from enemy action, but 12 men died from heat-stroke.

On 14 July a flank attack dislodged another rebel force from its position at Aong. Two days later the British found the Nana Sahib himself, the mutineers' leader, blocking the road into Cawnpore with 8000 men and eight guns. Havelock used a feint to the mutineer's centre to distracted the rebels' attention, while his main body of the relief column swung off the road to the right and rolled up the Nana Sahib's line as the 78th Highlanders, followed by the 64th, put in a ferocious bayonet charge. A second charge routed reinforcements that the Nana Sahib had summoned from the city.

The British entered Cawnpore the following day. The stench and sights where the women and children had been killed were sickening, and mutilated corpses filled the well to overflow. Men from the 84th recognised some of the regiment's womenfolk and children among the victims. Until now, neither side had in fact shown much mercy, but from this point on, nothing less than the extermination of the mutineers and their supporters would suffice for the British.

On 25 July, leaving a small garrison to hold Cawnpore, Havelock commenced his march into Oudh, fighting several successful actions but running short of artillery ammunition. With the rebels massing to his front, his lines of communication under threat, and the Nana Sahib raising a fresh army at Bithur on his flank, Havelock reached the conclusion that he would have to fall back on Cawnpore until he received reinforcements and fresh supplies. In a message to Lucknow, he asked whether it was possible for Inglis to break out and join him. Inglis told him that, burdened as he was with sick and wounded plus hundreds of women and children, breaking out was not an option, but he hoped that by placing everyone on half rations he could hold out until 10 September.

As soon as his supply situation had eased a little, Havelock moved against the Nana Sahib, who was now on his home ground and had collected about 4000 men and several guns. It was Nana Sahib's misfortune that he was a better mass murderer than he was a tactician, for he chose to fight in front of an unfordable stream crossed by a single bridge. An hour's fighting broke the mutineers, who were driven into the stream or across the bridge and through the town. The British then burned the Nana Sahib's palace to the ground. On 15 September reinforcements arrived, including the 5th (1/Royal Northumberland Fusiliers), the 90th (2/The Cameronians (Scottish Rifles)), 2/3rd and 1/5th Batteries Bengal Artillery, and a contingent of Sikhs from the Punjab. With them came Major General Sir James Outram, designated commander of the enlarged force and Civil Commissioner for Oudh.

Outram and Havelock knew each other well and had served together during the recent campaign in Persia. As Havelock had been responsible for the first clear-cut victories since the mutiny began, Outram did not wish his arrival to be seen as a reflection on Havelock. The two agreed that Outram should accompany the column as a volunteer, but that Havelock should remain in command until they had relieved Lucknow.

Inglis was still holding out in Lucknow when the column, now 3000 strong, moved off on 18 September. It dispersed an enemy force at Mangalwar on 21 September and two days later found the rebel army drawn up four miles south of Lucknow. Estimates put that army's strength at 10,000 infantry with ample artillery and 1500 cavalry. A marsh protected its front and its left rested on the former summer palace of the kings of Oudh, the Alambagh, which was enclosed by a high wall with a turret at each corner. Once again, Havelock demonstrated his tactical ability. He decided to attack the enemy right with a wide turning movement. While this was in progress, rebel guns, previously concealed by trees, opened fire on the marching column and inflicted serious casualties. Major Vincent Eyre's 1/5th Battery quickly silenced its opponents then turned its attention to the enemy cavalry. Unable to charge because of the marsh and unwilling to endure the hail of shot, the rebel horsemen fled. The mutineer infantry, having lost both their artillery and cavalry, crumbled as the flank attack developed and Outram at the head of the Volunteer Cavalry, now 168 strong, chased them as far as the city. A good day's work ended with more good news: Delhi had fallen to the British (see the section 'The Siege of Delhi', earlier in this chapter).

Havelock began the final phase of the operation on 25 September. He planned to storm the bridge over a canal marking the southern boundary of the city, then fight through the gardens of the palaces and other buildings beside the river until they reached the Residency. The fighting was bitter in the extreme but the plan worked, thanks to the close-quarter blasting of the British artillery. The gun crews suffered cruelly, but volunteers replaced those who had been shot down, while the infantry, with vengeful yells of 'Remember Cawnpore!', flung the rebels out of one position after another at the point of the bayonet. At last they reached the Residency gates amid scenes of jubilation.

The cost of the final breakthrough amounted to a horrific 31 officers and 504 men killed or wounded. This alone meant that Outram was now too weak to comply with his orders to evacuate the Residency. In effect, the relief amounted to nothing more than a reinforcement. If the mutineers rejoiced that Havelock and his men, so long a thorn in their side, were now penned inside the Residency, their joy was short-lived, as outlined in the next section.

Campbell is coming, hurrah! Hurrah!: The Second Relief

On 27 October the British received word that the advance guard of a second relief column, with Brigadier General Hope Grant in command and consisting of units that had taken Delhi, had reached Cawnpore. On 6 November Hope Grant sent another message to the effect that he was well on the way to Lucknow, and was simply waiting for newly arrived reinforcements from England under the redoubtable General Sir Colin Campbell, the recently appointed Commander-in-Chief India.

On the morning of 10 November, two bedraggled figures arrived at Campbell's camp with a request to see the General. One was a native spy in Outram's service, the other towered over him and, although he was wearing native clothes, a mixture of oil and lampblack stained his skin and a turban concealed his head of fair hair. His name was Thomas Kavanagh (a clerk by trade – not a soldier), and he and his comrade had slipped out of the Lucknow defences the previous night to guide the relief force in. Leaving Lucknow, Kavanagh and his accomplice were picked up by a rebel patrol, talked themselves out of trouble, lost their way, and finally floundered through a swamp before reaching British lines. Campbell said that their achievement was 'one of the most daring ever attempted'. Although a civilian, Kavanagh received the Victoria Cross (see the sidebar in Chapter 13) as he was under military command at the time of his exploit.

Campbell made excellent progress and had 5000 men and 49 guns available for the final advance on the Residency. He decided to accept Outram's advice and make this as close to the river as possible, even if it meant storming several riverside palaces he knew had been put in a defensible condition. On 14 November the British drove the enemy from the walls of the Dilkusha Park, and then from the Martiniere School. The following day they brought the heavy baggage and provision train into the Dilkusha Park, a necessary step because Campbell intended evacuating the Residency as soon as he had broken through.

Campbell was a patriotic Scot who favoured his fellow Scots above all others, but above all he favoured his beloved 93rd. He ensured that its men were always in the thick of the fray, and they never let him down. On 16 November they led the attack on the Secundrabagh palace, lying within a high-walled enclosure of strong masonry some 110 metres (120 yards) square, loopholed all round, and garrisoned to capacity with mutineers. Two hours of concentrated gunfire battered a small hole between 0.9 metres (3 feet) and 1.2 metres (4 feet) square in the wall beside the gate. The 93rd's pipers had roused them to fighting madness, so that when Campbell's drummer beat the advance they surged forward with a howl of pent-up rage. One after another, the kilted figures, berserk with a fury that those within could never match, swarmed through the breach.

The fight for the gates was bitter in the extreme, but when the British threw them open the rest of the 93rd, followed by the 53rd (1/The King's Shropshire Light Infantry), the 4th Punjabis, and a composite battalion, poured through, hounding the mutineers across the courtyard, up stairs, along passages, and from room to room. The British didn't knowingly leave a rebel alive in the Secundrabagh. They carried some 2000 rebel bodies out afterwards, but a photograph of the interior, taken months later after the carrion had done their work, shows the courtyard still littered with skulls and bones. Considering the nature of the fighting, British casualties were remarkably light – the 93rd, for example, sustained only 22 killed and 75 wounded.

It was now afternoon and Campbell decided to tackle the Shah Najaf, a domed mosque inside a garden, surrounded by a loopholed masonry wall surmounted by a parapet. Once again, the 93rd led the assault, followed by a composite battalion, once the attached naval guns under Captain Peel, RN, firing at point-blank range, had knocked a breach in the walls. This proved to be more difficult than expected. The crowds of mutineers on the walls, blazing away with their muskets at the British infantry, caused serious casualties, so the British fired rockets, clearing the wall like magic. The British heard the rebel buglers inside sounding the advance, and for a moment the enemy appeared about to make a determined sortie. Then silence ensued. After a while, a patrol under Staff Sergeant John Paton discovered that the mutineers had escaped through a gate at the rear. The British promptly occupied the building, and reached Outram's garrison the following day. The events of 16 November 1857 produced the greatest number of Victoria Crosses ever won during a single day.

Evacuating Lucknow

The evacuation began as soon as Campbell's force arrived. It was a model operation conducted without the mutineers' knowledge. Sadly, Havelock, worn out by strain and the effects of dysentery, died on 25 November. Two days later, leaving a garrison of 4000 men and 35 guns with Outram at the Alambagh, which was much easier to defend and relieve than the Residency, Campbell set out on the return march to Cawnpore. On the way, he learned that one of the rebels' best commanders, Tantia Topi, had attacked the small garrison left behind at Cawnpore with 14,000 men and 40 guns.

The rebels had driven the garrison back into its entrenchments, but it was still holding its own when Campbell returned. Having sent the women, children, sick, and wounded off to the safety of Allahabad on 3 December, he was able to give Tantia Topi his undivided attention. On 6 December he drove in both wings of the rebel army while Peel's guns punched holes through its centre. The British pursued the fleeing rebels, who lost all their supplies, for 22 kilometres (14 miles).

Campbell returned to Lucknow at the head of a 20,000-strong army in March 1858. The recapture of the city cost him 1200 casualties, but his men killed thousands of rebels and the rest fled. This time, the prize agents were slow off the mark, for so great was the quantity of loot that they were quite unable to assess its value. Shortly after (by coincidence, of course) a number of heavily mortgaged estates at home suddenly found themselves running at a profit.

Fighting in Central India, 1858

Although the British decisively defeated the mutineers at Delhi and Lucknow (see the preceding sections), at the beginning of 1858 large areas of Central India remained in rebel hands.

The officer selected to restore British power in Central India was Major General Sir Hugh Rose, who did not have wide experience of active service and whose appointment as commander of the Central India Field Force was far from universally welcome. The snobbery between the Indian and home establishments was very much two-way traffic and people who had been in India for less than a year were not considered capable of doing things the 'Indian' way. Rose couldn't have cared less and did things his way. He was intelligent, competent, vigorous, and possessed of an iron will.

Rose achieved so much with so little. When he assembled his force at Mhow it contained a substantial contingent that the Nizam of Hyderabad had supplied. The 1st Brigade, under Brigadier General Charles Stuart, contained half the 14th Light Dragoons (later Hussars), the 86th (2/Royal Irish Rifles), one troop of the 3rd Bombay Light Cavalry, two regiments of Hyderabad

Contingent Cavalry, the 25th Bombay Native Infantry, the 1st Troop Bombay Horse Artillery, two field batteries of the Hyderabad Contingent, and some Madras sappers and miners. The 2nd Brigade, under the command of Brigadier General Charles Steuart, contained half the 14th Light Dragoons, part of the 3rd Bombay Light Cavalry, one regiment of Hyderabad Contingent Cavalry, the 3rd Bombay European Regiment, the 24th Bombay Native Infantry, a battery of the Bombay Horse Artillery, a field battery of the Hyderabad Contingent, a company of Madras sappers and miners, and a siege train. This small force, which any opposition it encountered was likely to dwarf, took the field on 6 January 1858:

- Rose's first priority was to relieve the garrison of Saugur, which had been under siege for seven months. First, however, he had to take the fortress of Rathgur. The siege train began battering its walls on 26 January and three days later had opened a breach. This was the moment that the Rajah of Banpur chose to show his hand, closing in to attack the British rear. Leaving the siege guns at their work, Rose detached a force of cavalry, horse artillery, and infantry to meet the threat. At the first shot Rajah's men took to their heels, with Rose in pursuit. On the afternoon of 30 January he put them to flight again.

- Rose relieved Saugur on 3 February amid scenes of jubilation. Next, he took the fortress of Garrakota, 40 kilometres (25 miles) to the east, because it lay on the flank of Rose's intended line of march. Forty years earlier a British force far larger than Rose's had failed to capture it and since then it had been strengthened with outlying earthworks. For all that, the rebels weren't much interested in fighting. After being worsted in an artillery exchange, they abandoned the fortress on the night of 11 February.

Everything was going according to plan for the Central India Field Force. Rose was all set to continue his advance into the state of Jhansi, considered to be the centre of rebel activity in Central India, but had to bide his time until a column under Brigadier General George Whitlock arrived in support – which it did at a leisurely pace. Rose was incandescent with rage, but used the time to collect adequate supplies and transport. The rebels also put the delay to good use, fortifying two passes through a range of hills, both of which led into Jhansi. Rose feinted towards one and attacked the other. The attack failed, but succeeded the second time. The rebels hastily abandoned both passes and every fortified place between them and the city of Jhansi save for the fort at Chanderi, which the 1st Brigade took after a four-day siege.

Action in Jhansi

When he had reached a point some 22 kilometres (14 miles) from Jhansi, Rose received orders to go to the assistance of the loyal Rajah of Charkheri, whom Tantia Topi was besieging. As Charkheri lay 130 kilometres (80 miles) off his route, Rose doubted whether he could get there in time. He also believed that the capture of Jhansi would cut the heart out of rebel activity in Central India and destroy the prestige of its *Rani* (princess), who had done much to incite rebellion across much of the country (see the sidebar, 'The Rani of Jhansi'). Jhansi was heavily fortified and its citadel towered on a granite rock above the city. No fewer than 12,000 men manned its defences and the Rani's formidable presence kept them at their posts. The Rani also asked Tantia Topi to come to her assistance, which he did as soon as he had taken Charkheri.

Rose's siege guns opened fire on Jhansi on 25 March. Five days later a huge bonfire in the distance signalled the approach of Tantia Topi's army, consisting of 22,000 men and 28 guns. The position of the tiny Central India Field Force could now be said to be somewhere between a rock and a hard place. Rose kept his siege guns in action and deployed just 1500 men opposite the two fords of the river Betwa that he knew Tantia Topi would have to use. By means of a feigned withdrawal he drew the rebel advance guard across the river during the afternoon and evening of 31 March.

Rose intended attacking at first light, but when the rebels themselves advanced to the attack covered by the fire of their many guns, he ordered his infantry to take cover. Then, at the critical moment, he ordered his whole line to charge. This was the last thing that the rebels expected. Taken aback, they broke at the first shock and the British bundled them back across the river, in which many of them drowned. In an effort to halt the pursuit, Tantia Topi set fire to the tinder-dry underbrush and made a disorderly retreat amid clouds of acrid smoke. The Battle of the Betwa cost him 1500 killed, an unknown number of wounded, and all his artillery. British losses came to 19 killed and 66 wounded.

The Rani of Jhansi

Jhansi became one of the Honourable East India Company's dependent princely states in 1817. When the Rajah died without issue in 1853, his Rani, 30-year-old Lakshmi Bai, requested that the succession should pass to her adopted son. That was not permissible under the law of lapse and the Company annexed the state. Despite its having granted her a handsome pension, the Rani remained bitter towards the Company and the British in general. When the 12th Bengal Native Infantry and the 14th Irregular Cavalry mutinied at Jhansi, she provided charismatic leadership for them and indeed every disaffected element across Central India. Reportedly she reneged on a safe conduct granted to the Jhansi garrison's British officers and their families, who were savagely massacred days after the mutiny, and mutilated her male prisoners, but no proof of either allegation exists. Many officers serving with the Central India Field Force had a high regard for her. The fact that she dressed and fought like one of her own cavalry troopers added to her glamorous image.

Morale inside Jhansi collapsed. The British breached its walls on 3 April. Three days of street fighting followed and Rose's men showed the garrison no mercy. The Rani managed to escape, accompanied by a small escort.

Rose had incurred 343 casualties in the siege of Jhansi and his men were in serious need of rest. Reinforcements were now reaching India in large numbers and the arrival of several companies of the Highland Light Infantry made good his losses. On 25 April Rose began the 165-kilometre (103-mile) march on Kalpi, where the rebels had concentrated. The new arrivals must have found the march a horrific experience, for they made the first part of it through semi-desert with wells 13 kilometres (8 miles) to 16 kilometres (10 miles) apart in temperatures well in excess of 100 degrees.

Fighting in Kalpi

In Kalpi the Rao Sahib, nephew of the Nana Sahib, and the Nawab of Banda had sided with the Rani and Tantia Topi. The rebels undertook serious training, established a large supply depot, and their leaders agreed to engage the Central India Field Force at Kunch, 67 kilometres (42 miles) to the south. They would force Rose to fight with the desert at his back and believed that his defeat would spell complete disaster for the Central India Field Force.

Tantia Topi established a strong position to the south of the town, in an area consisting of temples, woods, and gardens presenting difficulties to an attacker. Unfortunately for the rebels, Rose had no intention of dancing to their tune. Having examined their position carefully, he decided that they were concentrating too much of their strength in the centre. His brigades made 22-kilometre (14-mile) approach marches under cover of darkness and at first light on 7 May fell on both enemy flanks. An hour's fighting so unsettled the rebels in the centre that they began to retreat along the road to Kalpi. A mutinied regiment that remained perfectly steady, firing and retiring by sections in accordance with its training, covered this retreat. It evoked respect, but a charge by the 14th Light Dragoons rode over it, then destroyed an attempt to form a new rearguard. The rebel army degenerated into a running mob, abandoned its guns, and was pursued by the British for 11 kilometres (7 miles). Over 600 rebels were killed and many more wounded at Kalpi. The British loss came to 62 killed and wounded, but Rose was compelled to grant his men 24 hours' rest in which to recover. He had himself fallen from his horse four times during the day as a result of heat exhaustion.

The British march in pursuit from Kunch to Kalpi was even worse than that from Jahnsi to Kunch (see the previous section). At one time half the 25th Bombay Native Infantry had fallen out, so you can imagine what the newly arrived British troops, less used to Indian temperatures, went through.

Luckily, reinforcements arrived with a column operating on the opposite side of the Jumna river, including the 88th (1/The Connaught Rangers) and a Camel Corps consisting of 200 men of the Rifle Brigade and 100 Sikh policemen.

The Rao Sahib laid out the defences of Kalpi to the south of the town. They consisted of five lines of trenches providing a defence in depth based on a series of ravines running down to the Jumna. Rao Sahib calculated, correctly, that the Central India Field Force simply could not afford the number of casualties that it would incur in fighting its way through the complex. Having got this right, he got it wrong by throwing away his advantage and attacking the British lines at 10 a.m. on 22 May, believing that his opponents would be laid low by the noon heat. They weren't, but the rebels pressed their attack so hard that they came within 18 metres (20 yards) of the guns. At this point Rose brought up 150 men of the Camel Corps. They dismounted behind a ridge and the General led them in a bayonet charge down the forward slope. The enemy gave way immediately, and although Rao Sahib mounted further attacks during the day, they were not pressed. Next morning, the British found that the mutineers had abandoned the town and its arsenal during the night.

Ending the mutiny at Gwalior

As the Central India Field Force had taken its final designated objective, Sir Colin Campbell decided to break it up. In what he intended – prematurely – to be a farewell speech, Rose summarised its achievements. These included:

- ✓ Capturing over 100 guns
- ✓ Marching 1600 kilometres (1000 miles)
- ✓ Regularly beating an enemy who outnumbered it many times
- ✓ Restoring law and order across a huge area
- ✓ Taking several fortresses
- ✓ Tramping through deserts and jungles

Hardly had the force begun to disperse than it was recalled. The loyal Mahrajah of Gwalior had had to flee when his army mutinied and joined the rebels whom the British had recently defeated at Kalpi. Tantia Topi was in command of the new rebel army – which says more about the shortage of suitable candidates than it does about his CV as a general. Sir Colin Campbell reacted quickly and despatched three converging columns into the area, including the Central India Field Force.

Movement took place at night due to thermometer-bursting temperatures. On 16 June Rose ejected the rebels from the Morar Cantonments, 8 kilometres (5 miles) east of Gwalior city. The following day the approach of a second column under Brigadier General M.W. Smith resulted in a cavalry combat at Kotah-ki-serai. During this a trooper of the 8th Hussars shot one of his opponents, little realising that he had inflicted a mortal wound on the Rani of Jhansi (see the section 'Action in Jhansi', earlier in this chapter, for more on her). The rebels never recovered from her loss. On 19 June Rose took some dominant ground overlooking Gwalior. Below them, the mutineers were visible in full flight, flinging away their weapons as they ran. Rose sent his cavalry and the 2nd Brigade in pursuit, now under the command of Brigadier General Robert Napier. They caught up with Tantia Topi, who had managed to rally 4000 men, at Jawra Alipur on 22 June. When Napier's cavalry, just 560 strong, bore down on the rebels in a dashing charge, the rebels took to their heels, abandoning 25 guns and everything else.

The Indian Mutiny was all but over. The surviving mutineers fragmented into armed gangs. Their demands lost them the support of local people and they were hunted down until, by the middle of 1859, the entire subcontinent was pacified:

- ✔ **Tantia Topi** (whose real names were several and too many to recount) fled into Rajputana after his defeat at Jawra Alipur and sought refuge with an old chum, the Rajah of Nawar. The Rajah had once been actively anti-British, but seeing the way the wind was now blowing he decided to earn himself some brownie points by handing him over. Tantia Topi went to the gallows on 18 April 1859.

- ✔ **The Rao Sahib** pretended to be a religious ascetic living in the jungles of the Punjab, but in 1862 he too was betrayed, tried, and hanged.

- ✔ **The Nana Sahib** was said to have sought refuge in Nepal, where he died in October 1858, but people claiming to be him made regular appearances for many years to come.

Waving Goodbye to John Company, 1860

Following the Great Mutiny the governance of India passed from the Honourable East India Company (popularly known as John Company) to the British Crown.

The Company's European regiments became Queen's regiments without the permission of their members. Normally, the men would have expected to receive their discharge from the Company's service, then re-engage into the Queen's service and receive a bounty. The change denied them this prize and they became undisciplined and insubordinate. At length, the government agreed to grant them a discharge and a free passage home. As over 10,000 of the 15,000 Europeans accepted the offer, this cost rather more than payment of re-enlistment bounties would have done in the first place. Both sides almost certainly ignored the proviso that on discharge the men were not permitted to re-enlist. The result was that in 1860 all the Company's artillery batteries transferred to the Royal Artillery. Three cavalry regiments became the 19th and 20th Light Dragoons (later Hussars) and the 21st Light Dragoons (later Lancers). A number of infantry regiments also transferred to the Army List at the same time, becoming the Royal Munster Fusiliers, the Royal Dublin Fusiliers, and the second battalions of several other regiments.

Because, or perhaps in spite of, the fact that they had spilled so much bad blood, the post-mutiny relationship that developed between the British and their Indian subjects was a good one that lasted for the remaining 90 years of the Raj. A shortage certainly never occurred in volunteers for the Indian army that fought in so many wars for the Queen Empress and then the King Emperors.

Chapter 15

Home and Away: Reorganisation, Re-Equipment, and More Trouble in India

The final 40 years of the nineteenth century were a period of constant change – political, social, and technical. The boundaries of the British Empire extended at an unprecedented rate, almost by accident, and the British army was almost continuously employed somewhere in the world. This chapter examines the nature of the changes that the army had to absorb as well as the nature of warfare in Afghanistan and on the North West Frontier of India.

In the mid and late nineteenth century, the British army were fully equipped with rifles rather than muskets (rifles being preferable due to their *rifling* – grooves in the barrel, which sent the bullet spinning with more accuracy than smoothbore muskets). For more on weapons, see the section 'Shootin' Fastest And Bestest'. At home and for some foreign campaigns, the British army still wore their traditional red coats, but dull-toned khaki uniforms were introduced for some regiments in India.

Addressing Matters Close to Home

Although France had been Great Britain's principal ally during the Crimean War (see Chapter 13), the British didn't trust the French and it didn't help that their ruler, Napoleon III, was a dodgy character who not only liked to fight wars but was an international wheeler and dealer – he'd somehow managed to inflict an Austrian Archduke on the Mexicans as their Emperor, without their permission!

Alarmingly, the French Navy had begun building excellent ironclad warships, forcing the Royal Navy to follow suit. The question was, why did the French want these warships? The answer seemed to be for an invasion of England. One result of this development was that the British built numerous modern forts in Portsmouth and other naval bases, many of which remain to this day. Another result of French actions was the volunteer movement. All over Britain regiments formed from volunteers anxious to play a part in the defence of their country. In the towns and cities rifle units were very popular, and many of these chose to dress themselves in grey uniforms. In the country, the yeomanry was joined by freshly raised regiments, many wearing odd uniforms of their own design that may have included a hussar jacket and a dragoon helmet. Some units had a rich patron who supplied everything that was needed at his own expense, while in others the volunteers made a financial contribution. The government provided musketry training for potential instructors, while retired senior non-commissioned officers suddenly found themselves hired to knock the new recruits into shape. In the event no invasion happened, but the units remained in being for possible use in a national emergency.

Other events changed the overall look and structure of the British army at this time, as outlined in the following sections.

Shootin' fastest and bestest

The birth of industrialised warfare began with two inventions:

- The drawn brass cartridge case activated by a firing pin or percussion hammer
- Efficient breech-closing mechanisms

As the bullet itself was pinched into the head of the cartridge case, this meant that the rate of fire of a unit equipped with breech-loading rifles was many times that of a unit armed with muzzle-loaders. In the British Army the breech-loading Snider replaced the Enfield rifle in 1866. In 1871 the Martini-Henry, the first hammerless rifle, followed, then in 1888 came the Lee-Metford, the forerunner of the Lee-Enfield, which served throughout the First and Second World Wars. The last two rifles were equipped with *magazines* capable of holding between eight and ten rounds, enabling an even faster rate of fire to be maintained. They also established the rifle ammunition standard calibre of .303-inch (7.7 millimetres), which lasted until the 1950s. Likewise, revolving chambers and spring magazines increased the firepower of pistols.

It's called a 'machine gun'

Rapid-fire systems, involving several gun barrels firing in succession, were almost as old as gunpowder itself. The problem was that once all the barrels had been fired, the gun needed reloading, so multiple barrels weren't much of an advantage. The first practical application of the idea was by an American of British descent, Dr Richard Gatling, in 1862. Gatling used several barrels that revolved around a central axis when a crank handle was turned. Ammunition was fed from above and each barrel fired in turn. The British Army used the Gatling in a number of campaigns, as did the Royal Navy. Other contemporary systems that the Royal Navy employed afloat and ashore were the Gardner and Nordenfeldt guns, which used barrels positioned side by side and were loaded and fired by the operation of a lever. All three guns were likely to jam at critical moments. Technically, they were really manually operated rapid-fire systems rather than machine guns.

In 1884 the Army adopted its first true machine gun. This was a water-cooled weapon developed by another American, Hiram Maxim. Once the first round was fired the weapon used its own recoil forces to operate the ejection, loading, and firing mechanisms. Belt-fed, the gun fired at the rate of 600 rounds per minute and soon replaced the Gatling, which only produced 200 rounds per minute.

Loading shells front and rear

In 1859 William Armstrong produced a practical breech-loading, rifled gun. The field artillery was equipped with the 12-pounder version of this and the horse artillery with the 9-pounder version. However, strongly conservative elements within the Royal Regiment of Artillery were only too keen to point out the complex process involved in the manufacture of such guns, including the lack of gas-tight breech mechanisms. They also expressed a dislike of the 'new-fangled' idea of rifled gun barrels, despite proof that shots from rifled guns fell within more concentrated areas than those of smooth bores.

The upshot of complaints by conservative gunners was a reversion to muzzle loading in the 1870s, although rifling was retained. By the 1880s better manufacturing techniques produced more powerful guns with secure breeches, so it was back to rifled breech-loaders again. For breech-loaders, the term *quick firing* came into common use during this period, although it actually meant guns that employed one-piece ammunition, incorporating the shell and propellant case, which loaded faster than the older system of loading first the shell and then the bagged charge. Advances in chemical science produced better propellants (some of them smokeless) and more powerful ammunition.

Another area in which the Royal Artillery, not having fought a western enemy since the Crimean War (see Chapter 13), was behind was the acceptance that with longer-range field guns, batteries no longer needed to take their place in the line beside the infantry. Provided that their fire could be controlled, batteries could do their work just as well from further back.

Introducing new uniforms

Shortly after the Crimean War a tunic replaced the coatee and a lower shako replaced the Albert Pot. In 1878 a spiked helmet replaced the shako, although in the Royal Field Artillery and specialist corps a ball took the place of the spike. Dragoon and dragoon guard regiments adopted a similar helmet to the Household Cavalry and rifle regiments wore a sealskin cap. Others retained their traditional headdress. This was the army's last home-service full dress uniform, which continued to be worn until 1914 when khaki replaced it, with the exception of the Brigade of Guards' ceremonial uniforms.

Abroad, soldiers wore the scarlet tunic on active service in conjunction with a sun helmet during the Zulu War, the First Boer War, and the early campaigns in Egypt (see Chapter 16). A khaki drill or grey cotton then replaced the scarlet. In post-mutiny India, khaki drill and sun helmet quickly became the norm save for ceremonial occasions.

Mr Cardwell knows best

The sort of army that had done so well under Wellington's command (see Part III) was just not suitable for post-Industrial Revolution Great Britain in the last two quarters of the nineteenth century. Edward Cardwell, Prime Minister Gladstone's Secretary of State for War from 1868 to 1874, was undeniably a good appointment for the army's long-term interests. Cardwell could see exactly what was needed and he set about reforming the army:

✔ **Sorry, your money's no good any more.** One of the things that the Crimean War brought into sharp focus was that the practice of obtaining commissions and promotions by purchase (see Chapter 7) could, from time to time, throw up buffoons like Lords Lucan and Cardigan (see Chapter 13). Obviously, when such people reached high rank they could cause serious problems, and their lordships had actually done so. Strenuous arguments were put forward in defence of the purchase system, but despite these objections Royal Warrant abolished it in 1871.

The Royal Artillery and Royal Engineers lay outside the system and obtained their commissions after passing through the Royal Military Academy at Woolwich. Everyone else, with the exception of medical officers and chaplains, now had to pass the course at Sandhurst. In the event, much the same sort of people came forward as potential officers, although some, including a gentleman cadet named Winston Churchill (British Prime Minister in the Second World War), found difficulty with the exams and got very poor marks.

✔ **Numbers are out, names are in.** In 1881 Cardwell made a radical alteration to the infantry's regimental system. The first 25 line regiments already possessed two battalions, and he now paired off the remainder to form two-battalion regiments, the idea being that while one battalion was serving overseas the other remained at home and provided reinforcements for its partner battalion as required. Many regiments resented the loss of their old numbers and individuality. Some regiments disliked each other so heartily that they fought on sight and could not be posted to the same garrison, let alone amalgamated. Others found their enforced 'marriages' difficult and took time to settle down together.

Regiments already had county names that were largely ignored. Now they received county titles instead of numbers and the specified counties became their home and recruiting ground. This was a shrewd move on Cardwell's part, taking account of the fact that men fight better accompanied by their friends, neighbours, and kindred, among whom they have to live afterwards. Militia and volunteer battalions were also allocated to their respective county regiments. The system was a good one that developed regimental spirit even further. It served well throughout two world wars and beyond.

✔ **You don't know you're born, lad!** Until 1847 men joined the army for 21 years or until they were considered too old or decrepit for further use. After 1847, the term of engagement for the infantry was 10 years and 12 years for other arms. This failed to produce a trained reserve to call on in wartime. Under Cardwell, the basic term remained 12 years, but it was divided into six years *with the Colours* (actually in the army) and six with the reserve, later changed to seven and five. This not only encouraged recruiting among men less willing to commit themselves to a longer term with the Colours, but also began to build up a substantial Regular Army reserve.

Cardwell also removed some of the harshest aspects of military discipline. In 1868 he abolished flogging in peacetime, and the punishment was discontinued altogether in 1900. Curiously, it remained a civil punishment until after the Second World War. Tattooing or branding the face with a red-hot iron for desertion and other serious crimes was also abolished. In 1878 Cardwell established the Army Pay Department, forerunner of the Royal Army Pay Corps, ensuring soldiers received what was due to them.

Seeing Action on the North West Frontier

No one could pretend that the Indian Mutiny had not happened (see Chapter 14 for full details), no matter how hard British and Indians alike strove to restore a working relationship. The important thing was to ensure that such a mutiny did not happen again, and that could only be done by taking precautions. The proportion of British to Indian troops was increased, usually to one battalion in each Indian infantry brigade. With the exception of mountain batteries, artillery remained in British hands and the squadrons within each cavalry regiment came from different races or religions.

Usually there were no more than a dozen British officers in each Indian regiment. Whereas formerly these officers were Honourable East India Company appointments, now they passed through Sandhurst and served with a British regiment in India before they were invited to stay for a time with the Indian regiment of their choice. They were assessed for suitability and if their application was approved they were transferred to that regiment and required to pass an examination in Urdu, the language of the Indian Army. They also spent a great deal of time learning about the regiment, its personalities, and the way it operated in the company of its *Viceroy's Commissioned Officers* (VCOs), who were highly respected Indian officers of great experience who had their own officers' mess. The status of the VCOs (the Viceroy was the senior representative of the Crown in India) lay approximately between that of British warrant and commissioned officers.

Following the Mutiny, no fighting happened in India itself, but lots could be had on the North West Frontier. The North West Frontier was a school for soldiers and generals alike right up to Indian Independence (see Chapter 25). There, the tribes regarded fighting as fun, especially if it involved a blood feud or two and, better still, the British. Amid these wild mountains, ambush, treachery, and torture combined oddly with an unbreakable code of hospitality, but the situation kept everyone on their toes. The tribes were numerous and their members gave trouble at the drop of a hat. Serious provocation such as the murder of a British official, raids on civil communities, or attempts to levy duty on the tribes' own account could mean the British mounting a punitive expedition.

Penetrating tribal territory was dangerous for the unwary and the dissidents always seemed to know at once when a regiment was new to the Frontier. The old hands protected their route by placing strong picquets on the high ground on either side of the route until the column had passed.

Then, covered by shellfire from the column's guns, the picquets were called down before the enemy overran them. Despite this, an enemy who was adept at concealment and an above-average shot could still inflict casualties. Mounted officers were obvious and prominent targets. A crack was heard, a puff of smoke rose among the rocks, and then, as the poet Kipling put it, 'ten thousand pounds of education went rolling in the dust' (see the sidebar 'Mr Kipling writes exceedingly good poems' for more on him). When a British force reached the tribal heartland, it burned villages and their watchtowers until the tribe decided to submit. The elders arrived and a *jirga* (conference) was held with the column commanders, deciding what reparations the tribe was to make. The elders promised to be good, and the troops marched off, being sniped at regularly along the way. Then, a year or two later, the whole process was repeated.

Mr Kipling writes exceedingly good poems

Rudyard Kipling (1865–1936) was born in India but educated in England. He returned to India in 1882 and worked as a journalist there until 1889. Anglo-Indian society was hierarchical and Kipling's profession placed him quite low in the pecking order, enabling him to socialise with other British ranks in a manner that would otherwise have raised eyebrows. Most private soldiers were men in their early 20s who conducted their conversation, heavily larded with oaths, in a mixture of English and Urdu. In India, the soldiers Kipling talked to came from the East Surrey Regiment and the Northumberland Fusiliers, who were in garrison together at Mian Mir, but it is also clear from Kipling's poems that he spoke to the gunners of a mountain battery. He also came into contact with soldiers when he returned to London, and in South Africa, which he visited during the Second Boer War.

In Kipling's *Barrack Room Ballads* we hear the authentic voice of the soldier, which is not so very different today. *Tommy,* one of his most famous poems, tells of the soldier's hurt when civilians at home look down on him, and his contempt for those same cheering civilians who wave him off to war.

Not even the staunchest anti-imperialist would dream of accusing Kipling of racism. His poems *Gunga Din* (about a regimental *bhisti* or water carrier) and *Fuzzy Wuzzy* (about the Hadendowa tribesmen of the Eastern Sudan who wore their hair in a huge fuzzy afro) are works of genuine admiration as expressed by the men in the ranks.

Kipling lived through the high noon of the British Empire. Queen Victoria's Diamond Jubilee in 1897 marked its zenith. Shrewd observer of human affairs that Kipling was, he knew that empires do not last and his poem *Recessional*, written specially for the Jubilee, reflects this.

The Second Afghan War, 1878–1880

When Sher Ali came to power in Afghanistan in 1863, he immediately became involved in a dynastic struggle with his nephew, Abdur Rahman. When Sher Ali began to get the worst of things he opened negotiations with the Russian Tsar's representatives, ignoring British warnings that they regarded such a course of action as a hostile act (remember that Britain and Russia were engaged in the Great Game at this time – see Chapter 12 for more).

Three British columns crossed the frontier immediately. In the south, General Sir Donald Stewart's Kandahar field force entered Kandahar unopposed in January 1879. In the centre, Major General Frederick Roberts's Kurram field force marched from Kohat over the Peiwar Kotal, outflanking its defenders and forcing them to retire after a brisk action on 2 December 1878. In the north, the Peshawar Valley field force, under the command of the one-armed Lieutenant General Sir Sam Browne – the inventor of the cross-belt that still bears his name – marched on Jellalabad through the Khyber Pass. On 21 November 1878 the force made an unsuccessful attack on the fort at Ali Musjid, which the Afghans abandoned during the night. Sher Ali fled north and died at Mazar-i-Sharif in February 1879.

Defending the Kabul Residency

Sher Ali's son Yakub Khan, acting as Regent, accepted a treaty under the terms of which a British *Resident* with wide-ranging powers, including control of Afghanistan's foreign policy, was installed at Kabul, in exchange for a £60,000 subsidy. If this seemed like a reasonable solution to a little local difficulty, in reality it was like throwing a lighted match into a barrel of gunpowder.

The British Resident, Sir Louis Cavagnari, reached Kabul on 24 July 1879, accompanied by a small personal staff and an escort of 25 cavalrymen and 50 infantry drawn from the Corps of Guides, under the command of Lieutenant Walter Hamilton, VC. For a while, all remained quiet despite the sullen atmosphere prevailing in the capital. Then, at the end of August, several Afghan regiments from Heart province marched in on a routine exchange of postings (remember that Afghanistan had its own army, which was not under British control). Their pay was seriously in arrears and they were in a foul mood, beyond their officers' control. They began by jeering at the Kabuli regiments that Roberts had defeated at Peiwar Kotal. Then they received some wages, but it was only a fraction of what they were owed. That blew their collective fuse. Someone shouted that the British had plenty of money, so the Afghans charged round to the Residency. Some started looting, but the sentries opened fire and drove them out.

After their initial setback, the Afghans arrived in force, bringing with them their weapons and the city's mob. The building lacked a perimeter wall and was overlooked from several angles, but Hamilton did what was possible to improvise defences. From the fragmentary evidence available, it seems that the Afghans' incessant fire steadily reduced the Guides' numbers and killed Hamilton, Cavagnari, and his staff. The Afghans brought up a cannon to pound the building. The Guides made several sorties out of the Residency, but these won them only temporary relief. By evening the Residency was burning fiercely. All hope gone, the last few men on their feet, led by a Sikh, Jemadar Jewand Singh, charged out into the mob and died fighting. Lying sprawled in every attitude of death all round the Residency were no fewer than 600 Afghan bodies. In the event only seven of the Residency's inhabitants survived the attack. The British Commission of Inquiry set up to examine the incident commented that 'the annals of no army and no regiment can show a brighter record of bravery than has been achieved by this small band of Guides'. The entire escort was awarded the Indian Order of Merit, the Indian Army's supreme award for valour at the time.

Retaking the Kabul Residency

A 7500-strong punitive expedition was sent out in response to the fall of the Kabul Residency (see the previous section). This, commanded by Sir Frederick Roberts, routed an Afghan force of comparable size at Charasia on 6 October 1879 and captured all its artillery.

One point of interest about the battle at Charasia is that it was the first action in which British troops used the heliograph for communication. The *heliograph* was a signalling apparatus that reflected flashes of sunlight from a movable mirror mounted on a tripod, enabling Morse code to be used.

Roberts's expedition occupied Kabul and hanged the ringleaders of the attack on the Residency in front of its ruins. Yakub Khan (ruler of Afghanistan), now seriously frightened, sought British protection and indicated his willingness to abdicate. Roberts's doubts about the Regent's sincerity were fully justified, for Yakub Khan remained in constant contact with anti-British elements among his former subjects. Nevertheless, Roberts agreed that the British troops should spend the winter in the partially fortified Sherpur *cantonment* (a military station) a mile to the northeast of Kabul. Roberts had something of a secret weapon in his armoury, namely a supply of the new *star shells* for his mountain batteries. These burst high above the battlefield like fireworks and produced brilliant balls of light that floated slowly to the ground.

Thousands of Afghans were arriving in Kabul daily, and sniping at the British began. Roberts mounted an unsuccessful sortie from the cantonment on 14 December and, encouraged by this, the enemy isolated the cantonment. Just before dawn on 23 December an enormous crowd of baying Afghans, estimated to number 100,000, surged forward to storm the walls. There was a series of cracks overhead as the artillery's star shells burst. To their astonishment and horror the Afghans found themselves starkly illuminated against the snow. Sustained volley firing ripped through them and high-explosive shells blew gaps in their ranks, but they kept on coming until 10 a.m. An hour later, they came on again but were noticeably less keen. The British shelled the Afghans as they tried to form up again and at 1 p.m. the Afghans began streaming away. Roberts sent out the 9th Lancers, the Guides Cavalry, and the 5th Punjab Cavalry, who chased the Afghans over the horizon. Roberts lost just three men killed and 30 wounded.

Throughout the siege of the Sherpur cantonment, Roberts rode round the perimeter, passing the time of day with the troops and encouraging them. Both he and his mount seemed completely oblivious to the sustained crack of incoming bullets that accompanied them everywhere, so they acquired suitable nicknames – the 'Iron Man on the Wooden Horse'.

Intriguing Afghan politics

After Roberts's victory at Kabul (see the previous section), a new king needed to be appointed. Abdur Rahman was acceptable to the British and to some Afghans. Unfortunately, Yakub's brother Ayub, the governor of Herat, considered that his claim to the throne was a better one. He had a large following in southern Afghanistan and became a natural focus for internal dissent and anti-British feeling. British intelligence sources indicated that Ayub planned to march through the country to Kabul via Kandahar, defeat Abdur Rahman, and assume the crown himself. At the end of May 1880 Ayub was on the point of leaving Herat; as his army had to march 560 kilometres (350 miles) to reach Kandahar, plenty of time appeared to exist to prepare a suitable reception for him. The governor of Kandahar, Sher Ali (not the Sher Ali mentioned earlier in this chapter, but another chap of the same name), decided that a show of force would discourage anyone planning to join the rebels. He marched out of Kandahar with his provincial troops and established a position at Helmund, 130 kilometres (80 miles) to the northwest of Kandahar. From this point, everything started to go wrong:

- ✔ The Afghans didn't like Sher Ali because he cooperated with the British.

- ✔ The local people didn't like having Sher Ali's army quartered on them.

- ✔ Sher Ali's army wasn't really interested in fighting Ayub Khan.

Sher Ali wrote to Lieutenant General P.M. Primrose, who commanded the British troops at Kandahar, requesting assistance. The prevailing opinion in senior political and military circles was that Sher Ali must not be seen to fail through a lack of British support, so on 4 July a column consisting of one infantry and one cavalry brigade, under the overall command of Brigadier General George Burrows, set off to join him.

The Maiwand disaster, 27 July 1880

When Burrows joined Sher Ali on 11 July, the governor's provincial troops were clearly on the point of mutiny, so he disarmed and dispersed them. Unfortunately, Sher Ali's men left behind a battery of smooth-bore guns, having made off with horse teams and cut up the harness. It may have been better to *spike* (disable) the guns and leave them where they were for the moment, but Burrows decided to take them along, forming a Smooth Bore Battery. No horses could be spared for the abandoned ammunition wagons, so an inadequate supply of ammunition was carried in the column's transport.

Burrows's orders were to attack Ayub if he felt strong enough. However, the orders also specifically stated that the enemy must be prevented 'by all possible means' from reaching Ghazni. As Ghazni lay two-thirds of the way along the road from Kandahar to Kabul, Ayub apparently intended to by-pass Kandahar altogether. This was not the case, but Burrows had to allow for it and based his subsequent moves on this assumption. The local people saw his actions as a retreat and went off to join Ayub in large numbers. Ayub's army contained no fewer than 10 Kabuli and Herati infantry regiments, plus 4000 cavalry and 36 guns, of which three were breech-loading 14-pounder Armstrongs, far more powerful than anything that Burrows possessed. This gave Ayub a basic strength of about 25,000 men, but additions may have increased the total to 35,000.

Ayub's army included a large number of *ghazis*, the nineteenth-century equivalents of the modern suicide bomber. Dressed in white robes to signify their ritual purification, they charged heedless of wounds, wielding wickedly curved knives. Ghazis were very difficult to stop and terrifying to those who had never experienced such an attack before.

By 23 July the opposing cavalry screens were in contact. Ayub was heading for the town of Maiwand. From there he could go either to Kandahar or Ghazni. Burrows delayed issuing orders for two days, and then decided to block Ayub's path by establishing a position along a dry ravine between the hamlets of Khig and Mundabad. Burrows set his troops in motion towards this ravine early on the morning of 27 July. Many of the men went without breakfast and others did not have the chance to fill their water bottles on what promised to be a scorching day.

At about 10.30 a.m. dense clouds of dust were seen approaching from the north. If Burrows had stuck to his original plan his force may have had some chance of survival. As it was, having witnessed the delaying action being fought by his artillery and cavalry on the dusty plain to the north of the ravine, he rashly allowed the rest of his force to be drawn into that struggle:

- **Enveloped on both flanks, Burrows's troops became the target of the Afghan infantry and artillery, which were deployed in a half-circle around the British.** Burrows's regiments fought back hard and inflicted losses.

- **By 1.30 p.m., the Smooth Bore Battery had expended its limited ammunition.** When it limbered up to return to the reserve ammunition area to replenish, the inexperienced 30th Bombay Native Infantry (Jacob's Rifles) thought that the artillery was about to pull out. Their officers only just held the Rifles in place.

- **By 2 p.m. one third of the 1st Bombay Native Infantry (Grenadiers) were down, as were one fifth of the Rifles.** The Rifles were commanded by a *jemadar* (the Indian equivalent of a lieutenant) after a roundshot killed their only British officer. The 66th (2/Royal Berkshire Regiment), secure in a dry watercourse, was as yet hardly touched, but both artillery batteries had lost a quarter of their strength.

- **Shortly after 2.30 p.m. Ayub launched a mass attack.** The combined British fire tore the Afghans apart and for a moment the enemy seemed to be on the verge of collapse. Then, on the left, two companies of the Rifles, shaken by the sight of the onrushing ghazis, broke and bolted into the ranks of the neighbouring Grenadiers, breaking their formation. Within seconds, the Afghans had closed in, hacking and stabbing. Two guns were lost but the British brought the rest out with great difficulty. Nuttall (leading the cavalry) ordered a charge, but at the critical moment Nuttall himself swerved away to the right. Most of his troopers followed him. Later, he claimed that he was trying to clear his brigade's front. As it was, his regiments galloped away to Mundabad and nothing persuaded them to return to the field.

- **Covered by the 66th, the broken Rifles and Grenadiers fled to Mundabad.** The 66th, perfectly steady amid the chaos and carnage, retired to the ravine. Crossing this obstacle, the regiment became split into two parts:

  - One part continued to cover the general withdrawal through Mundabad.

  - The other part, about 130 strong and including the Colour party, became involved in a one-sided fight among the mud-walled gardens of Khig. The Colours passed from hand to hand as their bearers were killed in turn, until finally no one was left to take them. Of that portion of the 66th, only two officers and nine men were still on their feet. Recognising that recovering the Colours was now impossible, they fought their way clear but Afghan cavalry surrounded them. The British died fighting back to back in a tight little knot. Weeks later, dead horses still ringed the spot.

If the victorious Afghans had not paused to loot the baggage, it is unlikely that any of Burrows's men would have survived. In the event, the British faced a night of being sniped at and thirst-tortured marching from well to well. Some of Nuttall's troops reached Kandahar during the early hours of the morning. Primrose sent out a relief force, and the provision of water did much to restore discipline. By mid-afternoon on 28 July, after 33 hours of marching and fighting, much of the time without food or water, the last British survivors trudged through the gates of Kandahar.

Of the 2565 men who fought at Maiwand, 962 were killed, including a party of 150 Rifles and Grenadiers who lost their way during the retreat and were massacred. Only 161 of the wounded survived the battle and the horrors of the retreat. Seven guns were lost or abandoned and over 2000 horses and transport animals were killed or captured. It took Ayub a week to clear the field of his own dead, including 1500 of his regulars and between 3000 and 4000 ghazis. When he did resume his advance on Kandahar, he had to leave 1500 of his more seriously wounded behind in Maiwand.

Marching from Kabul to Kandahar

In Kandahar, General Primrose immediately sent a signal to the Commander-in-Chief India, General Sir Frederick Haines, informing him of the Maiwand disaster, and put the city into a defensible condition. At Haines's suggestion, Lieutenant General Sir Donald Stewart, now commanding the British troops in Kabul, quickly organised a flying column under Roberts (see the section 'Retaking the Kabul Residency', earlier in this chapter), recently knighted and promoted, giving him the pick of the troops that were present. Roberts's mission was to relieve Kandahar as quickly as possible. The column consisted of one cavalry and three infantry brigades, three British and one Indian mountain batteries. It had to march 500 kilometres (313 miles) over terrain that included mountains and deserts, and it had to travel light.

The logistic planning for the march to Kandahar was a triumph. All transport consisted of pack animals. British officers were allowed only one mule each for their personal effects, and British soldiers were permitted 11 kilograms (24 pounds) of baggage per man, Indian soldiers 9 kilograms (20 pounds). Infantrymen each carried 70 rounds of ammunition, with a further 30 rounds per man in regimental reserve and 100 rounds in the Ordnance Field Park. The mountain batteries each had 540 rounds of ready-use ammunition, with a further 30 rounds per gun in reserve. Each company was allocated one mule to carry the arms of sick or wounded men. As no wheeled transport was permitted, special provision was made for the field hospital, including 2192 bearers, 115 *doolies* (litters to be carried on the shoulders), 286 ponies, 43 donkeys, 3 bullocks, and 6 camels. The column's pack animals included 2740 horses and ponies, 4511 mules, and 912 donkeys. The troops carried basic marching rations, but the commissaries bought livestock for slaughter, grain, and firewood from local sources along the way.

The march was not comfortable. At noon temperatures were scorching, but at night they dropped nearly to freezing point. The torment of sandstorms added to the choking dust kicked up by thousands of animals. The troops had to cross long stretches of the desert without water. Along the way, the garrison of Kalat-I-Ghilzai, including two detached companies of the 66th, reinforced the column. The British established heliograph contact with the Kandahar garrison on 27 August. Ayub abandoned the siege and withdrew to a low ridge 6.5 kilometres (4 miles) northwest of the city. Four days later, led by the pipers of the 72nd and 92nd Highlanders (respectively 1/The Seaforth Highlanders and 2/The Gordon Highlanders), the British column marched into Kandahar. It had marched the 500 kilometres (313 miles) in just 21 days, including one rest day, a truly remarkable feat for any army.

Roberts now commanded two infantry divisions, two cavalry brigades, and six artillery batteries, a total of 14,000 men and 36 guns, including two big 40-pounders. He had no intention of letting Ayub rest and the following morning led out his troops to do battle. Ayub's strength had dropped to 5000 regulars, about 10,000 ghazis and irregulars, and 32 guns. His men resisted the British attack to the best of their ability, but as the old saying had it, an Afghan attacked was far less formidable than an Afghan attacking. The British drove Ayub's men off their position, and the Afghans abandoned their camp and all their artillery, including the two guns belong the E/B Battery taken at Maiwand. The 3rd Bombay Light Cavalry and the 3rd Scind Horse also had their revenge for Maiwand, cutting down 350 of the fugitives as they ran. In total, Ayub lost about 1200 killed and wounded. Roberts's losses amounted to 35 killed and 213 wounded.

Ayub no longer presented a threat. Abdur Rahman was steadily bringing the rest of the country under his control and was clearly a man with whom the British could do business. He agreed to eliminate the Russian influence in Afghanistan in return for the British not forcing a Resident on him. As it happened, the Russians were just as unpopular as the British, so the decision involved no great hardship for the Afghans. The Second Afghan War had run its course.

The Great Frontier Rising, 1897–1898

In 1897 the tribal areas of the North West Frontier were abuzz with rumours. The rumours started because the previous year Greece and Turkey had gone to war. The Turks had won and massacred some of their opponents. Great Britain had protested formally and that annoyed the Sultan. As the Sultan was a very important figure in the Muslim world, the protest also annoyed the frontier mullahs, notably Sayid Akbar (known as the Mad Mullah of Swat), and the Haddah Mullah in the country of the Mohmands. This was a wonderful time, they said, to drive the infidels from their land, and by that they meant Hindus as well as Christians.

The rising began on 10 June with an attack by the Wazirs of the Tochi valley on a small British force escorting a political agent. It spread rapidly from tribe to tribe over an area 320 kilometres (200 miles) in length. To bring the rising under control took more than 60 infantry battalions (twice the infantry strength of the modern British army), supported by cavalry, artillery, and engineers, over a period of eight months.

The British were armed with the Lee-Metford magazine rifle, capable of a higher rate of fire than the tribesmen were used to. The Lee-Metford fired the soft-nosed *Dum-Dum* bullet, named after the arsenal near Calcutta where it was manufactured. The bullet spread on impact, delivering a terrific blow. Whereas ghazis had often kept coming when hit by earlier types of ammunition, the Dum-Dum bowled them over and they didn't get up. The Maxim machine gun also simply kept firing (see the section 'It's called a machine gun' earlier in this chapter for more on Maxims), providing a fresh addition to the fire fight.

The principal operations involved in suppressing the rising were as follows:

✔ **The Tochi field force.** This force, under the command of Major General G. Corrie Bird, occupied the Tochi valley until January 1898. The force destroyed Maizar, the village where the attack that set off the uprising took place (see the start of this section).

✔ **The Malakand field force.** The rebels attacked the posts of Malakand and Chakdara in the Swat valley several times at the end of July and the beginning of August 1897. The rebels admitted losing a total of 3700 men in these attacks. For the loss of 5 killed and 10 wounded, 60 men of the 11th Bengal Lancers and 180 men of the 45th Sikhs inflicted 2000 of the rebel losses. A punitive expedition, consisting of three brigades under Brigadier General Sir Bindon Blood, took the field immediately and was involved in heavy fighting until October. Blood then formed the Buner Field Force from many of the same units and engaged in subduing the Bunerwals until the middle of January 1898.

✔ **The Mohmand field force.** The Mohmands attacked a police post at Shabkadr Fort on 7 August 1897. The Peshawar Movable Column relieved the fort two days later. The Mohmand Field Force formed under Brigadier General E.R. Ellis on 15 September and operated until the beginning of October, imposing fines on the rebels. At Samana Ridge on 12 September, thousands of Orakzai and Afridi tribesmen attacked a signal station held by a detachment of 21 men of the 36th Sikhs. The garrison survived for several hours, but its ammunition ran out and the rebels brought down a section of wall, enabling them to swarm inside. Even when the post was burning fiercely, the Sikh survivors refused to surrender and died fighting. The nearby Forts Gulistan and Lockhart were relieved after a day's fighting by troops under the command of Brigadier General A.G. Yeatman-Briggs.

✔ **The Tirah field force.** The British decided that the Orakzais and Afridis must be punished by invading their homeland in the Tirah. This was no easy matter, as together the two tribes were capable of producing some 50,000 warriors. The British therefore required a much larger than usual force for the task. The Tirah Field Force, under the command of Lieutenant General Sir William Lockhart, contained two divisions and supporting formations, producing a total of 35,000 troops and 20,000 followers. Its advance commenced in early October 1897. On 20 October the 1/The Gordon Highlanders and 1/2nd Gurkhas stormed the precipitous Dargai Heights, lying across the axis of advance. During this attack, one of the most famous episodes of the Victorian era, Piper George Findlater of the Gordons, though shot through both ankles, propped himself against a rock and continued to play as his regiment fought its way upwards, earning himself the award of the Victoria Cross.

Regular skirmishing marked the force's further advance, but by December the Orakzai were willing to submit. The Zakha Kell Afridis, were not, and the British had to make a further advance into the Bazar valley in January 1898. Following a stiff fight at the Shin Kamar Pass, the Afridis agreed to submit, and this brought the Frontier rebellion to a close. During its existence, the Tirah field force sustained the loss of 287 killed, 853 wounded, and 10 missing.

Chapter 16

Boots, Boots, Boots, Boots: Marchin' Over Africa

With the exception of South Africa, which lay on the sea route to the Far East, for the first half of the nineteenth century the remainder of Africa lacked the political and military importance that India enjoyed. That changed as the newly industrialised nations sought markets for their goods throughout the world and their populations emigrated in search of a better life. Then some of the major European powers, keen to enhance their prestige, began to found colonies of their own.

Great Britain was forced to react and absorb the remaining areas of Africa into its Empire. Some areas were of little or no financial benefit and Britain acquired them simply to stop other people getting their hands on territory that could be developed in such a way as to threaten British interests. Inevitably, friction occurred with the indigenous population, and in the Sudan a form of violent Islamic fundamentalism exacerbated the problems. Equally, in such a vast area as Africa many small conflicts existed that have long been forgotten. Some were attempts to drive out the newcomers, some were police actions, and some arose from colonists' attempts to improve their position. Too many of these happened to record them in detail, so this chapter deals with the major military events, of which there were more than enough.

Some campaigns saw the army kitted out in dull grey or brown khaki uniforms, but at other times they wore their traditional red coats; helmets were now worn by most troops, as shown in Figure 16-1.

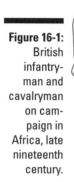

Figure 16-1:
British infantry-man and cavalryman on campaign in Africa, late nineteenth century.

Rescuing Hostages in Abyssinia, 1868

In the 1860s Abyssinia was a Christian country ruled over by King Theodore III, a not-so-modest chap who liked to be called 'King of Kings' and the 'Chosen of God'; his ambition was to wage a successful war against his Muslim neighbours. Theodore wrote a friendly personal note to Queen Victoria asking for her support. The Foreign Office failed to pass it on to Her Majesty. When Theodore didn't get a reply he took it that the queen had deliberately snubbed him and he became very angry. The last straw came in January 1864 when the British Consul, Captain Charles Cameron, crossed the frontier from Abyssinia to visit Kassala in the Sudan; Theodore saw this as an Anglo-Muslim plot to overthrow him. He promptly imprisoned Cameron on the Consul's return, along with his staff, their wives, missionaries, and anyone else who seemed slightly involved, and kept them in chains.

When diplomatic pressure for the captives' release failed, force had to be used. But two problems existed:

✔ Abyssinia did not have a coastline. Nevertheless, the Egyptians permitted the British to use their harbour at Zula on the Red Sea, which solved that problem.

✔ The Abyssinian terrain itself, which consisted of towering mountain ranges, rushing torrents, and few tracks considered usable for a modern army. In fact, the British had to traverse almost 650 kiloometres (400 miles) of this sort of going to reach Theodore's capital, Magdala, at an altitude of 2750 metres (9000 feet) above sea level.

The task fell to the Bombay army, under its Commander-in-Chief, General Sir Robert Napier. Over 4000 British and 9000 Indian troops were involved, plus a naval brigade armed with rockets. Napier was by training a military engineer and, appreciating the physical difficulties, his force included a large contingent of engineer units. Assembling the troops was the easy part, however. Napier also paid particular attention to the logistical aspects of the expedition, incorporating over 26,000 bearers and labourers, 19,580 transport horses and mules, 6045 camels, 7086 bullocks, 1850 donkeys, and 44 elephants.

Landing at Zula in December 1867, the expedition advanced slowly but methodically inland into Abyssinia, sometimes traversing narrow gorges, sometimes moving along narrow tracks above sheer precipices, but always climbing. It soon became apparent that the tribal chiefs along the way did not like Theodore and were happy to cooperate with the British. No opposition arose until the column reached Arogee on 10 April 1868, where Theodore had deployed his army. Theodore had a few guns, which his army had sited badly on hilltops from which they could only deliver a largely useless plunging fire, and about 5000 infantry, of whom half carried firearms of varying vintages. When the Abyssinians launched an attack, the rapid, controlled fire of British infantry, Punjabi pioneers, and the naval brigade's rockets tore through their ranks. Theodore's men fled, having sustained the loss of 700 killed and 1200 wounded. Napier's casualties amounted to 2 killed and 18 wounded.

Theodore handed over the British hostages, but declined to surrender. To relieve his feelings he flung several hundred of his Abyssinian prisoners over a 300-metre (100-foot) cliff. Napier, recognising that the king was completely unbalanced, decided to put an end to the whole business by storming Magdala on 13 April. When his last followers deserted him, Theodore shot himself, using a pistol that Queen Victoria had sent him as a present some years earlier. The expedition's personnel losses from all causes, including disease, came to fewer than 400, of whom only 48 were fatalities. In modern parlance, the battle had cost an arm and a leg, but the prestige it generated was enormous.

The Ashanti War, 1873–1874

Of the many small campaigns fought during Queen Victoria's reign, one of the most interesting and instructive is the Ashanti War of 1873–1874, which took place in the Gold Coast (now Ghana). The Ashanti tribal confederation lost much of its income on the abolition of the slave trade, and was in the habit of demanding tribute, which was nothing more than protection money, and taking hostages in order to ransom them. In 1873 the Ashanti confederation was ruled by King Kofi Karikari. Its raids into British- administered territory near the coast reached such serious proportions that the British decided to mount a punitive expedition under the command of Lieutenant General Sir Garnet Wolseley.

With some justice, this area of Africa was termed the White Man's Grave because of the many tropical diseases endemic there. The British War Office had very serious reservations about committing British troops, but at length it despatched the 23rd (1/Royal Welch Fusiliers), the 42nd (1/The Black Watch), and the Rifle Brigade. For their own sake, Wolseley kept the troops at sea until he was ready to commence the 160-kilometre (100-mile) march to the enemy's capital, Kumasi. In addition, he had available the 1st and 2nd West Indies Regiment, which had an excellent reputation and a higher resistance to disease, two locally raised regiments, and a naval brigade of sailors and marines. Wolseley decided to leave the West Indians and some of the locally raised infantry to guard his line of communication while he advanced with the rest of the men.

The axis of British advance lay along a track that passed through thick tropical rain forest. Wolseley denied the enemy the chance to mount ambushes by having his main column use the track, with subsidiary columns moving parallel to the track through the jungle. The three columns pushed out skirmish lines towards each other. The result was a sort of hollow square with guns or rockets on the main track and at each of the forward corners of the square. The reserve was situated some distance behind and the baggage brought up the rear. Forward progress was slow because of the need for units to keep pace with each other. A major disadvantage was the inability to see far in any direction.

On 31 January 1874 the British encountered the main body of the Ashanti army near a village called Amoaful. The area consisted of tall trees covered and interlaced with creepers and vines, with a dense undergrowth below. At the moment of contact the Black Watch were in the lead, and they fought their way slowly forward against an enemy who contested every small rise and clump. Frequently, the only sight of an opponent was a cloud of powder smoke hanging in the air. As fighting spread round the square, the noise level became deafening. The reason for this was that the Ashanti used huge powder charges in their ancient muskets, which sounded like small cannon when fired. The Ashanti unwittingly fired high, continually showering the Black Watch with branches, leaves, and twigs. After five hours of this, punctuated by British mountain guns banging away, the British reached and took the village. Most of the Ashanti disappeared, but some attempted an attack on the previous night's British camp at Quarman, only for the 2nd West Indies Regiment to beat them off. Estimates put the cost of the day's fighting at between 800 and 1200 Ashantis killed and the same number wounded. Wolseley lost 4 killed and 194 wounded.

Wolseley decided to capitalise on his victory and advance immediately on Kumasi. The local word was that if you were interested in human sacrifice, Kumasi was *the* place to be. When the British reached the capital on 4 February it was completely deserted, but around a big fetish tree several thousand skeletons and decomposing bodies confirmed the place's evil reputation. In King Kofi's palace they found yet more grisly souvenirs. Wolseley blew up the palace, burned down the city, and began his march back to the coast before the rainy season began. On 13 February Kofi came in to surrender, signed a treaty of submission, and paid the British a modest indemnity. By then the British troops were on their way home, and some of them were already showing signs of fever. Unfortunately, two further expeditions (in 1895–1896 and 1900) were necessary before the area was considered fully pacified.

The Zulu War, 1879

Sir Bartle Frere, Great Britain's High Commissioner in South Africa, believed that, sooner or later, the formidable Zulu army would invade the territories for which he was responsible and that the best course of action was to destroy this army as quickly as possible. He was tragically wrong, as the Zulus wished to maintain friendly relations with the British.

King Cetewayo's Zulu army of 40,000 *assegai-* (spear) and shield-armed warriors was the most formidable native army in Africa. Frere not only disregarded the instructions of his own government to maintain peace in South Africa, he also ignored the advice of those who knew the Zulus well. He belonged to that breed of politician who are determined to go to war, however dishonest the cause and whatever the cost to those who fight it. He picked on several minor issues, none of which provided any justification for hostilities, and sent Cetewayo an ultimatum the terms of which he knew were unacceptable.

The British Commander-in-Chief South Africa was Lieutenant General Lord Chelmsford. His limitations as a commander included a lack of imagination, an inability to read a battle beyond the range of his binoculars, and, worst of all, a fatal tendency to underestimate the enemy. The troops he had available included 6000 regulars and colonial volunteers, 9000 native troops raised by levy, 20 field guns, and 10 rocket launchers. His plan was for three columns to penetrate Zululand from Natal and the Transvaal, then converge on Ulundi, Cetewayo's capital, there to destroy the Zulu army. On 6 January 1879 British troops began crossing the Zulu frontier.

The Battle of Isandhlwana, 22 January 1879

Chelmsford and his staff chose to accompany the Central or No 3 Column of the British troops, crossing into Zululand at Rorke's Drift. Colonel Richard Glyn commanded the column, consisting of the 1st and 2nd Battalions of the 24th, N/5 Battery Royal Artillery with six 7-pounder guns, mounted infantry, and local volunteer units, engineers, and two battalions of the Natal Native Contingent, a total of about 4700 men of whom 1852 were Europeans. By 20 January a camp was established at Isandhlwana, the name given to the hill towering over the site. A saddle joined the hill to a ridge named the Nqutu Plateau, to the northeast. To the east was an extensive plain intersected by two *dongas* (watercourses).

Too much of a field-day atmosphere pervaded the camp. A number of Boers, hereditary enemies of the Zulus, were present and the lax British attitude appalled them. Instead of *laagering* or forming a circle with the wagons to provide an immediate defence in the event of the enemy rushing the camp, the British parked the wagons uselessly behind the tents, posted no sentries, and actually withdrew cavalry *vedettes* (mounted sentries) from the Nqutu Plateau.

On 21 January Chelmsford received false information that a Zulu force was a short distance away. He immediately formed a column with Colonel Glyn to confront it, and marched off into the pre-dawn darkness. Remaining in camp were five companies of the 1/24th, one company of the 2/24th, six Natal Native Contingent companies, most of the Natal Mounted Police, and two of N Battery's guns, amounting to 600 British infantry, 600 native infantry, 100 cavalry, and 70 gunners under the overall command of Lieutenant Colonel Henry Pulleine of the 1/24th. Before he left, Chelmsford ordered up reinforcements from Rorke's Drift under Colonel Henry Durnford's command. Although Durnford was senior to Pulleine and could have taken command of the camp, he did not press the point when he reached Isandhlwana.

Chelmsford was heading off on a wild goose chase, unaware that the main Zulu army, 20,000 strong, was lying concealed close to the British camp. The Zulus' intention had always been to overwhelm the camp at Isandhlwana, but, being deeply suspicious people, the moon's phase suggested to them that an attack on 22 January was not propitious. Moon's phases or not, mounted British scouts from the camp (not Chelmsford's column) discovered their hiding place and the Zulus had no alternative but to attack:

✔ **With a great roar, the Zulus swept over the plateau using their tradition *buffalo* formation.** This involved:

- The army's two wings pushing forward, as the buffalo's horns, to encircle the enemy.

- The centre, as the buffalo's chest, smashing into the enemy's main body.

- The reserve or loins delivering the *coup de grâce*.

In the attack on the British the right horn passed behind Isandhlwana Hill and the left horn struck Durnford, who on his own initiative had left the camp with some of his men, including the rocket detachment. The detachment was able to fire one rocket before the Zulus overran and speared its men. Durnford and the survivors fell back on the camp.

✔ **Pulleine just had time to deploy his companies.** Unfortunately, gaps of between 200 and 300 metres lay between them and their line was at least 1000 metres from the camp, which meant a very long run in both directions for the ammunition replenishment parties. Nevertheless, the British were delivering deadly volleys while N Battery's two 7-pounders were blasting case-shot through the Zulu ranks. Severely shaken, the Zulus halted between 150 and 300 metres from the British lines.

> ✔ **With the battle on a knife edge, unbelievable stupidity on the British side took a hand.** Neither the 1/24th's or the 2/24th's quartermasters would issue ammunition to parties from the other battalion, and they had no intention of supplying Durnford's men at all until he forcibly requisitioned some of their boxes. Even then, the lids were screwed down and no screwdrivers were available to open the boxes with. The British firing line spluttered into silence. The Zulus understood what that meant and charged. Their own accounts tell how the 24th's companies fought and died where they stood, two British officers attempting to save the 24th's Queen's Colour (see the sidebar, 'Melville, Coghill, and the Queen's Colour'). By 1.30 p.m. the camp had fallen.

During the battle and the pursuit, 52 British officers and 1277 other ranks died, of which 21 officers and 578 other ranks belonged to the 24th Regiment. The lowest estimate of Zulu dead was 2000, the highest 3000. Of those in the British camp at the time of the attack, about 350 managed to escape across what became known as Fugitives' Drift. Only five British officers and six privates of the 24th survived Isandhlwana. They included two bandsmen, Glyn's soldier servant, and three wounded men who 'played dead' when the Zulus overran the rocket detachment. That any escaped at all was thanks to the self-sacrifice of Durnford and his men. One good thing that emerged from the battle was that ammunition boxes were redesigned with lids secured by knock-off clamps rather than screws.

Chelmsford received details of the massacre from an officer who had returned to the camp to collect rations and narrowly escaped death or capture. Chelmsford and Glyn's column reached Isandlwana at about 8 p.m. Stripped and mutilated bodies lay everywhere. The contents of looted wagons lay strewn about. The flickering of countless Zulu camp fires in the hills told Chelmsford that he dared not remain for long, but he allowed his weary troops several hours' sleep. In the direction of Rorke's Drift, back towards British Natal, a brighter glow rose and fell on the horizon, making him fear the worst (see the following section).

Melville, Coghill, and the Queen's Colour

Pulleine, knowing all was lost, ordered Lieutenants Melville and Coghill to save the Queen's Colour of the 1/24th (the Regimental Colour had been left behind in Helpmakaar, Natal). Lieutenant Melville was swept off his exhausted horse in the swollen river and lost his grip on the Colour. Lieutenant Coghill returned from the far bank to rescue him, but they were quickly surrounded and killed, taking some of their opponents with them. The Colour floated downstream and was later recovered from the bottom of a pool.

The Defence of Rorke's Drift, 22–23 January 1879

The first that those at Rorke's Drift – a Swedish mission station on the Buffalo river being used as a British camp and hospital – knew of the disaster at Isandhlwana was the arrival of two Natal Native Contingent officers on lathered horses at about 3.15 p.m. One, Lieutenant James Adendorff, volunteered to assist in the defence of the post, while the other galloped on to warn the inhabitants of Helpmakaar.

Present at Rorke's Drift at this time were Lieutenant Gonville Bromhead's B Company 2/24th, a Natal Native Contingent company under Captain George Stephenson, Lieutenant John Chard of the Royal Engineers, Surgeon Major Reynolds, Assistant-Commissary James Dalton (a former infantry sergeant major), the Reverend George Smith (a missionary who had volunteered his services as chaplain), and the incumbent missionary, Otto Witt. As an irregular officer, Stephenson was not eligible to command the post, so this duty fell to Chard, who was three years senior to Bromhead. The officers agreed that the only possible course of action was to defend the post, which contained a small hospital and a storehouse. Loopholes were knocked into the walls of the building, and a barricade of *mealie* (corn) bags was erected. Abutting the eastern face of the perimeter was a small stone-walled kraal that the officers also decided to defend.

Scouts on a hill known as the Oskarberg, to the south of Rorke's Drift, spotted large numbers of Zulus fording the river to the east. Stephenson and his 300-strong Natal Native Contingent company took to their heels, as did Witt. For a little while Chard had commanded more than 500 men. Now he had only 139, including 35 sick or wounded.

Approximately 4500 Zulus were bearing down on the post. They belonged to the right horn of their army and had passed round the back of Isandhlwana Hill. They had therefore not been able to 'wash their spears' in the enemy's blood, in the Zulu phrase. The British presence at Rorke's Drift gave them the opportunity to do so:

> ✔ **The first Zulu attack began at 4.30 p.m. British musketry ripped through the Zulu ranks, but still they came on.** Those who reached the chest-high barricades immediately found that they needed to use at least one hand to scramble over, and were promptly spitted on the long British bayonets. As attack followed attack, Chard and Bromhead formed one tiny reserve after another and rushed to any threatened point.

✔ **The hospital was the scene of some of the most heroic acts of the entire battle.** Its rooms all had barricaded doors that faced outwards. No internal communication existed between them, and by 5 p.m. the Zulus were swarming round the building. Bromhead led several counter-attacks that drove them off for a while, but finally the Zulus succeeded in setting fire to the thatch. This meant that those defending the building could only evacuate the bedridden patients to safety by knocking holes through the partition walls, dragging the patients through, and lowering them from a window inside the British perimeter. While this was taking place, the defenders also had to fight off Zulus who pressed closely from room to room. At length the hospital was cleared of the living and Chard gave the order to withdraw inside a smaller perimeter where they could make a last stand.

✔ **The Zulus made six major attacks on the shrunken defences during the night, but the flames from the hospital illuminated these before they could be pressed home.** Each time the Zulus were driven back with heavy losses. Between attacks, those of the enemy who had firearms sniped at the defenders from the darkness. At midnight Chard led a sortie that recovered a water cart lying outside the barricade, enabling his men to slake their terrible thirst. After 2 a.m. the Zulus no longer made any serious assaults. By 4 a.m. it seemed as though they had gone. Fearing that the apparent lack of enemy activity may be a ruse, neither Bromhead nor Chard was prepared to let the men rest or sleep. At 7 a.m. the weary defenders saw a large body of Zulus on the high ground over-looking the post, but the enemy moved off out of sight. Those in the little garrison must have wondered what the coming day held for them.

Long before dawn on 23 January, Chelmsford began marching towards the post from the wreckage of Isandhlwana. Marching in the opposite direction were those Zulus who had spent the night attacking Rorke's Drift. The two columns passed each other within shouting distance, but both had seen too much death in its many forms and for the moment were prepared to live and let live. Dreading what they might find, Chelmsford's vanguard approached the post warily. Haggard, exhausted, and powder-grimed men greeted them by climbing onto heaped mealie bags, waving their helmets, and cheering lustily. Incredibly, the garrison of Rorke's Drift sustained the loss of only 15 men killed and 12 seriously wounded, two of them fatally. Nearly 400 dead Zulus lay in the immediate vicinity of the post, 100 more near the drift, and more still on the Oskarberg and in the surrounding bush. The exact number of Zulu dead and seriously wounded remains unknown.

For those in Britain, the astonishing defence of Rorke's Drift went some way to balance the horrific news of the disaster at Isandhlwana. In Germany, the Kaiser ordered this story of inspired junior leadership, determination, and expert improvisation to be read at the head of every regiment in his army.

Ending the Zulu War

The Zulu victory at Isandhlwana cost one tenth of the male Zulu population of military age killed there or at Rorke's Drift. A similar percentage were struggling to recover from their wounds. The wailing in the *kraals* (native villages) continued long after the battles. The greatest blow, however, was to Zulu morale.

The British public was also deeply shocked by the defeat at Isandhlwana and reinforcements were on their way to South Africa. But before final plans were made, the legacy of Chelmsford's failed invasion of Zululand had to be tidied up:

- **At Nyezane,** Colonel Charles Pearson's No 1 Column had also been under attack on 22 January, but he had held his ground. Hearing that Chelmsford was temporarily halting the invasion, Pearson sent part of his column back into Natal, but established a fortified position with the remainder at Eshowe, where he remained under siege. When reinforcements began to arrive, Chelmsford successfully marched to Pearson's relief, defeating a Zulu force at Gingidlovu on the way.

- **At Hlobane,** Colonel Evelyn Wood's No 4 Column had some success on 21 January, but withdrew on learning of the disaster at Isandhlwana. Chelmsford ordered Wood to create a diversion while he relieved Pearson at Eshowe. The diversion consisted of an attack on Hlobane on 28 March, under the command of Colonel Redvers Buller. The attack failed and Buller withdrew with difficulty and at heavy cost. Suitably encouraged, the Zulus attacked Wood's base at Khambula next day, but the British repulsed them at a loss to the Zulus of 800 dead, plus many more killed during the pursuit. Wood's losses were 18 killed and 11 mortally wounded.

- **At Intombe River** on 12 March, Zulus attacked a supply convoy bound for the Luneburg garrison, killing over half of the escort provided by the 80th (2/South Staffordshire) Regiment.

Chelmsford had now received sufficient reinforcements to resume his advance into Zululand, using two divisions and Wood's force from Khambula. The only incident of note during the advance on the Zulu capital Ulundi was the death of the Prince Imperial, son of the former Emperor Napoleon III, who was killed in an ambush. The British force, containing 4165 Europeans and 1152 Africans, approached the royal *kraal* in square formation on 3 July. Some 20,000 Zulus swarmed to attack it. In fighting that lasted for 90 minutes, the British killed an estimated 1500 Zulus and wounded as many. A ruthless pursuit, carried out by the 1st Dragoon Guards and 17th Lancers, added yet more to the total. The British loss came to 13 killed and 78 wounded. This was the decisive battle of the war, and the British captured Cetewayo shortly afterwards.

The First Boer War, 1880–1881

In 1877 the British government annexed the bankrupt Boer Republic of the Transvaal and began to put its finances in order. Unfortunately, the Boers, whose forebears had trekked hundreds of kilometres to escape British rule in the Cape, didn't want to be annexed. By the end of 1880 the Boers decided that the British presence must be ejected from their country.

On 20 December a supply convoy was heading for the British garrison at Pretoria, escorted by 264 men of the 94th (2/The Connaught Rangers). At Bronkhorst Spruit, a Boer with a white flag of truce asked the escort commander to turn back. The commander of course declined. The Boers opened fire from cover and 15 minutes later 155 of the British column's officers and men were either dead or wounded. The remainder surrendered, and the First Boer War was under way.

Introducing Boer commandos

The Boers lacked conventional military forces, but when threatened formed local units known as *commandos*. The commandos had served the Boers well against the Zulus and other native tribes.

Most Boers were farmers and lived much of their life on horseback. They were fine shots and expert at making good use of any scrap of cover available. When they went to war they did so in hard-wearing civilian clothes and slouch hats. They couldn't believe their luck that soldiers in red coats should provide such wonderful targets by advancing upright in straight lines. They also had the advantage of numbers, being able to field thousands of well-mounted riflemen against the 3500 British troops in garrisons scattered across the Transvaal.

The Battles of Laing's Nek and Majuba Hill, 28 January and 27 February 1881

Major General Sir George Pomeroy-Colley, senior officer in Natal and the Transvaal, assembled a force and began marching to the relief of the now-besieged British garrisons in Transvaal. Finding his path barred by 2000 Boers occupying Laing's Nek in the Drakensberg Mountains, on 28 January 1881 Pomeroy-Colley launched a frontal attack with the 58th (2/Northamptonshire) Regiment and the 3/60th (King's Royal Rifle Corps). The attack failed disastrously, with the loss of 180 British killed or wounded. The Boers sustained only 41 casualties.

On 7 February Colley fought an action at Ingogo that succeeded in preventing a Boer commando breaking away to the south and menacing his communications, but the British again sustained the greater losses. Negotiations now began between the Boers and the British government. Officially, a truce came into force while these took place, but Colley decided to render the Boer position at Laing's Nek untenable by occupying the dominant Majuba Hill. On the night of 26 February he led a 400-strong composite force, drawn from the 58th, the 60th, and the 92nd (2/The Gordon Highlanders), up the hill. At dawn on 27 February the Boers observed the British presence and sent a far larger number of men to fight their way up to the summit. So accurate was the Boers' fire that it was almost impossible for the British to make any effective reply. In the end, the British survivors had to make a disorderly retreat down the reverse slopes. British losses included 90 killed, including Colley, 133 wounded, 58 captured, and 2 missing. They killed one Boer and wounded five more.

The besieged garrisons held out until the subsequent peace treaty formally recognised the independence of the Transvaal, then marched to British-held Natal.

Invading Egypt, 1882

British policy in the Middle East had been to shore up the ramshackle Ottoman Empire as part of the Great Game against Russia (see Chapter 12). Egypt was always a vital element in this strategy, and its importance increased when the Suez Canal was completed in 1869, as this provided a new and vital lifeline to India and the Far Eastern portions of the British Empire. Unfortunately, Egypt was saddled with a crushing burden of foreign debt. The administration of government finance became a British and French concern, particularly after the British government purchased a controlling interest in the Suez Canal Company. Egypt's internal administration was inefficient and corrupt, and discontent was especially strong among the middle-ranking officers of the Egyptian army. Although Egypt was still nominally a province of the Ottoman Empire, the officers bitterly resented the appointment of Turks to senior appointments. Under the leadership of Colonel Achmet Arabi Pasha, the Egyptian army staged a coup in 1881 under the popular slogan 'Egypt for the Egyptians'. Matters soon got out of hand. In May 1882 rioters attacked foreign businesses and the mob killed some 50 Europeans.

British and French warships arrived off Alexandria, but the French declined to take part in punitive measures and sailed away. On the morning of 10 June Admiral Sir Frederick Beauchamp Seymour, commanding the British squadron, demanded the surrender of the Egyptian coastal forts. When the Egyptians ignored his ultimatum, the warships opened fire and by dusk had silenced the Egyptian guns. Arabi withdrew from the city and mob rule ensued until Royal Marine and naval landing parties went ashore on 14 June. They also assisted troops under Major General Sir Archibald Allison to establish defences around Alexandria, and even produced their own armoured train, of sorts. Arabi expected the British to advance on Cairo from the direction of Alexandria, but they disappointed him. Some landed at Alexandria as a feint on 12 August, but the rest of the army disembarked at Ismailia, half-way down the Suez Canal, on 20 August. The result was that even before serious fighting had begun, Arabi discovered that he had been outflanked. It says much for Victorian imperial administration that it was possible to concentrate 16,400 men from Britain, 7600 from Mediterranean garrisons, and almost 7000 from India for this task under the command of General Sir Garnet Wolseley.

After Arabi's troops had been worsted in skirmishes at Kassassin, he withdrew his army inside a well-constructed line of entrenchments dug along the top of a shallow ridge at Tel-el-Kebir. The position, held by 22,000 men with 60 guns, was about 6.5 kilometres (4 miles) long, with its right resting on the Cairo–Suez railway line and its left on the highly toxic Sweet Water Canal.

Wolseley decided to storm the entrenchments in a dawn assault following a night approach march, believing that his men fought better in the cool of the early morning. He had 17,000 men and 67 guns available for the assault. They moved into the assembly area, 9 kilometres (5.5 miles) short of the Egyptian position, during the night of 12/13 September and formed up in the order they would go into action. The cavalry brigade was on the right, then the 1st Infantry Division, then the 2nd Infantry Division, then a brigade-sized force across the Sweet Water Canal to keep pace with the advance. The general calculated that the troops would cover 1.6 kilometres (1 mile) every hour and, wishing to arrive within striking distance of the objective minutes before the sun rose, he set them in motion at 1.30 a.m. The great mass of marching men was within 150 metres of the Egyptian trenches before the enemy spotted it. A blaze of rifle and artillery fire came from the parapets, but it made no difference. A wave of yelling British infantry swamped the position and cleared it with the bayonet. Arabi's men broke and fled, leaving behind 2000 dead, 500 wounded, and all their artillery. Wolseley's losses included 58 killed, 379 wounded, and 22 missing, most incurred during the opening minutes of the engagement. The cavalry pursuit extended as far as Cairo, where Arabi surrendered his sword the following day.

The Battle of Tel-el-Kebir marked the beginning of 70 years of continuous British military presence in Egypt. At the time, no thought of such a prolonged commitment existed, but a series of unpredictable events led to continuity. In fact, hardly had Wolseley unpacked his trunks in England than incidents in the Sudan ensured his sailing for Egypt again.

Send Sir Garnet! The Sudan, 1884–1885

The Egyptian administration of the Sudan was even more corrupt than that of Egypt itself had been. During 1881 a wave of Islamic fundamentalism swept the Sudan, led by an ascetic named Mohammed Ahmed, better known as the Mahdi or Expected Guide. The Mahdi declared a holy war against the Turks (as he called the Egyptians). His followers, who became known as *dervishes*, defeated government troops on several occasions and captured the town of El Obeid, dismembering its governor as a warning to anyone else who tried to oppose them. At El Obeid they acquired a quantity of field artillery, several machine guns, and 6000 rifles. The Egyptian government despatched a 9000-strong force under Colonel William Hicks, a retired Indian army officer, to restore order. On 3 November 1883 the rebels surrounded Hicks's troops at Sheikan, near El Obeid, and massacred them two days later. Yet more armaments fell into the hands of the Mahdists.

The eastern Sudan, bordering the Red Sea, was also in a state of open rebellion. On 4 February 1884 a 3600-strong force under Valentine Baker, a former British officer now serving the Egyptians, fled when a dervish force one third its size attacked it at El Teb. Baker kept his head and managed to fight his way out with about 1000 of his men, but he lost all his artillery and machine guns.

Sir Evelyn Baring, the British government's agent in Egypt, was of the opinion that the British should withdraw the surviving garrisons in the Sudan, with the exception of the port of Suakin on the Red Sea (considered essential as part of the scheme for the evacuation of the rest of the Sudan). With reluctance the Egyptians accepted the decision. Major General Charles Gordon, who had served in the Sudan during the previous decade and was greatly respected there, undertook the task.

Gordon was mercurial, stubborn, wilful, and not the man for the job of evacuating the Sudan, for no sooner had he reached Khartoum than he decided that rather than abandon the city and its inhabitants to the Mahdi, he would defend it, confident that a British expeditionary force would be sent to his relief. This was the very situation that British Prime Minister William Gladstone had sought to avoid. Unfortunately for Gladstone, the public was on Gordon's side, especially after the Mahdist army isolated Khartoum in May. Gordon, an engineer by training, did everything possible to improve Khartoum's fortifications, and by means of spies managed to get despatches out to Baring in Cairo, always in the vain hope that the relief force was just over the horizon. In the eyes of the British press and public, he was a high-principled Christian officer who quite rightly refused to abandon those in need.

The political pressure on Gladstone mounted until he could no longer resist. In August he reluctantly gave way, peevishly restricting the size of the relief force to 10,000 volunteers to be selected from the entire British army. There was no shortage. In command was Sir Garnet Wolseley, who reached Cairo on 9 September. From the outset, Wolseley was aware that the chances of saving Gordon were shrinking with every day that passed. The quickest way to Khartoum was from Suakin across the desert to Berber on the Nile and then upstream. For tactical reasons, that was out of the question. The alternative was straight up the Nile from the railhead at Wadi Halfa. The problem with that was that six major sets of rapids, known as *cataracts*, existed between Aswan and Khartoum, and these had to be negotiated slowly. Wolseley was nothing if not thorough, ordering a large number of flat-bottomed Canadian boats and 300 Canadian boatmen to travel up the river (some of the boatmen, who had never heard of Egypt, assumed that it lay within the Arctic Circle and dressed accordingly). With infinite labour, the British force reached Korti.

On 17 November, Wolseley received a note from Gordon, expressing doubts that he could hold out beyond 14 December. Wolseley despatched:

- ✔ His main body on the slower route round the Great Bend of the River Nile

- ✔ A flying column ('Desert Column') across the arc of the Great Bend to rejoin the river within striking distance of Khartoum.

The Desert Column's objective was not to relieve Khartoum, but to reinforce it until the spring, when the level of the Nile rose at the cataracts and Wolseley was able to complete the relief.

Khartoum or bust!

Brigadier General Sir Herbert Stewart commanded the Desert Column, consisting of a Camel Corps and attached personnel, including a naval detachment with a Gardner machine gun. The column's strength was about 2000 men, plus 300 locally recruited camel drivers, interpreters, and guides. When they finally set off during the night of 9 January 1885 (after some initial delays), some doubt existed whether any of its members would ever be seen again. The column was marching straight into the enemy's heartland and its prospects of survival, let alone those of the small detachments it left behind to guard the wells along the way, seemed suddenly remote. During the early stages of the march, acute thirst was a far greater problem than the dervishes. The Mahdi knew the column's movements, but he intended to let it continue until it reached the limit of its resources, then destroy it, just as he had Hicks.

Some 12,000 dervishes were waiting to fall on Stewart when the moment was ripe. That moment almost arrived on 17 January when the column won a desperate battle near Abu Klea. The struggle became even more desperate when the column's Gardner gun jammed after firing only 30 rounds, enabling the dervishes to penetrate Stewart's square, from which the British only drove them after savage hand-to-hand fighting. The dervishes lost 1100 killed and a similar number wounded. British losses were 74 killed and 94 wounded. The column fought off further attacks at Abu Kru on 19 January and Gubat, where it reached the Nile, on 21 January. During these skirmishes Stewart received a mortal wound and command passed to his deputy, Colonel Sir Charles Wilson.

Four of Gordon's small steamers, sent down from Khartoum to meet the column, arrived. Wilson embarked a handful of seamen and 20 men of the Royal Sussex Regiment on two of these steamers. The troops wore scarlet tunics borrowed from the Guards in place of the grey khaki that the entire Camel Corps wore, because Gordon had once said that the sight of a few red coats would convince the Mahdi that Great Britain meant business. The reality was that Gordon's reputation for piety and benevolence were spoken of with respect throughout the Sudan, and this troubled the Mahdi a great deal more. Surely it did not seem good for one holy man to kill another, even if their beliefs differed? For some time the level of the Nile had been so low that Khartoum's water defences presented little or no obstacle, but rather than storm the city, the Mahdi seemed content to let starvation do its work. However, when he learned that the disciplined firepower of comparatively few British soldiers had killed over 2000 of his followers and wounded many more, he knew that he could delay no longer. On 26 January the rebels stormed Khartoum and its massacred its garrison. They ignored the Mahdi's instructions to spare Gordon's life.

Wilson's two steamers approached Khartoum the following day. They came under rifle and artillery fire, as they had many times, and replied with their own weapons. The difference was that the Egyptian flag no longer flew over the Governor General's palace, and much of the fire came from inside the city's fortifications. With a heavy heart, Wilson recognised that he was too late and reversed course. The steamers reached apparent safety, but were both wrecked near the Shabluka Cataract. In due course, the party was rescued and returned to their own lines, but only after a series of adventures that a thriller writer would consider overblown.

Meanwhile, the River Column under Major General W. Earl had defeated a dervish force at Kirbekan on 10 February, Earl being killed as he led the final advance. With Gordon's death, however, the entire purpose of the expedition had disappeared. Both the River and the Desert Columns were withdrawn into Egypt, where British troops assisted in the defence of the frontier. The dervishes had followed up the withdrawal, but the British defeated them at the Battle of Ginnis on 30 December 1885, an engagement that would long since have been forgotten if it had not been the last time that British infantry went into action in their traditional scarlet. Skirmishes continued along the frontier for the next few years, culminating in a seven-hour engagement at Toski on 3 August 1889 in which the British decisively defeated the dervishes with the loss of 1000 dervishes killed, including one of their most famous leaders, Wad-el-Nejumi.

The British electorate punished Gladstone for his failure to send a relief force earlier, and Queen Victoria expressed her displeasure publicly. Wolseley was bitterly disappointed by his inability to rescue Gordon, but the public knew that he had done everything humanly possible.

Sallying from Suakin against Osman Digna

Away from the rush to Khartoum (see the preceding section), the British still held Suakin, but were opposed by Osman Digna, the Mahdi's governor in the Eastern Sudan.

A colourful rumour had it that Osman Digna was actually a Frenchman named George Vinet; he was certainly a slave trader whose business the British had ruined, and for that he was prepared to harm them in any way possible. His influence among the local tribes was great and he had no difficulty in attracting the Beja hillmen to the Mahdi's cause. Because of their wild, frizzed hairstyle the British called them *Fuzzy Wuzzies* and came to regard their suicidal courage with the greatest respect.

Suakin was a nasty, hot, unhealthy, coral-built port around which, for the next few years, more battles were actually fought than took place on the Nile. A British garrison under Major General Sir Gerald Graham took possession of Suakin in the spring of 1884 and moved out to confront Osman Digna's dervishes. Graham had 4000 men at his disposal, plus four guns and several Gatling and Gardner machine guns, fighting the Dervishes at:

- ✔ **El Teb, 29 February 1884:** 6000 dervishes, plentifully armed with captured firearms, six guns, and one Gatling, assailed Graham's square. This action, the Second Battle of El Teb, was a resounding defeat for Osman, who lost most of the modern weapons and ammunition taken from Baker earlier in the month, plus more than half his men. Graham's casualties amounted to 34 killed and 155 wounded.

- ✔ **Tamai, 13 March 1884:** Osman gathered his strength for a second round when Graham resumed his advance. 12,000 dervishes attempted to swamp two British squares in furious attacks, one square being temporarily broken in hand-to-hand fighting before the position was restored. The dervishes overran two of the Gatlings and turned them on their owners, who were extremely fortunate that the dervishes were unable to operate them properly. At length Osman's men retired, leaving 2200 of their number dead around the squares. Graham lost a total of 214 killed and wounded.

After Tamai, Graham wanted to press on to Berber, but Gladstone's British government forbade him to do so and he retired to Suakin. For the next year Suakin, held by a much-reduced garrison, remained in a state of siege.

At the beginning of 1885 the British decided to support Wolseley's troops on the Nile by tying down Osman Digna with a renewed offensive from Suakin. This time the government gave Graham, now a lieutenant general, 13,000 men, including a brigade from India. Graham defeated one concentration of Mahdists at Hasheen on 20 March, but two days later the dervishes surprised one of his own detachments at Tofrek, under the command of Major General Sir John McNeill. This detachment just managed to hold its own and finally drove the dervishes off. Skirmishing continued until May, when Gladstone used a brush between Russian and Afghan troops at Penjdeh as an excuse for abandoning the campaign on the pretence that India was under threat.

Reconquering the Sudan, 1896–1898

The Mahdi died shortly after the capture of Khartoum. The Khalifa Abdullahi ibn Mohammed succeeded Mohammed Ahmed and ruled the Sudan with a blend of puritanical religious fervour and sadistic cruelty. In 1896 the British government decided that it had to reconquer the Sudan for political rather than philanthropic reasons:

- The Italians had sustained a serious defeat at the hands of the Abyssinians at Adowa in 1892 and it was desirable to re-establish the prestige of the European powers in the area.
- The French were showing an interest in establishing control of the upper reaches of the Nile and the British were determined to stop them.

No one suggested that reconquering Sudan would be easy, however. The Khalifa had available an army of no fewer than 60,000 ferocious warriors, with 40,000 firearms, including 22,000 comparatively modern Remingtons. In addition, the dervishes possessed 61 cannon, six Krupp field guns, and eight machine guns – although they had little use for firepower save as a prelude to a fanatical attack with sword and spear.

The burden of reconquest fell mainly on the Egyptian army. British officers and NCOs had completely reconstituted this army and brought it to a high level of discipline, efficiency, and morale. It now consisted of eight Egyptian and six Sudanese infantry battalions, a small camel corps, six squadrons of cavalry, four artillery batteries, and transport troops. One British battalion, 1/North Staffordshire Regiment, served as divisional troops for much of the initial phases of the advance on Sudan.

The army's *sirdar* or commander-in-chief was General Horatio Herbert Kitchener, who had served under Wolseley during the Gordon relief expedition and the operations around Suakin (see the section 'Send Sir Garnet! The Sudan, 1884–1885', earlier in this chapter). His glaring eyes, dour manner, and lack of social graces ensured that he was never a popular figure. He was not a particularly able tactician either, but he was an expert in the fields of supply and transport, and this proved to be the key to winning the forthcoming campaign. Kitchener had an excellent network of spies in the Sudan, run by his Chief of Intelligence, Major (later General) Reginald Wingate, so that little happened even in Omdurman, the Khalifa's gloomy capital across the river from the ruins of Khartoum, that did not reach Kitchener's ears shortly afterwards. Above all, Kitchener regarded the abandonment of Gordon as a national disgrace that he was absolutely determined to expunge.

Steaming along Kitchener's desert railway

When the campaign against Sudan began in June 1896, both Kitchener and the Khalifa were determined to fight the decisive battle near Omdurman. The Khalifa believed that the Sirdar would be at the extreme limit of his supply line and at his weakest, just as Hicks had been (see the section 'Send Sir Garnet! The Sudan, 1884–1885', earlier in this chapter). For his part, Kitchener had already decided to harness the most modern means of transport available not just to keep his army supplied, but to reinforce it with fresh British brigades, so that when he fought the critical battle he would possess twice the strength with which he had begun the campaign.

Dervish outposts offered varying degrees of resistance to the advance, but Kitchener's men took them just the same. These successes further built up the Egyptians' morale. When Dongola fell on 21 September, Kitchener took a courageous decision that eventually won him the campaign, namely to build a 380-kilometre (235-mile) railway through the arid and empty desert between Wadi Halfa and Abu Hamed. Work on the railway began on 1 January 1897. It progressed at an average rate of 1.6 kilometres (1 mile) per day and by July was well on the way. The following month the army's advance guard, which had moved up river with a gunboat flotilla, captured Abu Hamed. Events now speeded up. Unexpectedly, the enemy abandoned Berber, 220 kilometres (135 miles) beyond, which the Egyptians occupied on 13 September. On 31 October Kitchener's line reached Abu Hamed. This made the position of Osman Digna (still fighting after his defeat by Graham – see the section 'Sallying from Suakin against Osman Digna', earlier in this chapter) in the eastern Sudan untenable and he had to withdraw to Omdurman.

The Khalifa could not afford to ignore this threat. Unfortunately for him, he seriously underestimated the extent of the threat and despatched only 16,000 men under the Emir Mahmoud and Osman Digna to destroy the railway, which the British were now extending southwards to Berber. Kitchener's intelligence provided adequate warning. He despatched one British brigade up the line while a second prepared to follow as quickly as possible. Wily Osman dug himself in behind a thorn *zariba* (stockade) backing on to the dry bed of the Atbara river. Kitchener had prepared a warm reception for Osman, but when the latter failed to materialise Kitchener decided to attack. At 5.45 a.m. on 8 April 1898 Kitchener's artillery opened a two-hour bombardment of Osman's zariba. At 8 a.m. the British and Egyptian infantry stormed the defences and within 30 minutes had cleared the interior. Dervish losses amounted to 3000 killed and 2000 captured, including Mahmoud. The Anglo-Egyptian army sustained fewer than 600 killed and wounded. The road to Omdurman now lay open.

The Battle of Omdurman, 2 September 1898

Kitchener was not inclined to advance further until he was absolutely certain of victory. The second British brigade arrived, but the troops were not set in motion again until August. The gunboat flotilla bombarded Omdurman on 1 September. Simultaneously, 11 kilometres (7 miles) downstream Kitchener's army was constructing a zariba centred on the village of Egeiga, around which it curved in a half-moon with both flanks resting on the Nile. The British held the left of the line and the Egyptians the right. Outside the zariba was a featureless plain, lacking cover but punctuated here and there with shallow depressions. Some 3 kilometres (2 miles) to the southwest lay a rocky feature known as Djebel Surgan, about 75 metres (250 feet) high, while a similar distance to the northwest were the Kerreri hills.

At dawn on 2 September the Khalifa led out his army. He relied solely on the fanaticism of his 60,000 warriors and left his artillery to follow on. At 6.25 a.m. with the enemy's range at 2500 metres (2700 yards), the British and Egyptian artillery opened fire. The gunboats joined in and shortly after the Maxim machine guns, both ashore and afloat, went into sustained fire. At 6.35 a.m., with the range at 1800 metres (2000 yards), 1/Grenadier Guards commenced volley firing. By 6.45 a.m. the whole Anglo-Egyptian line was ablaze, yet still the dervishes came on. But by 7.30 a.m. those of them that were able turned away and walked off. Few had come within 700 metres (800 yards) of the British, or within 350 metres (400 yards) of the Egyptians.

The next stage of the battle is remembered for tactical decisions that varied between the bungling and the brilliant:

✔ **To the north of the zariba, the Egyptian cavalry not only completed a successful withdrawal across the Kerreri hills, but also provoked a large portion of the dervish army into following them, temporarily removing it from the main arena of the battle.** The slowly plodding Camel Corps, however, had to attempt a difficult withdrawal towards the northern face of the zariba. The dervishes pursued the Corps so vigorously that it was in real danger of being surrounded and massacred. Luckily, the captains of several gunboats tore the enemy's packed ranks apart with their concentrated fire, but it was a very close-run race.

✔ **With the main dervish attack beaten back, Kitchener ordered the 21st Lancers, on the extreme left of his line, to worry the enemy on their flank and head them off from Omdurman.** The regiment was the most junior cavalry regiment in the army and had never been in action before. The Lancers had not long left the cover of the zariba when their scouts reported a body of 700 dervishes drawn up in a *khor* or hollow to their right front.

In fact, the dervish strength was 2700, mostly hidden, and those few dervishes who were visible opened fire. Unable to resist the challenge, the Lancers charged at once. Suddenly the British realised that dervishes 12 deep packed the khor. After two minutes of stabbing and hacking, the horsemen fought their way through and up the far bank of the khor. Lieutenant Winston Churchill (future Prime Minister, troop leader at Omdurman, and Sudan Correspondent of *The Morning Post*) sensibly chose to sheath his sword and shoot his way through the mass with a privately purchased Mauser automatic pistol. Colonel R.M. Martin, commanding the Lancers, brought his men round on to the enemy's flank and opened brisk fire with carbines. Sullenly, the enemy retired towards Omdurman. The Lancers lost 21 killed and 46 wounded, but no fewer than 119 of their horses were killed or too seriously injured for further use. It was 9.30 a.m. before the regiment was ready to move off and it was hardly engaged again for the remainder of the battle. Martin had made a mistake that deprived Kitchener of a cavalry regiment when he needed one most, and the Sirdar was far from pleased.

✔ **With the main dervish attack apparently repulsed, Kitchener ordered his infantry to leave the zariba and wheel left towards Omdurman.** The decision was dangerously premature, for it ignored those dervishes, some 20,000 in number, who had tried to pursue Egyptian cavalrymen across the Kerreri hills. These dervishes now returned to the main battlefield, where they immediately attacked Colonel Hector Macdonald's

1st Egyptian Brigade on the extreme right of Kitchener's line. Macdonald had risen from the ranks and was a very capable commander; his battalions were already engaged with dervishes to the west, but to meet the new threat he coolly changed front so that his brigade resembled an L. He then opened tremendous fire, with his Maxims and attached artillery in support. Despite this, by the time the first reinforcements reached Macdonald, the dervishes were within 27 metres (30 yards) and his riflemen were down to six rounds apiece.

The Camel Corps came up, dismounted, and extended Macdonald's line to the right, followed by 1/The Lincolnshire Regiment. The 4th Egyptian Brigade, which had been left guarding the zariba, closed in on the action from the east, while the 1st British Brigade (1/Royal Warwickshire Regiment, 1/Seaforth Highlanders, and 1/Cameron Highlanders) fell on the dervishes' flank and dispersed them. By 11.30 a.m. the battle was over. The British resumed the advance and took Omdurman during the afternoon.

Nearly 10,000 dervishes died during the battle and perhaps twice that number sustained wounds of varying severity. The Anglo-Egyptian army lost 5 officers and 43 other ranks killed, plus 428 men wounded. His power broken, the Khalifa was hunted down and died fighting. Kitchener continued up river to meet Major Marchand, the officer commanding a small French detachment on the Upper Nile. The two got on well and agreed that the whole question of territorial rights in the area was one for the politicians to settle, which they did in Great Britain's favour. It provided a satisfactory end to an (almost) flawless campaign.

The Second Boer War, 1899–1902

The discovery of gold in the Transvaal drew outsiders to the country like a magnet. It was not long before these *Uitlanders* (foreigners) threatened to outnumber the native Boers. Understandably worried about losing their national identity and way of life, the Boers made matters very difficult for the newcomers, taxing them while simultaneously denying them political rights and skewing the law against them. Most stubborn of all was the Transvaal's president, Paul Kruger, who saw a threat to his country's existence when the British annexed neighbouring territories in 1895. He commenced a dialogue with the Germans, which did not at all please the British Foreign Office.

Over New Year 1896, at the urging of empire-builder Cecil Rhodes, Dr Leander Starr Jameson led an entirely private invasion of the Transvaal with 500 men in the hope of encouraging the resident *Uitlanders* to rise and overthrow the Boer government. They did not. Boer commandos rounded up Jameson and his men and forced them to surrender at Doornkop on 2 January 1896. The Boers handed Jameson over to the British to deal with. The British gave him a year's imprisonment, but regarded him as a hero. Events quickly went from bad to worse. Kaiser Wilhelm II of Germany, Queen Victoria's unstable grandson, rashly sent Kruger a telegram hinting that he may consider making the Transvaal a German protectorate. To the British public, that was like a red rag to a bull. The second Boer republic, the Orange Free State, openly sided with Kruger, creating a real danger of the large and sympathetic Dutch population in the British territories to the south responding favourably to a Boer invasion. Only 10,000 British troops were spread across the entire vastness of southern Africa, so the government despatched reinforcements because of the danger of internal unrest. On 9 October 1899 Kruger issued an ultimatum in a fit of hubris, demanding that the British withdraw within 48 hours. Naturally, Great Britain ignored the ultimatum and on 11 October found itself at war with the two Boer republics.

The easy victories of the First Boer War (detailed earlier in this chapter) probably influenced Kruger's decision to go to war, together with the fact that at this stage the Boers fielded some 50,000 men, mostly armed with the latest German clip-loading Mauser rifle, who outnumbered the small British garrisons. The Boers still fought in locally raised commandos as mounted infantry who made the most of their mobility and were expert at concealing their positions. Their artillery, however, was a regular force equipped with modern guns that were dispersed in action, making them difficult to spot. In comparison, British infantry advanced in line and presented a splendid target for any marksman. British cavalry continued to regard the lance and the sword as its primary weapons, with a lesser reliance on firearms. The artillery fought its batteries wheel to wheel, making them easier to spot than their Boer counterparts. The British army was involved in a new kind of warfare against the tricky Boers and couldn't produce results until it understood and adopted some of its opponents' methods. In fairness, however, no grounds exist for believing that any other western army could have done better.

Opening moves

By the end of October 1899 after some early skirmishes, most but by no means all of which ended in favour of the Boers, most of the original British troops in South Africa were under siege in Kimberley and Ladysmith. Good tacticians though they undoubtedly were, the Boers were poor strategists and the sieges, once begun, became matters of bombardment, counter-bombardment, digging, sniping, attack, and counter-attack. Some Boers did move south along the railway from Ladysmith to Durban, but halted after they had taken Colenso on the Tugela river, which offered a good position from which to defeat relief attempts. The British sent an armoured train up the line to investigate, but the Boers ambushed it at Chieveley. Among those captured was the *Morning Post's* roving correspondent, Winston Churchill (who saw action in the Sudan, but was now a civilian). The Boers took him to Pretoria but he managed to escape and make his way to freedom through Portuguese territory. The incident did his subsequent political career no harm at all.

Defending Mafeking

On 13 October 1899 some 8000 Boers under Generals Piet Cronje and Koos de la Rey laid siege to Mafeking, in British territory just across the border from the Transvaal. Frankly, the place was simply not worth all that trouble – it resembled an American Wild West township and its only real importance was that it contained a railway workshop. The Boers hated the town, partly because Jameson had launched his abortive raid from there (see the previous section), and partly because the Baralong tribe had a village close by and had worsted the Boers in several years of sporadic fighting. If the Boers had not expected an easy victory over the little British garrison, they would certainly not have bothered. Yet far from winning a victory, the Boers became tied down in a siege that became symbolic to both sides.

The one British professional present was the garrison commander, Colonel Robert Stephenson Smythe Baden-Powell, although some of his men had previous service in the Army or the Royal Navy. Baden-Powell's troops had been raised locally in recent months and included 21 officers and 448 men of the Protectorate Regiment, 5 officers and 77 men of the Bechuanaland Rifles, 10 officers and 81 men of the British South African Police, and 4 officers and 99 men of the Cape Police. In reserve were 450 men of the Railway Volunteers and the Town Guard.

As the siege progressed, Baden-Powell mobilised the town's boys as messengers; they became the forerunners of the world-wide Scout Movement that he later founded. An armoured train was also available, for which the British constructed an additional spur to bring its weapons within range of more sectors of the defence. Baden-Powell constructed inner and outer defences, laid dummy minefields, taking steps to ensure that the Boers believed they were real, and used a stock of carbide (employed in bicycle lamps at the time) to made searchlights. When the siege began he started a newspaper telling everyone what was happening, and an internal postal service using specially printed stamps. There was no area into which his inventive mind did not reach, including ingenious ways of eking out the garrison's food supplies.

Baden-Powell beat off the enemy's attacks and made the Boers' lives a misery with constant sorties and raids. In due course, Piet Cronje took himself off to Kimberley with many of the besiegers, but Mafeking continued to tie down large numbers of Boers. The British press eagerly reported details of the siege. When the Boers abandoned the siege on 16 May 1900 the news generated a wild, joyful riot in London that lasted all night: In British eyes, Baden-Powell was a hero who had been the plucky underdog from the beginning. He deserved to win, he had won, and that was that.

Struggling on through Black Week, 10–15 December 1899

General Sir Redvers Buller, VC, commanded the army corps despatched from England to bolster troops in South Africa. In some ways he was a good choice, as he had wide experience of African wars and was popular with the troops. In one important respect he was not ideal, however: He had proved himself to be an excellent second-in-command, but when it came to exercising command himself he was a ditherer.

The situation Buller was presented with made too many demands on the resources he had available. His original intention was to concentrate his troops for an advance on Bloemfontein, the capital of the Orange Free State, but the situation in Natal was potentially dangerous, and in diamond-rich Kimberley, 950 kilometres (600 miles) to the west, Cecil Rhodes – who possessed a very loud political voice – was demanding immediate relief.

Uncertain what to do, Buller tried to deal with everything at once:

- ✔ **Lieutenant General Sir William Gatacre was to remain on the defensive south of the Orange river, covering the approach to Cape Colony from Bloemfontein.** On 10 December 1899, Gatacre disobeyed his orders and attempted to recapture the railway junction at Stormberg. Having lost his way during a night approach march, he ordered his troops to assault a Boer position on top of a precipitous rock face. Not surprisingly, the assault failed. His orders to withdraw did not reach 700 men still on the feature and they had to surrender. In addition, the Boers killed or wounded 135 of his men. The humiliating reverse cost Gatacre his job.

- ✔ **Lieutenant General Lord Methuen was to relieve Kimberley.** On 11 December, Methuen launched an attack on the Boer positions at Magersfontein. The Boers, under the command of General Piet Cronje and Jacobus de la Rey, were well concealed. They also possessed excellent fields of fire, of which they took full advantage when Methuen's brigades advanced in neat lines. The Highland Brigade in particular suffered cruel losses, the Boers pinning it down for much of the day and then forcing it into a disorderly retreat. Altogether, Methuen lost 120 killed, including Major General Andy Wauchope who had commanded a brigade at Omdurman (see the section 'The Battle of Omdurman, 2 September 1898' earlier in this chapter), and 690 wounded. The Boers lost 87 killed and 213 wounded, mainly from artillery fire.

✔ **Buller himself, with the remainder of his force, concentrated on the relief of Ladysmith.** On 15 December Buller, with 21,000 men, 5 field artillery batteries, and 14 naval guns on travelling carriages, tried to force a crossing of the Tugela river at Colenso without adequate reconnaissance, maps, or knowledge of either the ground or the Boer positions. Everything that could go wrong somehow did. One brigade marched into a loop of the river from which no way across existed and was subjected to intense fire from three sides. Ten guns were lost, 143 men were killed, 755 were wounded, and 240 were posted missing. The enemy had consisted of just 6000 Boers and 8 guns under General Louis Botha. This defeat so shook Buller that he sent a signal to Lieutenant General Sir George White, commanding the besieged Ladysmith garrison, advising him to surrender. White may not have been one of the army's top commanders, but he had no intention of giving up and ignored the signal. One point of interest relating to the battle was the presence of Mohandas (Mahatma) Gandhi, the father of Indian Independence, with a contingent of Indian volunteer stretcher bearers in British service.

Taken together, the three defeats in six days became known as *Black Week*. To a British public used to tales of victory, they came as a profound shock. Other nations rejoiced at the sight of two insignificant African republics humbling the mighty British Empire. Obviously, the situation required a drastic solution. The government restricted Buller's authority to Natal and appointed 68-year-old Field Marshal Lord Roberts as commander-in-chief. Roberts received the news of his appointment on the day he learned that his son Frederick had died of wounds received while trying to bring out the guns at Colenso.

Taking the initiative from the Boers

Roberts, taking charge after Black Week, appointed Kitchener as his Chief of Staff and reached Cape Town on 10 January 1900. He had already decided that the solution lay in mobility allied to an indirect approach, as opposed to the frontal assaults that had so far proved to be such a dismal failure. His intention was to relieve Kimberley first, then drive on Bloemfontein. He concentrated his forces, now numbering 37,000 men, south of Kimberley and began the task of raising and training a mounted infantry regiment.

The British beat off a Boer attempt to capture Ladysmith on 6 January. Buller, who had recovered his nerve somewhat, tried to break through the enemy at Spion Kop (Spy Hill) on 23 January. The summit of this hill became the scene of a murderous close-range fire fight and both sides simultaneously abandoned the position. The Boers, however, quickly realised their mistake and reoccupied the feature. British losses included 243 killed and wounded plus 300 captured, while the Boers lost 335 killed and wounded. Buller tried again on 5 February, with equally indecisive results.

The initiative now passed to Roberts:

- ✔ **During the early hours of 12 January, Roberts' cavalry division, under the command of Major General John French, headed east to Waterval Drift on the Riet river, only to find the crossing in enemy hands.** Leaving one brigade to watch the Boers, French led the other two brigades east to De Kiels Drift, which they crossed without incident. On learning of this, the Boers at Waterval Drift faded away and by afternoon the entire British division was across the Riet.

- ✔ **On 13 January, French swung north, covering 40 kilometres (25 miles) of sun-scorched *veldt* (grassland) to secure Rondeval and Klip Drifts over the Modder river.** While French rested the following day, Cronje sent back troops to seal off the penetration, but they were too few to make much difference.

- ✔ **On 15 February, the division charged along a shallow valley and smashed through the enemy line out into the open.** Together, speed and dense clouds of dust provided a defence against Boer marksmanship. The British lost only a handful of men and horses. By mid-afternoon they had relieved Kimberley. Cronje began withdrawing towards Bloemfontein along the Modder, but the slow pace of his ox-drawn wagons hindered him. Roberts followed closely with his infantry while French, striking southeast from Kimberley, brought him to a standstill at Paardeberg.

- ✔ **On 18 February, Roberts, temporarily unwell, handed over to Kitchener, who launched a frontal attack on Paardeberg incurring pointless casualties.** Returning to duty, Roberts decided to bombard the Boer position into surrender. As the *laager* (Boer encampment) also contained women and children, the gunners did not welcome the task. Cronje could have broken out, but he declined to abandon his wounded and his men's families. He held out until 27 February, then surrendered. The British had killed or wounded 1000 of Cronje's men and marched 4000 into captivity. By coincidence, the surrender took place on the anniversary of the Battle of Majuba Hill, which the Transvaal Boers celebrated as a national day (see the section 'The Battles of Laing's Nek and Majuba Hill, 28 January and 26 February 1881' for this battle in the First Boer War). Elsewhere, Buller finally succeeded in breaking through the Tugela line on 18 February and relieved Ladysmith ten days later.

The tide had turned. Roberts advanced into the Orange Free State, took Bloemfontein on 13 March, and reached Kroonstad on 12 May. Buller continued to mop up in Natal. Both commanders then pushed into the Transvaal. Johannesburg fell on 31 May, then Pretoria, where 3000 British prisoners were released, on 5 June. Roberts and Buller joined forces at Vlakfontein on 4 July. The last formal actions of the war took place at Diamond Hill on 9 June and Bergendal on 27 August 1900, dispersing the remnants of the Boers' field armies. President Kruger escaped through Portuguese territory. Great Britain formally annexed both Boer republics and on 29 November Roberts departed for home, leaving Kitchener to tie up the loose ends. Unfortunately, the most difficult phase of the war was about to begin.

Fighting the guerrilla war

A number of the more prominent Boer commanders, including Botha, De Wet, and De La Rey, refused to accept that the British had beaten them. They rallied their commandos and began to raid the British lines of communication, almost at will. Given the vast areas in which they were able to operate, they possessed the initiative and could strike where and when they wanted. Dealing with this type of warfare involved the British in developing new tactics that not only required time to produce results, but also large manpower resources.

Kitchener first established lines of manned *blockhouses* to guard the railways, heavy timber structures used for defence with loopholed walls. Life in these was monotonously boring and months passed without anything of interest happening, if it happened at all. Initially, the commandos received food and support from their own people. Obviously, this had to stop and Kitchener resorted to measures first adopted by the Spanish army against Cuban rebels a few years early. These involved concentrating the Boer families in camps. The tragic and unintended consequence of this was that as many as 20,000 people died when epidemics of disease broke out, despite the attempts of the authorities to control them. Likewise, the commandos used abandoned farm buildings as shelter, so the British burned these down. This was always an unpopular but necessary duty. Next, hundreds of kilometres of barbed wire, originally designed as quickly erected cattle fencing, was used for military purposes for the first time, dividing large areas of the veldt from each other and so inhibiting the commandos' free movement. Increasing numbers of trained British mounted infantry units became available as the months passed, and Kitchener used their mobility to conduct drives within the enclosed areas, pushing the Boers back against the blockhouse stop line.

Gradually the British whittled away the commandos' strength until by the spring of 1902 Kitchener had taken some 40,000 men of the commandos prisoner. On 31 May the Boer leaders accepted the inevitable and surrendered at Vereeniging. Their stubborn courage had earned them the respect of their enemies. Among the generous peace terms they were granted were funds with which to repair their property and the right to buy now redundant army horses at giveaway prices. Their language and culture were guaranteed. As a result of this, when the two former republics were absorbed into the Union of South Africa in 1907, few objections were raised.

Part V
The First World War

In this part . . .

Technical advances produced a situation in which the powers of defence were greater than those of the attack, enabling defending armies to kill their opponents on an industrial scale. During the First World War the British Army expanded to its greatest size ever and sustained its heaviest casualties. It also found an answer to the deadlock of trench warfare – the tank, which did not become available in war-winning numbers until 1918.

During the last months of the war the British became the senior partner on the Western Front and led the final advance that resulted in the Armistice. In addition, the British and Indian Armies destroyed the Ottoman Empire, the collapse of which was followed by that of Germany's remaining allies.

Chapter 17

'Hangin' On the Old Barbed Wire': The Western Front, 1914–1917

In This Chapter

▶ The opening phases of the Western Front, 1914

▶ Trench warfare, 1914–1917

▶ The Battle of the Somme, 1916

▶ Other Western Front battles, 1917

---

*W*hen Archduke Franz Ferdinand of Austria-Hungary was assassinated in 1914, diplomacy failed to prevent a general drift into war. On the one side, initially, were Great Britain, France, Russia, and Serbia, joined later by Italy, Romania, and Greece. On the other were the German and Austro-Hungarian Empires, joined by the Ottoman Empire and Bulgaria. A major war had not taken place in Europe for 40 years, and cheering crowds greeted its outbreak in all the combatants' capitals, not having the slightest idea of what the battlefield had in store for them. For more information on the complex causes of the First World War, see Sean Lang's *European History For Dummies* (published by Wiley).

This chapter and Chapter 18 deal with the campaigns of the *Western Front* (France and Belgium). Chapter 19 tackles the British action spilling over into the rest of the world.

Of all the armies entering the war in 1914, only the British Regular Army consisted entirely of professionals and recalled reservists. It went to war wearing a practical, durable woollen khaki service dress. It had learned a great deal from the Boers (see Chapter 16). The infantry, for example, had perfected the technique of firing 16 aimed rifle rounds a minute, producing a firestorm guaranteed to shoot any attack flat, and learned the value of concealment. The First World War also saw the following developments in the British army:

> ✔ The introduction of the tank (for more see the section 'The Battle of the Somme, 1916', later in this chapter, and Chapter 19).
>
> ✔ Aerial warfare (see the sidebar 'Enter the aeroplane!').
>
> ✔ The vanishing role of cavalry on the modern battlefield.

Enter the aeroplane!

Great Britain entered the war with two air forces – the Royal Flying Corps, which belonged to the Army, and the Royal Naval Air Service, a branch of the Royal Navy. Both had operational squadrons in France and Belgium from the beginning. Air reconnaissance or scouting for the Army was an obvious role for the air forces and the generic name for the first fighter aircraft was *Scouts*. During the early days of the First World War, aircraft also dropped small bombs, grenades, and boxes of *flechettes* (small, weighted arrows) on the enemy's marching columns. Inevitably, they encountered enemy aircraft. The observers from each side banged away at each other with pistols, rifles, and shotguns without doing much damage, then went home. Such contests became more serious when their cockpits were fitted with rearward-facing machine guns, and downright dangerous when *interrupter devices* enabled pilots to fire forward-mounted machine guns through the propeller. This initiated the era of the dogfight, as each side sought to maintain air superiority over the trench lines.

The availability of machine guns, magazine rifles, quick-firing artillery, and barbed wire meant that the powers of the defence were stronger than those of the attack. The problem was that during the past 60 years fate had placed the generals under a tragic delusion: The side that kept attacking had won the American Civil War, the Austro-Prussian War, the Franco-Prussian War, the Russo-Japanese War, and even the Second Boer War, despite the fact that by far the heavier casualties were also among the attackers. The business of the generals was to win wars and they believed that they could only achieve this by doing likewise.

In due course, the British Regular Army was followed into action by the Territorial Force, as it was then known. Lord Haldane created the Territorial Army in 1907 from various volunteer units around the country. County associations became responsible for raising territorial units that ultimately formed 14 infantry divisions and 14 mounted brigades, based on the 14 military districts into which the country was divided. The old volunteer battalions became part of their county regiment, with the object of increasing efficiency by closer ties. This produced a regimental structure of, for example:

- ✔ 1st and 2nd (Regular) Battalions
- ✔ 3rd (Militia) Battalion
- ✔ 4th and 5th (Territorial) Battalions

Other roles for the air forces included spotting for the artillery, shooting down the enemy's observation balloons, photo reconnaissance, and ground attack. The Royal Naval Air Service broke new ground by forming an armoured car division in 1914, the original objective being to rescue pilots forced to land between the armies. Most Royal Navy Armoured Car Division squadrons transferred to the Army and served in other theatres of war, although one squadron headed for Russia where it enjoyed an adventurous career both before and after the Revolution. In 1918 the Royal Flying Corps and the Royal Naval Air Service merged to form the Royal Air Force as an independent arm in its own right.

All Noisy on the Western Front

The British army that went to France in August 1914 was called the BEF (British Expeditionary Force, although Kaiser Wilhelm gave it a different name – see the sidebar 'The Old Contemptibles'). Its first commander was Field Marshal Sir John French, who had relieved Kimberley with his Cavalry Division during the Second Boer War (see Chapter 16). It consisted of a Cavalry Division of five brigades under Major General E.H. Allenby, I Corps under Lieutenant General Sir Douglas Haig, and II Corps under General Sir Horace Smith-Dorrien. Following the first battles, III Corps under Major General W.P. Pulteney joined these. The recently formed Royal Flying Corps contributed the 2nd, 3rd, 4th, and 5th Aeroplane Squadrons.

The Battle of Mons, 23 August 1914

The German *Schlieffen Plan* (requiring the right wing of the German armies to swing round through Belgium, turning the left wing of the French armies with the object of pinning them back against the Swiss frontier) determined the course of the early fighting. The British Expeditionary Force came into the line on the left of the French and on 23 August 1914 II Corps became engaged with the IV, III, and IX Corps of General Alexander von Kluck's German First Army. The fighting took place along the original line of the Mons–Conde Canal to the west and north of Mons, Belgium. By later standards, the battle was a mere skirmish, but British rifle fire inflicted some 3000 casualties and convinced the Germans that British infantry battalions possessed far more machine guns than the two that were standard issue. British casualties amounted to 1600 killed and wounded. The British Expeditionary Force then had to conform to the withdrawal of the French army on its right and pull back.

> ## The Old Contemptibles
>
> Kaiser Wilhelm II was said to have described the British Expeditionary Force as 'a contemptible little army'. Having hammered German conscript regiments into the ground, BEF members took a perverse pleasure in the title. Wilhelm later denied that he had ever made such a remark, but after the failure at Ypres he is on record as yelling hysterically at his generals that the British were 'trash and feeble adversaries, unworthy of the steel of the German soldier', and very foolish he must have felt afterwards. Strictly speaking, only members of the British Expeditionary Force that went to France in 1914 were eligible to call themselves Old Contemptibles, and they took immense pride in the fact for the rest of their lives.

The Battle of Le Cateau, 26 August 1914

Mons did not halt von Kluck's advance, but it cost him time, and that was the one thing he could not afford. After a gruelling retreat in scorching weather, the British Expeditionary Force turned to give battle again at Le Cateau on 26 August. Although, once again, only Smith-Dorrien's 40,000-strong II Corps was involved, it was the largest battle fought by the British Army since Waterloo (see Chapter 11). Von Kluck's IV, IV Reserve, and part of III Corps, a total of 140,000 men, opposed the British. Hard fighting enabled the British Expeditionary Force to break out of a double envelopment and disengage, although the cost was 7812 casualties and 38 guns lost. The fighting also imposed a far more serious check on von Kluck, whose report paid the British Expeditionary Force an unintended compliment by claiming that nine divisions had engaged him when only three were present. He also made a serious error of judgement in believing that he had defeated the British Expeditionary Force and that it was retreating to the Channel ports. In fact, I Corps had not even been seriously engaged and the British Expeditionary Force was actually withdrawing south to conform with the movement of its allies.

The Battle of the Marne, 5–10 September 1914

The Battles of Mons, Le Cateau, and other factors seriously disrupted the German army's plan. A series of engagements between 5 and 10 September, known collectively as the First Battle of the Marne, altered the whole complexion of the war on the Western Front. A newly formed French army attacked von Kluck's right, forcing him to turn and meet the threat. As a result, a gap opened between his First Army and General von Bulow's Second Army on von Kluck's left. Into this marched the British Expeditionary Force, splitting the German line while the French went over to the offensive. German command ordered both armies to withdraw. The Schlieffen Plan (see 'The Battle of Mons, 23 August 1914', earlier in this chapter) had failed and no alternative plan existed.

The British Expeditionary Force's part in the Allied advance enabled it to force a crossing of the river Aisne, but German resistance stiffened on the plateau beyond and both sides began to dig trenches for their own protection and construct barbed-wire entanglements in front of them. By 27 September no further movement was possible. During this three-week period estimates put each side's casualties at half a million.

The First Battle of Ypres, 18 October–30 November 1914

After the first trenches were dug at the Marne, both armies made repeated attempts to turn the other's northern flank, continually digging in until the trench lines eventually reached the sea. Because the British were sensitive about the Channel Ports falling into enemy hands (thereby cutting their supply lines), the British Expeditionary Force, now consisting of four corps and a cavalry corps, transferred to this sector. Continuous and very determined German attacks on the salient around the city of Ypres involved two armies (Duke Albrecht of Wurttemberg's Fourth and Crown Prince Rupprecht of Bavaria's Sixth), both of which were heavily reinforced. The battle lasted from 18 October to 30 November.

By the end of the battle the original British Expeditionary Force was 'used up'. It had sustained 58,155 casualties (in addition to the 50,000 casualties that the two French corps holding part of the line incurred) and some of its units were indeed reduced to a handful, but enough remained to train and provide a stiffening for the huge armies that were in process of forming. German casualties spiralled to a shocking 130,000. Many were young, idealistic, but inexperienced recruits, including a high proportion of university students, serving in the newly raised reserve corps that formed Wurttemberg's army. Against this, on 11 November the repulse of several regiments of the crack Prussian Guard, the elite of the Imperial German Army, provided convincing proof that the German offensive was doomed to failure.

Digging In to Trench Warfare

After the First Battle of Ypres (see the preceding section), little significant movement occurred on the Western Front for the next three-and-a-half years. The trench lines stretched from the North Sea to neutral Switzerland. They became deeper as the army dug reserve and communication trenches, and the barbed wire entanglements grew wider. In the hope of achieving a break-through, artillery bombardments became heavier and heavier. It became a gunner's war in which some form of artillery activity took place every day, even when the generals were not contemplating major offensives.

Air-burst shrapnel shells were in use in such quantities that steel helmets made a return to the battlefield in 1915. Artillery officers became adept at controlling the fire of unheard-of numbers of guns of every type. The result was that the battlefield quickly began to resemble a moonscape, and the drainage that farmers had installed over centuries was so badly smashed that low-lying areas became quagmires in winter. Various weapons also came into their own in trench warfare – see the sidebar 'The tools of the trench trade'.

Cavalry officers spoke wistfully of creating mayhem in the enemy's rear areas once the army had achieved a breakthrough, unwilling to admit that a few machine guns and the simplest barbed-wire fence would soon put a stop to that sort of thing. In fact, logic dictated that for the moment a clean break-through was impossible. Even if they did penetrate the opposing trench lines, armies relying on horse-drawn artillery could not get their guns forward across the wastes of no-man's land before the enemy rushed reinforcements into the area and sealed off the penetration. It was not a situation any of the generals had been trained to cope with, yet the politicians and the public insisted that they keep on trying.

Coping with shell shock

At a personal level, wounded men received better attention than ever before, but at first little understanding existed of minds unhinged by *shellshock* (mental disturbance induced by prolonged exposure to mortal danger, partic- ularly artillery fire). Generals wondered why soldiers had not suffered from shellshock in earlier wars. The reason was that the soldiers of earlier wars had only been exposed to mortal danger for comparatively short periods, while modern trench warfare exposed men to it day in and day out for sometimes lengthy periods, steadily eroding their reserves of courage and shredding their nerves. The first to exhibit symptoms of shellshock received little sympathy and were actually accused of shirking.

The tools of the trench trade

It goes almost without saying that one of the objects of war is to make life as unpleasant as possible for the other side. Poison gas was used in the First World War, but its release was a haphazard affair that could go badly wrong if the wind direction changed; as the war progressed it became possible to fill shells with small quantities of gas and deliver them precisely on to an objective. The flamethrower, used mainly by the German army, was another weapon that men hated and feared. Conversely, no one was keen to volunteer to use a flamethrower because the back-pack fuel tanks identified the operator immediately and he became everyone's favourite target. Other tools of trench warfare included grenades and mortars – both used in earlier warfare (see Chapter 7). Mining (again, used in earlier warfare – see Chapter 4) was tried as a method of destroying a section of the enemy's front line, beneath which huge quantities of explosives were detonated. Trench raiding at night was a regular feature of war on the Western Front, usually to take a prisoner for interrogation; in the narrow confines of a trench, rifles and bayonets were too cumbersome for trench raiding, so men armed themselves with knives, clubs, and axes that they could wield freely at close quarters.

Despite the horrors of trench warfare, many survivors recalled with sincere pleasure the comradeship they enjoyed during that period of their lives. The mental toughness of their generation was reflected in the black humour of their songs. For example, went the ditty, if one was looking for 'the old battalion' they could be found 'hangin' on the old barbed wire' on the far side of no-man's land, while one refrain sung cheerfully by burial parties was: 'The bells of hell go tinga linga ling / For you but not for me'.

'Your Country Needs You!'

The poster showing Kitchener's stern face and the slogan 'Your Country Needs You!' is still familiar today. During the early months of the war, Kitchener asked for 100,000 volunteers with which to expand the army, and then asked for another 100,000. He got them all, many times over, although some had to wait months before they received uniforms, weapons, and constructive training.

The government encouraged potential recruits to enlist with others from the same neighbourhood, occupation, or sporting interest, in what were termed *pals' battalions*. They came from every social class and were indeed representative of the nation in arms. They received instruction from officers and non-commissioned officers who had already seen action, or older, experienced former soldiers who acted as instructors for the duration of the war. Enthusiasm was the hallmark of the New Army battalions. Some regular officers expressed doubts about the men's abilities, which proved unjustified when the time came to test them.

By the beginning of 1916, the flood of volunteers had shrunk to a trickle that could not replace the daily wastage. The government therefore introduced *conscription* (enforced military service), initially for bachelors only.

 The British First and Second Armies were formed at the end of 1914 and the Third Army in 1915. Territorial regiments were arriving at the front, but in the opinion of Kitchener, now serving as Secretary of State for War, the New Army would not be ready for active service until 1916. In the meantime, the armies in France and Belgium took over more of the front line and mounted several limited offensives designed to tie down German troops and take some of the pressure off the French and the Russians, who had already sustained several catastrophic defeats and were beginning to totter.

The Second Battle of Ypres, 22 April–25 May 1915

In March 1915 Sir Douglas Haig's First Army captured the village of Neuve Chapelle, to the south of Ypres, in a three-day battle that cost 12,892 casualties and exhausted artillery ammunition stocks to the point that the French postponed further offensive action for two months.

On 22 April the Germans renewed their attacks on the Ypres salient, releasing poison gas for the first time on the Western Front. On the French sector, the better part of two divisions panicked and fled. Fortunately the Germans were slow to exploit this, but they did make some local gains. The burden of the fighting fell on Smith-Dorrien's Second Army. On 27 April, Smith-Dorrien was replaced by Lieutenant General Sir Herbert Plumer following a clash of personalities between the former and Sir John French, the BEF's commander. Plumer withdrew to a more tactically suitable line on 6 May.

The Second Battle of Ypres continued until 25 May. The Germans made some gains at the cost of 35,000 casualties, but were unable to eliminate the salient. In the long term, their use of gas released from cylinders was a serious tactical error, as the prevailing wind favoured the Allies. British and French losses were respectively 59,275 and approximately 10,000, one reason being that the more numerous German artillery dominated the battlefield.

The Battle of Loos, 25 September– 8 October 1915

Haig's First Army failed in its attempts to capture Aubers Ridge and the village of Festubert. The British sustained over 29,000 casualties and, once again, their stock of artillery ammunition came close to exhaustion. By September it had recovered sufficiently for the First Army to launch a major attack on Loos as part of the Allied effort to keep Russia in the war. The battle began on 25 September following four days of preliminary bombardment and saw the first British use of poison gas. The Allies made some gains on the first day, but the French failure to capture Vimy Ridge, overlooking the battlefield, prevented further progress. On the second day two exhausted divisions ran straight into German reinforcements, who shot the Allies to pieces. The battle spluttered on until 8 October, when heavy autumn rain brought an end to the fighting. The First Army sustained 60,000 casualties, twice that of the enemy. As a result of recriminations following the battle, Haig replaced French as Commander-in-Chief of the British Armies in December.

The Battle of the Somme, 1916

The first half of 1916 brought no hint of light at the end of the tunnel. On 1 June the British Grand Fleet fought a major action with the German High Seas Fleet off the Jutland peninsular. The Germans fled back to harbour, never to emerge again, but they lost fewer ships and seamen than the British did. The general feeling among the British was that the result was not satisfactory. While the Royal Navy did still rule the waves, the enemy's *U-boats* (submarines) were sinking more and more merchant ships, while the results of a British naval blockade were more apparent in Germany itself than at the front. Trouble in Ireland also gave some concern to the British (see the sidebar 'The Easter Uprising, 1916').

On 5 June 1916 Kitchener, leading a mission to Russia aboard the cruiser *Hampshire*, drowned when the ship struck a mine shortly after leaving Scapa Flow. He had seemed to be reassuringly permanent and the British public regarded his loss as a catastrophe, which perhaps overstated the case a little.

To relieve pressure on the French fighting the bloody battle of Verdun, an Allied offensive was launched on the Somme sector. It was decided that the objective was to be the high ground of the Thiepval–Pozieres ridge. General Sir Henry Rawlinson's British Fourth Army would deliver the main attack, with two divisions of General Sir Edmund Allenby's Third Army protecting his left flank. On the Allied right, General Fayolle's French Sixth Army would advance either side of the river Somme. Once the offensive was under way, a breakout force, consisting of the Cavalry Corps and two of Rawlinson's infantry divisions, would form under Lieutenant General Hubert Gough and be known as the Reserve Army.

This offensive was to be the first major test for Kitchener's New Army divisions. Some regular commanders and their staffs so lacked confidence in the ability of these formations to execute such elementary tactical movements as controlled rushes by groups across fire-swept ground that they insisted on their attacking in straight lines at walking pace. Also available were ten Commonwealth divisions (five from Australia, four from Canada, one from New Zealand) and a South African brigade.

Starting the Somme offensive

The offensive was planned to commence on 29 June but was postponed until 1 July.

In places, the Germans had dug trenches on the reverse slopes of the ridge and concealed them, while air reconnaissance revealed that the front and second lines of defence extended to a depth of 450 metres (500 yards). Barbed-wire entanglements were 45 metres (50 yards) deep, sometimes shaped so that attacks were channelled into killing grounds swept by concealed machine guns. Hundreds of fortified machine gun posts existed, some of them inside reinforced concrete blockhouses. And huge dugouts lay some 9 metres (30 feet) or more beneath the surface, complete with running water, ventilation, electric lighting, and emergency rations. The attackers were told that the prolonged preliminary bombardment, audible in England, would cut the enemy's wire, smash his strongpoints, destroy his communications, neutralise his artillery, and reduce his will to fight. On reaching the enemy trenches, it was unlikely that they would find anyone alive. As the bombardment lifted, officers' whistles shrilled and the first British and French assault waves clambered out of their trenches.

Across *no-man's land* (the area between the opposing trench networks), the Germans came tumbling up from their deep dugouts into fresh air and daylight, glad to be free from their claustrophobic subterranean prisons and anxious to hit back. The bombardment had failed.

The Easter Uprising, 1916

Tens of thousands of Irishmen served in the British Army and, whether their persuasion was for _Home Rule_ (meaning Irish, not British, government) or not, they were prepared to wait for the war to end before pursuing the issues of their domestic politics further. But at Easter 1916, a group of Nationalists staged an armed rebellion in Dublin. Although the government put down the rising without undue difficulty, hanging the ringleaders was a mistake as it made martyrs of them. Discipline in the Irish regiments was not affected, but the incident left Irish soldiers unsettled in their minds as to what the future might bring (for more on what came to pass, see Chapter 20).

On the right, the French broke through the enemy's first line with a series of disciplined rushes. On their immediate left two New Army divisions of XIII Corps, the 18th and the 30th, achieved the only British success of the day. They did it by ignoring their fatuous instructions to walk in extended lines and by using their initiative:

- ✔ The 18th had only 180 metres (200 yards) of no-man's land to cross and they covered it at a run, arriving before the enemy had time to get their act together.

- ✔ The 30th had twice that distance to cover, but found that the wire had been sufficiently cut for them to press home their attack. However, even these gains cost XIII Corps some 6000 casualties.

Elsewhere, the story of the battle was one of supreme courage rewarded with terrible failure. Rifle and machine gun fire cut down each stolidly advancing wave of attackers as they appeared. The German artillery's defensive barrages created impenetrable walls of blast and flying steel. Inexperienced groups crossed the enemy's front-line trenches without clearing the deep dugouts, so they were shot down from behind when the defenders surfaced, or were cut off, surrounded, and forced to surrender. Wherever some small success was achieved, it was quickly eliminated by counter-attacks.

By 10 a.m. the action was all over. Along 30 kilometres (20 miles) of front no-man's land was strewn thick with khaki forms, sprawled among the thick growth of scarlet poppies or caught in the enemy's wire entanglements. Of them, no fewer than 19,240 were dead. Survivors crawled or limped back to their own lines or waited patiently for darkness in whatever cover shell holes provided.

Everyone knew a major disaster had occurred, but its sheer scale was not apparent for some days. Roll calls revealed battalions reduced to company strength with just two or three officers left, companies reduced to platoons, and platoons to a handful of men. When at last the full extent of the carnage was apparent, in addition to the dead, 33,493 men had been wounded, 2152 were missing, and 585 were known to have been captured. At 57,470, the total casualties incurred on 1 July 1916 were the highest in the entire history of the British army.

Turning the tide

The battle continued over the next few weeks, with smaller attacks against local objectives. The German doctrine was to recover lost ground immediately with counter-attacks, which exposed their infantry to the same sort of fire that the British endured on 1 July. On 11 July the Allies had their reward: The Germans suspended offensive operations against Verdun. The French went over to the offensive, recovering much of the lost ground, and the British maintained their pressure on the Somme. Now they were bleeding the German army dry.

On 14 July Rawlinson introduced a new tactical concept, a night attack delivered behind a *creeping barrage* in which artillery fire advanced through the enemy position by agreed bounds in accordance with a timed programme. The infantry, aware of the timing, were able to follow the barrage closely. By 8 a.m. the next morning the British had broken the German second line on a frontage of 5500 metres (6000 yards). Rawlinson ordered the cavalry forward to exploit the gap, but they were positioned some 16 kilometres (10 miles) behind the line. They did not arrive until 7 p.m. and by then the opportunity to take its designated objectives, Delville Wood and High Wood, had vanished because enemy reinforcements had plugged the gap.

On 15 July the Allied command ordered the 1st South African Brigade to take Delville Wood at all costs. They succeeded, although their casualties were high. The Germans were desperate to recapture the position, but failed. At one point estimates say that 400 shrapnel, high-explosive, or gas shells were blasting the wood every minute. Many of the South Africans were crack shots who collected five or six rifles from the dead and wounded and kept them loaded ready to repel the next attack. When the brigade was finally relieved on 21 July, its numbers had been reduced to 29 officers (only 8 of whom were unwounded) and 751 other ranks out of an original strength in excess of 2500.

Throughout the remainder of July and on into August and September, the Allies continued to mount local attacks eating away at the enemy's front line. Having lost the protection of their deep dugouts, the Germans took to holding their line with a series of linked strongpoints and counter-attack groups just behind. This policy increased their casualties to even higher levels than before.

Bringing on the tanks

On 15 September 1916, Haig mounted an attack on the Flers–Courcelette sector that, while its results were insignificant by Western Front standards, changed the face of warfare: Haig used tanks (see the sidebar 'Let's call it a tank!' for more on early armoured fighting vehicles) for the very first time.

Haig's plan allocated 17 tanks each to XIV and XV Corps and divided a further 15 between III Corps and the Canadian Corps. Of these, only 32 reached the start line. Nine more broke down and five became ditched. Another nine were unable to keep up with the infantry but were able to assist with the subsequent mopping up. The remainder achieved results out of all proportion to their numbers. Zero hour was set for 6.20 a.m., but the main assault was preceded by a preliminary attack timed for 5.15 a.m. against an enemy position known as Hop Alley, to the east of Delville Wood. This was carried out by Captain H.W. Mortimore's section of three tanks and two companies of 6/King's Own Yorkshire Light Infantry. One of Mortimore's tanks broke down immediately and another became ditched shortly after, but he continued across no man's land in his own tank, D1. Ahead, machine guns opened up. His own gunners replied, evidently to good effect, because the infantry charged past with fixed bayonets and secured the objective. Mortimore then positioned his vehicle astride another trench, which he raked with his machine guns. He recalled that the enemy's reaction was either complete bewilderment, fear, blind panic, or passive surrender. When the main attack began he joined the general advance, but had covered only 270 metres (300 yards) when a shell hit D1, broke the starboard track and blew in the sponson, killing two of the crew. Mortimore continued to engage targets until the infantry had passed through. Elsewhere, three tanks penetrated Flers and suppressed the opposition so effectively that the infantry were able to take possession of the village by 8 a.m. Later, two continued the advance to Gueudecourt, which would have fallen if the infantry had been able to keep up. As it was, the enemy's artillery knocked out both tanks, but not before they had done considerable damage. The hamlet of Gueudecourt fell on 26 September, largely because of the action of a single tank, D4, commanded by Second Lieutenant C.E. Storey, which turned parallel to the formidable Gird Trench, crushing its wire and firing heavily into the trench itself.

The appearance of the tanks had caused panic among the enemy, but the experience was restricted to the few of them in the immediate vicinity. When the Germans carried out a technical evaluation of knocked-out tanks, they discovered that their thin boilerplate hulls were vulnerable to not only to field guns but also to a powerful type of ammunition used to engage armoured bunker slits. What was more, the tanks were obviously unreliable in the mechanical sense. The Germans therefore reached the disastrous conclusion that there was no point in embarking on a tank-production programme of their own. The British conclusions were simple and to the point. Where tanks had been used, success had followed and infantry casualties had been light. Where they had not been used, the reverse applied. As for the technical problems, they were resolved, and the British tank-production programme was accelerated.

During October a series of local attacks finally cleared the Thiepval–Pozieres Ridge. The autumn rains began to make movement on the battlefield difficult. During the third week of November, Gough's Fifth Army, as the Reserve Army had become, took Beaumont Hamel, which had been one of the first day's objectives. As a result of the battle of the Somme, the Allies had gained a strip of territory some 32 kilometres (20 miles) long and up to 11 kilometres (7 miles) deep, at a cost, respectively, of 418,000 British and 194,000 French casualties.

Let's call it a tank!

Ever since trench warfare set in, the British and French armies appreciated the need for a fully tracked vehicle to negotiate the shell-torn ground of no-man's land, crush barbed wire, cross trenches, and eliminate machine-gun posts with its fire. The British were ahead in the race and had produced a viable design within a year, a remarkable achievement when one considers that it can take up to 20 years to get a modern tank design into production.

No one person was responsible for producing the first British tank. Many people had a hand in the effort, including Colonel Maurice Hankey, Lieutenant Colonel Ernest Swinton, and Winston Churchill, then at the Admiralty, all of whom were then serving on the Committee of Imperial Defence. Swinton had actually proposed the sort of vehicle described above as early as September 1914 and the idea dovetailed with some of Churchill's own thoughts. On 20 February 1915 Churchill set up a Landships Committee under Eustace Tennyson d'Eyncourt, the Director of Naval Construction, the members of which included William Tritton, the Managing Director of William Foster & Co Ltd, agricultural machinery manufacturers from Lincoln; Colonel R.E.B. Crompton, whose experience of land traction went back as far as the Crimean War; Flight Commander T.G. Hetherington and Lieutenants

W.G. Wilson and A. Stern, all of the Royal Naval Air Service, which was already actively employing armoured cars.

Swinton, a Royal Engineer officer, decided to compress the shape of the tracked wheel into a rhombus so that the bottom run was shaped like an arc taken from an 18-metre (60-foot) diameter wheel, while the vertical step from the ground to the forward track horns was more than adequate for surmounting parapets and crossing trenches. No one has yet succeeded in designing a tracked vehicle with a better cross-country performance. Armament consisted of two naval 6-pounder guns mounted in *sponsons* (projecting housings) on either side of the hull and four Hotchkiss machine guns.

Trials in January 1916 were satisfactory and the army ordered 100 of the vehicles. A dense cloak of security now enveloped the project while the vehicles were being built and crews and their instructors were recruited to man them. The word landship provided too obvious a clue to the vehicles' purpose, so the army spread a rumour that they were simply large mobile water cisterns or tanks intended for use by the Russian army. A photograph exists of one of the first tanks in Foster's yard, clearly inscribed in Cyrillic characters, 'With Care to Petrograd'!

Haig's view was that victory could only be obtained by defeating the main mass of the enemy, and that lay in France. He had gone some way towards achieving that, for the 650,000 casualties inflicted on the German army during the battle of the Somme included a high proportion of professional junior officers and non-commissioned officers. Signs were also appearing that the German soldiers' morale had begun to crack. Generals Hindenburg and Ludendorff concluded that German troops' endurance of heavy artillery bombardments followed by sustained infantry attacks could not be maintained for much longer. In February 1917 they voluntarily gave up several more kilometres of territory and pulled back to a shorter but stronger defence line. For the British, the consequences of the battle of the Somme were less apparent, although they marked a watershed in the nation's history. The endless casualty lists in the local press suggested that the country had sent forth its best and they had been wasted. Innocence and idealism died together on the Somme. With only a few exceptions, the British never again quite trusted their leaders, political or military, in the way they had prior to the battle.

The Battles of 1917

Following the Battle of the Somme (see the previous section), British forces engaged in more major actions on the Western Front during 1917:

- **Arras and Vimy Ridge.** On 9 April 1917 two British armies, General Sir Edmund Allenby's Third and General Sir Henry Horne's First, opened an offensive to secure Vimy Ridge, near Arras. It succeeded primarily because of the meticulous planning that went into its preparation. With 5000 guns, the British artillery outnumbered the German artillery by four to one. The British knew the position of the German batteries and neutralised most of them, while a newly developed gas shell greatly reduce the efficiency of the remainder. The Allies had dug miles of tunnels in which the assault troops sheltered immediately prior to the attack. Sixty tanks were available and, although most bogged down in the bad, shell-torn ground, the appearance of the remainder was decisive.

  The capture of Vimy Ridge itself by Lieutenant General Sir Julian Byng's Canadian Corps was one of the First World War's most notable feats of arms – everything went according to plan and the attack succeeded. Having lost the summit, the Germans had to withdraw from their positions on the reverse slopes, which had become untenable. Only the British cavalry fared badly, an attempt by two of its brigades to exploit a breach in the line at Monchy-le-Preux being halted by machine gun fire that inflicted heavy losses.

  By 15 April the offensive had run down. British and Canadian casualties amounted to 20,000, while General Baron von Falkenhausen's German Sixth Army sustained 27,000 losses.

- **The Nivelle offensive.** General Robert Nivelle, who had replaced 'Papa' Joffre as French Commander-in-Chief, claimed that his methods held the key to successful offensives. When his army tried these between 16 and 20 April, all they produced were 120,000 casualties. As a result, between 29 April and 20 May the French army was in a state of mutiny, although it agreed to fight if attacked. Incredibly, the French concealed this fact from the enemy, although they requested increased British pressure to tie down the German reserves.

- **Messines Ridge.** Haig planned a major offensive out of the Ypres salient, but before this could take place General Sir Herbert Plumer's Second Army had to secure Messines Ridge, south of the salient. Once again, the army took great care in the preparations for the assault. Extensive tunnelling beneath the enemy front resulted in the explosion of 19 mines packed with over 450,000 kilograms (1 million pounds) of explosive just before the main assault on 7 June. As a result, the British blew the Germans' forward defences out of existence and made an advance of 4 kilometres (2.5 miles) on a 16-kilometre (10-mile) frontage the first day. The fighting continued for a week, by which time the British had sustained 17,000 casualties and the Germans 25,000, including losing 7500 men as prisoners.

- **The Third Battle of Ypres (Passchendaele).** The six-week delay between the capture of Messines Ridge and the opening of the Third Battle of Ypres, better known as Passchendaele, cannot altogether be justified, as much of it was taken up with bickering between the generals, and between the generals and the politicians. The first objective was a low ridge on which the village of Passchendaele stood. Once that was taken, the next steps involved a breakout from the salient to clear the Belgian coast of the enemy and continue as far as the Dutch border. At a time when an advance of a kilometre or two was hailed as a great achievement, this was ambition gone stark, staring mad.

Passchendaele, even more than the Somme, has come to epitomise the utter misery of trench warfare on the Western Front, as well as the courage and endurance of those involved. The battle began on 31 July and the Allies made good progress. Then the rain began, and it kept on raining. Years of shellfire had destroyed the countryside's drainage system. The ground simply refused to absorb the continuous downpour. Whole areas turned into a bog in which men and horses vanished if they stepped off defined tracks. Tanks sank up to their roofs. The front line was a series of shell holes connected by flooded scrapes. Woods became a collection of shattered stumps. Farms and villages were reduced to fragments of wall or areas of mud stained with brick dust. Fighting apart, day-to-day living was a constant struggle.

The ordeal went on and on until the Canadian Corps finally took Passchendaele on 6 November, and the battle was officially declared to be at an end four days later. If anything good can be said about it, it succeeded in occupying the enemy's attention at a period when the French armies were slowly recovering their ability to fight offensively. The British Second and Fifth Armies lost 80,000 men killed and missing, 230,000 wounded, and 14,000 captured. The French First Army, operating to the north of the salient, sustained approximately 50,000 casualties. The German Fourth and Sixth Armies had 50,000 men killed and missing, 113,000 wounded, and 37,000 captured.

✔ **Cambrai.** More than any other, the officers of the Tank Corps, now commanded by Brigadier General Hugh Elles with Major J.F.C. Fuller as his Chief of Staff, insisted that fighting wars in this way was no longer necessary. So far, tanks had been committed to the fighting in small numbers on ground that virtually guaranteed failure. All the Tank Corps wanted was a chance to show what it could achieve en masse over good going. General Sir Julian Byng, commander of the British Third Army, supported the idea and selected the firm chalk downland of the Cambrai sector for the attack.

At 6:20 a.m. on 20 November, following a short bombardment that did not spoil the going, 378 of 476 tanks available rolled forward into the assault, led by Elles personally. With little difficulty they smashed through the enemy wire and crossed the German trenches, forging on into their rear areas with guns blazing. By noon they had ripped a hole 9.5 kilometres (6 miles) wide and 6.5 kilometres (4 miles) deep through the front of the German Second Army. The total cost had been 4000 casualties, including 648 of the tank crews. A similar breach during the Third Battle of Ypres needed three months and approximately 250,000 casualties to achieve. Tank casualties at Cambrai included 65 written off or seriously damaged by enemy action, 71 broken down, and 43 ditched. German losses, including a high proportion of prisoners, came to 10,500. The captured equipment included 123 guns, 79 trench mortars, 281 machine guns, and large stocks of ammunition and stores. For the only time during the war, the church bells in Britain rang out to celebrate a victory.

The celebration was short lived. On 30 November the Germans launched a counter-offensive that astonished everyone with its speed and weight. Using tactics pioneered against the Russians, they recovered much of the lost ground, and a little more besides. The technique involved a carefully orchestrated artillery programme after which specially trained storm troop units by-passed centres of resistance, leaving them to be dealt with by follow-up waves, and quickly worked their way into the opposing artillery and administrative zones, supported throughout by waves of ground-attack aircraft. By rounding up 63 assorted tanks and crews, the Allies halted the counter-offensive on 7 December. A further consequence of the battle was that the German army decided, very late in the day, to form its own tank units.

The year 1917 ended on an ominous note for the Allies. In October the Italian Army was routed at Caporetto. As a result of this, British divisions that could ill be spared from the Western Front were sent to Italy to help stabilise the line. The French army was gradually recovering its morale, but Russia had collapsed and was wracked by revolution and civil war. That meant that scores of German divisions could be transferred to the Western Front, lengthening the odds against the remaining Allied armies. On the other hand, the United States, with its huge manpower and material resources, had entered the war against Germany. The problem was that the American Regular Army was tiny. It would take time to raise and train new armies, and even when they had been shipped across the Atlantic they would still lack many of the things now considered essential in modern war, from tanks to steel helmets. On 31 December 1917 the shrewdest fortune teller with the highest-powered crystal ball on the market could not have predicted the outcome of events the following year, which are dealt with in Chapter 18.

Chapter 18

Storm Troopers and Tank Attacks: The Western Front, 1918

. . . .

In This Chapter

▶ Ludendorff's offensives

▶ Allied counter attacks

▶ The Battle of Amiens

▶ Breaking the Hindenburg Line

▶ Defining the legacy of the First World War

. . . .

As Field Marshal Hindenburg's Chief of Staff, the German General Erich Ludendorff had a significant say in what happened in the war. Ludendorff believed that with the transfer of divisions from what had been the Eastern Front before Russia's collapse in 1917, the Germans could win the war in the West. He considered the British to be the principal enemy, and if the Germans beat the British, he reasoned, the French would seek terms. So confident was he that he rashly promised his troops that their efforts would bring victory. After the initial scramble and relentless trench warfare of 1914–1917, the Western Front offered something different in 1918, so it gets a chapter all to itself. That something was mobility in various forms, an element unknown to most soldiers on this battlefront since the autumn of 1914.

Figure 18-1 shows British infantrymen in the First World War. Tanks and aircraft grew in importance, and towards the end of the war, as the stalemate of the trenches was left behind, cavalry made a return, too. In addition to the heavy tanks used in 1916 and 1917, the fast, light Whippet tank made an appearance in 1918.

Figure 18-1:
British
infantry-
men, First
World War.

The German army developed its own breakthrough technique employing three elements:

- **A carefully orchestrated artillery programme.** Colonel Bruchmuller, something of an artillery virtuoso, commanded a travelling circus of heavy guns that moved up and down the front as required, and absorbed the local artillery units into his plan. Depending on the area of front to be breached, he tailored the programme to include high explosives, phosgene gas, and smoke shells, with the object of leaving the defenders shocked, choking, and blind when the attack went in.

- **Deep penetration by storm troop battalions.** This involved forming battalions of storm troopers, recruited from young, fit men of proven initiative. Their favourite weapons were the grenade, of which each man carried at least one bag full, the light machine gun, and the man-pack flamethrower. They advanced in groups, usually at a run with slung rifles, taking advantage of the available ground cover. If they encountered opposition, they worked their way round it, leaving the follow-up waves of infantry to deal with it. Continual movement was the essence of their tactics, the ultimate object of which was to destroy brigade and divisional headquarters.

- **Continuous support by ground-attack aircraft.** This technique consisted of battle flights of up to six aircraft, trained to strafe enemy troops in the immediate path of the storm troopers from a height of 60 metres (200 feet). This produced less satisfactory results than the Royal Flying Corps' squadrons, which attacked at ground level, and this difference led to complaints from the storm troopers that the battle flights were not doing their job properly.

Thanks to politicians retaining a needlessly large number of troops for home defence, the manpower resources of the British armies in France and Belgium had become stretched to their limit. The nine battalions now forming each infantry division contained, on average, 500 men in contrast to the 1000 with which they had gone to war. With this in mind, the British introduced a new defensive layout that unintentionally favoured every aspect of Ludendorff's plans:

✔ First was a *forward zone*, consisting of strongpoints that were little more than fortified outposts. These actually provided the storm troopers with the very opportunities they sought to infiltrate.

✔ Second, three or four kilometres behind but still within range of the German artillery and lacking dugouts, lay a battle zone trench system containing about one third of the defenders.

✔ Thirdly, beyond this, a rear zone was intended to house the reserves, but in places this consisted of little more than a line of spit-locked turf.

The Ludendorff Offensives, March–June 1918

Ludendorff's first offensive, lasting from 21 March to 5 April, effected a breakthrough on a 95-kilometre (60-mile) front and penetrated to a depth of 65 kilometres (40 miles). The British lost all the gains they had so painfully made on the Somme and the Germans all but destroyed Gough's Fifth Army. The Allies sustained 255,000 casualties, including 90,000 taken prisoner, and the loss of 1100 guns. Together, self-sacrificial stands and small *ad hoc* groups made up of stragglers, cooks, drivers, clerks, storemen, and mess waiters thrust into the gaps managed to hold the line in desperate fighting. The offensive failed in its primary object of separating the British and French armies by a drive on Amiens and the Somme estuary. German losses were also heavier than they had allowed for, amounting to 250,000, mainly in the storm troop battalions. On 9 April Ludendorff tried again. His second offensive recovered all the ground lost at Passchendaele, reduced the Ypres salient to a rump, recaptured Messines Ridge, and inflicted 82,000 casualties. It did not, as planned, break through to the Channel ports and it cost 98,000 men. The sidebar 'Tank versus tank' highlights one of many actions fought during this period.

Between 27 May and 6 June, Ludendorff struck at the French on the Chemin des Dames sector in the hope of them withdrawing their reserves from Flanders, enabling him to strike a decisive blow against the British. He gained ground, at considerable cost, but now found himself without sufficient troops to man the salient that he had formed. Ludendorff then mounted a fourth offensive with the object of shortening the line between two salients. This failed because the Allies were by now familiar with the German methods and were prepared to meet the attack.

Tank versus tank

When the Germans began to produce tanks of their own, it was inevitable that tank would meet tank on the battlefield sooner or later. The meeting happened at Villers-Bretonneux, east of Amiens, on 24 April 1918. Here, in the Bois de l'Abbé, the crews of the three Mark IV tanks of No 1 Section, A Company, 1st Battalion Tank Corps were recovering from the effects of gas shells. Commanded by Captain J.C. Brown, the section consisted of two *female tanks* (armed solely with machine guns) and one *male tank* (armed with 6-pounder guns and machine guns). Second Lieutenant Francis Mitchell commanded the male tank.

On learning that the Germans were leading their attack with tanks, No 1 Section moved out to meet them at 8.45 a.m. Four German tanks were present, all A7Vs, the abbreviated title of the German design committee. The A7V consisted of a large, box-like armoured superstructure mounted on an extended commercial tractor chassis, armed with a 57-millimetre gun in the front plate and machine guns, and no fewer than 16 men manned it.

Only Mitchell's tank competed on equal terms. The Germans soon forced the two females out of the action by blowing holes through their armour. Mitchell's left 6-pounder gunner began ranging on an A7V. He scored three hits, the tank lurched to a standstill, and the crew made

off as fast as they could run. Mitchell now engaged two more A7Vs. One, after absorbing some punishment, backed away and the other turned and followed it. Unknown to Mitchell, a fourth A7V, named Elfrieda, had overturned in a sandpit before getting into action.

Later that morning a British reconnaissance aircraft spotted two storm troop battalions resting in a hollow near Cachy, just a few hundred metres from the scene of the tank battle. The pilot dropped a message to a company of the Tank Corps' 3rd Battalion, suggesting that if the tanks hurried they would catch the enemy in the open. The company was equipped with Whippet light tanks (developed to work with the cavalry), and its commander, Captain Thomas Price, seized the opportunity at once. In line abreast with 35 metres (40 yards) between them, his seven tanks tore through the hollow twice, machine guns blazing. They killed or wounded over 400 of the storm troopers. An A7V that had remained in the area knocked out one tank that ignored Price's instructions to avoid showing itself on the skyline, and damaged three more. The last act in this, the first tank battle in history, was the diffident return of 11 survivors of the crew belonging to Mitchell's first tank victim, after dark. They had been told to go and get their vehicle, or else — luckily for them, they managed it.

German morale nose-dived. The promised victory had not materialised. Most of the storm troopers were now dead, the remainder of the German army was of lesser quality, and the manpower reserve provided by the Eastern Front divisions had been used up. Letters from home complained about shortages of food and other things brought about by the British blockade. The Americans were reaching Europe in large numbers and being equipped by the British and French, who seemed to possess all the tanks, guns, rations, and supplies they needed. For the average German soldier in the middle of 1918, the future was bleak.

The Allies Fight Back

The shape of things to come became apparent on 4 July, when 60 of the new Mark V tanks supported an attack by ten Australian battalions and four American companies on a 5.5-kilometre (3.5-mile) frontage. The objective was the village of Le Hamel, situated on a low ridge to the northeast of Villers-Bretonneux, 2.5 kilometres (1.5 miles) behind the German lines. Incredibly, the Allies took the village within an hour. The Australians sustained 775 casualties and the Americans 134. The tank crews had 13 men wounded. Shellfire damaged five tanks, but the British recovered all of them. The German losses included 1500 men taken prisoner, 2 field guns, and 171 machine guns. Two weeks later the French and Americans struck a hammer blow into the flank of a salient south of Soissons. Their assault, spearheaded by 346 tanks, punched a hole 6.5 kilometres (4 miles) wide in the enemy defences. During the next few days the offensive ran down, enabling the Germans to retreat in good order to a shorter line. Despite this, they left no fewer than 25,000 prisoners in Allied hands.

On 23 July the Tank Corps' 9th Battalion won a unique distinction during the Battle of Sauvillers (sometimes called Moreuil). On loan to the French 3rd Division, the Corps led a successful attack at small cost to its allies, taking 1858 prisoners, plus 5 field guns and 275 machine guns. The battalion's losses were 54 men killed or wounded and 11 of its 34 tanks knocked out. Delighted, the French awarded the battalion a corporate Croix de Guerre as well as conferring on its men the honour of wearing the 3rd Division's insignia as an arm badge.

As a result of these successes, Ludendorff realised that the battle had begun to turn against him. Gibbering with rage, he declaimed:

> It is to the tanks that the enemy owes his success . . . As soon as the tanks are destroyed the whole attack fails!

It wasn't quite as simple as that and in a little while he was given something to really gibber about – the Battle of Amiens (see the next section).

The Battle of Amiens, 8 August 1918

The local successes of July prompted General Sir Henry Rawlinson, commanding the Fourth Army, to suggest that the British III Corps, the Australian Corps, and the Canadian Corps mount a major offensive east of Amiens, spearheaded by the Tank Corps. His choice of Dominion troops was deliberate, partly because their divisions were still largely up to strength and partly because they had retained their offensive spirit. Most British formations, on the other hand, were still recovering from the enemy's spring offensives and were seriously short of men.

The Allies accepted Rawlinson's suggestion. Four tank battalions (1st, 4th, 5th, and 14th) were allocated to the Canadian Corps on the right, four more (2nd, 8th, 13th, and 15th) plus the Austin armoured cars of the Tank Corps' 17th Battalion to the Australian Corps in the centre, and one tank battalion (10th) to the British III Corps on the left. The Cavalry Corps, given the task of exploiting the breakthrough, was allocated the 3rd and 6th Battalions, both of which were equipped with the Whippet light tank. In total, the attack would be made by 324 Mark V or V* heavy tanks, with a further 42 in immediate reserve, 96 Whippets,120 supply tanks, and 22 *gun carriers* (cut-down Mark Is designed to carry 60-pounder guns or 6-inch (15-centimetre) howitzers across no-man's land). The Fourth Army had 684 heavy guns and 1386 field guns available, while the neighbouring French First Army, which was to extend the attack southwards, had another 826 heavy and 780 field guns. An elaborate deception plan drew the enemy's attention elsewhere. Newly arrived artillery batteries, for example, simply registered their designated targets then lapsed into silence. The tanks arrived by train during the night of 6/7 August. As they dispersed to their assembly areas, the rumble of engines and the squeal of tracks were drowned out by the noise of low-flying aircraft. Opposite the Allies was General von der Marwitz's Second Army, consisting of 11 divisions each with an average strength of 3000 men. Recent failures and news of growing unrest at home had demoralised the infantrymen, although the machine gunners and artillery were as reliable as ever. A new anti-tank rifle had been issued, but this did not compensate for a general nervousness among the Germans about tank attacks.

At 4.20 a.m. on 8 August the Allied artillery exploded into life. In a morning mist that smoke shells made thicker, long lines of tanks and infantry moved forward in the wake of a rolling barrage. The Germans could hear the distinctive sound of engines and tracks long before they could see anything of the

attackers. Then, quite suddenly, the huge shapes burst out of the grey curtain at point-blank range, crushing wire, straddling trenches, spitting machine gun fire, high-explosive shells, and scything case shot. Hundreds threw up their hands in surrender at once. Between 6.30 and 7 a.m. the Allies overran the German front line so easily that it might never have existed. At 6.45 a.m. the mist had begun to clear and as the tanks probed deeper the German field gunners could see them. In the fight that followed, no quarter was given or expected. When the battle was over no fewer than 109 tanks had become blazing wrecks or were too badly damaged to continue, but the enemy's divisional artillery regiments had ceased to exist. The advance rolled on. By 11 a.m. the Allies had taken the second designated objective. By 1 p.m. they had taken the third.

A gap 18 kilometres (11 miles) wide and 11 kilometres (7 miles) deep now existed in the German line. The Cavalry Corps had reached the front too late to do any good at High Wood during the Somme battle, and they were late again at Cambrai (see Chapter 17 for these battles). Now, they were on time and desperate to show what they could do. In places they did well. They captured a large railway gun and field batteries trying to escape to the rear and rounded up prisoners by the score. Sadly, the bottom line was that cavalry and tanks were simply not compatible. When little or no opposition existed, the horsemen cantered ahead, leaving the Whippet tanks, capable of only 8.3 miles per hour at best, far behind. When the cavalry encountered serious resistance, they were pinned down and had to wait for the Whippets.

The official German report on the day's fighting made it clear that the Second Army sustained a disastrous defeat. It recorded the total losses of this sector at between 600 and 700 officers and 26,000 and 27,000 men, plus 400 guns and an enormous quantity of machine guns, mortars, and other equipment. It further stated that over two-thirds of the personnel casualties resulted from mass surrenders. Others who had not surrendered simply abandoned their weapons and took to their heels. The report actually underestimated the scale of the losses. The true casualty figure was in the region of 75,000, including almost 30,000 prisoners. Ludendorff described 8 August as 'The Black Day of the German army'. Officers were horrified when troops retiring from the battle yelled insulting remarks at divisions moving forward to plug the gap, calling them blacklegs and scabs. 'Our war machine was no longer efficient,' concluded Ludendorff.

On 9 August the Allies had only 145 tanks available. Next day the number was even lower and as fresh German divisions moved into the gap, the battle ran down. British casualties totalled 22,000 killed, wounded, and missing, while those of the French First Army were about half that figure. Haig had every cause for satisfaction. Together, the mass surrenders and interrogation of prisoners revealed that, at long last, he had broken the German will to fight.

Breaking the Hindenburg Line

In the weeks following the Battle of Amiens the Allied offensive became general along the Western Front. Much of the burden fell on the British armies. Mobility was back on the battlefield and the British adapted quickly to its demands. Throughout August and September 1918 the advance continued. Tanks led local attacks that steadily gnawed away at the German defences. On 29 September a second tank battle took place near Cambrai when groups of German tanks, most of them captured British vehicles, led a counter-attack. The Tank Corps' 12th Battalion met them and sustained some loss, but destroyed six of the eleven enemy tanks. The Germans had begun to fight harder once more, not because they had any hope of victory, but because their leaders had told them they were now defending the Fatherland. Despite this, the Allies had broken through the formidable defences of the Hindenburg Line by 5 October. Simultaneously, in Flanders, the British and Belgian armies finally broke out of the Ypres salient. In late October and early November, the pace of the advance was beyond even that of the Whippet tanks. Whenever the cavalry were not held up, they followed the German armies as the enemy retreated towards their homeland. When the Allies reached Mons, the Belgian town may have stirred memories among some of the troopers. After all, for the British Army, the war had started here, over four years earlier.

On 6 October Germany indicated that it welcomed an armistice. The Allies replied that they would not negotiate with a military dictatorship. Ludendorff resigned on 27 October to permit negotiations to continue, but his gesture was too late. Two days later the German High Seas Fleet, rusting at its moorings since Jutland (see Chapter 17), mutinied. Riots, rebellions, and mutinies in the cause of peace spread like wildfire across Germany. On 9 November a republic was proclaimed. Next day Kaiser Wilhelm formally abdicated, then scuttled off to neutral Holland. The new government finally agreed terms with the Allies and an armistice came into effect at 11 a.m. on 11 November. Haig considered that the humiliating terms that the victorious Allies imposed on Germany would simply lead to another war, and he was right (see Part VI).

Reflecting on the War: Lions, Donkeys, and Poets

Hardly a family in Great Britain did not lose at least one of its members during the First World War. The trauma remains deep-seated within the national consciousness. Very few war memorials existed prior to 1918. Subsequently, they appeared in every city, town, village, hamlet, and even in the workplaces of those who had been killed. In such times of raw grief, thinking of rational explanations was difficult when the nation had suffered nearly one million casualties.

A popular saying was that during a conversation between Hindenburg and Ludendorff they described the British Army as 'lions led by donkeys'. No such conversation ever took place, but the phrase entered common usage. Of course, the prior experience of most generals had not prepared them for the realities of trench warfare, and some were incompetent or promoted beyond their abilities as the army expanded, but the same was true of every army in the field. What is interesting is that the generals were considered competent enough before trench warfare set in during the autumn of 1914, and also when mobility returned to the battlefield in 1918.

Most staff officers performed to the best of their abilities, but others worked their way into staff jobs that offered safe, comfortable billets and the opportunity for a spot of bureaucratic empire building. The staff lived and worked well behind the lines, in or near their general's chateau, generally in some style. The troops resented their clean-shaven, spick-and-span visits to the front line, which the occupants shared with greedy lice, well-fed rats, and corpses, not simply because they were tactless, but because the orders they brought usually meant trouble of one sort or another for someone. Staff offers wore the same red band around their service dress caps and the same red lapel tabs as their generals. Such, however, was the dislike and contempt of the front-line soldier for the staff, expressed in the song 'The First Staff Officer Jumped Right Over the Second Staff Officer's Back', that these distinctions were withdrawn after the war.

Too much, perhaps, has been made of the generation of poets who served during the war. The views they expressed were personal, and many were writing in the late 1920s when the war may have been won but the peace had been lost. At such a time, all the effort and sacrifice of the war must have seemed pointless.

Chapter 19

Turkey With All the Trimmings: The Middle East and Beyond, 1914–1918

*A*lthough the war is mostly remembered for the action on the Western Front (see Chapters 17 and 18), during the First World War British and Commonwealth troops also fought in other places. This chapter considers these campaigns.

When Great Britain linked itself with France and Russia (Turkey's traditional enemy – see Chapter 13) in the Triple Entente, the Turks viewed this action almost as treachery by an old friend. When war between the United Kingdom and Germany became inevitable, the Royal Navy requisitioned two dreadnought battleships that British yards were building for Turkey. These would have been the pride of the Turkish navy and their loss caused widespread anger throughout the Ottoman Empire. As a gesture of friendship, Germany despatched the battlecruiser *Goeben* and the light cruiser *Breslau* as gifts for the Turkish navy. They eluded British warships in the Mediterranean and sailed through the Dardanelles, which Turkey immediately closed in contravention of an international agreement. On 29/30 October 1914 the two ships, now nominally Turkish but retaining their German crews, bombarded Russian positions on the Black Sea coast. The Turkish government ignored an Allied ultimatum and on 31 October hostilities between Turkey and the Allies commenced, opening up a whole new front of the war.

In the Middle East these campaigns involved not only the British and Indian Armies, but also the first major deployment for the Australian and New Zealand Armies, who quickly established their formidable reputation as fighting soldiers.

Defending Egypt

British concern in Egypt centred on the defence of the Suez Canal, the lifeline to the British Empire in the Far East. To the east, the Sinai Desert offered the defenders of the canal some protection, but an army could cross the desert, provided it made adequate logistic preparations. In this respect, the Turks were at something of a disadvantage. Even so, the Turks were determined to bring the war to the British in Egypt. In the circumstances, they could consider nothing more than a raid. Even then, the best that the Turks could expect was to halt canal traffic by means of sinking captured ships and damaging installations. They set no firm objectives. In fact, the Turkish leaders seemed happy to think about such things when the moment came. No one knew much about the British defences, or had considered that warships may form part of these. The approach was unbelievably amateur.

Attacking the Suez Canal

In mid-January 1915 the Turkish VIII Corps, under the command of Djemal Bey with a team of German advisers led by Colonel Freiherr Kress von Kressenstein, left its base at Beersheba and commenced a march across the Sinai – avoiding the coastal route that put marching columns within range of British naval gunfire. The central route was cool enough in winter and heavy rain had filled the pools and cisterns along the way. To be on the safe side, no fewer than 5000 water-carrying camels were taken on the march. If Djemal and Kressenstein had hoped to achieve surprise by using this route they were sorely disappointed, for seaplanes flying off the canal regularly reported on their march. The defenders therefore had plenty of time in which to complete their preparations.

On 3 February the Turks launched a series of uncoordinated attacks on the canal along a wide front. Heavy fire from warships and troops dug in on the west bank defeated them. Just three assault boats managed to complete the crossing of the canal. The British killed or captured all their occupants as soon as they set foot ashore. Having sustained 2000 casualties for no return, Djemal made a leisurely withdrawal to Beersheba. British casualties amounted to only 163.

Fighting in the Western Desert

Hardly had the British dealt with the threat to the Suez canal (see the previous section) than Lieutenant General Sir John Maxwell, responsible for the defence of Egypt, faced another threat – this time from the Western Desert. The powerful Senussi Moslem sect that lived there was engaged in a prolonged guerrilla war against the Italian authorities in Libya, who were allies of the British. An amicable relationship had always existed between the Senussi and their British neighbours in Egypt, but that changed when war broke out. The Sultan of Turkey held the office of *Caliph* (spiritual leader of the Moslem world), and his advice to the Grand Senussi, Said Ahmed, was that they must declare a holy war against all infidels and not just the Italians. To that end, German U-boats delivered artillery, machine guns, and ammunition to deserted stretches of coastline, together with military advisers, to aid the Senussi against the British.

Matters began to come to a head when a U-boat sank HMS *Tara*, a British armed boarding vessel in the Gulf of Sollum. The survivors were landed at Bardia and handed over to the Senussi. A British envoy went to the Grand Senussi with a request for their release. Said Ahmed regretted that he could not comply, as the Turks had left the seamen in his care as hostages. He was, in fact, under the influence of two Turkish senior officers, Nuri Bey and Ja'far Pasha, who pointed out, correctly, that the British were not doing at all well at Gallipoli or Mesopotamia (see later in this chapter). An invasion of Egypt, they promised, would bring about the collapse of the weakened British, particularly if the large number of Senussi supporters in Egypt rose against them. Convinced, the Grand Senussi announced that the holy war had begun.

Campaigning with the Western Frontier Force

The British garrison at Sollum beat off an attack by the Senussi on the night of 17 November 1915 and was then evacuated by steamer. Next day the British also repulsed an attack on Sidi Barrani. Maxwell knew that if he despatched sufficient troops to defeat the Senussi he would be left with too few to mount counter-insurgency operations, should the need arise. Nevertheless, he placed a number of Territorial infantry battalions and Yeomanry cavalry regiments under the command of Major General A. Wallace and designated them the Western Frontier Force. Wallace managed to halt the Senussi advance after fighting a number of sharp actions west of Mersa Matruh. The situation stabilised further when South African and New Zealand infantry reached the front, followed by troops returned from Gallipoli.

The Western Desert Gentlemen's Armoured Car Club

The Western Frontier Force included a Royal Naval Air Service armoured car squadron formed to meet the emergency, but this saw little fighting because the winter rains turned the going into a quagmire. In January 1916 the squadron went up the Nile to Upper Egypt where Senussi bands had occupied several oases. The Duke of Westminster's armoured car brigade (formerly No. 2 Squadron Royal Naval Armoured Car Division) replaced it, consisting of three batteries each of four Rolls-Royce armoured cars and a small headquarters, supported by an echelon of Model T Ford tenders. The unit was the closest thing imaginable to a gentleman's club, as the Duke had chosen his officers and men with care. Most came from cavalry and yeomanry regiments, with a leavening of chauffeurs, professional motor drivers, and mechanics.

Major General W.E. Peyton relieved Wallace, who was suffering from ill health, on 10 January 1916. Maxwell now felt that the Western Frontier Force was strong enough to take the offensive and ordered Peyton to recapture Sollum. As air reconnaissance revealed that the main Senussi camp was located at Agagya, southeast of Sidi Barrani, Peyton led out a column to deal with this first. On 26 January a hard-fought action took place at a ridge 8 kilometres (5 miles) north of the camp. Some 1500 of the enemy held the ridge, supported by artillery and machine guns. During the action, Brigadier General Lukin's South Africans stormed the enemy position at the point of the bayonet. As the Senussi withdrew, the Dorset Yeomanry charged into the enemy mass, cutting down 300 of them, capturing Ja'far Pasha, and chasing the rest across the desert. The regiment sustained 58 personnel casualties, but the loss of 85 horses reduced its strength by half.

The British occupied Sidi Barrani on 9 March and recaptured Sollum without a fight five days later. The Senussi had crossed the frontier into Libya, no doubt thinking that they were safer on Italian territory. Peyton, however, was determined to destroy their field army and doubted whether the Italians would raise too many objections. When aircraft reported a large enemy camp at Bir Wair, he despatched the Duke of Westminster's armoured cars to attack it (see the sidebar 'The Western Desert Gentlemen's Armoured Car Club'). The going was excellent, enabling the cars to close in at high speed. They found that the Senussi had abandoned the camp at Bir Wair and were retreating westwards. The Duke caught up with them near a well named Bir Azeiz. The Senussi were holding a rocky position fronted by rough going and opened fire with their mountain and machine guns at once. The cars fanned out from column into line and went straight for the enemy, maintaining a continuous fire with their own machine guns. When the British shot down the enemy's heavy weapons crews, the entire Senussi army broke and ran. Hundreds were killed or wounded during the pursuit. The booty for the British included three 4-inch (10-millimetre) guns, nine machine guns, a large quantity of small arms, and 250,000 rounds of ammunition. Two of the Duke's men received superficial wounds.

In March, the surviving crew of the *Tara*, horribly emaciated, half naked, starving, and suffering from dysentery but waving and cheering, were rescued from Bir Hacheim, taken back to Sollum, and put aboard a hospital ship for passage to Alexandria. On 26 July a joint operation with the Italians, supported by naval gunfire, ejected the Senussi from the Wadi Saal. Lying between Bardia and Tobruk, this was a landing place at which armaments and ammunition destined for the Senussi were put ashore from U-boats. The wadi contained numerous caves closed by stout wooden doors, each containing a treasure trove of munitions.

Heading into the desert

By the end of November 1916, the British had also recaptured the oases in Upper Egypt. Said Ahmed now accepted that getting involved in someone else's global war was not a good idea, and withdrew his troops to the Siwa oasis. Together with the neighbouring oases of Girba and Jarabub, this not only lay 320 kilometres (200 miles) south of Mersa Matruh, but was also 300 metres (1000 feet) below sea level. No army had ever penetrated this far south across the desert, and Said Ahmed had every reason to feel secure.

That was not the case, for in Cairo the British had decided to bring the Senussi war to an end by means of a motorised raid. The Duke of Westminster's armoured car brigade led this, together with three light car patrols equipped with Model T Fords mounting a Lewis gun. Under the command of Brigadier General Hodgson, the force assembled at Sheka, 300 kilometres (185 miles) south of Mersa Matruh, on 2 January 1917. The following day it began to fight its way down the difficult pass to Girba, while a diversionary patrol set off in the direction of Jarabub. The passage was difficult, sometimes requiring picks, shovels, and crowbars to clear obstacles from what was really nothing more than a camel track. Too late, the Senussi realised what was happening. They failed to prevent the cars from reaching the valley below the escarpment, and after a day's hard fighting the British broke their resistance. Said Ahmed abdicated in favour of his cousin Said Idris, who had of a more neutral turn of mind.

For the remainder of the First World War, light car patrols that ranged far and wide kept the peace in the desert. They little knew it, but the army would use the detailed maps they produced again during the Second World War (see Part VI), while their experience provided a thorough knowledge of how men and machines could be made to operate efficiently in such difficult, demanding circumstances.

Landing in the Dardanelles

By the end of 1914, two schools of thought were beginning to influence the British direction of the war:

- ✔ The Westerners, as they were called, believed that they could only win victory by defeating the main mass of the German army in France and Belgium.

- ✔ The Easterners, on the other hand, thought that if they defeated its weaker Turkish and Austro-Hungarian allies first, they would isolate Germany and force the Kaiser to sue for peace.

One thing was certain: Russia was not equipped to fight an industrialised war and had to be supplied with what the country needed to carry on fighting. The Black Sea ports offered the best way to do this, but Turkish control of the Dardanelles and the Bosphorus denied access to them

Optimism gone mad – the Dardanelles plan

Winston Churchill, First Lord of the Admiralty, believed that the Royal Navy's battleships were capable of fighting their way through the Dardanelles, then crossing the Sea of Marmara and bombarding Constantinople. This would solve two problems at once:

- ✔ The Sultan's government would request an armistice.

- ✔ The supply route to Russia would be wide open.

If the Turks had been complete fools, the plan may have worked. Unfortunately, they were not. Under the direction of General Liman von Sanders, they laid no fewer than 11 minefields on the approach to the narrowest part of the straits and strengthened their coast defence batteries on both shores. Nevertheless, during late February and early March 1915, Royal Marine landing parties silenced the outer forts and destroyed the guns within. That was the easy part. The British minesweepers were simply North Sea trawlers that had been conscripted along with their crews. They drew too much water for the job and were not powerful enough to work in the currents running through the straits. Worst of all, when they tried to sweep towards the inner forts, mobile howitzer batteries, whose positions were difficult to locate, constantly harassed them.

In the belief that the inner forts were causing the problem, the British decided to batter them into submission. On the morning of 18 March no fewer than 18 British and French battleships, accompanied by cruisers and destroyers, sailed into the straits. They met a fierce response from the Turks' coastal defence batteries, but by 4 p.m. the inner forts were silenced. As they turned away to allow the minesweepers to continue their task, three battleships, HMS *Irresistible, Ocean,* and the French *Bouvet,* ran over an uncharted minefield and sustained damage from which they sank with heavy loss of life. As for the minesweepers, the elusive howitzer batteries drove them off once again. The straits could not be forced, and that was that.

Getting everything wrong: Gallipoli

If the Royal Navy could not force the Dardanelles, went the argument, the British had to find some other way of getting to Constantinople. Someone put forward the crackpot idea of landing troops on the Gallipoli peninsula, from which they could march to Constantinople. No one present knew much about the peninsula. In fact, it was ideally suited to the Turkish defence:

- ✔ The peninsula consisted of a central spine to which steep ridges separated by gullies rose sharply from the sea to the west and the Dardanelles to the east, making it easier to defend.

- ✔ No maps existed and while some detailed knowledge of the terrain did exist, no one passed it on to those who were to do the fighting. As a result, objectives were set without any appreciation of the physical difficulties involved.

- ✔ The British had seriously underestimated the will of the Turks to fight in defence of their homeland.

Reluctantly, the War Cabinet sanctioned the venture, although some senior officers believed that a better use of the troops was on the Western Front.

Major General Sir Aylmer Hunter-Weston's 29th Division was to land at various beaches around the tip of Cape Helles, while Lieutenant General Sir William Birdwood's Australian and New Zealand Army Corps (ANZAC) was to land between Gaba Tepe and Ari Burnu. The entire operation was under the command of General Sir Ian Hamilton, a man of wide experience and undoubted courage, but lacking in decision and drive. Preparations took place on several islands off the Turkish coast. Neither service had any experience of mounting amphibious operations on this scale, and the necessary command, control, and communications network existed only as a sketchy framework. No purpose-built landing craft were available. The troops were to go ashore sitting upright in unprotected ships' boats or lighters. A variation existed in the converted *collier* (coal ship) *River Clyde*, which had four sally ports cut in its sides. The intention was that the troops aboard would leave through these when the ship grounded. They would then run along gangways down to *lighters* (flat-bottomed barges) forming a bridge to the shore.

When the landings took place at dawn on 25 April, everything that could go wrong did go wrong. In some cases the troops landed in the wrong place, in others machine guns created carnage in the packed boats, and in others the attackers were pinned down at the water's edge in coves that formed natural killing grounds. The *River Clyde*'s sally ports were natural aiming points. The Turks shot down so many of those who emerged from them that the British suspended landings from the ship until nightfall. On the Australian sector the Turkish 19th Division, commanded by Colonel Mustapha Kemal, one of the Ottoman Empire's most able soldiers and the first president of the new Turkey, launched a counter-attack. The Australians shot down the Turks in droves or killed them in savage bayonet fighting, but Kemal's vigorous defence ensured that the ANZAC lines remained where they were for the rest of the campaign. Elsewhere, chances were missed to occupy features that were later considered vital objectives. The only redeeming feature amid the day's bloodstained chaos was the courage of the troops: On W Beach, for example, 1/Lancashire Fusiliers, one of the 'Unsurpassable Six' Minden regiments (see Chapter 8), won their celebrated six VCs before breakfast.

The 29th Division managed to link its small beachheads, but never held more than a few square miles at the tip of Cape Helles. From this point on, barbed wire and machine guns guaranteed the sort of stalemate that existed on the Western Front. Throughout the months that followed, both sides displayed suicidal courage, piling up casualties without result. In an attempt to turn the Turkish flank, the 10th and 11th Divisions of Lieutenant General Sir Frederick Stopford's IX Corps landed at Suvla Bay, north of the ANZACs, during the night of 6/7 August. Thanks to the provision of armoured lighters the troops reached the shore safely, but then the same sort of inertia that prevented exploitation of the earlier landings seems to have gripped their commanders. Their beachhead was linked to that of the ANZACs, but the Turks quickly contained it and therefore rendered its possession useless.

Hamilton had written to Kitchener the previous month, commenting that the campaign had degenerated into a pointless killing match. Suvla Bay was the last straw for the War Cabinet, who relieved Hamilton of command on 15 October. His successor, General Sir Charles Monro, recommended evacuation and this was approved the following month. Suvla Bay and the ANZACs were evacuated on the night of 19/20 December and Cape Helles on 8/9 January 1916. The British and Dominion armies sustained 200,000 casualties at Gallipoli, while the French incurred a further 40,000 on their sector of operations. No accurate record exists of Turkish losses, but 300,000 is a reasonable estimate, of whom one-third were killed. Despite incurring the heavier loss, the Turks were entitled to feel pleased with themselves and could claim to have seen off the Royal Navy and Hamilton's troops as well. Amid the recriminations following the defeat, Winston Churchill had to resign his position as First Lord of the Admiralty and went off to command an infantry battalion in France for a while.

Fighting in Mesopotamia

Safeguarding the Middle East's oil supplies for the Royal Navy was a keystone of British policy. As part of this strategy, the British had occupied Basra and the Shatt-al-Arab waterway in Mesopotamia (modern-day Iraq) without difficulty in November 1914. They defeated weak Turkish counter-attacks with such ease that the Government of India, responsible for the security of the area, reached the mistaken conclusion that the enemy troops were representative of the Turkish army as a whole. As a result of this, it took the decision to extend the scope of operations to include an advance on Baghdad, the loss of which would be a serious blow to Turkish prestige throughout the entire Muslim world. The unforeseen and unwelcome consequence was that Great Britain had to open a fresh war front.

In the spring of 1915 Lieutenant General Sir John Nixon commanded the British army in Mesopotamia. It consisted of two Indian infantry divisions (Major General Charles Townshend's 6th and Major General George Gorringe's 12th) and a cavalry brigade. Nixon's career in the Indian Army had been long and honourable, although those who knew him best regarded him as impetuous, lacking in strategic sense, inclined to base decisions on wishful thinking, and seriously ambitious. This was to have unhappy consequences when allied to Townshend's personality. If Nixon's ambition was a driving force, Townshend's was nothing less than a mania: What he wanted most of all was glory and lots of admiration. Compared to Nixon and Townshend, Gorringe was a refreshingly normal, capable divisional commander.

In May, Nixon ordered Townshend's division to break through the Turkish position at Qurna and advance up the Tigris to Amara, thereby consolidating his hold on the captured territory further south. Unexpectedly, Turkish resistance collapsed completely on 31 May. Townshend embarked troops aboard any vessel he could lay his hands on and set off upstream. Passing Ezra's Tomb on 1 June, he reached Amara two days later and received the immediate surrender of the 2000-strong garrison. During the 130-kilometre (80-mile) advance the British disabled the Turkish gunboat *Marmaris* and captured the steamer *Mosul*. The episode became known as 'Townshend's Regatta'. The public loved it.

Baghdad or bust: Take one

Townshend fell victim to the torrid, unhealthy Middle East climate for a while and went to India to recover. He returned to find that Gorringe's division had taken Nasiriya on the Euphrates in July 1915. Nixon now felt that to secure the south of the country it was necessary for Townshend's division to take

Kut-al-Amara. That was easier said than done, because the Turks had constructed a strong fortified zone on both banks of the Tigris, some kilometres below the town. Under the command of a Turkish general named Nur-ed-Din, 6000 men and 30 guns held this zone. On 27 September, Townshend made a feint attack against the entrenchments on the right bank. Nur-ed-Din moved up his reserves to meet the threat. That night, two of Townshend's brigades crossed a bridge of boats two miles downstream. They then carried out a successful night march and fell on the Turkish left flank at dawn. After hard fighting they took the position and held it against counter-attacks. Air reconnaissance on the morning of 29 September revealed that the enemy was retreating through Kut.

Marching into trouble

Nixon believed that the road to Baghdad was wide open and ordered Townshend to take it. To his credit, Townshend pointed out the serious dangers involved in overextending the advance, but his warning fell on deaf ears. After spending five weeks in preparation, the 6th Indian Division and the cavalry brigade set off to the north. At about the same time, Nixon received intelligence reports indicating that 30,000 good-quality troops under the command of Khalil Pasha, one of the best generals in the Turkish service, were converging on Baghdad. Townshend was obviously marching straight into trouble, but Nixon made no attempt to recall him.

On reaching Ctesiphon, 50 kilometres (30 miles) south of Baghdad, Townshend discovered that the Turks had constructed entrenchments on both banks of the river. In November he fought his way through at the cost of heavy casualties and most of his ammunition stock. When air reconnaissance revealed fresh Turkish formations streaming out of Baghdad on 25 November, he wisely decided to withdraw.

Defending Kut – for all the wrong reasons

Townshend fought a successful holding action on 1 December 1915. He entered Kut the next day and immediately decided to compensate for his failure to capture Baghdad by conducting a heroic defence of the town, just as he had defended Chitral Fort on the North West Frontier in 1895. In fact, he had no need at all to defend Kut: If he wanted to halt the enemy's advance, better defensive positions existed downstream. What he really wanted was lots of good personal publicity. Tamely, Nixon approved his decision and made an empty promise to relieve him within two months.

Townshend's men beat off a Turkish assault on 24 December, so the Turks decided to starve Kut into surrender and concentrate on defeating Nixon's relief attempts. To emphasise the drama of his situation, Townshend reported that his garrison had just one month's food supply in hand. The truth was that he did not seriously cut the rations until early April 1916. In response to the plea, Nixon ordered Lieutenant General Sir Fenton Aylmer, commanding the relief force, to attempt a breakthrough. The attempt was premature and failed, as did every subsequent attempt. Aylmer requested that sorties by the Kut garrison should coincide with his attacks. It made sound military sense, but Townshend wanted to sit tight and be relieved in style, just as he had been at Chitral. Throughout the siege, he submitted regular demands for his own promotion. When his rival Gorringe took over from Aylmer and received promotion, Townshend openly wept at the news. When rations became short in April, an attempt was made – the first in history – to supply the trapped garrison by air, but the amount of rations deliverable by air fell far short of the consumption rate.

The War Cabinet was furious that Nixon and Townshend had allowed what had been intended as a sideshow to develop into a full-blown campaign, but it could hardly leave the Kut garrison to its fate. The government rushed reinforcements into Mesopotamia and Nixon's deteriorating health enabled him to make a dignified exit, his replacement being General Sir Percy Lake. On 24 April the British made a last-ditch attempt to run a supply steamer through to Kut. The attempt failed. By now some 23,000 casualties had been sustained in attempts to relieve the 8000-strong garrison of a town nobody wanted. No point lay in continuing and Kitchener told Lake of this decision that night. Lake informed Townshend early on 26 April that his men were to make no further relief attempts. Predictably, Townshend blamed the relief force, then opened negotiations with the Turkish commander. He offered him £1 million in gold in exchange for the garrison's freedom and its guns. Interesting through the offer was, Constantinople wanted the famous General Townshend and his men as trophies. All the Turks agreed to was the exchange of 345 of the garrison's hospital cases for an equal number of fit prisoners and a promise that they would treat the garrison as honoured guests. Townshend declaimed that he would go into captivity with his 2070 British and 6000 Indian soldiers, even if it killed him. Instead, he let the Turks treat him like royalty and spent the rest of the war in a luxurious villa on an island in the sea of Marmara. His men died in their thousands from starvation, disease, lack of medical facilities, and the brutal indifference of their guards. The British public never forgave Townshend and he slid into the obscurity he had always dreaded.

Baghdad or bust: Take two

The British public, unused to their armies surrendering, were shocked by Townshend's defeat (see the previous section). Coming as it did hard on the heels of the Gallipoli debacle (see the section 'Landing in the Dardanelles', earlier in this chapter), it caused additional damage to British prestige throughout the Middle East and the country dare not risk a further reverse. Khalil, the Turkish commander, decided not to exploit his victory at Kut. Instead, reacting to Russian incursions in Asia Minor and Persia, he withdrew many of his troops from the Tigris, leaving only three divisions under Kiazim Karbekit to hold the line at Hanna.

In August 1916 Lieutenant General Sir Frederick Maude relieved Lake. Maude was an officer as far removed from generals of the Nixon and Townshend sort as it was possible to get. He was cold, uncommunicative, and he understood that he could not gain lasting success without a sound logistic infrastructure. He was also an able administrator whose plans left nothing to chance, and was as good as Kitchener in this respect . His major fault was a tendency to meddle in the internal workings of his subordinate formations instead of letting them get on with their respective jobs.

By December 1916 Maude's army was 166,000 men strong, two-thirds being drawn from the Indian army, and consisted of two corps and a cavalry division. He also had armoured cars, river gunboats, and a narrow-gauge railway to support him. Kiazim, seriously alarmed by these developments, asked Khalil to reinforce him. Khalil, overconfident in victory, replied that the Hanna lines were impregnable and that no reinforcement was necessary.

Maude's offensive

Having spent some time studying Kiazim's defensive layout, Maude reached the conclusion that the enemy had put everything in the shop window and left nothing in reserve. The strength of the Turkish defences still lay on the left bank of the river, but those on the right bank were not as formidable as they had once been. Maude decided to fight his way through the right bank defences one section at a time, steadily working his way upstream until he was beyond Kut, then cross. This could force Kiazim to abandon his positions on the left bank, or trap him if he failed to withdraw in time.

Maude's offensive opened on 13 December with a feint on the left bank. As Maude had hoped, Kiazim responded by concentrating his troops there. On the right bank, the British made progress slowly and step by step, so as not to alert the Turks to their real intentions. However, by the third week of February 1917 the advance had reached a point some kilometres north of Kut. Having endured weeks of artillery pounding from across the river, on 23 February the defenders of the Hanna defile finally left their trenches. Simultaneously, to the north, the British 14th Division crossed the river at the Shumran Bend and put in a pontoon bridge. Kiazim, suddenly realising the terrible danger he was in, abandoned the Kut sector altogether, harried by the British cavalry division. At the Nahr Kellek Bend British gunboats caught up with Kiazim's marching column and engaged it with sustained fire from their main armament and automatic weapons until it disintegrated in rout.

Capturing Baghdad

Maude paused at Aziziyeh for several days to replenish his supplies. He resumed his advance on 5 March 1917, brushing aside Turkish attempts to form a new front. Two days later, he reached the banks of the Diyala, a tributary of the Tigris that flowed in from the northeast, and was able to make out the distant domes and minarets of Baghdad itself. Khalil was personally conducting the defence of the city, but Maude pushed his 13th Division across the Diyala to make a holding attack while the cavalry and two infantry brigades recrossed the Tigris and by-passed the city. Khalil, believing that he was in danger of falling into the same trap as Kiazim, hastily abandoned his positions and withdrew out of harm's way. Maude entered Baghdad on 11 March.

Horrified by the loss, the Turks pushed a corps down the Diyala in the hope of recapturing the city. The Cavalry and 13th Divisions defeated this at Delli Abbas and by the end of April the Turks began to withdraw. Meanwhile, the advance upstream from Baghdad continued. The British captured Samarra on 24 April, but with the onset of the hot season active operations ceased for several months.

Maude had inherited a demoralised army and led it to victory. Tragically, he did not live to see the end of the campaign. Despite his reserved nature, his troops sincerely regretted his death from cholera on 18 November. Lieutenant General Sir William Marshall succeeded him.

During the final year of the First World War Mesopotamia became less important to both sides. Palestine had a higher priority for the Turks and because the fighting was going badly for them there, Palestine received reinforcements that the Turks had originally earmarked for Mesopotamia. Marshall was able to maintain the initiative and throughout 1918 he steadily strengthened his hold on the upper reaches of the Tigris and the Euphrates.

Campaigning in Palestine

Following the evacuation of Gallipoli (see the section 'Landing in the Dardanelles', earlier in this chapter) and the arrival of fresh Imperial troops, it became possible to establish an Egyptian Expeditionary Force under the command of General Sir Archibald Murray in the spring of 1916. In Murray's view, a renewed Turkish advance from Palestine would enter Sinai between El Arish and El Kusseima, so he decided to establish his own front line between those two points. Doing so required an immense logistic effort. This began with hiring thousands of labourers who started building a standard-gauge railway at El Kantara on the east bank of the Suez Canal. This extended steadily across the Sinai at the rate of 80 kilometres (50 miles) per month. In parallel, the expeditionary force laid a freshwater pipeline, complete with storage tanks, a portable reservoir holding 2.25 million litres (0.5 million gallons), and batteries of standpipes. Beyond the railhead, an efficient Camel Transport Corps supplied the forward troops. Murray also established a logical casualty-evacuation system. In short, he did everything possible to avoid the disgraceful episodes that had taken place during the early phases of the Mesopotamian campaign. Murray made his methodical advance with the infantry divisions closest to the coast and railhead, while the cavalry and Camel Corps covered the open desert flank.

An Australian regular officer, Lieutenant General Harry Chauvel, commanded the cavalry, and many regarded him as the greatest cavalryman of the modern era. Most of his troopers were Australian Light Horsemen or New Zealand Mounted Rifles. Used to the outdoor life, they were tough, aggressive, and natural hard riders. They rode large, hardy horses called Walers that were more at home in the demanding Middle Eastern climate than other breeds. Some of the men were veterans of the 2nd Boer War and Gallipoli. Visiting British officers were shocked by the informality of their discipline, but it was effective. Their level of personal initiative was also higher than in more traditionally minded cavalry regiments. They were trained to fight a fast-moving mounted infantry battle. They had an unwritten law that no man, wounded or not, was allowed to fall into Turkish hands, and they took tremendous risks to keep that promise. Chauvel's command also included British yeomanry regiments that were more flexible in their approach than their Regular Army counterparts. Later, they were joined by Indian cavalry regiments used to soldiering in hard climates. Chauvel's divisions formed the Desert Mounted Corps.

Fending off early Turkish advances

Kress von Kressenstein, de facto commander of the Turks' Sinai sector, was fully aware of Murray's intentions. On 3 August 1916 he launched a spoiling attack against the railhead, which had now reached Romani. His troops contained many Gallipoli veterans who pressed home their attack, only to be halted by the dogged defence of the 52nd (Lowland) Division. Chauvel's Light Horsemen then closed in and counter-attacked from the southwest, forcing the enemy off a vital ridge. Having sustained the loss of 5000 killed or wounded and a further 4000 taken prisoner, Kressenstein had to disengage and withdraw. At a stroke, he lost half his entire force. The British loss came to 1130 killed or wounded.

Kressenstein abandoned El Arish without a fight. However, he retained a toehold on Egyptian soil at Magruntein, 40 kilometres (25 miles) beyond El Arish and just south of Rafah. Chauvel captured Magruntein after a day-long fight on 9 January 1917. The way was now open for a British invasion of Palestine. Prime Minister Lloyd George, an Easterner by instinct (see the section 'Landing in the Dardanelles', earlier in this chapter, for more on this), approved a plan for a limited offensive with the town of Gaza as its objective.

The First Battle of Gaza, 26 March 1917

Gaza sprawled across a low hill some two miles from the sea, a ridge to its east being dominated by the shrine of Ali el Muntar. South of the town were three more ridges, from east to west the Sheikh Abbas, the Burjabye, and the Es Sire. Elsewhere, almost impenetrable cactus hedges separated the numerous fig and olive orchards. The Turkish garrison consisted of just 3500 men and 20 guns.

Murray waited until his railhead had caught up with him, then launched his attack at dawn on 26 March, shielded by a dense sea mist. The infantry of the 53rd (Welsh) and 54th (East Anglian) Divisions advanced on the left, while the ANZACs swung round the eastern end of Sheikh Abbas to take Ali el Muntar ridge. Throughout the day Turks put up a determined resistance. They conducted a determined counter-attack against the ANZACs, but this came to grief after bayonets were crossed in savage hand-to-hand fighting. By dusk the Welshmen of the 53rd Division had joined the ANZACs on Ali el Muntar and were looking down into the defenceless streets of Gaza.

Incredibly, Murray ordered a general withdrawal. The troops queried the order, but they had to obey. The instruction originated in a headquarters that was 24 kilometres (15 miles) behind the fighting, where the commanders of the two infantry divisions decided that if the troops had not physically captured Gaza by sunset, they should pull out to prevent them being trapped between the garrison and the reinforcements that Kressenstein was bringing up. As if one blunder wasn't enough, another compounded it. At about the same time as the withdrawal order was issued, radio operators in Cairo intercepted a transmission from the German commandant of Gaza to Kressenstein. The transmission made clear that the Turkish situation was desperate and that if the British continued to attack the sender would have to ask for terms. Thanks to what amounts to criminal negligence, the radio operators did not relay the message to the front until midnight, and by then the damage was done. The Turks could hardly believe their luck and followed up the withdrawal next day, pushing the British line further away from Gaza.

British losses in the First Battle of Gaza came to 523 killed, 2932 wounded, and 412 missing. The Turks lost 301 killed, 1085 wounded, and 1061 missing. Not wishing to report failure, Murray submitted a despatch claiming a partial success that just fell short of a complete disaster for the enemy, whose casualties he wildly exaggerated. He received messages of congratulation from the King and Lloyd George.

The Second Battle of Gaza, 17 April 1917

Kressenstein promptly set about turning Gaza into a fortress, extending the defences inland to Beersheba. This left Murray with no alternative other than a frontal assault, although in theory the arrival of eight tanks made his task easier. The Second Battle of Gaza began on 17 April and involved direct assaults by the infantry of the 52nd (Lowland), 53rd (Welsh), and 54th (East Anglian) Divisions. They faced defences similar to those on the Western Front, if not so well developed. The tanks, distributed along the front in penny packets, were unable to strike a concentrated blow, although they did achieve some local successes. By the time the battle ran down two days later the British had dented the Turkish front but not broken it. British casualties included 509 killed, 4539 wounded, and 1576 missing. The Turks lost 402 killed, 1364 wounded, and 245 missing. This time Murray was unable to hide the truth and he was dismissed. If his vanity had temporarily got the better of his judgement, he deserved a great deal of credit for bringing his army across Sinai in good order.

Taking the Gaza Line

Murray's replacement was General Sir Edmund Allenby, who had recently commanded the Third Army at Arras on the Western Front (see Chapter 17). Big, bluff, and energetic, his bellow when angry earned him the nickname of The Bull. The two reverses at Gaza had damaged the morale of his new command and he saw that his first task was to restore spirits. He immediately chased his General Headquarters Staff out of its comfortable quarters in Cairo and re-established it just behind the lines at Rafah, where the troops got used to seeing him.

Reinforcements had arrived from Salonika and Aden, bringing the strength of the British army up to three corps. Allenby accepted a suggestion that the capture of Beersheba would turn Kressenstein's line. The plan was for the Desert Mounted Corps to carry out a long approach march through the desert and then launch an immediate attack from the south and southeast, while XX Corps brought further pressure to bear on the Turkish left. Simultaneously, on the Gaza sector, XXI Corps would mount a diversionary attack, supported by a heavy bombardment.

Allenby struck on 31 October. Despite achieving tactical surprise as they emerged from the desert, the ANZAC and Australian Mounted Divisions had to overcome stiff opposition from the enemy's outposts. Nevertheless, the 4th Light Horse Brigade made a dashing charge, with the men holding their unsheathed bayonets as though they were sabres. The torrent of horsemen swept over two lines of trenches and on into Beersheba itself. This thunderbolt attack so startled the Turks that resistance collapsed and the British took the wells intact.

The Turkish Gaza Line had now been knocked off its hinges. XX Corps began to roll up the defenders and push them away to the northwest. Then something quite unexpected happened. On 1/2 November XXI Corps' diversionary attack suddenly developed into the real thing. Allenby had insisted that all the tanks were under the command of the 54th Division, and they punched a hole clean through the Turkish defences. He reinforced their unexpected success and, unsettled by indirect pressure from the Beersheba direction, the Turks began pulling out. On 7 November XXI Corps hardly had to fight to take possession of Ali el Muntar ridge. Taken together, the actions that broke the Gaza–Beersheba Line became known as the Third Battle of Gaza. On 9 December the Turks abandoned Jerusalem. In military terms, the loss of the city meant little, but following the loss of the other Holy Cities of Mecca and Baghdad the damage to the morale of the Ottoman Empire was immense.

In total some 17,000 British casualties were sustained during Allenby's 1917 offensive. The Turks, however, sustained 25,000 casualties and their morale was badly shaken. Kressenstein was dismissed. General Erich von Falkenhayn, the former Chief of German General Staff who had overrun Romania the previous year, took his place. When the Gaza Line disintegrated, he was commanding a force of 14 Turkish divisions and the 6000-strong German Asia Corps, known collectively as the Yilderim (Lighting) Army Group. This was earmarked for the recapture of Baghdad, but Falkenhayn considered that the situation in Palestine was potentially more dangerous and he redirected the group there. The creaking railway system failed to prevent the Germans reaching the front before Jerusalem fell, but the troops enabled Falkenhayn to create a new front north of the city, stretching from the sea to the Jordan valley. Torrential rain brought further operations to a standstill.

Battle of Megiddo, 19–21 September 1918

During the first half of 1918, Ludendorff's offensives on the Western Front in Europe overshadowed everything else (refer to Chapter 18). Allenby had to send reinforcements to France to help hold the line, but apart from mounting two raids across the Jordan on Amman, neither of which produced lasting results, his men remained largely inactive. With the passing of the crisis on the Western Front, Chauvel's cavalry corps was brought up to its maximum strength and enabled Allenby to plan an autumn offensive aimed at the complete destruction of the Turkish army group. In simple terms, the Desert Mounted Corps would exploit an infantry breakthrough on the coastal sector with a huge wheel to the east, severing the Turks' lines of communication and taking the Jordan Valley as its objective. The function of the newly formed Royal Air Force's Middle East Detachment, consisting of seven squadrons under Major General Geoffrey Salmond, was first to destroy the enemy's telephone communications, and then *strafe* (bomb and machine gun) his columns behind the front until their will to fight had been broken.

Building up to Megiddo

As a prelude to the breakthrough, the British mounted an elaborate deception plan to convince the Turks that the blow would fall in the Jordan Valley. The ANZAC Mounted Division moved into the area and began simulating the presence of the whole Desert Mounted Corps with dummy gun parks, battery positions, horse lines, camps, and a buzz of activity. Simultaneously, the Arab army advancing north through the desert beyond the Jordan intensified its efforts against the Hejaz Railway (see the later sidebar 'With Lawrence in Arabia' for more on the Arab army's role). Lieutenant General Sir P.W. Chetwode's XX Corps held the right of Allenby's line, responsible for 70 kilometres (45 miles) of front. To its left, concentrated on a 25-kilometre (15-mile) frontage, was Lieutenant General Sir Edward Bulfin's XXI Corps. Immediately behind Bulfin was the Desert Mounted Corps (4th and 5th Cavalry Divisions and the Australian Mounted Division).

Across no-man's land, squabbles had seen General Liman von Sanders, who had successfully defended the Gallipoli peninsula, replaced Falkenhayn as Turkish commander. The experience at Gallipoli made him a firm believer in holding ground at any price. His preparations suited static defence rather than mobile warfare. Furthermore, Allenby's deception plan had convinced von Sanders that the British offensive would begin in the Jordan Valley and most of his strength concentrated in that area. Sanders' command consisted of three armies, none of which was stronger than a weak corps:

- ✔ On the right Djevad Pasha's Eighth Army of 10,000 men and 157 guns included most of the German Asia Corps and held a 30-kilometre (20-mile) front from the sea to Furqa.

- ✔ From Furqa to the Jordan Valley the front became the responsibility of Mustapha Kemal's Seventh Army of 7000 men and 111 guns.

- ✔ Across the Jordan was Djemal Kucuk's Fourth Army with 8000 men, including the German 146th Regiment, and 74 guns.

- ✔ In reserve were 3000 men and 30 guns. Sanders' General Headquarters was in Nazareth, too far behind the front. It was connected to HQ Eighth Army at Tul Karm and HQ Seventh Army at Nablus by telephone lines than ran through a main switchboard at Afula.

Fighting the main action

So thorough had Allenby's preparations been that the British had won the battle before it began. At 4.30 a.m. on 19 September the combined artillery of XXI and the Desert Mounted Corps began bombarding the forward trenches of the Turkish Eighth Army. At times, no fewer than 1000 shells per minute were exploding in the enemy positions. As the guns lifted their fire to targets in the rear, Bulfin's infantry swamped the stunned defenders. Chauvel's mounted columns began to pass through into the open country beyond, while the infantry divisions began wheeling eastwards to roll up what remained of Djevad's army. As soon as it was light enough to bomb, the Royal Air Force eliminated the central telephone exchange at Afula. In Nazareth, Sanders was ignorant of what was happening. At noon he was able to talk to Kemal, who told him that Djevad had been routed and that as the right flank of his own Seventh Army had been turned, he also had to withdraw. The only other piece of intelligence Kemal offered was that Allenby's cavalry was streaming forward.

For the Turks, the situation rapidly escalated from disastrous to catastrophic. The remnant of Djevad's army was moving eastwards along the Tul Karm–Mus'udye road. As well as complicating Kemal's withdrawal, this provided the Royal Air Force with a splendid series of targets that they strafed to destruction.

The night was one continuous movement for both sides. At 5.30 a.m. on 20 September the 5th Cavalry Divsison's 13th Brigade galloped into Nazareth itself. Sanders's staff put up a fierce but hopeless fight, while the general escaped to Tiberias by car. Elsewhere, the 4th Cavalry Division took Bet Shean (Beisan) and the Australian Mounted Division captured Jenin, both lying squarely across Kemal's intended line of retreat. Kemal, already fighting a skilful rearguard action against the British infantry, realised that he was in danger of being surrounded and decided to retreat eastwards towards the Jordan Valley.

At first light on 21 September, the Royal Air Force discovered Kemal's Seventh Army strung out along the Wadi Far'a. For four hours aircraft bombed and strafed the Turks' panic-stricken column continuously. The enemy became a dispersed mob of fugitives fleeing across the hills. When the British cavalry entered the valley it took possession of 90 guns, 50 lorries, 1000 carts, and much else besides. This was the first occasion in history when air power alone completed the destruction of an army.

Following up after the battle

In two days Allenby had destroyed two of his opponent's three armies and taken 25,000 prisoners. The fugitives were streaming across the Jordan fords and up the road to Damascus. In vain, Sanders tried to rally on a line based on the confluence of the Yarmuk and Jordan rivers, but this broke apart when the 4th Light Horse Brigade took Samakh on 25 September.

Now isolated, Djemal Kucuk's Fourth Armydid not have much longer to live. A force under the command of Major General E.W.C. Chaytor, including the ANZAC Mounted Division, an Indian and a Jewish brigade, crossed the lower reaches of the Jordan and received the surrender of the Turkish corps at

Amman without the need to fire a shot. Lawrence's Arabs (see the sidebar 'With Lawrence in Arabia') took Der'a on 27 September and Major General Sir George Barrow's 4th Cavalry Division joined them there the next day. Both then advanced directly up the parallel railway and road to Damascus. The 5th Cavalry and Australian Mounted Divisions also converged on Damascus, having passed between the Sea of Galilee and Lake Hula. They entered an undefended Damascus on 1 October. A few miles to the northwest of the city the Australian Mounted Division trapped what was left of the Fourth Army in the Barada Gorge and pounded it until wreckage and bodies blocked the road. Meanwhile, on the coast, the infantry took the ports of Haifa, Acre, and Beirut in rapid succession.

With Lawrence in Arabia

Thomas Edward Lawrence was born at Tremadoc, Wales, on 16 August 1888. His father was Sir Thomas Chapman, an Anglo-Irish baronet. Lawrence was educated at Oxford, where he developed his interest in archaeology and military history. In 1911 he joined an archaeological expedition led by Sir Flinders Petrie at Carchemish in Mesopotamia and spent his time exploring the area and learning to speak a number of Arabic dialects.

On the outbreak of the First World War, army intelligence employed Lawrence as a junior officer in Egypt. In 1916 Hussein ibn Ali, the Grand Sherif of Mecca, proclaimed Arab independence of Turkey. With the Arabian tribes supporting him, he occupied Mecca, captured Jeddah, and laid siege to Medina. Because of his knowledge of the Arabic language and culture, Lawrence was sent to meet the Emirs Feisal ibn Ali and Nuri es-Said, influential leaders in the Arab revolt, in Jeddah. Lawrence agreed to remain there as part of a team of British advisers. He quickly earned the trust of the Arabs and was given a small motorised force consisting of a Rolls-Royce armoured car battery, a Ford light car patrol armed with Lewis guns, two Talbot lorries mounting heavier weapons, and supporting transport. This force provided the mainstay of his operations, as many of the Arabs fought for plunder and vanished with their loot for a while after a successful raid. In July 1917 Lawrence played a prominent part in the Arab capture of the port of Aqaba. During the last year of the war, the Arab army operated on the right wing of the Allied advance through Palestine and Syria, and actually reached Damascus before the Allies. Lawrence, the supreme irregular, ended the war with the rank of colonel.

A convert to the cause of Arab nationalism, Lawrence felt that the various treaties the Allies signed at the Paris peace conference betrayed the promises he had made the Arabs on the Allies' behalf. In 1921 he served as special adviser on Arab affairs to Winston Churchill, then Colonial Secretary. Fate had thrust Lawrence to the forefront of affairs and that did not rest easily with his complex psyche. Seeking anonymity, he joined the Royal Air Force, but the press discovered his whereabouts and the air force discharged him. From 1923 until 1925 he served in the Tank Corps, again under an assumed name. In 1926 he joined the Royal Air Force again, spending two years on the North West Frontier of India. In March 1935 he left the air force and retired to his home in Dorset. He died from injuries sustained in a motorcycle accident later that year.

Allenby decided to continue the pursuit to the north, encountering only scattered resistance. British armoured cars reached Aleppo on 26 October. Three days later they took Muslimie Junction, through which passed the Turks' railway lifeline to the Mesopotamian Front. On 31 October Turkey requested an armistice, which the British granted. Since the beginning of the Battle of Megiddo, Allenby had destroyed three Turkish armies, advanced 560 kilometres (350 miles), and captured 76,000 prisoners, 360 guns, and 89 locomotives. No figures exist for the numbers of the enemy killed or wounded. The cost to his troops was 782 killed, 4179 wounded, and 382 missing. Megiddo was the crowning – and last – achievement of the British cavalry.

Megiddo should be remembered as the first time that all the elements of what became known as the *Blitzkrieg* technique (see Chapter 20 for more on this) came together. The fact that the battle employed horsed cavalry rather than tanks is not significant, the method of achieving the desired result was what counted. Blitzkrieg warfare features prominently in Part VI.

Engaging Enemies World Wide

As part of the overall Allied effort in the First World War, smaller numbers of British troops served in Italy and at Salonika in the Balkans. British and Empire troops also captured most of Germany's colonies during the early months of the war. In the Pacific these included part of New Guinea, the Bismarck Archipelago, Bougainville and Buka in the Solomon Islands, Samoa, and the Caroline, Pelew, Marshall, and Marianne Islands. The Japanese, with British assistance, took the German Treaty Port and naval base of Tsingtao on the coast of China. In Africa the German colonies included Togoland, the Cameroons, South West Africa, and East Africa (becoming Tanganyika under British rule, now Tanzania).

Only in East Africa did the war run its full course. There, the German commander, General Paul von Lettow-Vorbeck, led British, South African, and Portuguese troops a merry dance for years in the bush without their being able to pin him down. A master of improvisation, he salvaged the guns of the German cruiser *Konigsberg*, which British naval gunfire had sunk in the Rufuji river, fitted them with travelling carriages, and used them as heavy artillery. Lettow-Vorbeck was still at large when Germany requested an armistice and the German command had to order him to surrender, which he did on 25 November 1918.

Part VI
The Second World War (and Beyond)

The 5th Wave   By Rich Tennant

"That's the problem with these planes. The fuselage isn't long enough."

In this part . . .

Years of political neglect ensured that the British Army was ill prepared and underequipped for a second global conflict, although it did have a spectacular success against the Italians in North Africa. However, by 1942 Britain was able to take the offensive, despite the intervention of Japan, fighting successful campaigns in North Africa, Italy, northwest Europe, and Burma.

Following the end of the Second World War, the army's work involved ensuring a peaceful withdrawal from Empire, fighting a Cold War against communists, fighting real wars in Korea, the Falkland Islands, Iraq, and Afghanistan, defeating terrorism, and peace keeping. Despite constant reductions in its strength, the army undertook all these tasks successfully and with credit.

Chapter 20

Phoney War, Panzers, and Miracles: The Outbreak of the Second World War

*I*n 1919 the Treasury cut defence expenditure to the bone, using the excuse that Great Britain was not likely to become involved in a full-scale war for ten years. This notorious *Ten Year Rule* remained year after year until 1932, when Hitler came to power in Germany. The measure was simply an excuse for not spending money and deferring modernisation of the army.

Mechanisation of the forces proceeded at a snail's pace. For some years after the First World War, the army spent more on animal feed than it did on petrol. The numerous senior cavalry officers in high places did everything in their power to retain their traditional arm of service at the expense of the Royal Tank Corps, as it became in 1923. When, under Hitler, Germany began re-arming openly, the British government suddenly realised that years of deliberate political neglect had produced an army incapable of fighting a modern war. Several Territorial infantry battalions transferred to the Royal Tank Corps, and when the size of the Territorial Army doubled in 1939, their numbers doubled as well. In 1939 the British government made a sensible decision to form the mechanised cavalry regiments and the Royal Tank Corps (which became the Royal Tank Regiment) into the Royal Armoured Corps, to centralise training, administration, and other matters. At this point, time ran out and the Second World War began.

The causes of the Second World War have filled many books dedicated to the subject, so for more information, check out Keith D. Dickson's *World War Two For Dummies* and Sean Lang's *European History For Dummies* (both published by Wiley). For now, it's worth remembering that Britain, France, and some other *Allied* countries originally faced off against Germany, Italy, and other *Axis* countries (and that the Soviet Union, America, and later Italy joined with the Allies).

At the start of the Second World War, the British army consisted of:

- ✔ **Infantry:** British infantrymen started the Second World War equipped not unlike they were at the end of the First World War: steel helmets, rapid firing Lee-Enfield rifles, and khaki uniforms were standard issue. Figure 20-1 shows typical infantrymen of this period.

- ✔ **Cavalry:** By this time, the cavalry were re-equipping with tanks and armoured cars.

- ✔ **Artillery:** Early in the war, British artillery was towed by trucks, and self-propelled artillery came later in the war.

- ✔ **Tanks:** The Royal Tank Regiment (RTR) was still growing at the start of the Second World War, and the tanks it used in included heavily armoured Matilda tanks and lightly armoured Cruiser tanks.

For more on British tank theory between the wars and at the start of the Second World War, see Chapter 1. The British army developed its own special forces in the early stages of the Second World War – see the later sidebar 'Commandos and Paratroopers' for more information.

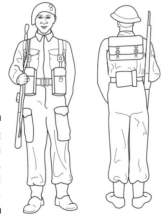

Figure 20-1:
British infantrymen, Second World War.

Campaigning between the Wars

The defeat of the Central Powers in 1918 did not mean that the army had nothing to do. Under the terms of the general peace agreements of the First

World War (see Part V), the British Empire absorbed several German colonies and reached its greatest territorial extent. The United Kingdom also had mandates to administer the Turkish provinces of Palestine and Mesopotamia. As increasing Jewish settlement in Palestine was already causing friction with the Arab population, this proved to be a poisoned chalice.

To avoid overstretching the post-war army, the Royal Air Force assumed responsibility for air policing Mesopotamia (renamed Iraq) and Aden. A Third (and brief) Afghan War began in 1919 with an incursion into British territory. Having experienced a taste of modern firepower and the Royal Air Force's ability to bomb deep inside Afghanistan, the Afghans called the fighting off and went home, forfeiting their British subsidies.

British troops were actively employed in dealing with civil wars of one kind or another, notably during:

- **International intervention in Russia, 1918–1919.** The Russian Civil War was raging and British troops formed part of the international interventionist forces. They fought on the side of the White Russian armies in the areas of Murmansk, Archangel, the Baltic, and South Russia. Unfortunately, the Whites could not agree on a joint strategy, or much else for that matter, whereas the Red Russian or Bolshevik armies were clear in their aims and, having the benefit of a central position within Russia, were able to deploy their troops more efficiently. One by one the White armies were defeated and the interventionist forces withdrew.

- **The Irish War of Independence, 1919–1921.** Executions following the Easter Rising of 1916 (see Chapter 17) and the imprisonment of hundreds of Irish nationalists afterwards swung public opinion in Ireland towards independence. Some nationalists favoured achieving independence by violent means and enjoyed the tacit support of some sections of the population. To assist in restoring order, some 8000 auxiliary policemen were recruited. They were called the *Black and Tans* because of the colour of their uniforms, and they were mostly ex-servicemen unable to settle down to civilian life. Both sides committed acts to be ashamed of, but the Black and Tans excelled in such activities and they alienated moderate Irish opinion. By 1921, neither side expected to win an outright military victory. The nationalist leaders concluded a treaty with the British government that recognised the right of six Protestant counties of Ulster to remain within the Union of Great Britain and Northern Ireland, while the remaining 26 counties gained self-governing dominion status as the Irish Free State, which eventually became the sovereign republic of Ireland in 1949. Ulster accepted the situation, but elsewhere a bloody civil war ensued between those Irishmen who accepted the provisions of the treaty and those who did not, ending in favour of the pro-treaty party in 1923 (the knock-on military effect of this partition is detailed in the sidebar 'The lost regiments').

The lost regiments

Granting independence to the 26 counties forming the Irish Free State in 1921 meant that the regiments with strong local connections in those areas could no longer exist within the British Army. Five regiments disbanded and those men wishing to continue their service with the British Army transferred to other regiments. The five regiments were:

✔ The Royal Irish Regiment

✔ The Connaught Rangers

✔ The Prince of Wales' Leinster Regiment

✔ The Royal Munster Fusiliers

✔ The Royal Dublin Fusiliers

The Irish Guards, though formed as recently as 1900, were not affected, nor were those regiments whose local connections lay in Ulster. The Army as a whole still draws recruits from both sides of the Irish border.

The Phoney War, 1939–1940

The Second World War started in September 1939. On the Western Front it was known as the *Phoney War* because, apart from patrol activity, absolutely nothing happened.

Despite being known as the Phoney War in France, the war was very real elsewhere:

✔ Under Adolf Hitler's leadership, Germany defeated the Polish army in September 1939 with the help of the Soviet Union. For the moment, Hitler and Josef Stalin, the Soviet dictator, maintained a truly insincere friendship.

✔ Germany invaded Denmark and Norway in April 1940. British forces went to the Norwegians' assistance, only to find that the Germans possessed tanks and adequate air support, whereas the British and Norwegians had neither. The result was an embarrassing evacuation of the British army by sea in June.

Germany's initial victories were fought using the same *Blitzkrieg* tactics that Allenby used at Megiddo (see Chapter 19). These consisted of a holding attack that coincided with a deep penetration elsewhere on the battlefront with the object of inflicting strategic paralysis on the enemy, both accompanied by dominant air support.

Nothing happened on the new Western Front for months and months. The Allies believed that if the Germans attacked, they would employ a mechanised version of the Schlieffen plan that had failed so narrowly in 1914 (see Chapter 17), sweeping through Belgium and on across France's northern frontier. The British Expeditionary Force (BEF), commanded by Field Marshal Viscount Gort, and the best French armies were to drive north into Belgium in response to this. Here's what followed:

- ✔ On 10 May 1940 the Germans launched their offensive in the West. They invaded Holland and captured Fort Eban Emael, the lynchpin of the Belgian frontier defences. As agreed, the BEF and the French drove north. It was then that the enemy sprung their trap.

- ✔ Powerful German *panzer* (armoured) divisions drove through the Ardennes Forest and on 13 May began assault crossings of the river Meuse. Holland surrendered the following day.

- ✔ From 16 May onwards, the panzer corps, with the close support of the dive bombers from the *Luftwaffe* (Germany's air force), smashed through the French front and began to carve a wide corridor across northern France to the coast.

- ✔ The Germans reached the coast at Abbeville on 20 May, having achieved in days what Ludendorff's storm troopers failed to do in weeks during 1918 (see Chapter 18). The Allied armies to the north of the corridor were now isolated within a pocket and, with the exception of the Belgians, cut off from their supply bases.

The BEF was seriously deficient in tanks. Apart from the light tanks in the divisional cavalry regiments, the equipment of the 1st Army Tank Brigade (consisting of the 4th and 7th Royal Tank Regiments) was mainly the slow, heavily armoured Matilda I and a few Matilda IIs, but the brigade was under strength. The 1st Armoured Division was not due to arrive from England until mid-1940. Initially, the French army had plenty of tanks, but the best of these had been destroyed in the frontier battles.

The Arras counter-attack, 21 May 1940

The Allies' planned response to the rapid German advance across northern France was to cut the 'Panzer Corridor' in two by converging counter-attacks from north and south, so isolating the panzer divisions closest to the coast. The southern counter-attack never got moving. The northern counter-attack force, under the command of Major General H.E. Franklin, moved off during the afternoon of 21 May. It consisted of two columns, plus supporting artillery and anti-tank batteries with each column.

The force descended Vimy Ridge and then began to wheel eastwards, passing south of Arras, with a view to forming a front facing east. In so doing, they ran into the flank of Major General Erwin Rommel's 7th Panzer Division and not only played havoc with its motorised rifle regiments, but also caused neighbouring German troops to bolt. To the Germans' horror, their 37-millimetre anti-tank guns were useless against the Matildas' thick armour. For a while, Rommel himself was under fire and his aide was shot dead beside him. Energetic commander that he was, Rommel concentrated all his artillery against the slow-moving British tanks. His 88-millimetre anti-aircraft guns were potent tank killers and his field guns, while unable to penetrate the British armour, were capable of immobilising a tank by blowing the tracks off. By 6 p.m. the British assault was at a standstill and during the evening the surviving tanks began to withdraw. As they did so, the riflemen of the Durham Light Infantry beat off German counter-attacks on the villages they had occupied. Rommel's own tanks, which he had despatched to the west during the morning, returned to the battlefield in an attempt to intervene. They ran straight into the British anti-tank gun screen and a French armoured formation covering the British right flank.

Altogether, Rommel's losses included approximately 600 personnel casualties and between 30 and 40 tanks. The real damage, however, was of a different kind. The higher German headquarters were already nervous about projecting their precious armoured formations so deep into enemy territory. Now, their worst fears seemed about to be realised. They recalled the 6th and 8th Panzer Divisions from the coast and directed them towards a crisis that was apparently developing in the Arras area, while with few exceptions they halted the onward drive of the remaining panzer divisions for 24 hours.

If Franklin's men felt that they had incurred heavy casualties to no purpose, they were wrong. They had bought priceless time for the BEF. On 22 May the Royal Navy landed garrisons at the ports of Boulogne and Calais. The determined resistance put up by these absorbed yet more of the panzer divisions' time. During that time the opportunity for the Germans to destroy the BEF began to evaporate.

The Dunkirk evacuation, 26 May–4 June 1940

On 25 May King Leopold of Belgium ordered the Belgian army to cease fighting. This left a yawning gap in the left flank of the Allied armies and insufficient troops were available to fill it. The following day the government told Lord Gort that his first priority was to evacuate as much of his BEF as possible to England. The BEF and its allies commenced a steady withdrawal to Dunkirk, where they established a defensive perimeter.

The panzer divisions halted to catch their breath and reform, perform some much-needed maintenance, and prepare for the next phase of the war in the west – the destruction of the remaining French armies south of the Somme. Reichsmarschall Hermann Goering assured Hitler that the Luftwaffe's aircraft were quite capable of breaking resistance within the shrinking Allied perimeter. As British units reached Dunkirk, they destroyed heavy weapons and vehicles to prevent them falling into enemy hands; lines of lorries driven across the sands at low water formed additional piers to evacuate troops from.

Admiral Ramsay, in charge of the evacuation, assembled over 1000 vessels, including destroyers and smaller warships, cross-channel ferries, pleasure steamers, coasters, trawlers, tugs, and craft as small as cabin cruisers. Their civilian owners manned many of the little ships. They declined to hand them over to the Royal Navy because they were determined to play a part in bringing their soldiers home. Some ferried men out from the beaches to larger vessels, but others returned to England fully laden. The initial hope was that up to 45,000 men might be rescued, but when the evacuation ended at 3.40 a.m. on 4 June, the ships had taken 200,000 British, 130,000 French, and 10,000 other Allied soldiers to safety. All their tanks, guns, and heavy weapons had to be left behind.

Commandos and paratroopers

With his strong sense of history, British Prime Minister Winston Churchill was aware of the long British tradition of carrying out raids on the enemy's territory. He requested volunteers from all over the army for this type of operation, implemented after the British withdrawal from Dunkirk. The units they formed were named *Commandos*, after the Boer units that tied down so many British troops during the Second Boer War (see Chapter 16). Both the selection process and the training the troops received were severe. The raids they carried out were desperate affairs. More often than not, they were successful. To Hitler's fury, they often made the German military machine look rather foolish. The raids also created a sense of insecurity in the enemy's coastal garrisons.

In due course, the Royal Marines also formed Commando units. Today's Royal Marine Commandos pride themselves on being the most thoroughly trained infantry in the world. Their members only receive the award of their green berets after successfully completing months of hard, demanding effort.

Both Germany and the Soviet Union possessed parachute troops. The Germans used theirs to good effect in Norway, Denmark, and Holland in 1940. Obviously paratroops held the key to certain tactical situations. The British Army began training its first parachute troops shortly after Dunkirk. The men were volunteers and underwent tough physical tests and training, as well as assessments of their mental attitude. The hard-earned maroon beret soon became the hallmark of the airborne soldier. The British Parachute Regiment formed on 1 August 1942. Its early operations quickly placed it in the front rank of shock troops. It maintains its reputation for hard, aggressive fighting to this day.

Throughout the evacuation Dunkirk was under heavy attack by the Luftwaffe. The Germans sank six British and three French destroyers and damaged 19, as well as sinking 56 other ships and 161 small craft. The apparent lack of British aircraft above the evacuation zone resulted in unjustified criticism of the Royal Air Force. In fact British fighters intercepted and broke up many German air attacks before they reached the beaches. Between 10 May and 4 June, 402 enemy aircraft were destroyed and a further 201 damaged, at a cost to the Royal Air Force of 141 aircraft.

Some British troops remained south of the Somme. The Germans trapped the 51st (Highland) Division, which had been serving on the French sector of the front, and forced it to surrender at St Valery, near Dieppe. The 1st Armoured Division, stripped of its infantry element to form the garrisons of Boulogne and Calais, reached France through Cherbourg. Its tanks, deficient in gunsights, radios, and many other essential items, mercifully saw little action before the French armies collapsed. The division was ordered back to Cherbourg to re-embark for Britain along with the base and administrative troops left in northern France – a total of 150,000 British and 20,000 Polish soldiers.

Standing Alone after Dunkirk

The campaign in France cost the British Army 4438 killed, 14,127 wounded, and 39,251 taken prisoner. In England, only three divisions with 500 guns and 200 tanks were available to meet a possible invasion by the Germans. Plenty of soldiers were around, but their divisions had to be reconstituted and re-equipped. For the moment, nothing existed to equip them with. Factories therefore had to continue producing weapons in quantity even if they were not the most modern available. For example, designs for 6-pounder tank and anti-tank guns had been approved, but because factories were still tooled up for 2-pounder production that had to continue out of sheer necessity.

Winston Churchill became Prime Minister on 10 May 1940. He had made mistakes in his career, and he would make more, but the hour had produced the man. He bore some resemblance to that traditional British symbol, the bulldog, and possessed its virtues of strength and stubborn courage. He saw Dunkirk as a deliverance and not a victory, and commented that evacuations did not win wars. His superb command of the English language enabled him to deliver speeches that rallied the nation behind him and gave people a sense of purpose, although he promised nothing for the immediate future but hard times.

Lend-Leasing

Under President Franklin D. Roosevelt, the United States maintained an attitude of benevolent neutrality towards Great Britain during this initial period of the Second World War. Churchill made an open request to the United States: 'Give us the tools and we'll finish the job.' Roosevelt was sympathetic and the *Lend-Lease Agreement* came into force. Under this agreement, the United State provided guns, tanks, motor vehicles, aircraft, food, fuel, and machine tools to any of the combatants who collected them, knowing full well that the Royal Navy's

blockade prevented any of these items reaching Germany. Some years earlier, Roosevelt commented that 'The business of America is business', so these supplies had to be paid for in due course. In effect, Great Britain's war effort was being bankrolled by the United States. The Americans charged a high rate of interest on the loan and in the aftermath of the war the British had to endure years of serious austerity to pay it back; the final payment was made at the end of 2006.

Throughout the summer of 1940 the Royal Air Force fought and won the Battle of Britain. During this aerial campaign fought for supremacy of the skies over Britain, the Luftwaffe was unable to obtain the air superiority necessary for an invasion, and by October the prospect of autumn gales in the Channel led Hitler to abandon the idea of invading the United Kingdom. The Luftwaffe continued to bomb British cities and inflict heavy civilian casualties. Again, contrary to German expectations, these attacks simply strengthened British determination to go on fighting.

With most of Continental Europe now under German occupation, Britain stood completely alone. Benito Mussolini, Hitler's Italian crony, declared war on the United Kingdom on 10 June, hoping to share in the eventual spoils. As the British already regarded Mussolini as a buffoon, the event tended to stiffen British resolve rather than add to the sense of isolation. Day by day, the British army was visibly recovering its strength – including hiring equipment from the US (see the sidebar 'Lend-Leasing'), and forming new special forces (see the sidebar 'Commandos and paratroopers'). Chapter 21 looks at the next significant theatre of war – the war in North Africa.

Chapter 21

Sun, Sand, Sea, and Tanks: The Middle East and North Africa, 1940–1943

*I*taly joined the war on Germany's side after the British withdrawal from Dunkirk (see Chapter 20); this made the North African theatre an area of key importance, as the Italian presence in Libya posed a serious threat to Egypt and Suez Canal, the British Imperial route to India and the Far East.

In June 1940, General Sir Archibald Wavell, Commander-in-Chief Middle East, commanded some 50,000 British and Imperial troops, spread across a wide area stretching from the Syrian border to Somaliland. Only 36,000 men, critically short of armour and artillery, were in Egypt itself, where the defence of the Suez Canal was once again the major consideration. Across the border in Libya was a 250,000-strong Italian army, while in Italian East Africa were a further 200,000 men, poised to strike into the Sudan, Kenya, and British Somaliland, the largest of whose garrisons numbered only 9000. Figure 21-1 shows some of the actions fought in this theatre of war.

In the Middle East and North Africa, the British army consisted of British Dominion and Indian troops. Special forces also served in this theatre of war (see the sidebar 'Desert Elites'). Mechanisation was the key to success in North Africa, and the main British tanks of this period were:

✓ **Cruisers:** Equipped the armoured divisions. Most were fast and armed with a 2-pounder gun firing armour-piercing rounds only. This meant that infantry and anti-tank guns could only be tackled using the tank's machine guns. Later models of the Crusader, which reached the desert in mid-1941, were up-gunned with 6-pounders.

- **Grants:** Equipped the armoured divisions. American lend-lease tanks (see Chapter 20) armed with a 37-millimetre gun in the top turret and a 75-millimetre gun in a sponson. The 75 millimetre was capable of penetrating German tanks at 780 metres (850 yards) and could fire a high-explosive shell. The Grant's frontal armour was also proof against the German 50-millimetre anti-tank gun at 900 metres (1000 yards). They arrived in North Africa in the spring of 1942.

- **Matildas:** Equipped the army tank brigades, which supported infantry operations. Slow but heavily armoured, the Matilda was known as The Queen of the Battlefield during the early stages of the desert war, but its reputation for invulnerability was dramatically ended when a battery of German 88-millimetre guns shot a squadron to pieces at Halfaya Pass in June 1941.

- **Shermans:** American lend-lease tanks used from 1942 until the end of the war. The Sherman was a versatile medium tank, although it tended to burn rapidly when penetrated; equipped with a 75-millimetre gun like the Grant, but positioned in the main turret.

- **Valentines:** Slow, well-armoured replacement for the Matilda. It was produced in large numbers and served in this theatre of war from late 1941 onwards.

Figure 21-2 shows some of the tanks commonly used by the British in this campaign.

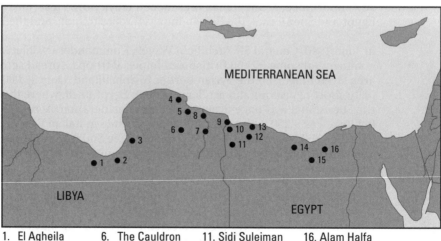

Figure 21-1: The War in the Desert, 1940–1942.

1. El Agheila	6. The Cauldron	11. Sidi Suleiman	16. Alam Halfa
2. Marsa Brega	7. Sidi Rezagh	12. Buq Buq	
3. Beda Fomm	8. Tobruk	13. Sidi Barrani	
4. Derna	9. Bardia	14. Tel el Aqqaqir	
5. Gazala	10. Sollum	15. El Alamein	

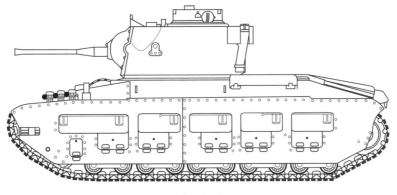

Matilda II

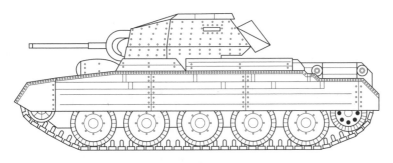

Crusader III

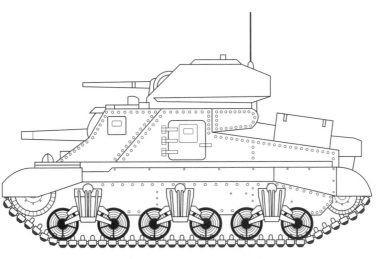

Figure 21-2:
British tanks
in the
desert.

Grant

Desert elites

Some people love the desert, others are scared stiff by it. By and large, the British seem to like it, just as they do the sea. One of the most famous desert travellers of the inter-war years was Major Ralph Bagnold, who probably knew more about the Western Desert than any man alive. In 1940 Bagnold received permission to form a unit capable of travelling the deep reaches of the desert and operating far behind enemy lines. He drew his recruits from volunteers throughout the army. His requirements were for trained soldiers with some practical knowledge of vehicle mechanics, but he was particularly seeking fit, intelligent men with stamina, imagination, initiative, iron determination, and the ability to act as part of a team regardless of rank. The vehicles he chose were Chevrolet or Ford 30 cwt trucks fitted with sand channels, radiator condensers, and a variety of automatic weapons. The unit was called the *Long Range Desert Group*. It reached its maximum strength of 25 officers and 324 men in March 1942. The group's basic unit was the Patrol, normally operating in two halves each of five or six vehicles. Operating from oases far to the south of the main battle area, Patrols used the vast empty desert spaces to penetrate far

into the enemy's rear and carry out intelligence-gathering missions including surveillance of traffic on the coast road, the insertion or extraction of agents or the SAS, and sometimes direct action including ambushes and harassing attacks.

Another elite, the *Special Air Service Regiment* (SAS), was the brainchild of a Scots Guards officer, Lieutenant David Stirling. He believed that a handful of highly trained and motivated men could achieve things that conventional troops could not. Allowed to raise and train a small unit known as L Detachment Special Air Service Brigade, Stirling looked for the same personal qualities as Bagnold did, but additionally trained his men in the use of captured weapons, explosives, and incendiary devices. His first major operation involved a parachute drop and ended in disaster. He then established a successful partnership with the Long Range Desert Group, which transported his teams to within marching distance of their objectives. Before the Desert War ended, the SAS had destroyed 400 German and Italian aircraft on the ground, plus many tons of aviation fuel, bombs, ammunition, and other stores.

Facing the Italians in Libya

In Libya, the Italians were not exactly brimming with confidence and looking forward to an easy victory. Only mechanised armies can fight desert warfare successfully, and the Italian army consisted mainly of infantry divisions that marched on foot.

They possessed a large number of L3 light tanks that were little better than tracked machine-gun carriers, and a regiment of badly designed M11/39 medium tanks. Some of their artillery weapons were elderly, but in general the Italian gunners handled their guns well and courageously.

The war began badly for the Italians when their anti-aircraft gunners shot down their own Commander-in-Chief, Marshal Italo Balbo, over Tobruk on 28 June 1940. His replacement, Marshal Rodolfo Graziani, inherited a demoralised army. On the day after Mussolini declared war, elements of the British 7th Armoured Division crossed into Libya. During the next few weeks they harried the Italians' frontier garrisons without mercy, struck deep into their territory, shot up vehicle convoys, and even captured a general who happened to be carrying plans of the Bardia defences. During this time the Italians suffered 3000 casualties, while 7th Armoured Division suffered only 150. German liaison officers reported the Italians as being nervous and depressed.

Despite all this, Mussolini ordered Graziani to invade Egypt or lose his job. With great reluctance, the Marshal crossed the frontier on 13 September, taking four days to march the 60 miles to Sidi Barrani, just halfway to the main British position at Mersa Matruh. Apart from establishing an advance post at Maktila, he flatly refused to go any further. He simply sat tight and established a chain of fortified camps stretching away southwest towards the distant escarpment. Meanwhile, although the Battle of Britain was still raging (see Chapter 20), Churchill took the courageous decision to reinforce Wavell with three armoured regiments, including the 7th Royal Tank Regiment equipped with Matilda IIs, the most powerful tanks in the British armoury. When they reached Egypt in early October, Wavell took steps to ensure that the enemy remained unaware of their presence.

On the night of 11/12 November 1940 the Fleet Air Arm's torpedo bombers crippled the Italian battle fleet in Taranto harbour. This meant that the Western Desert Force would receive close support from the Royal Navy's Inshore Squadron, consisting of gunboats and monitors, without Italian interference. Wavell, tired of waiting for Graziani to make the next move, decided to make that move himself.

The Battle of Sidi Barrani, 9–12 December 1940

Wavell had served under Allenby in Palestine, so unsurprisingly his planned attack bore a striking resemblance to the opening phase of the Battle of Megiddo (see Chapter 19). His plan involved passing the 4th Indian Division and the 7th Royal Tank Regiment through a gap in the Italian chain of camps. They would storm those camps to the north of the gap in turn. The 7th Armoured Division would pass then through the same gap, striking deeper, and swing north to the coast, isolating Sidi Barrani, which both divisions would then attack. Codenamed Operation Compass, the attack began on the morning of 9 December 1940.

Following a heavy bombardment, the tanks spearheaded the Indian Division's attack on the camp at Nibeiwa. They found the entrance blocked with 23 M11/39 medium tanks, all of which they knocked out before they could return fire or move. To their horror, the Italians found that they did not possess a gun capable of penetrating the Matilda's armour, although their gun crews bravely kept firing until they were shot down around their weapons. Seeing this, some Italians surrendered at once, but others continued to resist fiercely. Two hours of hard fighting by the tanks and the infantry were required before they fully secured the position. During the day, the remaining camps in the northern half of the chain offered varying degrees of resistance, but they were all taken in much the same way. Elsewhere, the 7th Armoured Division had reached the coast, severing Sidi Barrani's communications to the west and cutting its water pipeline. Next day, the British attacked the town's defences from the west and the south. Simultaneously, tanks moved round to the eastern perimeter to intercept the enemy's 1st Libyan Division, which was withdrawing from Maktila. Sidi Barrani fell as soon as its defences were penetrated, but the Libyans did not give up until the following morning.

On 11 December the Italians abandoned the last of their camps in the Sidi Barrani area and headed for the frontier with the 7th Armoured Division in pursuit. On 12 December the 7th Armoured Brigade was ordered to intercept the Italians at Buq Buq. It found the massed artillery of the enemy rearguard lining a low, semi-circular ridge overlooking a salt flat. Light tanks promptly charged across this, but broke through the thin crust and floundered. The enemy gunners immediately began pounding them to scrap iron. The situation eased a little when Royal Horse Artillery opened fire on the Italians. Meanwhile, the Allies worked their way round the flanks of the enemy position. The Italians swung their guns round to meet the threat, but were momentarily stunned when one of their ammunition lorries went up in a tremendous explosion. By the time the dust had settled the tanks had reached the gun line and resistance collapsed. A Hussar officer, evidently from an agricultural background, gave a radio report on the number of prisoners taken: 'Twenty acres of officers and a hundred acres of men.'

In four days Operation Compass, intended simply as a spoiling attack, had driven the Italians out of Egypt and yielded 38,000 prisoners, including four generals, while the enemy equipment captured or destroyed included 237 guns and 73 light and medium tanks. Wavell decided to reinforce its success. Within days, the Allies had captured most of the enemy posts across the frontier and the Italians had retired into Bardia.

Chasing 'Electric Whiskers'

A 17-mile anti-tank ditch surrounded Bardia, behind which lay barbed-wire aprons, minefields, concrete emplacements, and blockhouses with interlocking arcs of fire. Bardia's garrison consisted of a total of 45,000 men, backed by

400 guns and 100 armoured vehicles. In command was one of Italy's most famous soldiers, General Annibale Bergonzoli, better known as Electric Whiskers because of his dramatically forked beard.

The 7th Armoured Division quickly isolated the fortress and imposed a state of siege on 20 December 1940. Four troops of Matildas arrived to take part in thorough rehearsals for the planned assault. This was delivered by the 6th Australian Division at dawn on 3 January 1941, following a bombardment focused on the sector chosen for the break-in. After the infantry had rushed the nearest posts, three parties of *sappers* (military engineers) set to work – one to throw down the sides of the anti-tank ditch, one to build causeways on which the tanks could cross, and one to cut the wire with *Bangalore torpedoes* (long tubes filled with high explosive) and clear paths through the minefields. The Matildas and the Australian infantry then penetrated the defences, methodically clearing one position after another. To add to the Italians' ordeal, the combined fire of three battleships, seven destroyers, and the Inshore Squadron pulverised designated areas within the defences.

In places the enemy fought very hard indeed, but on 5 January the last resistance was overcome. Another 38,000 prisoners began the long walk into captivity, leaving behind immense quantities of military equipment, including 700 wheeled vehicles, many in working order. No one could find Electric Whiskers, who had somehow evaded capture and was walking to Tobruk. The Allies sustained 500 casualties including 150 killed.

Taking Tobruk, 6–22 January 1941

The 7th Armoured Division isolated Tobruk on 6 January. Tobruk's defences were similar to those of Bardia (see the preceding section) and were held by 25,000 men, supported by 200 guns and 90 armoured vehicles. In command was General Pitassi Mannella, known to his peers as the King of Artillerymen. He was less than pleased at being required to defend an area twice the size of Bardia with a force half the size of Bergonzoli's lost garrison. He was right to be aggrieved, for on 21 January the combination of thorough planning, impenetrable Matildas, and aggressive Australian infantry tore his defences apart. During the night the garrison tried to destroy its stores and set the grounded cruiser *San Giorgio* ablaze. Little further fighting took place and by 10 a.m. on 22 January the town and harbour were firmly in Australian hands.

The Italian Tenth Army occupied the line of the Wadi Derna, west of Tobruk. On 25 January the Australians closed up to it, but heavy artillery fire and fierce local counter-attacks prevented their making any headway. But then the situation changed dramatically. The Tenth Army's commander, General Tellera, fearing that British tanks might encircle his men from the south, withdrew during the night of 28/29 January. Graziani not only sanctioned the move but decided that such of Cyrenaica as remained in Italian hands had to be abandoned. Local

Arabs confirmed the suspicions of Major General Richard O'Connor, commanding the Western Desert Force, that the Italians were retreating into Tripolitania along the coast road. O'Connor immediately realised that this presented him with a chance to trap and destroy his opponents by sending 7th Armoured Division across the base of the Benghazi Bulge to Beda Fomm, while the Australians pursued the enemy along the coast road.

The Battle of Beda Fomm, 5–7 February 1941

7th Armoured Division's advance guard, named *Combeforce* after its commander, Lieutenant Colonel John Combe, reached Beda Fomm on the coast shortly after noon on 5 February and established a roadblock. Two hours later the head of the Italian column appeared. Its vehicles were halted by mines or gunfire. By radio, Combe suggested that the approaching 4th Armoured Brigade engage the enemy's steadily lengthening column from a series of ridges lying to the east and parallel with the road. At dusk its regiments were in action.

The presence of 7th Armoured Division came as a shock to the Italians, who believed that it was still north of Benghazi. The Italians planned to mount a holding attack on Combeforce while most of their tanks swung off the road at point that became known as 'The Pimple'. They would then smash their way through 4th Armoured Brigade's cordon, turn south, and attack Combeforce from the flank and rear.

The Italian attacks began shortly after dawn on 6 February, but foundered under steady tank fire of 2 Royal Tank Regiment's cruiser tanks. The trapped Italian column now stretched for 18 kilometres (11 miles). The 3rd Hussars shot up its centre while the 7th Hussars fastened onto its rear. Towards evening, very few of the British tanks had more than a few rounds of ammunition left and the regiments started to give ground, but at this critical moment reinforcements arrived. The demoralised Italians abandoned their attacks. At dawn on 7 February the remaining Italian tanks tried to batter their way through the roadblock in the wake of a heavy bombardment. For a while, every element of Combeforce had to fight for its life. Then, quite suddenly, white flags began to flutter along the Italian column. As General Tellera had been mortally wounded, Bergonzoli surrendered to Colonel Combe, who gave him breakfast. Everyone had heard of Electric Whiskers Bergonzoli and wanted to see what he looked like. Despite his flamboyant nickname, he turned out to be a rather dignified individual in his later middle years.

The Allies captured over 25,000 prisoners at Beda Fomm, plus 1500 wheeled vehicles and over 100 tanks. In total, since the start of Operation Compass, O'Connor's corps had taken over 130,000 prisoners, captured 380 tanks and

845 guns, advanced 800 kilometres (500 miles), and occupied half of Libya. The cost had been 500 killed, 1373 wounded, 55 missing, and a handful of tanks written off. In the wider sphere, the campaign exposed the Italian army's inability to fight a modern war. In Spain, General Franco, for long a potential ally of Hitler and Mussolini, announced that he was remaining strictly neutral.

Rommel Arrives in the Desert

As Commander-in-Chief Middle East, Wavell's responsibilities covered a huge area. Useless involvements in Greece and Crete, both lost to German invasion in 1941, detracted from the strength he had available to deploy in North Africa, which once again became the Middle East's most important theatre of war.

At the beginning of February 1941, Hitler offered to assist his ally Mussolini. The first the British knew of German involvement was an increase in the level of Luftwaffe activity in the area.

The German commander sent to North Africa was Lieutenant General Erwin Rommel. Ungovernable by nature, he decided to disregard his specific orders to avoid offensive operations until reinforcements had reached Libya. His nominal superior was Marshal Italo Garibaldi, and Rommel also ignored him. The British troops remaining in Cyrenaica were under the command of Lieutenant General Sir Philip Neame, who lacked experience of high command. His troops included 3rd Armoured Brigade, equipped in a manner that would have graced any self-respecting scrapyard: 5 Royal Tank Regiment possessed 23 clapped-out cruisers that had survived the earlier campaign, while the 3rd Hussars and 6 Royal Tank Regiment were equipped in part with useless light tanks and in part with Italian M13s captured at Beda Fomm.

On 24 March a German reconnaissance unit probed the British advance post at El Agheila. The troops holding it withdrew to the main defence line at Mersa Brega. The German 5th Light Division followed up and was halted there until Major General Gambier-Parry, in charge of the 2nd Armoured Division, gave the order to withdraw. This exposed British troops to the same sort of drive across the base of the 'Benghazi Bulge' with which O'Connor had destroyed the Italian Tenth Army (see the section 'The Battle of Beda Fomm, 5–7 February 1941', earlier in this chapter). Rommel saw this opportunity and took it with both hands:

 ✔ The 9th Australian Division avoided the trap and withdrew into Tobruk.

 ✔ The 2nd Armoured Division, subjected to order and counter-order, became fragmented. Its 3rd Armoured Brigade fought as well as it could, but shed broken-down tanks for kilometre after kilometre and virtually ceased to exist.

Next day the Germans captured Gambier-Parry and his divisional staff. They also overran the independent 3rd Indian Motor Brigade, which lacked artillery and anti-tank guns. About one third of its members evaded capture and reached Tobruk. Worse still, O'Connor had been sent forward to advise Neame and German motorcycle troops captured then both. With the exception of those troops preparing to defend Tobruk, the remnant of the British XIII Corps crossed the frontier into Egypt.

Holed up at Tobruk, April–December 1941

Admiral Sir Andrew Cunningham, the Commander-in-Chief Mediterranean Fleet, assured Wavell that Tobruk could be supplied by sea, so Wavell wasted no time in rushing reinforcements into the port. The garrison's strength now amounted to 25,000 men, 5 field artillery regiments, 25 cruiser tanks, 4 Matildas, 15 light tanks, and 30 Marmon-Herrington armoured cars manned by the King's Dragoon Guards.

The garrison's greatest asset, however, was its commander, Major General Leslie Morshead, who had served during the First World War and in civilian life was a shipping executive. His men called him Ming the Merciless because he bore a passing resemblance to the cruel, ruthless Emperor Ming, the arch-enemy of the science-fiction film hero Flash Gordon. Morshead made it clear to his officers that he would brook no retreat, no surrender, and no Dunkirk-style evacuation (see Chapter 20). As he didn't have enough troops to man the entire 48-kilometre (30-mile) perimeter of Tobruk, he decided to conduct a mobile defence, channelling any penetration onto tank killing grounds by a combination of minefields and natural obstacles. As his infantry lacked adequate anti-tank protection, he instructed them to let the enemy's armour roll past them and then surface to tackle its infantry. At other times they were to patrol aggressively, a policy that the Italians in particular found unsettling.

After the British defeated the enemy in tank battles involving 1 Royal Tank Regiment (see the sidebar 'Outgunned? By what?'), the arrival of 15th Panzer Division's infantry element from Tripoli enabled Rommel to attack the garrison again on 30 April. During the night an infantry attack secured a breach 2.5 kilometres (1.5 miles) wide in the outer defences of the southwestern perimeter; with a restored tank strength of 70, the German 5th Panzer Regiment passed through. One battalion, 40 strong, headed for Tobruk town, but was brought up sharp by a minefield and lost 17 of its tanks. The regiment's second battalion had swung right and begun rolling up the line of Australian defence posts. During a 5-kilometre (3-mile) run they neutralised five, but were brought to a standstill by artillery fire and tanks. The Germans retired to replenish their fuel and ammunition, but during the afternoon they returned to the attack, being driven back by the British. Both German battalions renewed the attack and a furious tank battle lasted until dark.

Outgunned? By what?

One of the myths of the Desert War in North Africa was that German tanks consistently outgunned their British opponents. This was simply not true. Technically the British tanks had marginally better weapons, and the cause of the myth was rooted in the enemy's *sword-and-shield* tactics. The German tank commanders were adept at feigning a retreat that drew the British armour within range of an anti-tank gun screen. The screen might consist of dug-in towed guns or *Panzerjager*, which were obsolete or captured tank chassis with an anti-tank gun mounted in an armoured housing. Both outranged the British tank guns and often fought from concealed positions. Even if they spotted the screen, British tank crews were at a disadvantage as at this period their tanks only fired anti-tank rounds.

Operation Battleaxe, 15–17 June 1941

Although Rommel had ended his advance, he took care to fortify positions on the frontier, including Halfaya Pass, Sollum, and Fort Capuzzo. Wavell wanted these as a springboard for his intended relief of Tobruk. He tried to take them in May (Operation Brevity) and again in June (Operation Battleaxe), without success, although the British did have local if temporary successes. But they lost a total of 91 tanks during Battleaxe, including a high proportion from mechanical failure. They claimed to have disabled 100 enemy tanks, which was probably close to the truth, but as the Germans were left in possession of the battlefield they were able to recover all but 12 burned-out hulks.

These failures infuriated Prime Minister Winston Churchill, who wanted to appoint a new Commander-in-Chief Middle East. However, Wavell had too many successes to his credit to sack him out of hand. Instead, Churchill promoted him sideways, ordering him to change places with General Sir Claude Auchinleck, Commander-in-Chief India.

Operation Crusader, 18 November–7 December 1941

After Battleaxe (see the previous section) the desert remained relatively quiet for the next five months. Both sides used the lull to build up their strength. During September and October most of the Tobruk garrison was relieved by sea, the 9th Australian Division being replaced by Major General Ronald Scobie's 70th Division and the Polish Carpathian Brigade. Further reinforcements included 4 Royal Tank Regiment, bringing the number of Matildas present to 69. Together, the garrison's armoured regiments formed the 32nd Army Tank Brigade under Brigadier A.C. Willison.

The British troops in the Western Desert were elevated to the status of being the Eighth Army. In command was General Sir Alan Cunningham, who had XIII and XXX Corps at his disposal. Auchinleck planned not only the relief of Tobruk but also the destruction of the Axis army. This was to be achieved by an advance of the entire Eighth Army across the frontier in conjunction with a breakout by the Tobruk garrison. The codename for the operation was Crusader. Auchinleck had resisted Churchill's pressure for early action, intending to mount his offensive in January 1942. However, the cost of keeping Tobruk supplied was high in terms of warships and merchant vessels sunk or damaged, while the Royal Air Force badly needed the airfields in Cyrenaica to provide air cover for Malta's vital supply convoys. Taking these considerations into account, Auchinleck decided to begin the offensive on 18 November.

The Battle of Sidi Rezegh, 21–23 November 1941

The Eighth Army crossed the frontier on 18 November before the enemy guessed what was happening. XXX Corps, containing most of the British armour, engaged the enemy first. At Bir el Gubi on 19 November, tank attack was followed by counter-attack and the British lost significant numbers of tanks. During the evening Gott switched 22nd Armoured across the battlefield, believing that together with 4th Armoured Brigades they would finish off 15th Panzer Division next morning. However, when dawn broke the only German tanks visible were those that the British had knocked out during the previous day's fighting. The reason was that 7th Armoured Brigade and the 7th Armoured Division's Support Group, containing much of the division's artillery, anti-tank guns, and motorised infantry, had enjoyed a clear run the previous day and were closing in on Sidi Rezegh airfield. Rommel ordered both panzer divisions to converge on the area as quickly as possible and as the fighting became more intense, Gott directed the 4th and 22nd Armoured Brigades there as well.

What followed during the next two days has been described as a multi-layered battle, in which formations on both sides found themselves simultaneously attacking in one direction and conducting a desperate defence in another. To put the matter at its simplest, in the north the Tobruk garrison began to break out against opposition from the Afrika Division, which was also trying to defend Sidi Rezegh against the 7th Armoured Brigade and the Support Group, who were in turn under attack by the 15th and 21st Panzer Division, whose anti-tank gunners were doing their best to hold off the pursuit by 4th and 22nd Armoured Brigades.

By the evening of 23 November things were beginning to look grim for XXX Corps:

- A South African brigade was overrun.

- The 4th Armoured Brigade still possessed a respectable tank strength, but was widely dispersed and was effectively out of action until its headquarters could be reconstituted.

✔ The 7th Armoured Brigade had suffered so severely that its personnel returned to Egypt after handing over its 15 remaining tanks.

✔ The 22nd Armoured Brigade had been reduced to 34 tanks, and the Support Group had received a severe mauling.

Rommel, too, had sustained losses, but with the arrival of the Italian Ariete Armoured Division from the south he still had sufficient tanks in hand to mount a drive eastwards, which would simultaneously re-establish contact with his frontier garrisons and pose such a threat to the Eighth Army's communications that Operation Crusader would have to be abandoned. His decision was based on the undeniable defeat of XXX Corps, but ignored the considerable presence of XIII Corps, which was still intact. It was a dangerous gamble based on overconfidence, and it was to lose him the battle.

Relieving Tobruk

If XXX Corps had been the hare, then XIII Corps was the tortoise. Its progress had been steady and methodical. On 22 November the frontier posts of Omar Nuovo, Libyan Omar, and Fort Capuzzo fell to its infantry attacks spearheaded by Matilda and Valentine tanks, and it cut off the Bardia garrison's water supply. The advance continued along the coast road. By the evening of 25 November it had forced the Axis infantry back against the Tobruk perimeter. Inside Tobruk, the breakout operation was suspended during the Sidi Rezegh battle. Now it was resumed. Shortly after noon on 26 November, the British took the escarpment at Ed Duda. That night, in a brilliantly conceived action, 44 Royal Tank Regiment's Matildas, spattering the ground ahead with machine gun fire, drove straight through the enemy positions at walking pace, accompanied by the New Zealanders' 19th Battalion. The defenders simply faded away into the darkness. By 1 a.m. on 27 November the Allies had relieved Tobruk.

The relief of Tobruk brought Rommel scurrying back from the frontier. The only result of his drive was that it had seriously unsettled Cunningham, who was promptly replaced as Army Commander by Major General Neil Ritchie. By then, however, the 7th Armoured Division had put its house in order and had sufficient tanks. During the next few days Rommel managed to hold off Gott and prize the New Zealanders away from the Tobruk perimeter. Against this, his army's losses were becoming insupportable. When the Eighth Army re-established contact with the Tobruk garrison on 5 December, the Germans had obviously lost the battle. On 7 December Rommel began an expertly conducted withdrawal from Cyrenaica, reaching the El Agheila defile on 1 January 1942. Operation Crusader had achieved its objectives, although it had proved to be a much tougher struggle than anyone had expected. Axis casualties amounted to 38,000 killed, wounded, and missing as against 18,000 British and Commonwealth losses.

The Battle of Gazala and the fall of Tobruk, 26 May–21 June 1942

In January 1942 history repeated itself in a most unpleasant way. Just as Wavell had been required to despatch assistance to Greece after Beda Fomm, now Japan's entry into the war forced Auchinleck to strip his command and send reinforcements to the Far East. During the next four months both sides prepared for a major offensive. By the last week of May the Eighth Army contained 125,000 men and 849 tanks, while the Axis army numbered 113,000 men and 560 tanks. The Eighth Army therefore possessed a numerical as well as a qualitative superiority. It should have won the subsequent battle without undue difficulty. Instead, it sustained the worst defeat in its history.

Shortly before the Battle of Gazala, the British received the Grant medium tank (see the start of this chapter for more details), and the 6-pounder anti-tank gun, the performance of which was much superior performance to that of the old 2-pounder. Across the lines the Germans had received some up-gunned PzKw III Model Js, plus 117 Marder tank destroyers (based on the obsolete PzKw 38T tank chassis and armed with a captured 76.2-millimetre Russian anti-tank gun rechambered to take German 75-millimetre ammunition).

The Axis strategy at Gazala contained two phases:

✔ The first phase, Venezia, involved the defeat of the Eighth Army and the capture of Tobruk.

✔ The second phase, Herakles, required a standstill in the desert while airborne and amphibious landings neutralised British-held Malta, the most heavily bombed place on earth and a perpetual thorn in the Axis flesh.

Rommel opened his offensive during the night of 26/27 May by sweeping round the southern flank of the British line. The Eighth Army was organised for attack rather than defence, so many units were in the wrong place to meet the Germans. As transport criss-crossed the desert in every direction to escape the Axis armour, one observer described the scene as resembling 'a confused musical ride' at the Royal Tournament. Despite being caught off balance, the 1st and 7th Armoured Divisions rallied and inflicted heavy losses on the enemy armour. By evening Rommel was pushed back against the Eighth Army's minefield. Desperately short of water, he considered asking Ritchie for terms. In the nick of time the Italian Trieste Division managed to clear a corridor through the mines.

Despite this, Ritchie still possessed a golden opportunity to destroy the Axis army. He lost it because the Eighth Army's two corps commanders were not only personal friends but also senior officers to him. He was, therefore, reluctant to employ the full weight of his authority. The result was that orders became subjects for protracted discussion. Time ticked by and Rommel's position, known as The Cauldron, remained unmolested.

By 1 June Rommel had recovered his strength. Ritchie did not make a move until 5 June, when the Germans easily repulsed a series of uncoordinated attacks on The Cauldron. The following day Rommel returned to the offensive, inflicting further loss on the British infantry. His lines of communication now clear, he repeated the thrust with which he had begun the battle. XXX Corps' three armoured brigades launched piecemeal counter-attacks on 12 June and the Germans defeated each in turn.

By now, a feeling had begun to spread throughout the Eighth Army that its generals were incapable of getting anything right. By the following evening the Army had only 70 tanks left and it abandoned the Gazala line during the night. Recognising that he had lost the battle, Ritchie initiated the army's withdrawal into Egypt, having reinforced the garrison of Tobruk.

The British had not anticipated a second siege of the fortress, but at 5.20 a.m. on 20 June, enemy dive bombers and artillery began blasting a gap on a narrow sector of the perimeter. By 8.30 a.m. both panzer divisions were through and pushing steadily north. The British 32nd Army Tank Brigade counter-attacked and fought itself to destruction. By 1.30 p.m. the Germans had reached the escarpment overlooking the harbour and at 6 p.m. they entered the town. Garrison commander Major General Klopper ordered a general surrender, which some of his garrison refused to accept, and some carried on fighting until 22 June. Several hundred men from various regiments broke out into the desert and eventually succeeded in rejoining the Eighth Army, but 32,000 marched into captivity.

Total Axis casualties for the period 26 May to 21 June amounted to 60,000. British losses during the same period came to 88,000. Coming as they did on top of equally bad news from the Far East (see Chapter 24), the Battle of Gazala and the loss of Tobruk were serious blows to British morale and marked the army's lowest point during the war. Rommel, on the other hand, was at the peak of his career and the capture of Tobruk won him his field marshal's baton. Ignoring the agreed strategy that the invasion of Malta was to follow the capture of Tobruk, he set off in pursuit of the Eighth Army. Once more, he ignored orders, but with Hitler as his personal patron who was going to argue?

First Battle of Alamein, 1–27 July 1942

On 25 June 1942 Auchinleck assumed personal command of the Eighth Army. That evening the Afrika Korps penetrated between X and XXX Corps at Mersa Matruh and a disorderly retreat followed. This ended at El Alamein, a little town lying on the railway some 95 kilometres (60 miles) west of Alexandria.

Here the negotiable desert narrowed to a 55-kilometre (35-mile) strip between the sea in the north and the impassable Quattara Depression to the south. Within this strip lay three ridges, Meteiriya in the north, Ruweisat some miles to the south, and Alam Halfa to the southeast. None was more than a swelling in the stony desert, but the overview they provided made their possession extremely important.

The First Battle of Alamein was actually a series of hard-fought actions that took place between 1 and 27 July. These were centred on Ruweisat Ridge and Tel el Eisa (Jesus Hill) in the north. While each side received reinforcements, neither was strong enough to defeat the other. By the end of the month both armies were exhausted and the front had lapsed into apparent stalemate. By then the battle had cost the Eighth Army 13,000 casualties and 193 tanks, while Axis losses amounted to 22,000 casualties (including 7000 prisoners) and up to 100 tanks.

Nevertheless, the British were in a better strategic situation as they were so close to their bases. They were also being reinforced at a rate that the Axis army, with its overextended lines of communication, could not hope to match. Now Rommel realised that he had fallen into a trap of his own making. He had already burned the fuel captured at Tobruk and only had a day's supply in hand at any one time. That meant that he could neither break through to Alexandria, as he had hoped, nor resume a war of movement that would leave his army stranded after a few hours' fighting. As luck would have it, for the moment both armies were more interested in digging in and increasing the depth of their minefields.

On 3 August Churchill arrived in Egypt, accompanied by General Sir Alan Brooke, the Chief of the Imperial General Staff. They both felt that a change was needed at the top. They replaced Auchinleck with General Sir Harold Alexander as Commander-in-Chief Middle East. Churchill then agreed to Brooke's personal choice for Commander of the Eighth Army, Lieutenant General Bernard Montgomery, who flew out from England and took over the Army on 13 August. Montgomery was determined to establish his own personality rather than Rommel's in the minds of his men. He discarded his general's 'brass hat' and toured units wearing the Royal Tank Regiment's famous black beret, adding his general's insignia to the regiment's badge. He was incisive, brisk, and brusque. He told the men that further withdrawals were out of the question. They would fight where they stood and they would win. The effect was remarkable. The men were jaded and cynical, yet they instinctively recognised that the new army commander meant what he said and was capable of delivering what he promised. Changes began to happen immediately. Out went tired or inefficient senior officers, even if they were old desert hands. A new wind of optimism blew through the ranks of the Eighth Army. It was tested at the end of August.

Rommel had saved just enough fuel for one last attempt to break through to Alexandria. On the night of 30/31 August, German and Italian tanks broke through the British minefields in the south under heavy fire. With dawn came air attacks. Losses were higher than had been allowed for, but the German spearhead swung north, heading straight for Alam Halfa ridge. Brigadier Roberts's 22nd Armoured Brigade was waiting for them. By 6 p.m. the mass of Axis armour was approaching the ridge. Both sides opened fire at 6.10 p.m. The British Grant tanks blew holes in the enemy ranks, but still the Germans came on. At one point it seemed that they may break through the brigade's centre. Roberts called the Royal Scots Greys forward and, just as their forebears had done at Waterloo (refer to Chapter 11), they came thundering over the crest, blazing away with every gun they possessed. The crisis was over and dusk put an end to the fighting.

Next morning, 15th Panzer Division tried to slide past the eastern end of the ridge. The British spotted them and a brisk fire fight ensued. Before long, the 8th Armoured Brigade closed in from the east. The fighting was inconclusive, but it convinced Rommel that he could go no further. He withdrew the way he had come, harassed on the ground and bombed from the air. By 2 September this battle all over. He losses included 3000 casualties, 49 tanks, 60 guns, and 400 lorries. The British lost 1640 killed and wounded, plus 67 tanks.

Second Battle of Alamein, 23 October– 4 November 1942

Under Montgomery, the Eighth Army began a programme of exhaustive training for the coming battle. The training involved not just the normal daylight attacks, but also tactics devised for night attacks. They involved the infantry leading with the tanks following close behind. When the objective had been taken, the tanks remained with the infantry to break up the inevitable counter-attack and did not leave until the infantry's own 6-pounder anti-tank guns had been brought forward and dug in. New weapons reaching the Eighth Army included the Sherman medium tank. Like the Grant, this was armed with a 75-millimete gun, but it was mounted in a turret with all-round traverse.

Montgomery's plan for Operation Lightfoot, as the opening phase of the Second Battle of Alamein was known, required XIII Corps in the south to mount holding attacks while XXX Corps in the north struck the main blow, capturing the minefields, and clearing two corridors through which the two armoured divisions of X Corps were to pass. Overall, Montgomery's intention was to fight what he called a 'crumbling' battle, attacking first in one place and then another, forcing Rommel to burn priceless fuel with counter-attacks until the British reduced his army to immobility. Rommel's fuel supply had barely kept pace with daily consumption; knowing what lay ahead, he had prepared the best defence he could, extending his minefields until they were between 3 kilometres (2 miles) and 8 kilometres (5 miles) deep, while along the front German units were interposed with Italian to provide a stiffening. Tired and ill with worry, Rommel left for home and sick leave on 23 September, handing over to General Georg Stumme.

Operation Bertram, October 1942

To convince the Axis commanders that he would begin the battle on the southern sector of the front, Montgomery set in motion the largest deception plan of the desert war. Codenamed Operation Bertram, it was under the control of Lieutenant Colonel Charles Richardson and bore a remarkable similarity to Allenby's plan at Megiddo (see Chapter 19). Its principal architect was a Royal Engineer officer named Jasper Maskelyne, who had been a stage magician in civilian life:

- ✔ In the north, the British disguised tanks as lorries and real lorries obliterated their tracks, and tents and more dummy lorries concealed stockpiled ammunition and stores.

- ✔ In the south they disguised lorries as tanks, their tyre marks masked by weighted trailers with track links fitted to the wheels. Dummy guns and 'supply dumps' multiplied, joined by dummy water-pumping stations, pipelines, and storage towers, serviced daily by real vehicles and 'labour gangs'. Simultaneously, bogus radio traffic between make-believe armoured formations on the southern sector indicated a build-up in preparation for an offensive.

The battle began at 9.40 p.m. on 23 October with a bombardment fired by 592 guns, 456 of them crammed into XXX Corps' sector. Resistance was fierce and progress was slower than expected. The following day Stumme sustained a fatal heart attack and General von Thoma, commander of the Afrika Korps, took over command of the Axis army. When Rommel returned to the front on the evening of 25 October, he was shaken by the sheer volume of the British artillery fire and depressed by the way in which the Eighth Army's carefully rehearsed infantry/tank tactics were remorselessly eating their way through his positions. He recognised immediately that he was engaged in 'a battle without hope'.

Defence of Outpost Snipe, 27 October 1942

On 27 October, while counter-attacking Briggs's 1st Armoured Division at Kidney Ridge, Rommel lost a disproportionate number of tanks to a single motor battalion. The previous night, 2/The Rifle Brigade had mistakenly occupied a hollow measuring 800 metres (900 yards) by 350 metres (400 yards), believing it to be a locality codenamed Snipe. The Riflemen had actually established their outpost in close proximity to the tanks of 15th Panzer and the Littorio Armoured Divisions. The enemy attacked at first light and attacked repeatedly during the day. When the riflemen and their attached gunners weren't under direct attack they were being shelled constantly until the hollow was a shambles of smashed guns, carriers, jeeps, dead, and dying. Even so, they destroyed tanks and kept on destroying them until the hollow was surrounded by wrecked and burning enemy armour. At 11 p.m. the outpost's survivors, now critically short of ammunition, withdrew from the hollow.

The defence of Outpost Snipe became a legend throughout the Eighth Army, so much so that a month later a Committee of Investigation visited the scene to verify the story and examine the wrecks. It concluded that 21 German and Italian tanks, plus 5 assault guns or tank destroyers, had been destroyed outright. In addition, evidence suggested that a further 15, and possibly 20, tanks had been knocked out and recovered, although few of these can have been repaired by the time the battle ended. The Battalion's commander, Lieutenant Colonel Victor Turner, who was seriously wounded during the action, received the Victoria Cross and decorations were awarded to a high proportion of his officers and men.

The fight for Thompson's Post, 28/29 October 1942

During the night of 28/29 October the 9th Australian Division attacked northwards towards the coast, isolating a heavily defended Axis locality named Thompson's Post. In bitter fighting, they wiped out one panzer grenadier battalion and trapped another, as well as an Italian Bersaglieri battalion. When they renewed the attack the following night, the Australians won a toehold north of the railway. From this they advanced due east across the rear face of Thompson's Post, but sustained crippling casualties and at first light were forced to retire. Undeterred, the Australians attacked to the north again, cutting the coast road.

Dawn was breaking when 40 Royal Tank Regiment, with 32 Valentine tanks, reached the area. On learning that the Australians were desperately short of men, the regiment's commanding officer brought his tanks across the railway and deployed them facing west to await the inevitable counter-attack.

The cutting of the coast road caused Rommel serious alarm. At about 11 a.m. the Germans began a series of counter-attacks lasting throughout the afternoon. British tanks, artillery, and bombing broke them all up. When dusk put an end to the fighting, a battered handful of tanks were all that reached the rally point. 40 Royal Tank Regiment's personnel casualties came to 9 officers and 35 men, a high proportion of the Valentines' three-man crews. The Australians, themselves the toughest of fighters with scant regard for those who failed to measure up, had watched the battle with something like awe:

> *The courage of these men made their action one of the most magnificent of the war*

wrote their official historian of the tank crews. The following day, however, the Australians had to give a little ground, enabling the garrison of Thompson's Post to escape during the night.

Operation Supercharge, 2 November 1942

Now Rommel's attention was so firmly fixed on the coastal sector (see the preceding section), Montgomery decided to mount a fresh attack further south. This was codenamed Supercharge and went in just north of Kidney Ridge.

The attack consisted of three phases:

- ✔ **Breaking into the enemy's position.** The 2nd New Zealand Division executed this first phase during the early hours of 2 November. By first light they had secured their objectives.

- ✔ **Overcoming the anti-tank gun screen.** This second phase involved Brigadier John Currie's 9th Armoured Brigade. Montgomery told Currie that if necessary he must accept 100 per cent casualties in breaking through the enemy's anti-tank gun screen. The brigade passed through the recently captured ground as dawn was breaking and smashed its way through the screen, losing 87 of its 94 tanks.

- ✔ **Destroying enemy armour in battle.** The penetration of the second phase attracted enemy armour like a magnet, as Montgomery had intended. Two brigades from the 1st Armoured Division activated the third phase at once. They passed through the wreckage of Currie's brigade to engage in a furious day-long battle that took its name from the nearby Tel el Aqqaqir.

The British sustained the heavier losses, but when the battle was over the Italian armoured divisions had ceased to exist and the Germans had been reduced to 24 tanks. In defiance of Hitler's orders, Rommel commenced his withdrawal shortly after. The battle had lasted for 13 days. The Axis army sustained 55,000 casualties, including 30,000 prisoners, of whom nearly 11,000 were German. The Eighth Army sustained 13,500 casualties, including approximately 4500 killed, mainly in the infantry divisions.

Pursuing Rommel to Tunisia

Without pausing, Rommel drove steadily westwards with what little remained of his army. He abandoned all his gains in Egypt and the whole of Cyrenaica as well. On the way he discovered that the Anglo-American First Army had landed in Morocco and Algeria on 8 November. He also found out that Hitler and Mussolini had decided to hold Tunisia as an Axis stronghold in North Africa. At Mersa Brega Rommel called a halt, as he had done in the past. The Eighth Army's supply services used every means at their disposal to keep the pursuit moving. Even so, only a limited number of formations could be supplied over the lengthening distance from the army's bases. Montgomery closed up to the Mersa Brega bottleneck and on 13 December the 2nd New Zealand Division embarked on a wide turning movement through the desert, forcing Rommel to withdraw another 320 kilometres (200 miles) to Buerat. On 14 January 1943 he was similarly levered out of this position and as Tripoli was not defensible, he retired across the Tunisian frontier. On 23 January units of the Eighth Army entered Tripoli unopposed. The war in North Africa had four more months to run, but the desert war was over.

The principal actions fought in North Africa took place in Tunisia at:

✔ **The Tebourba Gap, 30 November–3 December 1942:** British and American troops held the Gap against a fierce German counterattack (including the formidable German Tiger tank).

✔ **Kasserine Pass, 14–22 February 1943:** British and American troops halted the thrust of Rommel's German advance, although the Americans sustained serious casualties.

✔ **Medenine and the Mareth Line, 6–26 March 1943:** Rommel was repulsed by a textbook defence by Montgomery's Eighth Army, incorporating heavy artillery concentrations and concealed anti-tank guns opening fire at point-blank range.

After these actions, Montgomery's Eighth Army and Anderson's First Army prepared to bring the war in North Africa to its conclusion. The US II Corps moved to the northern end of the line, while 1st and 7th Armoured and 4th Indian Divisions were transferred from the Eighth to the First Army. After extremely hard fighting the hills dominating the Medjerda Valley (notably Longstop Hill) were taken by combined infantry and tank assaults. Tunis was taken by 7th Armoured Division on 7 May while, to the north, the Americans captured Bizerte. Recognising that the end had come, Axis soldiers began to surrender in drove, over 238,000 of them. By 13 May 1943 the war in North Africa was over.

Chapter 22

One Bloomin' Ridge After Another: The Italian Campaign, 1943–1945

*E*ven before the Axis surrender in North Africa (see Chapter 21), the Allies were deciding their next move. The Americans wanted to concentrate on building up forces in the United Kingdom in preparation for the invasion of France. The British took the view that this invasion could not take place before the summer of 1944. In the meantime, Churchill argued persuasively, a blow struck into what he called 'the soft underbelly of Europe' would shatter the Axis alliance and result in large numbers of German troops being tied down in Italy instead of being available for operations in western Europe when the time came. Churchill's view prevailed.

In Italy the internal organisation of infantry tank squadrons was changed to provide a balance between armoured protection and fine fire control. Squadrons consisted of a headquarters troop of three Churchill tanks, two three-tank Churchill troops, and two three-tank Sherman troops. This took account of the fact that while the Sherman lacked the thick armour of the slow, heavily protected Churchill, it possessed the better gun control equipment. About 120 Churchills had been re-armed with the superior 75-millimetre guns of Shermans written off in North Africa.

Warming Up for Italy: Sicily

Before the Allies could invade Italy, they had to take Sicily as a stepping stone from North Africa; and before they could take Sicily they had to neutralise the island of Pantelleria, lying between Sicily and Tunisia. A week's pounding by the Allied air forces convinced the garrison commander that resistance was pointless. The British 1st Division made an unopposed landing on Pantelleria on 11 June 1943. Shortly after, Allied aircraft began operating from Pantelleria and the nearby island of Lampedusa.

The invasion of Sicily proper was under the overall control of three British commanders: 15th Army Group, General Sir Harold Alexander; naval, Admiral Sir Andrew Cunningham; and air, Air Chief Marshal Sir Arthur Tedder. The 15th Army Group contained two armies, the Eighth under General Sir Bernard Montgomery, and the US Seventh under Lieutenant General George S. Patton. The invasion was the largest amphibious operation that the Allies had attempted so far.

The landings took place in poor weather on 9/10 July. The Allies met little opposition, as they took the Italians manning the coastal defences by surprise. During the next two days the Americans faced heavy counter-attacks at the port of Gela, but they held their ground with the assistance of naval gunfire. They then broke out of their beachhead and cleared western Sicily of the enemy. Meanwhile, the Eighth Army pushed northwards against increasing opposition and was brought to a halt south of Catania. On the night of 13 July, however, Allied commandos took the bridge at Lentini while paratroops took the bridge at Primasole. Patton's army now swung eastwards along the north coast of the island. This had the effect of turning the enemy's right flank. Colonel General Hans Hube, coordinating the Axis defence, now realised that he had to abandon Sicily. During the first two weeks of August, while the American advance continued, the Eighth Army fought its way past Mount Etna. By the time the Allies reached Messina on 17 August, however, the Axis army had carried out a model evacuation, shipping no fewer than 100,000 men, 9800 vehicles, and 50 tanks across the Straits of Messina to the Italian mainland.

The Allies sustained some 16,000 casualties. Axis losses totalled 164,000 killed, wounded, or captured, including 32,000 Germans. Most Italians did not want to fight and were happy to be taken prisoner.

Landing at Salerno

On 24 July 1943 the Italian army staged a coup and overthrew the Italian dictator Mussolini. His successor, Marshal Badoglio, informed Hitler that Italy would continue fighting, but opened clandestine negotiations with the Allies. They concluded a secret armistice on 3 September. On that day two of the

Eighth Army's divisions crossed the Straits of Messina to land in Calabria, on the toe of the Italian boot.

Field Marshal Albert Kesselring, German commander in southern Italy, took measures to delay the Allies' progress. Known as 'Smiling Albert' because of his frequently displayed teeth, he was a very shrewd operator indeed and recognised at once that the landing in Calabria was not the Allies' principal invasion effort. He expected this to be made in the Gulf of Salerno with the ultimate object of taking Naples, to serve as the Allies' principal supply port. Kesselring was right. On 8 September the terms of the armistice were published. With the exception of the Italian navy, which sailed for Malta, the Germans promptly and efficiently disarmed and confined the forces of their former ally.

On 9 September the Eighth Army's 1st Airborne Division landed at the Italian naval base of Taranto in the Gulf of the same name. The same day the Allied Fifth Army, commanded by Lieutenant General Mark W. Clark, landed in the Gulf of Salerno. The British X Corps, under the command of Lieutenant General Sir Richard McCreery, landed north of the Sele river. British commandos and their American equivalent, the Rangers, took the hills on the northern arm of the bay.

The Allies seriously underestimated the speed and strength of the German reaction. General Heinrich von Vietinghof, commanding the German Tenth Army, had four panzer and two *panzergrenadier* (armoured infantry) divisions at his disposal. From the high ground inland, the Germans saw exactly what was happening. They quickly sealed off the beachhead and subjected the Allies to heavy shelling and counter-attacks. One senior officer commented that the situation reminded him of Gallipoli (see Chapter 19). Despite naval gunfire support and complete air superiority, at times the Fifth Army seemed at danger of being driven into the sea. At one period the Allies seriously considered evacuation. Alexander, however, rushed reinforcements into the beachhead and the crisis passed.

With the approach of Montgomery's Eighth Army from the south, Vietinghof began to break contact and conduct a skilful withdrawal to the north. On 22 September the 78th Division landed at Bari on the east coast. The 1st Airborne Division established links with it and the main body of the Eighth Army, creating a front from coast to coast across the Italian peninsula. Clark finally broke out of the Salerno beachhead, taking Naples on 1 October. By then, however, the Germans had established a new defensive front along the line of the Volturno river.

The Allies sustained about 15,000 casualties in the Salerno beachhead in the period 9–18 September. The Germans sustained approximately 10,000.

Monte Cassino and the Gustav Line

Few landscapes in the world are as suited to defence as that of Italy. From the central spine of the Apennines, ridges extend down to the east and west coasts, while in the valleys between run rivers that can become torrents in winter. Having taken one ridge, an attacker is confronted with another, and another beyond that, and so on. This was not country in which to employ armoured divisions in their usual role; instead, their tanks were used as supplementary artillery, firing from reverse slopes to obtain extra range. Inevitably, the terrain made it an infantryman's war, and this meant that when major offensives took place, the crews of Churchill tanks, responsible for infantry support, were employed day after day and received little rest. The Churchill proved that it had no equals when it came to climbing hills.

The Fifth Army took two months of hard fighting to fight its way over the Volturno river. Kesseling used this time to create a fortified zone 16 kilometres (10 miles) deep, known as the Gustav Line. This ran from the mouth of the Garigliano river on the west coast, along its tributary, the Rapido, then over the Apennines to reach the east coast north of the Sangro valley. Near the western end of the line the Liri valley provided an obvious route to Rome, but was dominated by the towering Monte Cassino, crowned with its famous Benedictine monastery. In December, Montgomery left Italy for Britain to prepare for the cross-Channel invasion of France (see Chapter 23). Command of the Eighth Army passed to General Sir Oliver Leese.

From January 1944 onwards both the Fifth and Eighth Armies became involved in attempts to storm Monte Cassino and break through to Rome. The first Allied attempt lasted from 17 January until 12 February and involved the British, the Americans, and the French. Most of the gains they made they then lost to vigorous counter-attacks. Unjustified suspicions that the enemy was using the monastery led to the controversial decision to subject it to heavy bombing on 15 February. The Germans promptly dug in among the ruins, from which they were almost impossible to eject. Immediately after the bombing, Indian troops made limited gains north of Monastery Hill and New Zealand forces captured Cassino railway station, only to lose it again on 18 February. On 18 March, following a heavy air and artillery bombardment of the town, the New Zealanders recaptured the station and took the castle after three days of heavy fighting against the German 1st Parachute Division.

A lull followed, during which the Allies prepared for a major offensive. During the night of 11/12 May, 2000 guns pounded the German positions. The Polish isolated Monastery Hill, while British, French, and US troops crossed the Rapido to the west of the town and entered the Liri valley, to the complete surprise of the Germans, whose defences the Allies overran despite the enemy's hard fighting. By the morning of 18 May, the Allies had finally cleared the town of Cassino of Germans and the Polish flag was flying above the ruins of the monastery. During the four months of fighting the Germans sustained approximately 60,000 casualties while the Allies lost 115,000.

The Anzio Beachhead

On 22 January 1944 the US VI Corps, under the command of Major General John P. Lucas, landed at Anzio, 50 kilometres (30 miles) south of Rome. The intention was to outflank the Gustav Line and break the apparent impasse at Cassino by threatening the German rear. An important element of the plan was an early advance inland to secure the Alban Hills, which dominated the main road between Rome and Cassino. The effect of this would be to trap a major part of General Eberhard von Mackensen's Fourteenth Army as it attempted to withdraw.

Things did not work out this way, and the reason lay with Lucas, who was cautious, easy going and benign at a time when speed and aggression were most in demand. He just didn't do speed. Before the operation began he told his divisional commanders that rather than go for the Alban Hills, he preferred to consolidate a defensive perimeter. That should have disqualified him for the job immediately but it didn't, and he got his preference.

On 29 January the Allies began to advance out of the beachhead. On 3/4 February and again from 7–10 February the Germans mounted ferocious counter-attacks against the British in the Carroceto area. These resulted in some of the most desperate fighting of the entire war and the Allies held their positions with difficulty. At the time of the landings four German divisions were in the area. This figure rapidly grew to nine. With General Alexander's approval, Lieutenant General Clark began to pour reinforcements into Anzio. As the German artillery had the entire beachhead within range, it could hardly avoid hitting something or someone every time it fired. On 23 February, Major General Lucian K. Truscott replaced Lucas. Nevertheless, Anzio continued to be one of the most unpleasant places on earth.

The Germans could contain the Anzio beachhead or hold the Gustav Line, but they couldn't do both. When the Gustav Line gave way in May, they pinned their hopes for a successful withdrawal on a lay-back position called the Hitler Line. The most important sector of this lay between Pontecorvo and Aquina in the Liri Valley, where months of work had gone into the defences.

At 5.45 a.m. on 23 May the Allies attacked the Hitler Line. After an extremely hard battle, shortly after 4 p.m. the enemy ceased their fanatical resistance and slipped away. The cost to the attackers was high, in both casualties and tanks. In the North Irish Horse alone, 25 tanks had been lost, while 34 officers and men had been killed and 36 wounded. On the same day that the Hitler Line was broken, VI Corps broke out of the Anzio beachhead. It soon established contact with the US II Corps coming up from the south, but elsewhere its actions caused controversy. Clark thought that he deserved to be famous, and capturing Rome would do just that for him. Alexander's plan required VI Corps to thrust eastwards through the gap between the Alban Hills and the Colli Lepini to Valmontone on Route 6. This would achieve the isolation and destruction of several German divisions pulling back from the broken Hitler

Line. Clark, however, merely sent his 3rd Division, the Special Service Force, and part of 1st Armored Division in the direction of Valmontone. He wheeled the rest of VI Corps across the Alban Hills, where they encountered little resistance. Then he commenced his drive on Rome. Over at Valmontone, Mackensen deployed adequate forces to fend off attacks from the weak American units deployed against him.

Clark entered Rome on 4 June. His arrival caused a stir for a couple of days, then the Allies landed in Normandy and it was quickly forgotten (see Chapter 23). The irony was that if he had followed Alexander's orders to the letter, history would have put him down as one of the war's most capable generals, and he would still have been able to enter Rome. Anzio, therefore, did not achieve what had been expected of it, but it did tie down enemy divisions that could have been used in France, and in the end it did help to produce a victory of sorts. Between 22 January and 23 May the Allies sustained approximately 40,000 casualties in beachhead fighting, while the Germans sustained approximately 35,000.

Fighting through the Gothic Line

Beyond Rome, the Germans had carried out such extensive demolition on all the routes leading north that a pursuit in the conventional sense was impossible. Bridges, viaducts, culverts, embankments, and retaining walls were all blown, slowing the pace of the advance to a crawl. During this period the most effective piece of equipment in the Allies' advance guard was the bulldozer.

In due course, the Allies did close up to the next line of enemy defences, known as the Gothic Line. This was a zone 16 kilometres (10 miles) deep running from the Magra valley to the Foglia valley and a point on the Adriatic between Pesaro and Cattolica.

The defence works were similar to those in the Gustav and Hitler Lines (see earlier in this chapter), although more of them existed. Terrain factors made things even more difficult for an attacker: A turbulent history had resulted in many of the larger villages and country towns being built on hilltops and walled for their own defence. Not only were they difficult to capture, they dominated the roads in their immediate vicinity and made ideal artillery observation posts. Again, the agricultural step-terraces that are so much a feature of the Italian landscape inhibited cross-country movement, while the vineyards, with their narrow fields of vision between the lines of vines, provided ideal cover for ambush parties or *panzerfaust* (anti-tank) teams.

The operations required to break through the Gothic Line began on 30 August and ended on 28 October. The Allied intention was to maintain steady pressure on the central sectors of the line, while achieving a breakthrough in the east with the object of unleashing armoured formations into the Po valley. Every day, scores of small actions took place designed to wrest one feature or another from the enemy. The Germans bitterly contested every one, notably the Gemmano and Coriano Ridges, and gave ground very slowly. Total casualties are uncertain, but were heavy. By 21 September the Eighth Army had lost 14,000 men killed, wounded, or missing. At the beginning of October the Fifth Army calculated that on average each of its divisions was losing 550 men daily. On 25 September the German Tenth Army recorded that only 10 of its 92 infantry battalions possessed more than 400 men, while of the rest 38 had fewer than 200 men each.

Heavy autumn rain put an end to the fighting. The chance to release the armoured divisions into better tank country had passed, but the Allies were in an excellent strategic position from which to mount a successful offensive in the spring of 1945.

Assaulting the Po

After D Day, the press at home had been giving British troops in Italy less coverage than they deserved. 'We are the D Day dodgers/Out in sunny Italy' went their ditty. The problem was that in editorial eyes the small gains they were making daily were not as newsworthy as what was taking place in western Europe. They need not have worried, for in a few months they would be making headlines again. Winter saw changes on both sides of the line. In March 1945 Kesselring left Italy to take command in western Germany. His place was taken by Vietinghof, who sensibly wanted to withdraw across the Po. Hitler, by now completely divorced from reason, forbade any such plan. Among the Allies, Alexander became theatre commander, Clark took over as 15th Army Group Commander, and Truscott became commander of the Fifth Army.

Opposite the Eighth Army, the enemy front line ran along the flood banks of the river Senio. On 9 April 1945 the last offensive of the war in Italy began with Crocodile flame-throwing tanks projecting their flames across the river to land on the far bank. The 2nd New Zealand and 4th Indian Divisions then crossed in assault boats. After heavy fighting they won enough ground for the engineers to put across bridges that enabled the armour to cross. During the next 48 hours the enemy fought back hard, but eventually the advance reached the

Argenta Gap, the last major obstacle before the Po valley, situated between Lake Comacchio and the marshes of the Massa Lombarda, with the town of Argenta lying in its centre. On 11 April, Allied troops and commandos went across the lake in tracked landing vehicles to carry out assault landings in the enemy's rear. Simultaneously, other troops fought their way up the Gap, capturing Argenta and Consandolo. Resistance collapsed and the 6th Armoured Division, fighting together in its proper role for the first time since Tunisia, passed through to exploit towards and beyond the Po. The Eighth Army's pursuit of the broken German armies took it through Verona, Padua, Venice, and across the Piave. On 29 April Vietinghof agreed to an unconditional surrender that became effective on 2 May.

That wasn't quite the end of the campaign in Italy. Marshal Tito's communist partisans, having chased the Germans out of Yugoslavia, developed grand ideas about territorial expansion. They wanted Trieste, but the New Zealanders told them quite firmly that they couldn't have it. When 6th Armoured Division reached Austrian territory, they found that Tito's men had already arrived and were staking claims. The Yugoslavs were told to push off, but they argued. The Allies then told Tito's men that things would get very nasty indeed if they didn't leave, so they did. And that was that.

Chapter 23

Beachheads and Bridges: Normandy and Northwest Europe, 1944–1945

. . . .

In This Chapter

▶ Raiding Dieppe, 1942

▶ Landing in Normandy on D Day, 6 June 1944

▶ Attempting to breakthrough at Arnhem, 17–26 September 1944

▶ Crossing the Rhine and ending the war, 1945

. . . .

*A*fter Allied successes in North Africa and Italy (refer to Chapters 21 and 22), the scene was set for a re-entry into Europe, and by forcing Germany onto the defensive on home soil, ending the war. For more on Allied and Axis strategy, see Keith D. Dickson's *World War II For Dummies* (Wiley). Figure 23-1 shows where the key action took place in 1944–1945.

Table 23-1 shows the amount of hardware used when the Allies launched themselves into Europe via Normandy, at D Day. Figure 23-2 shows some of the commonly used British tanks for this part of the war.

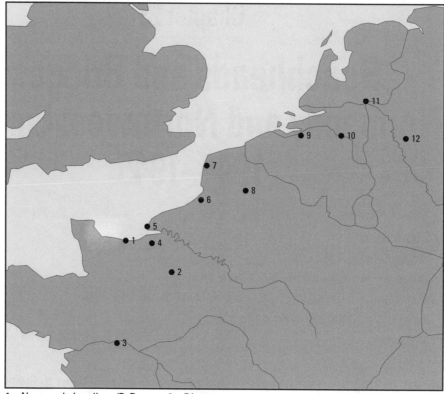

Figure 23-1:
The war in northwest Europe, 1944–1945.

1. Normandy Landings/D-Day
2. Villers Bocage
3. Mortain
4. Caen
5. Le Havre
6. Dieppe
7. Boulogne
8. Dinant
9. West Kappelle, Flushing, Breskens
10. Nijmegen
11. Arnhem
12. Remagen

Table 23-1	Shopping List for Invading France in 1944
Naval	
About 200,000 men (two-thirds British and Canadian) engaged in naval operations on D Day	

About 6900 ships, including:

7 battleships	2 15-inch gun monitors
23 cruisers	2 gunboats
103 destroyers	221 escorts
287 minesweepers	4 minelayers
1 seaplane carrier	8 headquarters landing ships
495 motor torpedo and motor gun boats	2 midget submarines (to be used as boundary markers)

Naval	
4126 landing craft of different types	736 ancillary vessels
10 hospital ships	59 blockships (to be sunk as part of artificial harbour breakwaters)

Land (troops put ashore on D Day)	
Approx 75,000 British and Canadians	Approx 57,000 Americans

Air	
Approx 14,000 sorties flown on D Day	

Approx 3700 allied fighters including:

15 squadrons covering shipping	54 squadrons giving beach cover
36 squadrons supporting ground operations	33 squadrons taking part in offensive operations
33 squadrons available for immediate deployment as required	

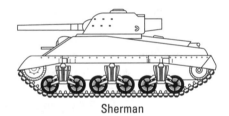

Sherman

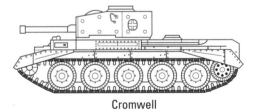

Cromwell

Figure 23-2:
British tanks
in northwest
Europe.

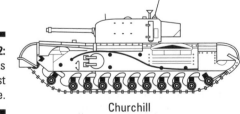

Churchill

Hobart's Funnies

Major General Percy Hobart began his career in the Bengal Sappers and Miners and then transferred to the Royal Tank Regiment. He was, therefore, uniquely qualified to carry out his task of designing armoured vehicles to deal with the Germans' defences. Gifted with a powerful intellect himself, he exploded with volcanic rage if people failed to grasp immediately what he was proposing. Not even senior officers escaped his fury, but he produced results.

The most versatile of Hobart's 79th Armoured Division's vehicles was the AVRE (Assault Vehicle Royal Engineers), developed as a direct result of the experience gained during the Dieppe raid. The hull of the Churchill tank was chosen because of its roomy interior, heavy armour, and adaptability. It was fitted with a specially designed turret mounting a 290-millimetre spigot mortar named a *petard*. This threw an 18-kilogram (40-pound) bomb and was capable of cracking open concrete fortifications, to a maximum range of 210 metres (230 yards). In addition, standardised external fitting enabled the AVRE to be used in a variety of ways. It could carry a fascine up to 2.4 metres (8 feet) in diameter and 4.2 metres (14 feet) wide that it could drop into anti-tank ditches, forming a causeway. It could lay a small box girder bridge with a 40-ton capacity across gaps of up to 9 metres (30 feet), and could be fitted with a bobbin that unrolled a carpet of hessian and metal tubing ahead of the vehicle, creating a firm track over areas of soft going. It could place demolition charges against an obstacle or fortification, then detonate them by remote control after it had reversed away. It could push mobile bridges into position, or be fitted with a plough that brought mines to the surface.

The division's standard mine-clearing tank was the Sherman Crab. This employed a powered rotating drum that beat the ground ahead of the tank with chains, detonating any mines in its path. The Crab was capable of clearing a lane almost 3 metres (10 feet) wide at a speed of 2 kilometres (1.25 miles) per hour and could fight as a conventional gun tank when it was not flailing.

The Allies required a tank to land ahead of or with the first assault wave. Following experiments, Hobart decided to adopt the DD (Duplex Drive) Sherman amphibious tank. When swimming, this was kept afloat by a collapsible canvas flotation screen and driven by twin propellers. Only a few millimetres of the screen appeared above the water, resembling a harmless ship's boat. Once ashore, the screen was collapsed, the drive to the propellers disengaged, and the tank proceeded normally on its tracks.

Together, the AVRE, the Crab, and the DD formed the basis of the Division's assault teams on D Day. Following the invasion they were joined by the Churchill Crocodile flame thrower (recognisable by its armoured trailer containing the flaming fuel and propellant gas cylinders), tracked landing vehicles named Buffaloes, Canal Defence Lights (Grants fitted with a powerful armoured searchlight), and Kangaroos (turretless tanks or self-propelled gun carriages stripped of their armament and used as armoured personnel carriers).

The Raid on Dieppe, 19 August 1942

Two years before D Day, on 19 August 1942, the 2nd Canadian Division and Commando units raided the French port of Dieppe. Stalin had complained that if the Allies didn't start a Second Front in Europe, the

Soviet Union would make a separate peace with Hitler. Preparations for return to France were still in the early planning stage, but to convince Stalin that a premature invasion would have catastrophic results, Churchill authorised the raid on Dieppe to demonstrate the sort of difficulties the Allies would face.

As expected, the raid on Dieppe achieved very few of its objectives and the Canadians sustained severe casualties. Against this, the Allies drew valuable lessons:

✔ **They could not expect to capture a port intact, so they decided to take their own pre-fabricated harbours, codenamed *Mulberries*, with them.** These consisted of breakwaters made from sunken blockships, quays consisting of concrete caissons or watertight chambers, and floating roadways.

✔ **The German's coastal defences, known as the Atlantic Wall, were so highly developed that they were capable of inflicting horrendous casualties on any landing force.** The Allies therefore designed armoured vehicles that were capable of dealing with every aspect of the defence, including mines, concrete bunkers, anti-tank walls, and anti-tank ditches (see sidebar 'Hobart's Funnies').

✔ **As the shortest sea crossing between England and France lay between Dover and Calais, it seemed logical for the planned invasion to take place in the Pas de Calais area.** That was what everyone, including the Germans, thought, so the Allies decided to land somewhere else, namely Normandy – but placed dummy tanks, lorries, guns, supply dumps, and camps in southern England for German reconnaissance flights to spot them, with the result that almost all the German armoured divisions congregated in the Calais area to oppose this dummy force.

D Day, 6 June 1944: The Greatest Amphibious Invasion in History

The Allied invasion of France, codenamed Overlord, was the largest amphibious operation in history. Getting everyone in the right place at the right time required organisational genius on a grand scale. In the period immediately prior to the departure of the invasion fleet, the army sealed off southern England while the divisions for the landing moved into their embarkation areas. It strictly forbade movement out of this secure area and suspended communication by telephone or post with the rest of the country until the landings had taken place.

The Allies had already conducted a month-long air offensive against road and rail communications in northern France, accompanied by a steady increase in French Resistance activity. General Dwight D. Eisenhower, the Allied Supreme Commander, appointed General Sir Bernard Montgomery commander of the cross-channel assault. On the German side, the Commander-in-Chief West was Field Marshal Gerd von Rundstedt. The Luftwaffe had only 319 operational aircraft available on D Day.

Shortly after midnight on 6 June, the US 82nd and 101st Airborne Divisions dropped on the western flank of the projected beachhead. Simultaneously, the British 6th Airborne Division dropped on the eastern flank and captured bridges over the Caen Canal and the River Orne. The seaborne landings commenced at half-tide, from 6.30 a.m. onwards, when most of the German beach obstacles were visible. Beyond the Vire estuary the US 4th Division landed on Utah Beach, then advanced inland. At 1 p.m. it made contact with the American paratroopers. By midnight it was holding a beachhead 6.5 kilometres (4 miles) wide and 14.5 kilometres (9 miles) deep. Across the Vire the unsubdued defences of Omaha Beach pinned down the US 1st and 29th Infantry Divisions. The Americans finally overcame these defences at the cost of over 3000 casualties, but at midnight their advance units were only 2.5 kilometres (1.5 miles) inland.

Further east, the British Second Army's landings had the benefit of a more prolonged naval bombardment and the presence of 79th Armoured Division's assault engineering teams with the leading elements. The 50th (Northumbrian) Division landed on Gold Beach, capturing Arromanches, and by midnight had reached the outskirts of Bayeux, which they took the following day. The Canadian 3rd Division came ashore on Juno Beach and, despite congestion, struck inland to a depth of 11 kilometres (7 miles). The British 3rd Division landed on Sword Beach and, with 6th Airborne Division, had advanced to within sight of Caen by midnight.

The Germans believed that the landings were simply a feint intended to draw their attention away from the Pas de Calais, which complicated their response. Hitler refused to commit his reserve panzer divisions until too late. During the afternoon, however, the 21st Panzer Division, which was on the spot, mounted a counter-attack from Caen into the area between the Juno and Sword beachheads, but was halted by the Allies and driven back. Additional factors limiting the German response were the Allies' complete air superiority and the tremendous weight of naval gunfire support available.

By midnight 57,000 American and 75,000 British and Canadian troops and their equipment were ashore. Allied casualties included 2500 killed and 8500 wounded, a fraction of those expected given the strength of the defences and poor sea conditions prevailing. The German loss remains unknown.

Pushing on through the hedgerows

Eisenhower believed that the British performed best in dogged, sustained fighting, while the Americans produced better results in fast-moving operations. That was how the campaign was planned. By launching a series of heavy offensives, the British would attract most of the German armoured formations in the west. When their preparations were complete, the Americans would break out of the western end of the beachhead and roll up the enemy's left flank.

While the Allies had achieved strategic surprise by landing in Normandy, it was very difficult country in which to fight. Much of the area consisted of narrow lanes and very small fields divided by hedges planted on top of earth banks. Visibility often did not extend beyond the next hedge. This type of country was known as *bocage*. In some places it was simply not possible to deploy major armoured formations, and this favoured the defenders. For the British and Canadian infantry, supported by three Churchill-equipped tank brigades, the battle was one of attrition in which casualties at times bore comparison to the daily losses on the Somme (see Chapter 17).

During the rest of June and most of July the Allied build-up continued. As more American armies reached France, leadership of the Western Alliance passed to the United States, which now had by far the greater number of troops in the field. In the meantime, Montgomery had mounted three major operations to tie down the enemy's armour:

- ✔ First came Epsom, lasting from 25 June until 2 July. This was mounted west of Caen and succeeded in crossing the River Odon and securing the notorious Hill 112.

- ✔ Next came Charnwood, aimed directly at Caen, between 4 and 10 July.

- ✔ Finally came Goodwood on 18 July. This took place east of Caen, in one of the few areas suitable for the deployment of armour on a large scale and involved the 7th, 11th, and Guards Armoured Divisions. Some ground was gained, but a massed anti-tank defence halted further progress on 16 August.

On 25 July the Americans began their breakout from the beachhead. Responding to their excellent progress, Field Marshal Gunther von Kluge, now commanding the German armies in the west, withdrew some armour from the British sector. His action was too little, too late. When he delivered his counter-attack at Mortain on 6 August, the Germans made some progress because poor weather stopped the Allied ground attack squadrons from taking off. These returned to the battlefield two days later and halted the counter-stroke. At the opposite end of the beachhead, the Canadian II Corps mounted a major offensive. The first phase of this, codenamed Operation Totalise, involved a daring night attack astride the Caen–Falaise road on 7 August. To reduce casualties, the infantry rode in Kangaroos (see the sidebar 'Hobart's Funnies', earlier in this chapter). The operation got off to a bad start when the US Air Force accidentally bombed the troops on their start line, but the advance reached a point halfway to Falaise. It was repeated under the codename Tractable on 14 August. This time air support consisted of area bombing to protect the flanks of the advance. Aware that they faced a strong anti-tank gun screen, the tanks fired smoke shells on the move to further blind their opponents and drove straight through it.

The Americans were now driving up from the south, while the rest of the British and Canadians continued to advance from the north. The Germans, an estimated 80,000 men, were now trapped inside a shrinking pocket, hammered incessantly by artillery and air attack. Perhaps 20,000 escaped by the time the Allies closed the last exit on 19 August. Of the rest of the Germans, 10,000 were killed and 50,000 surrendered. Amid the wreckage in the pocket were over 700 tanks and armoured vehicles of various types, 750 artillery weapons, and 7500 motor vehicles. No one counted the thousands of horse-drawn vehicles.

Pursuing through France and Belgium

With nothing to stop them, the armoured divisions of Montgomery's 21st Army Group raced north in a 480-kilometre (300-mile) drive. On 3 September they liberated Brussels amid scenes of rejoicing. So rapid was the advance that when units of 11th Armoured Division entered Antwerp two days later, they found they had forced the Germans to leave the docks more or less intact. For the moment, however, the Allies could not use them because the enemy was still present in strength on both banks of the Scheldt estuary.

Back in France, some tidying up remained. As all the Allies' supplies were still coming across the Normandy beaches, they needed to capture the Channel ports as quickly as possible. Hitler, recognising the ports' importance, had decreed that the Germans were to defend them to the last man. The British assaulted:

- ✔ Le Havre on 10 September. The AVREs, Crabs, Crocodiles, and Kangaroos (see the earlier sidebar 'Hobart's Funnies') of their assault teams sorted out the prepared defences so quickly that three days later the garrison surrendered. The chagrined Germans described their use, and particularly that of the Crocodiles, as 'unfair' and, best of all, 'un-British'!

- ✔ Boulogne on 17 September. The Canadians and the armoured assault teams opened their attack, and on 21 September the last of the garrison surrendered.

- ✔ Calais and Cap Gris Nez on 25 September. The Germans had flooded much of the surrounding area, making the approaches difficult, but the Allies realised at once that most of the garrison were elderly or invalids who lacked the will to fight. By 1 October the fight was all over and for the first time in four years shipping was able to pass through the Straits of Dover without the Germans' huge coast defence guns threatening it.

With the exception of Dunkirk, whose garrison represented no danger and was allowed to rot until the war ended, all the Channel ports were now in Allied hands. The enemy, however, had done such a thorough job of wrecking their facilities that it would be months before they became operational. The only alternative, therefore, was to clear the Scheldt estuary and open Antwerp. On the south bank resistance centred on the town of Breskens. On 6 October the Canadians cleared this and, shortly after, Buffaloes (tracked landing vehicles) lifted two of the brigades into the enemy rear; from then onwards the infantry, AVREs, Crabs, and Crocodiles took every neighbouring town and village, until by 3 November the area was clear. Across the Scheldt the Canadians cleared the South Beveland peninsula, the last operations taking place on 27 October. They enjoyed the support of almost everything 79th Armoured Division had to offer, including DDs and Buffaloes (for more on these vehicles see the sidebar 'Hobart's Funnies', earlier in this chapter).

To the west of South Beveland was the heavily fortified island of Walcheren. On 1 November the Allies made landings at Flushing and Westkapelle. That at Flushing went according to plan, but at Westkapelle the landing force ran into some of the heaviest coast defence fire of the entire war. Of the 27 LCGs (Landing Craft Guns), nine were sunk and eleven were put out of action with serious damage. The four LCTs (Landing Craft Tank) carrying the armoured assault teams had the worst landing in 79th Armoured Division's experience. They took a fearful battering, but managed to get a few of their vehicles ashore. The situation eased when commandos stormed each of the coast defence batteries in turn. They captured Flushing and the remaining Germans withdrew to the fortified town of Middleburg in the centre of the island. As flooded terrain surrounded the town, they must have felt secure. However, on 6 November Buffaloes closed in. Already demoralised and surprised by this turn of events, the Germans gave up without a fight.

Between 1 October and 8 November the Canadian First Army sustained 12,800 casualties. In return, they took over 41,000 prisoners and cleared both banks of the Scheldt. Minesweeping had begun even before Walcheren surrendered and the first cargoes reached Antwerp docks on 26 November.

Operation Market Garden, 17–26 September 1944

Decisive as the operations around the Channel ports were (see the previous section), they were overshadowed by dramatic events elsewhere. On 3 September 1944 Eisenhower assumed direct command of ground operations. He had insufficient fuel to keep both his army groups supplied, but he decided to allocate the bulk of what was available to Montgomery's 21st Army Group.

Montgomery proposed an operation that, if successful, would shorten the war by months. He suggested the use of three airborne divisions to create a corridor between the existing Allied front line on the Dutch border and Arnhem on the north bank of the Lower Rhine. XXX Corps, spearheaded by the Guards Armoured Division, would drive north up the corridor and relieve each airborne division in turn. The effects of this would be twofold. First, it would turn the northern flank of the notorious steel and concrete defences of the Siegfried Line; and second, possession of a bridgehead across the Rhine would permit a drive deep into the heart of Germany. Some felt that Arnhem was too ambitious an objective, but without Arnhem no point lay in mounting the operation at all. The codename for the operation was Market Garden. The plan received Eisenhower's approval and was put into effect very quickly.

The drops

The drops took place on 17 September. Near Eindhoven the US 101st Airborne Division secured the bridge across the Wilhelmina Canal. The US 82nd Airborne Division captured the bridge over the Maas at Grave, but became involved in bitter fighting for possession of that over the Waal at Nijmegen. At Arnhem, the British 1st Airborne Division dropped well to the west of the town, because of unjustified fears that the anti-aircraft defence closer to the bridges would cause heavy casualties. Although the landing achieved tactical surprise, the result of this decision was that the division had a long march into town, during which the Germans got their act together very quickly.

Unfortunately the immediate enemy consisted of the II SS Panzer Corps, refitting after their ordeal in Normandy. In addition, German units, including formidable Tiger tanks, converged on Arnhem from every direction. They halted 1st Airborne Division's advance and forced most of its units into a defensive perimeter in the suburb of Oosterbeek. For a while, General Urquhart, commander of the British 1st Airborne Division, was cut off behind enemy lines. Nevertheless, one group of paratroopers worked its way through the town, reaching the north end of the huge road bridge, holding it against all comers until 20 September, knocking out tanks, armoured cars, and half-tracks, inflicting 400 casualties, and taking 120 prisoners.

Meanwhile, XXX Corps had relieved the US 101st Airborne on 18 September. Next morning it broke through to the US 82nd Airborne, with which it spent the rest of the day fighting its way through Nijmegen, simultaneously fighting off counter-attacks from the Reichswald Forest to the east. The following afternoon US Parachute Infantry made an apparently suicidal crossing of the Waal in assault boats. They suppressed the opposition on the far bank, captured the north end of the railway bridge, and were quickly reinforced. At about 6.30 p.m. a Sherman tank troop of Grenadier Guards charged across the Nijmegen road bridge under heavy fire, routed the defenders at the far end, and went on to join the Americans, having lost two of its tanks. Little did the Grenadiers know that the enemy tried to detonate the bridge's demolition charges while they were on it. A member of the Dutch resistance who was later killed in the fighting may have cut the wires to prevent this.

Arnhem was now only 18 kilometres (11 miles) distant. On the morning of 21 September a squadron of Irish Guards' Shermans broke out of Nijmegen and took the Arnhem road. Unfortunately, this ran along the top of a causeway with deep water-filled ditches on either side, so that when anti-tank guns knocked out the leading tanks south of Elst the remainder were unable to deploy. The Irish Guards were now strung out along the embankment. No further movement was possible, because behind them several kilometres of closely packed vehicles stretched all the way back to the road bridge, creating a traffic jam of which the German artillery took full advantage.

Withdrawing from Arnhem

The original object of Market Garden had long since ceased to be attainable. The priority now was to extract as much as possible of the 1st Airborne Division, fighting its ferocious battle against immense odds at Oosterbeek. As a first step, a Polish Parachute Brigade was dropped at Driel, on the south bank of the Lower Rhine, almost opposite Oosterbeek, on the afternoon of 21 September. The question now was whether XXX Corps could reach Driel.

Next morning, elements of Major General G.I. Thomas's 43rd (Wessex) Division, led by armoured cars, took advantage of a heavy mist to work their way out of the bridgehead and through the enemy lines. Map reading on minor roads proved difficult, but by 8 a.m. the leading troop was receiving a delighted welcome from the Poles. The car's radios were used to establish a link with one of XXX Corps' artillery regiments, which began to pound the enemy attacking the Oosterbeek perimeter.

General Urquhart, commanding 1st Airborne Division, sent two of his staff officers across to Driel in a rubber boat. They said that the troops in Oosterbeek were short of ammunition, food, and medical supplies and could not hold out much longer. Meanwhile, Thomas had used two of his brigades to punch a hole through the Germans surrounding the Nijmegen bridgehead. A relief column pushed through consisting of light infantry, a Sherman squadron, and two DUKWs (amphibious troop carriers) laden with supplies. On the road to Driel they ambushed an enemy tank column that had tagged on behind them, destroying five of its number. More of 43rd Division followed, including an convoy carrying assault boats.

On the night of 25/26 September these boats ferried 2162 men of the 1st Airborne Division across from Oosterbeek. The rest of the division were either dead, wounded, or prisoners. In Arnhem itself, the Germans sustained some 3300 killed or wounded and an unexpectedly high number of armoured vehicles destroyed.

Arnhem was a battle of 'what ifs'. What if 1st Airborne Division had been dropped over the town instead of out in the country? What if the extravagant number of gliders that transported the corps headquarters from England had been used to deliver the division's full complement of anti-tank guns on the first day? What if Urquhart had not been cut off at a vital moment? What if II SS Panzer Corps had not been refitting on the spot? And, the biggest 'what if' of all, what if Market Garden had succeeded and the war shortened because of it? Then Montgomery would have been hailed as a genius and his coup regarded as one of the greatest strokes in military history. But then 'if' is the biggest word in the English language.

Fighting Through to Germany: The Last Winter

In the aftermath of Market Garden (see the previous section), the Allied priority was to widen the narrow corridor that had been created by XXX Corps' drive northwards. This became known as the *Airborne Corridor* and was cut by the enemy several times during Market Garden. The Corridor not only made life very difficult for those Germans to the west of it, it also enabled troops and stores to be assembled in the Nijmegen area for the projected drive into Germany itself (see the section 'Operation Veritable, 8 February–8 March 1945', later in this chapter). The Allies also had to secure the area between the Waal and the Lower Rhine, called The Island. With the exception of the operations to open the Scheldt (see the section 'Pursuing through France and Belgium', later in this section), winter weather and soggy going meant that no major developments took place on the British sector.

The Battle of the Bulge, 16 December 1944–16 January 1945

To everyone's surprise, Hitler used a period of fog, rain, and snow to mount a major counter-offensive, now known as the Battle of the Bulge, on 16 December. The German intention was to drive through the Ardennes, cross the Meuse, take Brussels, and throw the Allies out of Antwerp . . . using captured American fuel. The effect would be to cut Eisenhower's armies in two. Those to the north, mainly the British and Canadians, would be cut off and forced to surrender, and the Germans would return to the rip-roarin' days of 1940. At least, that was the dream of the deluded maniac that Hitler had become. The situation never came close to that, of course, but it was a dangerous, damaging offensive.

The Germans made a breakthrough on a sector of the front manned by inexperienced American divisions and made considerable progress. Beyond some redeployment, British troops were hardly involved, although the 11th Armoured Division was briefly engaged with the 2nd Panzer Division near Dinant on 24 December, forcing it to withdraw.

Eisenhower made Montgomery responsible for operations against the northern flank of the Bulge, while Omar Bradley, commanding the US 12th Army Group, continued to command in the south. Montgomery could be difficult at times, but the American officers who served under him on this occasion admired his perception, strength of purpose, and the results he achieved. By the middle of January 1945 the Germans were back where they started.

Operation Veritable, 8 February– 8 March 1945

While the Allies were reducing the Bulge (see the previous section), they were also preparing for the next phase of the campaign, involving an advance through the Reichswald, a forest east of Nijmegen. This contained the as yet incomplete northern section of the Siegfried Line, the defences of which had not developed to anything like the same extent as they had further south (see the section 'Operation Market Garden, 17–26 September', earlier in this chapter). When through the Reichswald, the advance would clear the left bank of the Rhine in preparation for a crossing in force. The operation, codenamed Veritable, began on 8 February 1945.

Operation Veritable used the British artillery's largest fire plan of the entire war. It lasted for two-and-a-half hours. The British laid a smoke screen 12,500 metres (13,500 yards) long in front of the German lines. The enemy, understandably thinking that an attack was coming in, surfaced from their dugouts and fired into the smoke, at the same time calling down their own artillery's defensive fire strikes. For ten minutes the British locating units pinpointed the position of the German guns, and then the whole shooting party started up again, smashing the guns to ruin while continuing to pound the defenders.

Incessant rain had turned the ground into a quagmire, and in some areas the enemy had breached the dykes and flooded the landscape, leaving farms and higher ground as islands. In places the only vehicles capable of movement were jeeps, the Churchills (initially designed for conditions similar to the Western Front in the First World War, described in Part V), and Churchill-based 'Funnies' (see the sidebar 'Hobart's Funnies', earlier in this chapter). Progress was sustained but steady, improving towards the end of the month when the water level dropped and the ground began to dry out. During the first week of March the enemy withdrew across the Rhine, leaving the left bank of the river in Allied hands. The British and Canadians sustained approximately 15,000 casualties during Operation Veritable. The Germans lost 22,000 men killed or wounded and the same number captured.

Crossing the Rhine

On 7 March 1945 the leading elements of the US First Army seized an unexpected opportunity to capture the Ludendorff Bridge at Remagen more or less intact. They supplemented the bridge by pontoons and by 21 March the bridgehead was 32 kilometres (20 miles) long by 13 kilometres (8 miles) deep. On 22 March Patton's US Third Army mounted a surprise river crossing and secured a second bridgehead at Oppenheim. The following day Montgomery's 21st Army Group obtained bridgeheads at Rees, Wesel, and Rheinberg.

Montgomery's assault crossing, codenamed Plunder, attracted the same detailed planning that went into the preparations for D Day. At 9 p.m. on the evening of 23 March, covered by the fire of 3500 heavy, medium, and field guns, four battalions of 51st (Highland) Division, mounted in 150 Buffaloes and accompanied by DD Shermans, secured a good beachhead near Rees. An hour later XII Corps employed all its artillery to cover 1st Commando Brigade's crossing at Wesel. The commandos crossed in 24 Buffaloes while a second wave followed in assault boats, the far bank illuminated by the top-secret Canal Defence Lights. At 2 a.m. on 24 March the 15th (Scottish) Division crossed near Xanten, using Buffaloes and assault boats. Simultaneously, the US Ninth Army put its 30th Division across north of Rheinberg and its 79th Division east of the town. Resistance to these crossings varied between stiff and indifferent. (See the earlier sidebar 'Hobart's Funnies' for more on DD Shermans, Buffaloes, and Canal Defence Lights.)

At 10 a.m. the US XVIII Airborne Corps (British 6th and US 17th Airborne Divisions) began dropping behind the Diersfordter Wald, opposite 15th Division, to capture bridges on the Issel river. Tanks were rafted across the Rhine almost at once, and construction work began on pontoon bridges. Distinguished visitors at the end of the first day included Winston Churchill, Eisenhower, and Montgomery. The bridgeheads were linked and expanded quickly. By 27 March the combined bridgehead was 56 kilometres (35 miles) wide and 32 kilometres (20 miles) deep. The British Second Army sustained 3868 casualties and took 11,161 prisoners during the river crossing and the expansion of the bridgehead.

Advancing across Germany to Victory

Very few people can name the battles that 21st Army fought during April 1945 when it broke out of its bridgehead and advanced northwest across Germany. Even fewer know of the attempted stand by the German army on the line of the river Aller, or the bitter fighting that took place around the little town of Rethem, or the use of Canal Defence Lights to cross the Elbe on 26 April (see the earlier sidebar 'Hobart's Funnies'). Some people know that Bremen fell on 28 April or that 7th Armoured Division occupied Hamburg on 3 May, and that on 4 May Field Marshal Montgomery received the surrender of all German forces in Northwest Europe at his headquarters. The war, to all intents and purposes, was over.

The journey from the Rhine to the Baltic was a strange one. The German civilians were sullenly indifferent, glad only that it was the British and not the Russians who were occupying their country. Towns and villages hung out white sheets, but Nazi fanatics were always willing to fight to the death while their world collapsed around them.

There was, too, a hint of things to come (see Chapter 25). On 2 May the Royal Scots Greys, with the 1st Canadian Parachute Battalion aboard their tanks, were told to head for the Baltic coast road at Wismar. Shortly after they had arrived, advance elements of the Russian III Tank Corps trundled into Wismar from the east; they were heading for Denmark and would have occupied it if they had got there. The arrival of the 11th Armoured Division at nearby Trevemunde next day ended any discussion on the subject.

Chapter 24

Welcome to the Jungle: The Far East, 1941–1945

*I*n 1940 the British, American, and Dutch governments banned the export of strategic materials to Japan and froze Japanese assets, due to the savagery of Japan's war with China, which had started in 1937. Japan, unable to trade for the supplies of rubber, tin, and oil needed to continue its war, decided to take these necessities by force. In Japanese eyes the attack on the US Pacific Fleet at Pearl Harbour on 7 December 1941, followed by the invasion of British, Dutch, and American territories, were not treacherous acts by a neutral country but courageous pre-emptive strikes. For more on Pearl Harbour and the outbreak of hostilities in the Far East, see Keith D. Dickson's *World War II For Dummies* (published by Wiley).

The war in the Far East relied heavily on infantrymen and artillery, but wherever tanks could be used they proved frequently to be a battle winner. The tanks most commonly used by the British in Burma were the reliable American-designed Stuart and Lee; Sherman tanks entered service later in the campaign. Burma also saw the British use of special forces in the jungle (see the sidebar 'The Chindits').

The Chindits

One man who did not believe that the Japanese were jungle supermen was Major General Orde Wingate. He believed that specially trained units, supplied by air, were capable of operating for long periods behind Japanese lines and causing damage quite disproportionate to the number of troops employed. He received permission to raise a brigade-size force, which became known as the Chindits from its distinctive arm badge, a *Chinthe* or stone lion that guarded the entrance to Burmese temples. In February 1943 the Chindits, organised into seven columns each of 400 men and 100 mules, crossed the Chindwin river into Burma. They fought several successful actions and wrecked the Mandalay–Myitkyina railway in several places. Wingate created the uproar he intended, for the Japanese hated having their communications interfered with as much as they loved interfering with other people's. By the time his Chindits returned to India in April, they had marched through 2400 kilometres (1500 miles) of nominally held enemy territory. It was a gruelling ordeal, and of the 2182 survivors, only 600 were fit enough for further active service, although many of them formed the nucleus of the division-size Chindit force that took the field in 1944.

The quality of the Japanese armed forces soon made itself felt. The British Royal Navy had initially trained Japan's Imperial Navy, which maintained high standards. It also possessed an extremely efficient naval air arm, operating from numerous aircraft carriers. In the air, the Zero fighter was faster and more manoeuvrable than anything the Allies had immediately available. Japanese soldiers favoured the German storm troop tactics of 1918 (see Chapter 18). They were highly disciplined, hardy, indifferent to all but crippling wounds, and willing to fight to the death for their Emperor, whom they considered to be a divine presence on earth. The idea of surrender was incomprehensible to the Japanese, and they regarded those who did surrender as men without honour.

Losing the Empire in the Far East (For the Time Being)

On 8 December 1941 the Japanese 38th Division invaded the mainland territories of the British colony of Hong Kong. The British garrison, which included a small Canadian brigade, withdrew to Hong Kong Island and rejected a demand to surrender. Japanese artillery, aircraft, and warships began to pound the defences. On 18 December the enemy succeeded in getting ashore. The garrison put up a stiff fight, but surrendered on Christmas Day. This was a sign of things to come, as the Japanese eyed up Malaya.

The Malayan Debacle, December 1941–February 1942

The General Officer Commanding Land Forces Malaya was Lieutenant General Arthur Percival. He was a man of courage and perception, whose warning that the jungle did not present an impenetrable obstacle to an invasion from the north the British government quietly brushed aside as being at odds with current thinking. He also asked for two armoured regiments, plus additional anti-tank and anti-aircraft guns, which he did not receive. Unfortunately, Percival lacked the drive, ruthlessness, and charisma needed to deal with the desperate situation that was about to arise. He was, tragically, the wrong general in the wrong place at the wrong time.

Percival had too few troops at his disposal and, worse still, most of his units were inadequately trained. His Indian battalions were newly raised and contained a high proportion of recently commissioned British officers who had yet to master Urdu, the Indian Army's common language, and were therefore unable to communicate with their men. The only armoured vehicles present were some tracked weapons carriers and a few armoured cars armed with machine guns. Perhaps worst of all was dangerous tendency to despise the Japanese.

Early on 8 December 1941 Japanese air attacks on Royal Air Force bases destroyed over half the available aircraft on the ground. Those that survived were no match for the enemy's Zeros. Simultaneously, Lieutenant General Tomoyuki Yamashita's Twenty-Fifth Army landed on the Kra Isthmus, just over the Thai border, and at Khota Baru. The battleship *Prince of Wales* and the battle cruiser *Repulse* sailed north from Singapore to destroy the Japanese invasion fleet. By now the ships had no air cover and on 10 December Japanese bombers and torpedo aircraft sent them to the bottom. In two days the invaders had achieved complete air and naval superiority.

On 11 December the Japanese 5th Division, having advanced south across the border with a spearhead of tanks, overran a screen of ten 2-pounder anti-tank guns, lined up across the road. No fighting occurred, because the gunners were all sheltering from the rain under nearby rubber trees. Roaring on, the tanks ploughed into the marching column of a retreating Indian brigade. Only 200 of the Indians succeeded in reaching their own lines. The rest, cut off, had to surrender. This incident set the pattern for the whole campaign. To deny his opponents time to consolidate new positions and maintain the momentum of his advance, Yamashita ordered his men to commandeer thousands of bicycles that they rode or pushed along any sort of track that provided reasonable going, or carried them when it did not. They fed so well on captured supplies that their own meagre marching rations went untouched. This enabled their supply services to concentrate on the delivery of ammunition.

The British defence of Malaya was road based. When the Japanese encountered opposition, they left about one third of their strength to conduct a holding attack. The remainder executed a wide loop through the jungle and rubber plantations to rejoin the road some kilometres to the defenders' rear, where they established roadblocks. The local British commander, engaged in holding off a frontal attack possibly supported by tanks, then faced the alternatives of either asking friendly troops beyond the block to clear the road, or fighting his own way out. Usually, he was left to his own resources. If he was unable to break the block, this meant abandoning all his artillery, anti-tank guns, motor transport, and stores. Such, too, was the pace of the Japanese advance that the British lost yet more equipment when jittery engineers blew bridges prematurely.

'Can't have you digging trenches on the golf course'

The sickly smell of defeat hung over Percival's troops, yet higher authority denied them sensible defensive measures to halt the enemy because they may give an impression of defeatism. For its part, some of the British civilian population in Malaya were in a state of complete denial. They lived a very comfortable lifestyle and were not going to allow the army to interfere with it. 'Can't have you digging trenches on the golf course, old boy – the Committee would never stand for it!' was a typical reaction, completely divorced from reality.

By the end of January the British decided to abandon the mainland and withdraw to Singapore Island. General Wavell, who had recently been appointed Supreme Commander Allied Forces South East Asia, felt that the Japanese would land on the island's northwest coast, but Percival thought that they would deliver the assault further east, a belief that Yamashita encouraged with ostentatious troop movements. British command decisions continued to be made in a grotesque climate of fantasy. Percival had not formed a central reserve, intending to defeat the landing at the water's edge. In fact, his men had done little or no work to construct defences on the vulnerable northern coast, the excuse being that it would seriously affect civilian morale while fighting was still taking place on the mainland. This overlooked the fact that massive demolitions were already taking place in the naval dockyard. In fact, many of the troops returning from the mainland already regarded themselves as beaten and were in no mood to sacrifice their lives in a futile last stand. Drunkenness, desertion, and indiscipline began to spread.

Yamashita chose the northwestern coast for his assault landing, as Wavell predicted. On the night of 8/9 February the Japanese 5th and 18th Divisions crossed the Straits of Johore in the wake of a heavy bombardment, swamping the Australian 22nd Brigade with sheer weight of numbers. Once again, reality seems to have taken a back seat. The Australians had been forbidden to use their searchlights without the permission of higher authority. No doubt that authority would have given permission, but shellfire had cut the all-important field telephone cables. It also beggars belief that the radios on which the Australians relied to control their artillery support had been withdrawn for servicing! The following night the Japanese Imperial Guard

Division secured a further beachhead in the area of 22nd Brigade's eastern neighbour, the Australian 27th Brigade. During the next few days the Japanese got their tanks ashore and made steady progress towards Singapore city. By 15 February they controlled the city's water reservoirs.

Surrendering Singapore

Percival considered that if the Japanese had to storm the city they would massacre the Chinese element of the population, just as they had done at Shanghai and Hong Kong. He asked Yamashita for terms, little knowing that the Japanese had only sufficient ammunition in hand for three days' serious fighting. Yamashita bluffed, promising only to safeguard the lives of soldiers and civilians. With that Percival had to be satisfied.

The surrender of Singapore was the greatest military defeat that the British Empire ever sustained. Some 130,000 soldiers, sailors, and airmen were now prisoners of war, including the entire British 18th Division, which reached Singapore from the United Kingdom only days before the general surrender. The consequences were far reaching. Australia and New Zealand turned to the United States for their defence, and British prestige throughout the Far East was so severely damaged that it never fully recovered.

Retreating from Burma, 1942

The British garrison of Burma was much smaller than that of Malaya and consisted of two untrained divisions, 17th Indian and 1st Burma. On 15 January 1942 the Japanese Fifteenth Army invaded Lower Burma from Thailand. The 17th Indian Division had to retreat across several rivers to avoid the Japanese outflanking them using jungle trails, just as they had in Malaya. Early on 23 February, the defenders of the only road bridge across the Sittang river came under such pressure that they blew it prematurely, leaving most of the division and its artillery and transport on the far bank. About 4000 men managed to cross elsewhere, most of them without their weapons.

Fortunately, the Japanese were exhausted and a pause ensued while their supplies caught up with them. During this an event occurred that ensured that the story of Malaya would not repeat itself in Burma. Brigadier Anstice's 7th Armoured Brigade had been bound for Singapore when news of Percival's surrender led to its being diverted to Rangoon. Its first task was to provide cover for the 17th Indian Division while it reformed. One squadron was located at Waw when the Japanese resumed their advance on 23 February. The British Stuart tanks' close-quarter fire cut great swathes through the Japanese infantry. When five of the enemy's light tanks tried to intervene, their crews were evidently clueless about fighting other tanks. The British destroyed four of their number and the crew of the fifth got out and ran off. After this, Japanese tankmen avoided contact with the Stuarts whenever possible.

The British retreat towards Rangoon continued. General Wavell wanted to hold the port, but Burmese commander Lieutenant General Alexander saw that its loss was inevitable and would simply present the enemy with a triumph similar to Singapore. The British decided to abandon the city and embark on an extremely long overland retreat to India.

On 7 March they encountered a roadblock at Taukkyon, 38 kilometres (24 miles) north of Rangoon. Attacks from north and south failed to clear it. They planned a major attack for dawn next day, but by then the Japanese had inexplicably vanished. The enemy had crossed the road earlier, leaving a flank guard to man the roadblock. When the last of the division had passed, the flank guard followed on, little realising that it had trapped almost all of Alexander's army, including the general himself. At Prome, Alexander handed over command to Lieutenant General William Slim on 19 March. The army was also redesignated Burcorps. Two Chinese armies, siding with the Allies, entered Burma in the hope of keeping open their vital supply artery, the Burma Road. On 22 March the remnant of the Allied air force, which had fought hard and inflicted heavy losses, was destroyed on Magwe airfield. For some reason, Lieutenant General Shojiro Iida, in command of the Japanese, considered the Chinese to be the more dangerous opponents. Concentrating three of his divisions, he routed the Chinese and cut the Burma Road at Lashio on 29 April. The remnant of the Chinese fled towards their own country, with the exception of one good-quality division that had been attached to Burcorps.

The British retreat continued with the Stuart tanks being constantly involved in numerous local actions and acting as rearguard. They made such a nuisance of themselves that on one occasion the Japanese attacked them with frangible (breakable) glass grenades containing liquid hydrogen cyanide.

On 30 April, Slim's rearguard passed through Mandalay, crossed the Irrawaddy river, and blew the Ava bridge. At Shwegin on the Chindwin the troops boarded river steamers that transported them upstream to Kalewa and safety. Before the evacuation was complete the Japanese appeared on bluffs overlooking the embarkation area. Counter-attacks failed to shift them, but during the evening the Allied artillery fired off its remaining ammunition in a whirlwind bombardment, the intensity of which seemed to stun the enemy. The Allied weapons were then thoroughly wrecked, as were all but one of 7th Armoured Brigade's Stuarts. The men marched up river to Kaing and crossed to Kalewa. The arrival of the monsoon prevented any pursuit by the Japanese and Burcorps retired unmolested to Imphal in Manipur.

So ended the longest retreat ever made by a British army. Burcorps had withdrawn 1600 kilometres (1000 miles) and, while defeated, had retained its cohesion to the end. It casualties included 4000 killed and wounded, and although 9000 men were listed as missing, many of them were Burmese soldiers who had simply gone home. Japanese losses in killed and wounded during the campaign came to 4597.

Ending the Myth of Jungle Supermen

By May 1942, Japan had overrun Malaya, Burma, the Dutch East Indies, and the Philippines. These easy victories seems to have warped the judgement of its rulers, for Japan continued to occupy territories across the South Pacific, ignoring the fact that it could not hope to defend all its gains at once. The drawn Battle of the Coral Sea on 7/8 May dented the myth of Japanese naval invincibility and the Battle of Midway on 4/6 June completely shattered it (both battles were fought between the Japanese and American navies). Afterwards, Japan still had some local successes, but its rising sun was now past its zenith. Nowhere was this clearer than in Papua and New Guinea (both administered by Australia), where the Japanese, deprived of air superiority and unable to feed from captured supplies, lost their reputation as jungle supermen.

Defending New Guinea

The Japanese objective was Port Moresby on the south coast in Papua, from which they could menace northern Australia. They wanted to take the port by amphibious landing, but they postponed the operation as a result of the Battle of the Coral Sea. Instead, the Japanese decided to capture Port Moresby by converging thrusts from Milne Bay on the eastern tip of the island, and from Buna on the north coast across the Owen Stanley mountain range.

Two Australian brigades held Milne Bay, with Major General Cyril Clowes in command. An American engineer regiment was constructing three airstrips in the area. On 25 August, Kittyhawk fighter bombers flying off the airstrips pounced on seven Japanese landing barges off the north coast of New Guinea, driving them ashore on Goodenough Island and setting them ablaze. The 350 infantrymen aboard were left stranded. However, a much larger Japanese invasion fleet did succeed in landing a regimental-sized group and several light tanks at Ahioma on the eastern shore of the bay during the following night.

The Japanese began advancing at once, but found that dense jungle restricted their movements to a narrow strip of land between the sea and the mountains. They preferred to attack at night, led by tanks that used their headlights and subjected the ground ahead to continuous machine-gun fire. The Australians had to give ground because their anti-tank guns could not be manhandled forward through the mud. Nevertheless, someone produced a Boys anti-tank rifle, a huge weapon with a kick like a mule. The Australians used this to knock out two tanks at point-blank range. More tanks became uselessly bogged down. On 31 August the Japanese, reinforced with 800 naval infantry, reached the nearest airstrip, which they attempted to capture in a series of charges. Clowes's brigade counter-attacked and shot the Japanese to pieces. During the next few days the Australians steadily pushed the enemy back. On the night of 5/6 September the Japanese left the island.

The Allies had won their first clear-cut victory over the Japanese, and killed over 600 of them. For the first time, the enemy had had to endure sustained artillery fire supplemented by continuous air attack in daylight hours, and was not able to develop his usual flanking tactics against the Australian positions. Australian losses amounted to 161 killed and missing and about the same number wounded.

In the meantime, the second and more important thrust at Port Moresby had already begun. On 21 July a 13,000-strong force known as the South Seas Detachment landed at Buna on the north coast. Major General Tomitoro Horii commanded this force, consisting of veterans from China, Malaya, and the Philippines. The Australian strategy was to inflict maximum casualties and delay on the enemy. On the narrow front both were possible, and air attacks inflicted further casualties on the Japanese. The first clash took place on 23 July at Awala, held by units of the Australian 30th Brigade. The Australians fell steadily back, being reinforced by the 21st Brigade at the end of August, and then by the 25th.

Chasing out the Japanese

By 17 September 1942 the Japanese had lost 1000 men killed and 1500 wounded, over three times the Australian losses. Their supply system had broken down, and they were riddled with disease, starving, and exhausted. At Imita Ridge, 48 kilometres (30 miles) from Port Moresby, a formidable defensive position confronted them. Luckily, Horii was spared the need to mount an attack, which would surely have ended in bloody failure, by a signal from Tokyo ordering him to withdraw from the Owen Stanley range. It seemed that Imperial General Headquarters was depressed by the failure of the Milne Bay landing and recent American successes on Guadalcanal in the Solomon Islands. If Tokyo was seeking to avoid another defeat, it was disappointed.

The Australians followed up the Japanese retreat towards the north coast, being supplied by parachute drop. The starving enemy were eating anything, including grass and wood, to fill their bellies. Beside the track lay skeletons of those killed during the earlier fighting, picked sparkling white by ants. Horii himself did not survive the retreat. He drowned trying to cross the Kumasi river by raft. The Japanese rushed reinforcements to Buna, which they had turned into a fortress. It now became the Allies' primary objective. The Australians and Americans closed in, but in November a general assault on the defences failed. However, on 9 December the Australians captured Gona on the northern flank of the enemy's perimeter. Reinforcements arrived from Milne Bay, including Stuart light tanks. The Allies gnawed their way through the defences until Buna itself fell on 2 January 1943. About 7000 Japanese died there. Some 1200 sick and wounded were evacuated by sea and 1000 escaped into the jungle.

The threat to Australia was lifted. For Japan, New Guinea became a lost cause claiming 100,000 lives. For the next 18 months the Allies made a series of landings along the north coast of the island, destroying one enemy garrison after another, isolating the battered and disorganised Japanese Eighteenth Army for the rest of the war.

Fighting Back into Burma, 1943–1944

For the British in Burma, success against the Japanese took longer to achieve than for the Australians in New Guinea (see the preceding section). In December 1942 the Allies decided to mount a limited offensive with the object of restoring morale. The area selected was the Arakan coast of Burma, an area of mangrove swamps, twisting tidal *chaungs* or shallow river beds, steep-sided ridges, and river valleys clothed in almost impenetrable jungle. Dry and dusty for much of the year, between May and September no fewer than 500 centimetres (200 inches) of rain can fall, washing out primitive tracks in a day. Some described the Arakan as not being fit to fight in, but for the Japanese it was an area of great strategic importance because it provided a route into the vulnerable regions of central Burma.

The Allied offensive involved Major General Lloyd's 14th Indian Division and its object was to secure the Mayu Peninsula. For a while, all went well then, in March 1943, the Japanese worked their way round Lloyd's flank and threatened to isolate him. He had to make a difficult withdrawal and by 12 May was back where he had started in December. Far from raising morale, the offensive actually lowered it, suggesting as it did that the Japanese were still the masters of jungle warfare.

The Admin Box, 6–25 February 1944

The Allies planned a fresh offensive in the Arakan for early in 1944. Three important factors differentiated this offensive from its predecessor:

✔ British and Indian troops were now fully familiar with Japanese methods and were trained to defeat them.

✔ The offensive included the 25th Dragoons, an armoured regiment equipped with Lee tanks.

✔ From December 1943, newly arrived Spitfire aircraft had chased the enemy's Zero fighters out of the Arakan skies, so even if British formations found themselves surrounded, they could still be supplied by air until relief arrived.

The enemy's response matched the scale of the new offensive. The Japanese quickly cut the communications of the 5th and 7th Indian Divisions, but to the surprise of senior Japanese officers, instead of embarking on the expected disorderly retreat, they seemed quite happy staying put and fighting things out. This meant that the Japanese troops could not feed themselves from captured Allied rations, as they had in the past. Indeed, once their meagre marching rations were consumed, they went very hungry indeed.

On 6 February the Japanese overran the 7th Indian Division's headquarters. The divisional commander, Major General F.W. Messervy, and most of his staff managed to reach the defensive box held by the division's administrative troops at Sinzewa. This 'Admin Box' measured 1370 metres (1500 yards) by 685 metres (750 yards) and a feature known as Artillery Hill divided it into two areas. Into this space crammed tanks, guns, transport, supply dumps, a field hospital, and headquarters. Low hills overlooked the interior from every direction. While Messervy continued to run his division by radio, the defence of the box was the responsibility of Brigadier G.C. Evans, a no-nonsense soldier who told his garrison that they could either fight hard enough to keep the Japanese out or risk captivity with the chance of being butchered.

By 7 February the Admin Box was completely isolated. It became the focus of fighting in the Arakan. Every day the Japanese shelled its packed interior, while their frenzied attacks were repelled by the defenders and the point-blank fire of the Lees. At night, when the tanks were less effective, the enemy was able to approach much closer before launching assaults. The result was vicious hand-to-hand fighting before the surviving Japanese faded into the darkness. To encourage his men, Evans started a daily competition, the winners of which were those defending the sector on which the highest total of fresh enemy bodies was found.

The night of 7 February witnessed one of the worst atrocities of the war. A mixed party of Japanese and *Jifs* (Japanese Indian Forces – Indian prisoners fighting against British rule) broke into the main dressing or first-aid station and slaughtered doctors, orderlies, and patients without mercy. They then dug in amid the shambles until a West Yorkshire company and a troop of Lees ejected them two nights later. The Allies killed some 50 of the Japanese, including an officer in possession of a complete set of orders for the enemy's counter-offensive. Until now, British and Indian troops had regarded the Japanese with a degree of respect, but after the dressing station massacre they saw the enemy as no more than dangerous animals to kill on sight.

As the fighting reached its climax, the Japanese found themselves not only under pressure from different directions but also fighting on the defensive. The 5th Indian Division detached a brigade, supported by tanks, to relieve the Admin Box. This involved crossing the Mayu Range by means of the Ngakyedauk Pass, known as the Okedoke Pass to British troops unable to master the jaw-cracking local pronunciation. At the summit a huge bunker complex confronted them, which even the Lees' guns were unable to subdue. However, some 20 medium howitzer shells methodically reduced the bunkers to smoking craters and the advance continued.

On 25 February the Admin Box was relieved. Its interior stank of death and cordite and was covered with smashed equipment and burned-out vehicles, while the new dressing station contained 500 wounded men. Despite this, everyone knew that the Japanese had taken a real beating. The Allies sustained 3500 casualties, but went on to take all their objectives. The Japanese 55th Division lost 5600 in killed alone and most of its emaciated survivors were unfit for duty. The 54th Division, rushed into the area to retrieve the situation, also suffered severely until the monsoon rains put an end to the fighting.

Kohima and Imphal

The Japanese planned an offensive aimed at establishing an impregnable defence line along the crest of the Naga Hills, on the border between Burma and India. They wanted to destroy any hopes the British may have had of reconquering Burma from the north. The plan, codenamed U-Go, was for three divisions to cross the Chindwin on a broad front: The 31st Division would then sever the British lines of communication by cutting the road at Kohima; simultaneously, the 15th Division would attack the Imphal Plain from the north and east, pressing Lieutenant General G.A.P. Scoones's IV Corps back against the 33rd Division, which would be closing in from the south and west. All this looked very fine on paper, but in practical terms the difficult nature of the country prevented the three divisions from cooperating with each other. As usual, Japanese rations consisted of little more than a picnic.

A factor that the Japanese did not know was that in northern Burma a Chinese/American army commanded by Lieutenant General 'Vinegar Joe' Stilwell was about to start driving south with a view to reopening the Burma Road supply route to China. Stilwell, a prickly old Anglophobe, didn't like anyone much, but curiously he got on quite well with General Sir William Slim, commanding the British Fourteenth Army. Slim agreed to mount the second Chindit expedition to support Stilwell. Slim's plans also included an advance by Scoones's IV Corps to the Chindwin, but when he learned of the Japanese advance he cancelled this and ordered Scoones to concentrate his divisions on the Imphal Plain.

The Battle of Kohima, 5–20 April 1944

The Japanese isolated the little hill town of Kohima on 5 April. The fight for Kohima possessed a savagery that has rarely been equalled. For 13 days the little garrison, with Colonel Hugh Richards in command, beat off frenzied attacks by an enemy many times their number. Hand-to-hand fighting took place both above and below ground as the Japanese tried to tunnel their way in and were met by counter-mines. One by one important features were lost, but somehow the garrison held on, supported by the mountain guns at Jotsoma, a defensive box 3 kilometres (2 miles) away.

Meanwhile, Lieutenant General Montagu Stopford's XXXIII Corps had assembled at Dimapur and was coming into action. It relieved Jotsoma on 14 April. On the night of 17 April, fearing that they were about to be frustrated, the Japanese launched mass attacks on the Kohima defences, overrunning what remained of the position, except for Garrison Hill. With the coming of daylight Richards believed that his exhausted men would never see another dawn, but at 8 a.m. the Allied artillery began hammering the Japanese as a prelude to the advance of 1/1st Punjabis, spearheaded by Lee tanks. By 20 April the relief was complete.

The Battle of Imphal, 10 April–22 June 1944

Down at Imphal, the battle began with a crisis on 10 April when the Japanese captured the detached Nunshigum ridge. This towered 300 metres (1000 feet) above the plain and dominated several airstrips on which IV Corps relied for its survival. A counter-attack failed the next day, but a larger attack was planned for 13 April.

Nunshigum ridge is 6400 metres (7000 yards) long, and its slopes presented a hard scramble even for infantry, but Brigadier Reginald Scoones (the Corps Commander's brother) had trained his tank crews in hill climbing and was confident that the Lees were capable of reaching the crest. At approximately 11.30 a.m. the tanks, manned by the 3rd Carabiniers' B Squadron, were proceeding along the knife-edge crest when their artillery and air support ceased. The enemy immediately counter-attacked on both flanks. The Allies beat them off with difficulty, but by then all of the Carabinier officers were dead, as were the commanders of two supporting 1/17th Dogra infantry companies. The success of the attack hung by a thread. Squadron Sergeant Major Craddock and two surviving Indian VCOs worked out a plan to continue the advance. Craddock would carry on the attack with the remainder of the tanks, beating in the bunker slits with gunfire, and the Dogras would go in with the bayonet. They tried this, and failed. They tried again, and the plan worked. By the time the fighting was all over, no Japanese were left alive on the hill. The enemy tried to recapture the feature that evening, without success.

After their failure at Nunshigum, the Japanese were thrown on to the defensive and routed out of their positions in a series of actions around the edge of the Imphal Plain. Whatever hopes they may have retained for the success of the U-Go offensive were shattered when the leading elements of XXXIII Corps, driving south from Kohima, reached IV Corps' perimeter on 22 June. The Japanese lines of retreat to the Chindwin were littered with countless bodies, abandoned tanks, guns, and equipment of every kind. In their deserted field hospitals, the wounded were shot to spare them the dishonour of falling alive into Allied hands. The Japanese army had sustained the loss of 53,000 dead, of whom perhaps half were battle casualties while the rest stemmed from starvation and disease. British and Indian casualties at Kohima and Imphal amounted to 17,000, but because of the medical services' efficiency many of the wounded returned to duty later in the campaign.

Destroying the Japanese Burma Area Army

Inevitably, the monsoon months of 1944 slowed down the advance of the Fourteenth Army following its victories at Kohima and Imphal (see the previous section). Nevertheless, Slim soon realised that the enemy had withdrawn beyond the Irrawaddy and intended to fight a decisive battle in the Mandalay area. Once he had established this, he was able to plan the master stroke of the entire campaign.

Supplies for the Japanese armies holding the line of the Irrawaddy had to pass through the road and rail communications centre of Meiktila. As Slim pointed out, Meiktila was the wrist through which the lifeblood flowed into the Japanese fist clenched around Mandalay. Slash the wrist, and the nerveless fingers would open of their own accord. He decided, therefore, that XXXIII Corps would close up to the river as the enemy clearly expected, while a dummy IV Corps radio network, operating from the Schwebo Plain, transmitted signals indicating that the corps was moving into the line beside it. In reality, while XXXIII was holding the enemy's attention, IV Corps was moving south in great secrecy along the Kabaw and Gangaw valleys towards Pakoku, where it crossed the Irrawaddy and established a bridgehead

On 9 January 1945, XXXIII Corps further attracted Japanese attention when 19th Indian Division secured a bridgehead 95 kilometres (60 miles) north of Mandalay. On 12 February, 20th Indian Division established a second bridgehead 65 kilometres (40 miles) west of the city. A week later Major General Cameron Nicholson's 2nd British Division landed several kilometres east of 20th Division. In each case, the Japanese reacted with frenzied counterattacks that simply piled up bodies around the bridgeheads' perimeters. By degrees, the British and Indians went over to the offensive, taking nearby villages and forcing the enemy to expend yet more of its manpower.

On 21 February, 17th Indian Division and 255 Tank Brigade broke out of IV Corps' bridgehead at Pakkoku and headed for Meiktila. This part of Burma consisted of semi-desert and was good tank country. What followed was a classic application of the blitzkrieg technique: Armoured cars of 16th Light Cavalry (the first Indian regiment to be officered entirely by Indians) probed ahead, accompanied by the Royal Air Force's forward air controllers. Overhead flew Messervy in a light aircraft, sometimes landing beside the leading tank squadrons to spur them on.

The capture of Meiktila, 28 February– 4 March 1945

On 24 February, Messervy's columns captured Thabukton airfield and promptly flew reinforcements in. The enemy knew that Meiktila was in real danger and they turned every house into a fortress. The Allies isolated the town on 28 February. During the next three days its 3000-strong garrison fought to the death amid the blazing ruins. The few survivors waded into a lake and shot themselves.

In the acrimonious aftermath of U-Go's disastrous failure (see the section 'Kohima and Imphal', earlier in this chapter), more Japanese generals' heads rolled than balls in a bowling alley. The new commander of the Burma Area Army, General Hayotoro Kimura, was not the cleverest man in Asia, but even he was horrified by the implications of losing Meiktila. Recapturing the town became a matter of the utmost urgency, but from where could he draw the necessary troops? Not from the Arakan, where General Christison's XV Corps was mounting a series of amphibious operations along the coast. And not from the Mandalay area, where his Fifteenth Army was losing its grip on XXXIII Corps' bridgeheads. He had to abandon northern Burma, from which the Japanese 18th and 49th Divisions were ordered to converge on Meiktila with all speed; he also ordered the 14th Tank Regiment, the only Japanese armoured unit in Burma, to do the same. Allied air attacks pounded the tanks into scrap iron by air attack when its commander rashly decided to make his approach march in daylight. Only seven Japanese tanks reached their destination.

The 'siege' of Meiktila was a non-event. Cowan's division received all the supplies it needed by air and its few casualties were evacuated. Daily sorties by columns of tanks, armoured cars, guns, and lorried infantry inflicted heavy casualties and prevented the enemy concentrating for an attack. Meanwhile, as Slim had predicted, the enemy's Fifteenth Army, starved of reinforcements, ammunition, and food, had suddenly collapsed. Stopford's divisions were bursting out of their bridgeheads and armoured columns were ranging across areas the Japanese had previously considered to be safe. The Allies took Mandalay on 20 March.

Driving to Rangoon

As Slim had intended, Kimura's army group had been smashed. The next task was to deny the Japanese any chance of recovery. That meant a dash to Rangoon, 480 kilometres (300 miles) to the south, and with the monsoon approaching the risk was finely balanced. There was no time to develop elaborate attacks. Opposition had to be by-passed, even if it meant leaving large bodies of the enemy behind.

By 11 April 1945, the Allies had outflanked and broken a hastily formed Japanese line at Pyawbwe. In the ensuing race IV Corps was the favourite and reached Hlegu on 3 May, having covered 480 kilometres (300 miles) in three weeks. On the more difficult Irrawaddy route, XXXIII Corps reached Prome. In fact, neither of them won. On 1 May the 26th Indian Division from XV Corps made an amphibious landing at the mouth of the Rangoon river. The following day air reconnaissance revealed that the Japanese had abandoned the city, so the 26th Division promptly occupied it.

Plenty of Japanese were still running loose, but they were starving, disorganised, and thought only of reaching the safety of Thailand. In effect, the campaign in Burma was over. The campaign was the last to be fought by the old Indian army, and from the manner in which its final stages were conducted it was more of a grand finale than a last hurrah. The war in the Far East ended on 15 August 1945, the Japanese conceding defeat after American bombers dropped atomic bombs on Hiroshima and Nagasaki.

Chapter 25

Around the World in 60 Years: Operations 1945–2006

In This Chapter

▶ Waving goodbye to the British Empire

▶ Conducting conventional wars

▶ Maintaining internal security and peace

*A*fter the end of the Second World War (see Chapters 23 and 24), the British army faced many commitments all over the world. In order to fulfil these commitments, the government initially retained conscription (renamed *National Service*). Most young National Servicemen, having had their careers interrupted, were irreverent in their attitude to the army, but when it came to actual fighting they proved to be just as good soldiers as their regular comrades. With the reduction in Imperial and other commitments, National Service began to run down during the late 1950s, leaving the army an all-regular volunteer force recruited by selection. Simultaneously, a process of downgrading of the army's size began and has continued ever since. Regiments have amalgamated time and time again. Only a tiny handful of the regiments who served the Empire and fought in two World Wars have succeeded in preserving their identity.

The military changes taking place between the end of the Second World War and the present day have been many and varied. In the late 1940s and 1950s, the British Army was equipped in a similar fashion to at the end of the Second World War, but since that time some of the technological advances made include:

✔ **Infantry weapons:** Automatic rifles (including the L1A1 and SA80), soldier-portable anti-tank missiles and rocket launchers, bullet-proof *flak jackets*, and equipment protecting against nuclear and biological attack, to name but a few.

- ✔ **Armoured vehicles:** Ever-advanced tanks, with bigger and better guns, and more advanced armour (such as the Centurion, Chieftain, and Challenger) have been joined by armoured personnel carriers and infantry fighting vehicles (such as the FV432 and Warrior), designed to transport infantry squads into action protected by armour and vehicle-mounted heavy weapons.

- ✔ **Helicopters:** These now have numerous battlefield applications, including the tactical transport of troops and providing immediate support for them from the air.

- ✔ **Missile systems and artillery:** Many new systems, both traditional guns and space-age missiles, are employed by the army. Some systems are towed by other vehicles, but many are now self-propelled on armoured vehicles.

So what actions have British troops been involved in? This chapter runs through the main actions of the British army after 1945 (Figure 25-1 shows the geographical spread).

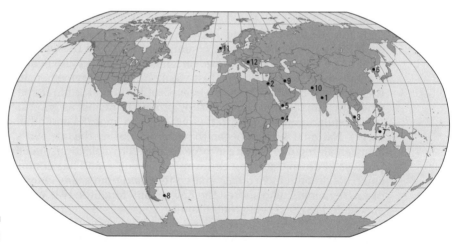

Figure 25-1:
British military actions, post-1945.

1. India and Pakistan
2. Palestine, Cyprus, Suez
3. Malaya
4. Kenya
5. Aden
6. Korea
7. Borneo
8. The Falkland Islands
9. The Gulf Wars
10. Afghanistan
11. Northern Ireland
12. Former Yugoslavia

Withdrawing from the Empire

After the Second World War, the Soviet Union and its Eastern European satellite countries were so menacing that the British had to maintain large forces in Germany. The Soviet Union, however, preferred to fight this *Cold War* by proxy rather than in person, involving British troops in a conventional war in Korea and a prolonged anti-terrorist campaign in Malaya. For more on the final days of the Empire, see Sean Lang's *British History For Dummies* (published by Wiley).

Palestine, 1945–1948

Palestine had never been a British colony, but the British had governed the country under a League of Nations' mandate after the dismemberment of the Ottoman empire, following the First World War. After the Holocaust in Europe killed so many Jews in the Second World War, large numbers of the survivors wished to emigrate to their spiritual home and form their own state. Uncontrolled immigration would have swamped the indigenous Arab population of Palestine, so a necessity existed to control immigration as fairly as possible. However, when the pressure exceeded reasonable proportions, the British had to turn away would-be entrants and house them in camps. This provoked bitter hostility among Jewish Americans, who gladly provided funds for their co-religionists to buy arms. Many Jews entered Palestine illegally, displacing Arabs. Terrorists on both sides attacked the British: The Arabs because they were letting too many Jews in, and the Jews because they were not letting enough in. And when Jew and Arab were not murdering British soldiers, they were murdering each other.

The situation in Palestine grew beyond control and the British government announced its decision to withdraw its troops when the League of Nations' mandate expired in 1948. Prior to embarkation to return home, the British presence concentrated in enclaves around Jerusalem, Jaffa, and Haifa. At this point the Jewish terrorists surfaced to try their hand at conventional warfare. Unfortunately for them, they weren't very good at it and left the British army seriously alone for its last two weeks in Palestine. Needless to say, the troops were delighted to leave.

India and Pakistan, 1947

India and Pakistan were the first former colonies to achieve independence, and understandably the rest of the countries in the British Empire wanted their freedom as well. The British government did not want to dispute the issue and merely insisted that the necessary political infrastructure had to be in place before each country became self-governing. The United Kingdom had promised to grant independence to India, and it did so in August 1947. Unfortunately, Hindu and Muslim politicians refused to work together in one state, so two nations – India and Pakistan – came into being. This resulted in large-scale population movements across the new frontier. So long as British troops were present little violence occurred, but after the troops withdrew the new national governments were not able to prevent horrific massacres of Muslims by Hindus and vice versa as ancient hatreds surfaced.

Some regiments of the old Indian army that recruited primarily in Muslim areas transferred to the newly formed Pakistan army. In cavalry regiments that contained both Muslim and Hindu squadrons, the religion of the majority determined the army in which the regiment would serve in future, those in the minority being posted to regiments across the border. When this happened soldiers on both sides wept openly, not only because of the lost comradeship but because they suspected that one day their respective politicians would make them fight each other; they were not disappointed. Nor did the new Indian army wish to retain all the existing Gurkha regiments, which recruited in Nepal, so the British army absorbed several of these regiments. As for the former British officers of the old Indian army, some stayed for a while as advisers to the new states, some retired voluntarily, and some transferred to the British army for the remainder of their service.

Malaya, 1948–1960

Hardly had the dust from Palestine settled than another, and far more serious, outbreak of terrorist activity took place in Malaya. The terrorists called themselves the Malayan Races Liberation Army, but they were nothing of the kind. They were almost exclusively Chinese communists, many of whom had taken part in a resistance campaign against the Japanese. Their targets were government officials, the police, the army, planters, and anyone who didn't agree with them, including their own people. They lived in the jungle, were highly organised, and were difficult to get to grips with.

On 5 April 1950 Lieutenant General Sir Harold Briggs was appointed Director of Operations. The British had already introduced detention without trial, issued identity cards (without which people were not able to purchase food), and instituted limited curfews. Briggs established greater cooperation between the armed services, the police, and the civil authorities, including sharing and coordinating intelligence. His greatest achievement, however, was a resettlement programme that, over a two-year period, moved Chinese squatters into protected villages. The army escorted food supplies into the villages, but did not allow any food out. Hungry, the terrorists were forced to operate in smaller groups.

However, on 6 October 1951 the terrorists scored a major success with the murder of the British High Commissioner, Sir Hugh Gurney. The following year, Briggs returned to Britain. The appointments of High Commissioner and Director of Operations were combined under General Sir Gerald Templar. The keynote of Templar's policy was winning the hearts and minds of the population, and particularly its Chinese element. This approach evidently worked when prosperity returned to those areas from which the British had cleared the terrorists.

The war moved deeper into the jungle. British troops set ambushes on tracks linking terrorist bases and villages known to be supplying the enemy. The British recruited trackers from Borneo, who proved adept at interpreting the slightest sign of terrorist presence. The terrorists moved yet deeper into the jungle and began to grow their own food. These gardens were visible from the air and indicated their presence. When a terrorist base was located, it received prompt attention not only from the Royal Artillery's guns, but also naval gunfire and air attacks.

In 1952 the Special Air Service Regiment, disbanded after the Second World War, reformed in Malaya, augmented by squadrons from Rhodesia and New Zealand. The following year helicopters enabled the British to insert troops deep into the jungle. By 1955, being a terrorist wasn't fun any more. But the British government brushed aside the terrorists' peace overtures and then kicked out the bottom of their collective bucket by announcing that it was to grant Malaya independence in 1957. Following Independence Day, terrorists began to surrender in large numbers. On 31 July 1960 the State of Emergency officially ended.

The terrorists had killed 3000 civilians, 1350 policemen, 128 Malayan and over 500 British and Gurkha soldiers. Some 12,000 communists took part in active operations. Of these 6710 were killed, 1290 were captured, and 2696 gave themselves up. We do not know the fate of the remainder.

Kenya, 1952–1956

Two battalions of the King's African Rifles served in Malaya (see the previous section). This proved to be of great value when, in 1952, similar problems arose in Kenya. The difficulties involved a large dissident group of the Kikuyu tribe that called itself the Mau Mau and practised black magic initiation ceremonies. Eventually, two British brigades and local troops deployed against them. Similar measures to those used in Malaya eroded the Mau Mau's strength, together with cordon-and-search operations and the use of *counter gangs* of captured Mau Mau who turned against their former comrades. By the end of 1956 the strength of the Mau Mau was broken.

Cyprus, 1954–1974

The *North Atlantic Treaty Organisation* (NATO) was an alliance of Western countries including Britain, who opposed the Soviet Union's communist *Warsaw Pact* in the Cold War era after the Second World War. Cyprus was an important NATO listening post for eavesdropping on the Warsaw Pact's radio transmissions.

At the end of March 1955 a group calling itself EOKA exploded bombs in Nicosia, initiating a terrorist campaign. The aims of EOKA were not just independence from Britain, but also union with Greece. The idea was not acceptable to the one-third of the island's population who were Turkish, nor to the Turkish government, and, once again, the British army and the police found themselves in the middle. By 1956 no fewer than four brigades were engaged in hunting terrorists, mainly in the Troodos mountains, with some success.

In 1960, following protracted negotiation with all the parties concerned, including the Greek and Turkish governments, Great Britain granted Cyprus independence on the basis of power sharing between the two communities, retaining two sovereign base areas at Dhekelia and Akrotiri as well as rights to maintain radar and radio stations elsewhere on the island. A Greek *coup d'état* in 1974 provoked a Turkish invasion that occupied the north of the island, creating the situation that exists to this day.

Aden, 1964–1967

The importance of Aden as a naval refuelling station disappeared when the United Kingdom withdrew from its Far Eastern colonies. During the early 1960s President Nasser of Egypt began meddling, not very successfully, in the affairs of neighbouring Yemen; nationalist elements there liked his proposal to absorb Aden and its protectorates into a Greater Yemen. With Nasser's secret encouragement, a major insurrection broke out in the Radhfan mountains in Protectorate territory to the north of Aden. This was successfully put down by a punitive expedition into tribal territory.

The violence moved into Aden colony itself, despite the fact that Britain had promised independence within a year or two. Two terrorist organisations, the Marxist NLF (National Liberation Front) and FLOSY (Front For the Liberation Of South Yemen), wanted control when the British left and seemed determined to prove their credentials by committing bigger and better atrocities than their rivals. The Aden Police were corrupt to the point of murdering a number of Royal Northumberland Fusiliers, an event that provoked wild rejoicing in Crater city. It evaporated suddenly when the inhabitants awoke one morning to find that Lieutenant Colonel Colin Mitchell's 1/Argyll and Sutherland Highlanders had taken over during the night.

In three years of conflict, 600 British casualties, including 90 killed, were sustained. During the autumn of 1967, British troops steadily withdrew inside an embarkation perimeter based on Khormaksar airfield. On the afternoon of 29 November the last company of 42 Commando left by helicopter and flew to the carrier HMS *Albion*. At midnight Aden and South Arabia became independent.

The 'Real' Wars: Great and Small

Britain has been involved in few conventional wars after the Second World War. This section gives the lowdown on where British soldiers have served in such wars.

Korea, 1951–1953

As part of the Russo/Chinese policy of expansion by surrogate means, communist North Korea was persuaded by those countries to invade non-communist South Korea in June 1950. The United Nations reacted quickly in arranging for the rapid despatch of military assistance to South Korea. The British sent troops from Hong Kong and in July 1951 these combined with the Australian, New Zealand, and Canadian contingents to form the Commonwealth Division alongside divisions from other countries.

Following some initial success, an amphibious landing at Inchon by the US Marines outflanked the North Koreans. The North Koreans fled and the UN forces chased them almost as far as their frontier with China, the Yalu river. American General Douglas MacArthur, commanding the UN forces, put forward several wild ideas for carrying the war into China, most of which the American Joint Chiefs of Staff vetoed. They did approve one suggestion, involving the bombing of the Yalu bridges, on condition that only the Korean end was bombed!

The Chinese were horrified that their Korean pals had taken such a beating, a disaster reflecting badly on the legend of communist invincibility. At the end of November they came swarming across the Yalu in huge numbers; so many, in fact, that part of the UN army had to be evacuated by sea from Hungnam. By January 1951 the Chinese had advanced into South Korea and temporarily taken Seoul, the capital, before the UN troops pushed them back. MacArthur began talking about nuclear strikes. That was too much for the Joint Chiefs of Staff and President Truman replaced MacArthur with General Matthew B. Ridgway.

Remembering the Glorious Glosters

On 22 April 1951 the Chinese attacked once more. Their 63rd Army, consisting of about 27,000 men, had the task of crossing the Imjin river and advancing on Seoul down the traditional invasion route, the effect being to trap the UN I Corps with its back to the sea. Directly in its path, however, was Brigadier Tom Brodie's 29th Brigade, consisting of 1/Royal Northumberland Fusiliers, 1/Royal Ulster Rifles, 1/The Gloucestershire Regiment, and a small Belgian battalion. On the right, the Fusiliers, Rifles, and the Belgians were almost swamped but retreated slowly, making the enemy pay for every metre of ground. On 25 April they were ordered to break contact and withdraw south. With tank assistance they managed to do so with difficulty.

On the left, the Glosters, under the command of Lieutenant Colonel James Carne, revealed the value of regimental tradition. At Alexandria during the Napoleonic Wars (see Part III) their two ranks had successfully fought back to back against separate French attacks, earning the famous back-badge that had adorned the regiment's headress ever since. Although the Chinese quickly isolated and surrounded the battalion and outnumbered the British by six to one at times, the battalion fought off human wave attacks for four days and nights. By the last morning the Glosters were concentrated on a single hill. They were no longer able to contact their supporting artillery because their radio batteries were exhausted. They had little ammunition left, and across the valley heard the Chinese buglers summoning their men for the final assault. The Glosters' drum major responded, sending the regimental call echoing defiantly around the hills. Seven times the Chinese masses charged up the hill, and seven times the Glosters pitched them off it. Then squadrons of American F-80 aircraft howled into the attack, blasting the packed ranks of the Chinese with napalm and strafing them with cannon fire. Suddenly all was very quiet. Carne had received permission to withdraw earlier that morning. His battalion had done its job and could do nothing more. The medical officer, the chaplain, and their helpers volunteered to remain with the wounded while the rest, in small parties, tried to reach the UN lines. A total of 58 Glosters were killed in the fighting and 30 more died in captivity. Only 63 got through to form the nucleus of the reformed battalion. Reports of the Glosters' stand spread around the world and met with something like awe. The Glorious Glosters, as they became known, received a very rare distinction for a British regiment, a US Presidential Distinguished Unit Citation. They had done their Napoleonic forebears proud.

As a whole, the 29th Brigade destroyed the Chinese 63rd Army, which withdrew and took no further part in the war in Korea. The following month the communists tried again and failed so badly that they began to surrender in droves. The front stabilised and *fixed position warfare* (trench warfare) set in. Even the Chinese huge manpower resources were unequal to the UN's massive artillery response.

Ending the Korean War

British regiments each served for approximately one year in Korea. During the war's final stages they were deployed on the hills west of the river Samichon. In the spring of 1953, ceasefire negotiations were reaching their final stages and the communists badly needed a success with which to improve their negotiating position. In May they mounted an attack in strength on a vital feature called The Hook. 1/ The Duke of Wellington's Regiment (60 per cent of whom were 19-year-old National Servicemen) threw the Chinese off the hill after fierce hand-to-hand fighting in bunkers and tunnels.

Total British casualties during the Korean War amounted to 793 killed and 2878 wounded and missing.

Suez, 1956

In March 1956 the last British garrison of the Canal Zone left Egypt. Shortly after, Egypt's President Nasser announced that he was nationalising the Suez Canal Company, of which Great Britain was a major shareholder. The British Prime Minister, Anthony Eden, over-reacted badly. His view was that Nasser needed to be taught a lesson. Just why is unclear, even with hindsight. The financial aspects of the transaction would have resolved in due course, and if Great Britain had wanted to retain physical possession of the Canal, why did the country withdraw its troops in the first place? After all, not much of the British Empire remained east of Suez (the traditional British route to the East).

The British government planned an invasion, but did not have sufficient resources to mount it. Months passed while it called up reservists and sorted the army out, and in that time world opinion turned against the venture. Eden did a shady deal with the French and Israelis, under which the Israelis would start a war with Egypt, and Great Britain and France would 'intervene' to sep-arate the combatants and ensure the safety of the Canal. They began this short-lived operation at dawn on 5 November. The United States threatened to wreck the British economy if the fighting continued, so imposed a cease-fire at midnight the following day. By then the British and French were halfway down the Canal with little to stop them.

The Suez incident emphasised Great Britain's loss of 'great power' status and destroyed the country's prestige throughout the area. Unfortunately, the American State Department seemed unfamiliar with the Arab belief that he who survives has won. Nasser, anxious to obtain funds for his Aswan Dam project, began playing the United States and the Soviet Union off against each other. The Russians won and for almost 20 years their influence was para-mount in many Middle Eastern countries.

Borneo, 1962–1966

President Ahmed Sukarno of Indonesia's ambition was to absorb the Malayan Peninsula, Singapore, and the three territories of British Borneo – Sarawak, Brunei, and North Borneo (now Sabah) – into a Greater Indonesian state. This was contrary to the wishes of Tunku Abdul Rahman, the Prime Minister of the Malayan Federation, which the three territories wanted to join. On 8 September 1962, a 4000-strong armed mob calling itself the North Kalimantan National Army (Kalimantan being the name of Indonesian Borneo) began running amok in Brunei town. British troops from Malaya answered the Sultan's call for assistance. They killed about 40 rebels, 2000 surrendered, and the rest fled into the jungle, where the British quickly tracked them down.

Sukarno declared that a state of confrontation existed between Indonesia and Malaya. His people, he said, were as thwarted and angry as he was and were volunteering to slip across the border and cause trouble. When the new, expanded Federation of Malaysia became a fact on 16 September, little doubt remained that a shooting war was about to break out. Nobody called it a war because Great Britain and Indonesia were not officially at war, and anyway much of what happened remained secret, so it continued to be a confrontation.

The British had become very experienced in jungle warfare (see the sections on Malaya and Kenya earlier in this chapter). In December 1962, Major General Walter Walker became Commander British Forces Borneo. His command expanded steadily until by March 1965 it contained 11 infantry battalions, half of which were British and the rest Gurkha, Malaysian, Australian, and New Zealand. Patrols from a composite British/Australian/NewZealand SAS squadron spent months at a time befriending border villages and sending back priceless intelligence. In addition, Walker had a unit of Border Scouts, 1550 strong, recruited from among indigenous tribes, two battalions of the Police Field Force, two regiments each of armoured cars, artillery, and engineers, 80 helicopters, and 40 fixed-wing aircraft including Javelin fighters. Offshore and on the rivers, the Royal Navy maintained a fleet of coastal minesweepers and patrol craft.

Much of the 1440-kilometre (900-mile) border separating Sarawak and Sabah from Kalimantan ran through wild, jungle-covered mountains, parts of which remained unmapped. As the enemy was only able to approach along established trails, the logical course of action was for the British to defend these with fortified bases from which they could watch the trails and patrol aggressively. The bulk of Walker's troops, however, were in camps further back, employed as rapid reaction forces capable of swift deployment by helicopter into a threatened sector.

In September 1965, some 200 Indonesian volunteers overran a small outpost at Long Jawai. Gurkhas were inserted by helicopter into ambush positions along the raiders' withdrawal route and killed all but a few of them. Three months later a repeat performance took place at the village of Kalabatan, from which only six of the enemy returned home. By March 1964, a shortage of volunteers led Sukarno to deploy regular army units that operated from bases across the border. The SAS raided these regularly with artillery support, following careful reconnaissance; the Indonesians didn't like what was happening and abandoned their bases.

Ambushes used the deadly *Claymore mine*. Detonated electronically, the Claymore's 700 steel balls blasted through its curved forward face in a 60 degree arc, killing everything within 45 metres (50 yards). Sensitive seismic detectors, capable of registering footfalls, warned the defenders of the enemy's approach along a track.

When Walker returned to Britain in 1965, Major General George Lea maintained his offensive policy to good effect. In March 1966 Sukarno was deposed in a coup. Five months later his successor formally ended the state of confrontation. Commonwealth casualties in this undeclared war amounted to 114 killed and 181 wounded. The Indonesians lost over 700 killed and 771 captured.

The Falkland Islands, 1982

In early 1982 a deeply unpopular military *junta* ruled Argentina. In an effort to restore its reputation, on 2 April the junta invaded the Falkland Islands, on which Argentina had a sentimental claim dating back to the Napoleonic Wars. The sustained reduction in British armed forces had given the junta the impression that Great Britain was a toothless old lion with no stomach for a fight. Yet hardly had the rejoicing ended in Buenos Aires than the shocking news came that a naval task force under Rear Admiral John Woodward was heading for the South Atlantic to recapture the Falkland Islands and their dependency, South Georgia.

Some post-war British Prime Ministers would indeed have responded with little more than a formal protest to the United Nations, but Margaret Thatcher was not one of them. Nor was she prepared to tolerate the sort of delays that had proved fatal during the Suez crisis (see the section on Suez, earlier in this chapter).

Recapturing the Islands

The British recaptured South Georgia without difficulty on 25 April 1982. On 2 May, following the sinking of its cruiser *General Belgrano*, the Argentine Navy retired from the conflict. On 14 May the British SAS raided Pebble Island and destroyed a squadron of enemy ground attack aircraft on its airstrip. This meant that the Argentine garrison of the islands had to rely on aircraft flying from Argentina, as the main airfield at Port Stanley was subjected to naval gunfire. During the night of 20/21 May the assault wave of the British task force entered Falkland Sound and landed at San Carlos on East Falkland. It consisted of Brigadier Julian Thompson's 3rd Commando Brigade (40, 42, and 45 Royal Marine Commandos, 2/ and 3/The Parachute Regiment). As the troops dug in, their heavy support weapons began coming ashore. The only serious resistance encountered came from the Argentine air force, which made several successful attacks on the British navy's escort vessels but failed to stop the landing.

The Argentine army had not fought a serious action within living memory. It consisted of regular officers (who received far better rations than their men, even in the field), regular non-commissioned officers, and conscript soldiers. It operated according to its training manuals and proved to be good for defensive purposes only. With the exception of a garrison holding Goose Green at the southern end of the isthmus connecting the two halves of East Falkland, most Argentine units on the island were dug in a series of high features overlooking Port Stanley. They really did not enjoy life on their 'beloved Malvinas', as the Argentines called the Falklands. The islands seemed to consist of solely of rainy, sleet-swept moorland with a high wind-chill factor, and their population seemed to consist of lots of sheep and penguins and a small but hostile British community.

The Battle of Goose Green, 28 May 1982

On 28 May 2/The Parachute Regiment, under the command of Lieutenant Colonel H. Jones, had the task of eliminating the Argentine garrison of Goose Green. This was not an easy task, because no room for manoeuvre existed on the narrow isthmus and the enemy had dug themselves in at the far end of it. Once again, tradition played a part in the battle. The paras had defended the bridge at Arnhem (see Chapter 23) and here too they meant business, even though the Argentines heavily outnumbered them.

The paras had to neutralise bunkers and trenches under heavy fire. At one period the battalion was pinned down, and Lieutenant Colonel Jones went forward, successfully unpinning his men at the cost of his own life. Under Major Christopher Keeble the attack got moving again. The battle became a contest of wills. The paras' mortars and Milan anti-tank guided missiles proved effective against the enemy's bunkers. A feigned Argentine surrender cost British casualties, and after this the British accepted no surrenders unless the enemy came forward with their hands raised. At the end of 15 hours' fighting, the Argentines were confined to a half-circle around Goose Green settlement. They screamed in fear as low-flying British Harrier aircraft strafed their remaining positions; their will had broken and they agreed to surrender at a formal parade next morning.

Goose Green cost the British 17 dead and 35 wounded. Argentine losses were 250 killed and missing, some 150 wounded, and about 1200 prisoners. The defeat was a shattering blow to Argentine morale.

The Battles around Port Stanley, 2–14 June 1982

As the paras fought at Goose Green, the rest of 3rd Commando Brigade had begun a 70-kilometre (45-mile) march across the island to Port Stanley. The islanders said it couldn't be done, and certainly not with the huge loads that the men were carrying. The commandos and paras, however, were superbly fit, and although some units received helicopter assistance, the rest completed the march entirely on foot. On 2 June commandos took the 450-kilometre (1500-foot) Mount Kent, providing views of Port Stanley on a clear day. They had penetrated the outer, and potentially most formidable, ring of Argentine defences at comparatively little cost.

Meanwhile, Brigadier Tony Wilson's 5th Infantry Brigade (2/The Scots Guards, 1/The Welsh Guards, and 1/7th Gurkha Rifles) had reached San Carlos, as had Major General Jeremy Moore, who was in overall command of land operations. A telephone call from a farm manager indicated that the enemy had abandoned the area of Fitzroy and Bluff Cove, to the southeast of Port Stanley. 3/The Parachute Regiment were lifted forward by helicopter to secure the area, while the two Guards battalions were shipped round to Bluff Cove in the logistic landing ships *Sir Tristram* and *Sir Galahad.* On 8 June, before disembarkation was complete, the Argentine air force attacked both ships. *Sir Tristram* was severely damaged and *Sir Galahad* became a raging inferno. The raid caused 146 casualties, including 63 killed, the majority of them Welsh Guardsmen. General Moore used the short operational pause to bring forward artillery and ammunition for the final assault on Port Stanley. During the same period the Gurkhas, of whom the enemy had an almost supernatural dread, cleaned out any remaining pockets of Argentines left behind by the British advance.

On the night of 11 June the assault began. 42 Commando took Mount Harriet and 45 Commando the Two Sisters without undue difficulty, but 3/The Parachute Regiment only took Mount Longdon after a hard fight. On the night of 13 June, 2/The Scots Guards fought and won an equally tough battle for possession of Tumbledown Mountain, while 2/The Parachute Regiment, with a troop of light tanks in support, took Wireless Ridge. In these battles some of those who thought that the bayonet was old-fashioned discovered that it could still perform its work efficiently.

By the morning of 14 June the only features remaining in enemy hands were Mount William and Sapper Hill. The Welsh Guards and Gurkhas were preparing to attack them when they saw hundreds of the enemy walking away from their positions towards Port Stanley. Later in the day the Argentine commander, General Mario Menendez, agreed to a general surrender.

Many commentators throughout the world had seriously doubted whether Great Britain was capable of projecting a task force 13,500 kilometres (8000 miles) to achieve a complete victory over an enemy that had had weeks to prepare its defences. The result led to intense study of the operation and the successful workings of British military professionalism. Curiously, it had all been rather like one of Queen Victoria's little wars (see Chapter 12).

The First Gulf War, 1991

Saddam Hussein, the dictator of Iraq, badly needed funds to pay for his recent inconclusive war with Iran. He thought the oil revenues of neighbouring Kuwait may provide an immediate answer, so on 2 August 1990 his army occupied the country against token opposition from the small Kuwaiti army, which withdrew into Saudi Arabia. Unfortunately for Saddam, the possession of oil is a very sensitive issue in the West. He chose to ignore United Nations Resolutions that he should withdraw, so the United States put together a coalition including Great Britain, France, Egypt, Syria, Saudi Arabia, Oman, Qatar, and the United Arab Emirates. As well as contributing naval and air contingents, Britain contributed its 1st Armoured Division.

On the night of 16/17 January 1991, while the land forces were assembling in Saudi Arabia, the Coalition powers launched a major air offensive against the Iraqi Army in Kuwait and targets in Iraq itself. While this attack was in progress, SAS patrols went behind the Iraqi lines to locate Scud missile sites. At the time, the Iraqi army was the fourth largest in the world. Some commentators managed to confuse size with excellence, describing it as formidable and its Republican Guard as 'crack'. In fact, the army's leadership was poor and it had never had to take on a first-class enemy. The Iraqis followed the Soviet approach to defence, so had packed Kuwait with bunkers, strongpoints, and dug-in armoured vehicles, which meant that air attacks could hardly fail to cause damage and casualties. You can imagine the earthquake effect of hundreds of tons of bombs unloaded from unseen B-52s flying at the edge of the stratosphere.

The Coalition offensive, planned by General Norman Schwarzkopf and codenamed Desert Sabre, began on 24 February. It took the form of an advance into Iraq followed by a huge wheel to the right into Kuwait. The British 1st Armoured Division was close to the hub of the wheel. In Germany it had trained extensively in night fighting and was very flexible in its operations. The advance met little serious resistance, although Saddam's engineers did manage to set fire to the Kuwaiti oil wells.

Most Iraqis, starving and with shattered nerves, simply wanted to give up. Those who tried to escape from Kuwait City along the road to Basra ended up in a huge traffic jam of wrecked and burning vehicles of every type that the coalition pounded incessantly from the air. As a captured Iraqi officer put it, the contest had been between a First World War army (his own) and a Third World War army. After 100 hours of fighting, Saddam accepted the UN resolutions relating to Kuwait as a matter of self-preservation. It worked. Kuwait was liberated and President George Bush Snr controversially ordered a ceasefire. The terms permitted Saddam to keep his helicopter gunships, which he used without mercy on Shia rebels in the south of Iraq. Some in the Arab world considered Saddam as a hero, simply because he stood up to the might of the coalition and survived. The business in Iraq remained unfinished (see the section 'The Second Gulf War, 2003', later in this chapter).

Iraqi losses in personnel, tanks, guns, and armoured personnel carriers were too great to quantify with any accuracy. Coalition losses were light. Very few British casualties occurred, but half derived from *friendly fire* when an American tank-buster aircraft attacked a British armoured column by mistake.

Afghanistan, 2001 onwards

On 11 September 2001, Islamic extremists flew two civilian airliners into the World Trade Center in New York, destroying the buildings and killing thousands of innocent people. America's understandable desire for revenge centred first on Afghanistan, ruled by a Muslim fundamentalist group known as the *Taliban*, who allowed an Islamic network called *Al-Qaeda* to train its members in terrorist techniques on Afghan soil. The American response, aided by Afghan forces hostile to the government, soon ousted the Taliban. The SAS made the principal British contribution, fighting a savage battle of extermination with Taliban/Al-Qaeda fighters amid the rocks, caves, and hills of Helmand province in the south of Afghanistan.

Somehow, the Taliban managed to infiltrate their way back into Afghanistan. By 2006 they were particularly strong in Helmand province, a poppy-growing area of vital interest to drug dealers. While the province is nominally a NATO (North Atlantic Treaty Organisation) responsibility, in practice the real fighting has been done by the British Army and Royal Marines. The fighting was the heaviest that British troops have been involved in since the Second World War, with the Taliban sustaining serious losses for little return. At the time of writing, an end to British commitment in Afghanistan seems remote.

The Second Gulf War, 2003

President George Bush Jnr turned his attention to Iraq, mindful of the unfinished business his father had left. Saddam Hussein was indeed still in power, but his grip on Iraq was such that neither Al-Qaeda nor any other terrorist group was able to operate inside the country (see the preceding section). The American and British governments:

✔ Peddled the story that Saddam possessed *weapons of mass destruction* and could launch them against the West within 45 minutes. The UN Weapons Inspectorate couldn't find them; it seems that no weapons of this kind existed. Iraq did possess some short-range tactical missiles, but had already surrendered these for destruction.

✔ Said that what they really wanted was regime change in Iraq because Saddam was a mass murderer. However, changing other people's regimes because you don't like them is illegal, so the politicians then said they were keen to bring western democracy to the Iraqi people.

The United Nations did not sanction an armed American and British invasion, but Bush and British Prime Minister Blair's administrations produced dubious evidence that Saddam was planning all sorts of evil. Despite serious public reservations, Great Britain found itself embroiled in an American war the legality of which remains highly questionable.

America and Britain assembled a coalition force in Kuwait. Operations against Iraq commenced on 20 March 2003 with a bombardment by cruise missiles and laser-guided munitions on targets in Baghdad and elsewhere. The basic strategy of the campaign was for the Americans to head straight for Baghdad, while the British contingent prevented the destruction of the southern Iraqi oilfields, took Basra, and captured the port of Umm Qasr, getting the docks back into working order. After the Americans had taken Baghdad on 9 April, the British pushed north from Basra to join them at Amarah.

Getting to that point was the easy part. Unfortunately, American politicians decreed that the coalition should disband the Iraqi army and police immediately. This proved to be a disastrous error of judgement. Suddenly, Iraq was full of armed men pursuing their own aims:

- ✔ Some were Saddam loyalists.
- ✔ Some represented a resistance to the coalition.
- ✔ Some were religious militias eager to do the bidding of their leaders.

In Basra and the south of Iraq, long British experience in counter insurgency maintained a more stable atmosphere than in other areas, where the American casualty lists lengthened by the day. By degrees, the insurgents learned that sniping at British patrols was very dangerous, so they resorted to roadside bombs. Saddam Hussein's capture in a hole in the ground on 12 December 2003 did not have a calming effect. Since then Muslim fighters and Al-Qaeda terrorists have swarmed into Iraq, while the Shia and Sunni Muslim sects do their best to destroy each other, and suicide bombers create indiscriminate slaughter.

No end to coalition involvement in Iraq seems to be in sight at the time of writing. On 1 October 2006 the number of Iraqi civilians killed since the invasion was put at a minimum of 50,000. American military deaths at the present time are in excess of 3000, while 236 British soldiers have lost their lives.

Peacekeeping Around the World

In addition to fighting in full-blown wars, and engaging in action to enable the withdrawal from Empire, the British Army has been involved in peacekeeping missions, too. This section details the main ones. The sidebar 'Punching above their weight' details some of the other military actions the British Army has been involved in after 1945.

Punching above their weight

This chapter only outlines the main events in the British Army's history after 1945. Every year, the army has been employed on active service somewhere in the world. Here are a few examples of the many other events it has been involved in:

- 1948: British Honduras

- 1948–1951: Eritrea

- 1951: Aqaba, Jordan

- 1957–1959: Muscat and Oman

- 1964: Zanzibar Revolution; Kenya, Uganda, and Tanganyika army mutinies

- 1970–1976: The Dhofar

- 1979–1984: Rhodesia/Zimbabwe

- 1980: SAS assault on Iranian Embassy in London to end a terrorist siege

Although Great Britain is no longer an imperial or even a great power, it still possesses the ability to punch above its apparent weight and to get good results.

Ulster, 1969–1998

In 1969 the civil rights movement took up the cause of Catholic grievances in Northern Ireland. These grievances covered many aspects of day-to-day life that were imposed by the Protestant majority in Northern Ireland, who felt that both the Catholic Republic of Ireland across the border and enemies within Northern Ireland itself threatened their way of life. When a Protestant mob attacked a civil rights march, rioting was inevitable, reaching such a pitch of intensity that large-scale inter-community violence would have followed if the British government had not shipped additional troops into the province quickly.

At first the Catholic community was grateful for the British Army's protection. No one expected this honeymoon period to last. The latest troubles gave the *Irish Republican Army* (IRA), an anti-British group that had begun to slip into folk memory, a new lease of life. It began orchestrating destructive riots that the British Army had to put down. The IRA therefore easily claimed that the army was an occupying force whose purpose was to oppress the Catholics. From this, sniping at soldiers on patrol and planting bombs were only a short step.

The Troubles lasted for 30 years, centring on the Catholic areas of Belfast and Londonderry and along the border with the Irish Republic, mainly in South Armagh. The British army and the police were involved in constant patrolling and surveillance, the pooling of intelligence gathered from many sources, ambush and counter-ambush, exercising restraint on the sorely tried Protestant community, and staying rigidly within the law. Politicians had to remove the causes of Catholic grievance, which in the long term removed the IRA's reasons for continued resistance.

By far the worst year of the troubles was 1972. On 30 January, now known as Bloody Sunday, the British Parachute Regiment were fired on while dispersing an illegal march. They returned fire and 13 people were killed. The subsequent inquiry concluded that no one would have died if the march had not been held, that the army had come under fire, that the soldiers had returned that fire in accordance with their standing orders, and that no breakdown of discipline had taken place. The incident still provokes intense controversy.

In the end, the Irish gunmen recognised that the democratic process would produce better results than their campaign of violence. Most soldiers actually welcomed their tours of duty in Ulster, partly because they were doing a useful job and partly because the tension kept their reactions sharp. In total, 1972 saw 10,628 shooting incidents and 1853 bombings. Among those killed were 103 regular soldiers, 26 members of the part-time Ulster Defence Regiment, 17 members of the Royal Ulster Constabulary, 223 civilians, 95 known republican gunmen, and three 'loyalist' gunmen. Finds included 1264 weapons and over 27 tons of explosives. 531 people were charged with terrorist offensives.

Yugoslavia, post-1992

The break-up of the old Yugoslavia into its constituent republics resurrected hatreds that the iron rule of the late President Tito had suppressed. Serb, Croat, Bosnian, Albanian, Muslim, and Christian all found reasons for killing their neighbours and burning their villages to the ground. British troops deployed by the United Nations to Bosnia and Kosovo as peacekeepers found themselves listening to both sides' atrocity stories, and sometimes witnessing the sickening results of those atrocities. At times they also found difficulty in keeping the warring parties apart or talking their way through roadblocks while escorting a convoy of humanitarian aid to a trapped community. The troops' duties required all their tact, persuasion, patience, strength of will, and fair mindedness. Their only thanks was the knowledge that they saved lives.

Part VII
The Part of Tens

In this part . . .

Here you can find ten successful generals, ten important and decisive British battles, and ten military museums worth visiting if you want to learn more about British military history, the British Army, its soldiers, and their weapons.

Chapter 26

Ten Great British Generals

. . . .

In This Chapter

▶ Spotting Britain's most able soldiers

▶ Figuring out what they did, and when

. . . .

Some warriors appear to be born to lead, and here's a list of those I believe to be the ten greatest British military commanders of all time. This is just my opinion, of course, and you may have your own thoughts on the subject. Each entry directs you to a chapter of this book to find out more.

King Edward 1 (Chapter 4)

As far as medieval generals went, Edward was in a class of his own. He not only understood the finer points of strategy when planning a campaign, he was also a sound tactician when he came to fighting battles. In addition, he understood an aspect of war that his contemporaries sometimes neglected. The castles of Conway, Caernarfon, and Beaumaris that Edward built in North Wales, each costing the medieval equivalent of a modern nuclear submarine, were actually the citadels of walled towns. Towns meant business, business meant prosperity, and prosperity meant that the Welsh were less likely to rise in revolt against the English. As Sun Tsu said, the best generals defeat their opponents without ever having to fight them.

Oliver Cromwell (Chapter 6)

Our image of Cromwell is of an unpleasant, warty man who left England strewn with ruined castles, had Charles I executed, and massacred Irish Catholics. But he was also a sound general who believed in thorough training and strict discipline. He was also an early practitioner of what is now called *C3*: Command, Control, and Communication. In brief, he was in complete control of his troops in action and they knew what he required of them. His Ironside cavalry, for example, did not go chasing after their beaten opponents in the style of Prince Rupert's cavaliers. Instead, they rallied and returned to the battlefield, where their arrival was often decisive.

The Duke of Marlborough (Chapter 8)

John Churchill, Duke of Marlborough, was responsible for restoring the international reputation of the British soldier to levels it had not reached since the days of the English archers. An expert strategist and tactician, he enjoyed an excellent working relationship with Prince Eugene of Savoy, forming a partnership that achieved numerous successes. He impressed on his officers that the most important part of their duties was looking after the welfare of their men. In this respect he paid such attention to detail that he became known as 'Corporal John' to the rank and file, with whom he was popular. He demonstrated his forward planning ability during the long march that ended with the Battle of Blenheim, when he arranged for fresh supplies of shoes to be available at various places along the route. Marlborough had political enemies at home, but as long as his wife Sarah remained on good terms with Queen Anne he was safe from their interference. Unfortunately, the two women fell out and Marlborough was recalled to England, receiving Blenheim Palace as a reward for his services.

The Duke of Wellington (Chapters 10 and 11)

Arthur Wellesley, later the Duke of Wellington, belonged to the Anglo-Irish aristocracy. It was while serving in India that he began to demonstrate his tactical ability. During the Peninsular War he developed his own distinctive way of fighting battles. This involved fighting defensively, preferably using the crest of a ridge for cover, followed by a swift but controlled counter-attack when the enemy attack failed. He did not undertake a general pursuit until it became obvious that the enemy was beaten. In this way he won the decisive victory of Waterloo, in which only a portion of his army was British. His troops respected him and were uneasy when he was not about, but cannot be said to have loved him. After his military career, Wellington's political opposition to the Reform Bill of 1832 made him unpopular for a while. In due course his popularity returned and huge crowds attended his state funeral in 1852.

General Sir Colin Campbell (Chapters 13 and 14)

Colin Campbell, later Field Marshal Lord Clyde, was the son of a Glasgow carpenter and served under Sir John Moore and Wellington during the

Peninsular War. He later served in America, China, and India. During the Second Sikh War he commanded an infantry division with the local rank of brigadier general. He retired after spending three years on the North West Frontier, but his best years lay ahead of him.

Aged 61, he was recalled to duty on the outbreak of the Crimean War, promoted to major general, and given command of the Highland Brigade. Colin Campbell's world was made up of two sorts of people – those who were Scots and those who were not. A strong empathy existed between him and his Highlanders, who broke the will of the Russians at the Alma; at Balaklava it was the 93rd Highlanders who, under Campbell's direct command, formed the original 'thin red line'. During the Indian Mutiny Campbell finally drove the rebels from Cawnpore and Lucknow. Queen Victoria ennobled him and gave him his field marshal's baton. The carpenter's son had come a very long way by the time he died in 1863.

Field Marshal Lord Roberts (Chapters 14–16)

William Sleigh Roberts belonged to an Anglo-Irish family. He was born in Cawnpore and spent most of his life in India. The first remarkable thing about Roberts was that he was small, with delicate health and poor vision in one eye. Today, he would probably not pass his medical examination. The second remarkable thing was that he was as brave a lion and loved a fight, especially if it was hand to hand. In this sort of fight he won the Victoria Cross during the siege of Delhi, saving the life of a loyal *sowar* (Indian cavalryman), recapturing a regimental Colour, and cutting down two mutineers.

Following the suppression of the Indian Mutiny, Roberts served in many of the Indian army's campaigns. His battles around Kabul and his march from Kabul to Kandahar during the Second Afghan War first earned him fame. The little man with a lot of fight in him caught the imagination of the press and public, who nicknamed him 'Bobs'. He became Commander-in-Chief India in 1885 and held the post for seven years. In 1892 he became Baron Roberts of Kandahar and Waterford. Roberts became a field marshal in 1895 and an earl and viscount in 1901. During the Second Boer War he was appointed the commander of British troops in South Africa. He achieved success at once, relieving Kimberley and obtaining the surrender of a Boer army at Paardeberg. He then went on to capture both Boer capitals before handing over command to Kitchener. Roberts was the last of Queen Victoria's heroes to be honoured personally by his Sovereign. He succeeded Wolseley as the Army's Commander-in-Chief, and died in the winter of 1914, having contracted pneumonia while visiting troops on the Western Front.

Field Marshal Lord Wolseley (Chapters 15 and 16)

Garnet Wolseley, the son of an army officer, was born at Golden Bridge, County Dublin. He first saw action during the Second Burma War, where he was severely wounded and mentioned in despatches. During the Crimean War he took part in the siege of Sevastopol. He served under Sir Colin Campbell during the Indian Mutiny, taking part in numerous actions, and was frequently mentioned in despatches. In April 1859 he was promoted to lieutenant colonel, achieving the rank in a remarkably short space of time. He next served in China and was present at the storming of the Taku Forts.

After spending some years in Canada, Wolseley was appointed Assistant Adjutant General in 1871 and worked on the practical details of the Cardwell reforms. In 1873–1874 he brought the Ashanti War to a successful conclusion. For this he received the thanks of Parliament, a grant of £25,000, and promotion to major general. Promotion to lieutenant general followed in 1868 and the next year, following reverses in Zululand, he was sent to South Africa to relieve Lord Chelmsford. However, by the time he arrived, the Zulu War was all but over. In May 1880 Wolseley was appointed the British army's Quartermaster General then, two years later, Adjutant General. He held this post for only a few months before conducting a short but brilliant campaign in Egypt against Arabi Pasha. He again received the thanks of Parliament and became Baron Wolseley. 1884 saw his return to Egypt as commander of an expedition up the Nile for the relief of General Gordon, besieged in Khartoum. Gordon, however, was dead by the time that the expedition's leading elements set eyes on Khartoum. The failure of the expedition depressed Wolseley, but the causes of that failure lay beyond his control. Once more, Parliament formally thanked him and he became a viscount. He did not see active service again, but served as Commander-in-Chief Ireland 1890–1895 and Commander-in-Chief of the Army 1895–1900.

Field Marshal Lord Allenby (Chapter 19)

Edmund Allenby's first career choice was the Indian Civil Service, but he had problems with the entrance examination and decided to become a soldier instead. Having passed out of Sandhurst, he joined the 6th Dragoon Guards. He saw active service during the Second Boer War and in 1914 he commanded the British Expeditionary Force's Cavalry Division. He was appointed commander of the Third Army, which he handled efficiently during the Battle of Arras in 1917. Allenby did not get on with General Haig, who posted him to Egypt as Commander-in-Chief in June 1917. He became known as 'The Bull', partly because of his build and partly because he was inclined to bellow when angry.

Allenby demonstrated his tactical flexibility during the Third Battle of Gaza/Beersheba, exploiting the success of what was originally intended as a feint attack. He took Jerusalem – the first Christian commander to do so since the Crusades – and probably could have finished off the Turkish army in Palestine in the spring of 1918 if he was not forced to send many of his experienced troops to counter German offensives in France.

Once his army's strength had been restored Allenby began to plan the Battle of Megiddo. The course of the battle is easily recognisable as an early application of the blitzkrieg technique used by the Germans in the Second World War. Allenby was promoted to field marshal and made Viscount Allenby of Megiddo. He subsequently served as British High Commissioner in Egypt, virtually ruling the country until it gained its independence. In the opinion of Field Marshal Earl Wavell, who served on his staff, Allenby was the best British General of the First World War.

Field Marshal Viscount Montgomery of Alamein (Chapters 21–23)

Bernard Law Montgomery, a clergyman's son, joined the Royal Warwickshire Regiment in 1908 and served with it during the early months of the First World War. In October 1914 he was badly wounded and served in staff appointments for the rest of the war.

Montgomery commanded the 3rd Division in France 1939–1940, and after Dunkirk he was promoted to lieutenant general and commanded first V Corps and then XII Corps, followed by South East Command. In August 1942 he went to Egypt to take over the Eighth Army. He restored its morale and instituted thorough training. Montgomery virtually destroyed Rommel's Axis army during the Second Battle of Alamein, then conducted a long advance across North Africa to Tunisia, bringing the campaign to a successful conclusion. Invasions of Sicily and Italy followed, before he left the Eighth Army to return home and prepare for the Normandy landings as commander of the 21st Army Group. Montgomery received his field marshal's baton in 1944. Following the campaign in Normandy he led his army group to victory in northwest Europe, receiving the enemy's surrender in May 1945 on Luneburg Heath.

Montgomery enjoyed the confidence of his troops, but he was a difficult man to like. His sharp, confident manner grated on some senior American commanders, and his attitude to his immediate superior, General Dwight D. Eisenhower, bordered on the insubordinate at times. Like all great commanders, including Allenby, he was utterly ruthless in sacking commanders whose conduct of operations fell short of his expectations. He became Viscount Montgomery of Alamein in 1946. After commanding the British

Army of the Rhine, Montgomery served as Chief of the Imperial General Staff between 1946 and 1948 before playing an important role in the development of NATO (the North Atlantic Treaty Organisation). He received many honours and awards, and after his retirement he wrote extensively on military matters. He died in 1976.

Field Marshal Viscount Slim (Chapters 21 and 24)

Like Montgomery, William Joseph Slim began his military career in the Royal Warwickshire Regiment. When the First World War broke out he was serving as a lance corporal in one of the regiment's territorial battalions. A minor misdemeanour cost him his stripe, but he was commissioned shortly afterwards. He was wounded in France and later served in Mesopotamia. When the war ended, the toss of a coin decided whether Slim stayed in the army or became a journalist. He joined the 6th Gurkha Rifles, remarking later that it is harder to become a good journalist than a good general.

During the Second World War Slim was wounded while serving as a brigade commander in the Sudan and Eritrea. In 1941 he commanded the 10th Indian Division during the Iraq revolt and the campaign in Syria. The following year he was promoted to lieutenant general and commanded I Burma Corps during the long retreat from Burma to India. His victories at Kohima, Imphal, Mandalay, Meiktila, and Rangoon cost Japan a complete army group and were a unique achievement in the Far Eastern theatre of war.

Slim became a Field Marshal and a Viscount shortly after the Second World War ended. He served as Chief of Imperial General Staff 1948–1952 and then as Governor General and Commander-in-Chief Australia 1953–1960. With his burly build he resembled a prosperous farmer, but the determined set of his jaw said that if he had indeed been a farmer, he would always have got top price for his produce. Admiral of the Fleet Earl Mountbatten, the Supreme Allied Commander South East Asia, believed that Slim was the war's best general. His men thought the world of him. They knew that he had learned the business of soldiering from the bottom upwards. They also knew he understood them and was aware of their thoughts. And they respected the way he talked to them, man to man, with no punches pulled. When Bill Slim died in 1970, his old Gurkhas and the members of the Burma Star Association felt that they had lost a member of their family.

Chapter 27

Ten Decisive Battles in British Military History

In This Chapter

▶ Discovering the most important battles fought by the British army

▶ Working out the battle's effect on history

*T*hroughout this book, you can read about many battles in British military history. This chapter lists the battles that I believe to be the most important, and tells you in which chapter you can find out more about that period.

Hastings, 1066 (Chapter 4)

The Norman Conquest provided England with a strong central government for the first time. In addition, the combination of Saxon stolidity and the Norman genius for organisation produced stability combined with progress. At this period, of course, England was only the central portion of the British Isles, but the Anglo-Norman influence spread steadily to Wales, Scotland, and Ireland.

Fought between: Anglo-Saxons versus Normans

Outcome: Norman victory

Bannockburn, 1314 (Chapter 4)

To every Scot, Bannockburn is the most important battle in the country's history, as it won Scottish independence from England. On the death of Queen Elizabeth I, King James VI of Scotland (the son of Mary Queen of Scots) ascended the English throne, from which he reigned over both countries.

Fought between: English versus Scots

Outcome: Scottish victory

Blenheim, 1704 (Chapter 8)

Blenheim was the first of Marlborough's great victories. It established the reputation of British troops in general, and the infantry in particular, to a level not achieved since the English archer dominated the medieval battlefield.

Fought between: British and allies versus French

Outcome: British victory

Saratoga, 1777 (Chapter 9)

The British defeat at the hands of American colonists during the fighting at Saratoga resulted in France, Spain, and Holland declaring war on Great Britain. In the circumstances, American independence was assured. The two branches of the English-speaking peoples – Great Britain and America – developed along similar but separate lines. Working together, they became a powerful factor in world politics. Two battles took place at Saratoga: Freeman's Farm on 19 September and Bemis Heights on 7 October.

Fought between: British versus American colonists

Outcome: American victory

Waterloo, 1815 (Chapter 11)

Wellington's victory at Waterloo ended 22 years of warfare with Revolutionary and Napoleonic France. Great Britain was already well on the way to becoming an industrialised nation. For most of the nineteenth century its undisputed command of the ocean trade routes enabled the country to amass vast profits as well as expand its empire. With the exception of the Crimean War, the British army was not involved in another continental war until the next century.

Fought between: British and Allies versus French

Outcome: British and Allied victory

Amiens, 1918 (Chapter 18)

The great British tank attack at Amiens finally broke the will of the German army to continue fighting in the First World War. General Erich Ludendorff, shocked by the sheer numbers of German officers and men willing to surrender, described 8 August as 'the Black Day of the German Army'. After Amiens, the British armies continued a slow but steady advance until the signing of the Armistice on 11 November 1918.

Fought between: British versus Germans

Outcome: British victory

Operation Compass and its Sequels, 1940–1941 (Chapter 21)

The destruction of the Italian Tenth Army by Generals Wavell and O'Connor produced results far beyond the battlefield. Hitler had to send German troops to North Africa to prop up his Italian ally, Benito Mussolini. General Franco, the Spanish dictator, had maintained a stance of hostile neutrality towards Great Britain, but now declared himself to be a 'non-belligerent'. If Franco had thrown in his lot with his fellow dictators, predicting the outcome of the war in the Mediterranean would have been difficult.

Fought between: British and Commonwealth troops versus Italians

Outcome: British victory

The Second Battle of Alamein, 1942 (Chapter 21)

1942 marked the turning point in the Second World War. To the British, the Second Battle of Alamein was the first occasion during the war in which they defeated a predominantly German army beyond hope of recovery. After that, the British saw victory as a probability. The Second Battle of Alamein is known as the British Empire's last battle. That is not entirely accurate, as Imperial and Commonwealth troops continued to fight until the war's end, but not necessarily in battle side by side.

Fought between: British and Commonwealth troops versus Germans and Italians

Outcome: British victory

Normandy, 1944 (Chapter 23)

The Normandy campaign was the beginning of the end for the German army in Western Europe. Professionals like Field Marshal von Rundstedt knew that the Wehrmacht could not support the demands of the Eastern Front, Italy, and Normandy at the same time and advised the German High Command to open peace negotiations. The High Command ignored his professional advice and the Allies completely destroyed the German armies in Normandy. During the Normandy campaign the United States, which contributed the greatest number of troops and material, became the leader of the western Allies.

Fought between: British, Commonwealth troops, and Americans versus Germans

Outcome: Allied victory

Meiktila, 1945 (Chapter 24)

The capture of Meiktila, leading directly to the disintegration of the Japanese Burma Area Army, was a brilliant demonstration of the blitzkrieg technique. It was the last major action to be fought by the old Indian army.

Fought between: British and Indians versus Japanese

Outcome: British victory

Chapter 28

Ten British Military Museums Worth Visiting

● ●

In This Chapter

▶ Taking a tour around Britain's best military museums

▶ Seeing the weapons, uniforms, and equipment up close and personal

● ●

Reading about British military history is one thing, but visiting a museum and seeing artefacts and uniforms with your own eyes really is something else. This chapter lists my favourite military museums in Britain, broadly in order of chronological interest, and gives contact details should you wish to find out more.

Housesteads Roman Fort, Northumberland

Sited on the most spectacular section of Hadrian's Wall, Housesteads is a great site to visit to find out about the Roman army in Britain. Vindolanda Museum (another important Roman site, housing the Roman Army museum) is nearby. Tel: 01434 344363; Web: www.english-heritage.org.uk

The Tower of London

The White Tower is one of the finest examples of a Norman keep enclosed by later medieval concentric defences. The Museum of the Royal Regiment of Fusiliers is also located within the Tower of London. Tel: 0870 756 6060; Web: www.hrp.org.uk

Caernarfon Castle

Many people consider Caernarfon in north Wales to be the finest of Edward I's castles. The Museum of the Royal Welsh Fusiliers is located in the Queen's Tower. Tel: 01443 336000; Web: www.cadw.wales.gov.uk

Edinburgh Castle

Edinburgh Castle occupies a naturally strong position made virtually impregnable by fortification. Within the Castle are the Museum of the Royal Scots Dragoon Guards (formed by the amalgamation of the 3rd Carabiniers and the Royal Scots Greys), the Museum of the Royal Scots Regiment, the Scottish National War Memorial, and the Scottish United Services Museum. Tel: 0131 225 9846; Web: www.historic-scotland.gov.uk

The Royal Armouries Museum, Leeds

A world-famous collection of arms and armour, with state-of-the-art displays showing how they were used. Tel: 0113 220 1916; Web: www.royalarmouries.org

Firepower! The Royal Artillery Museum, Woolwich

Displays include the evolution of artillery from the earliest guns to the present time, including weapons captured by the British army on campaign. Tel: 020 8855 7755; Web: www.firepower.org.uk

The Imperial War Museum, London

A museum covering all aspects of the World Wars and more recent conflicts involving the United Kingdom and the Commonwealth. The museum possesses an enormous photographic archive. Tel: 0207 416 5320; Web: www.iwm.org.uk

The National Army Museum, London

Exhibits providing information from the beginnings of the British Army to the present day, the Indian Army to 1947, and Colonial land forces. Tel: 020 7730 0717; Web: www.national-army-museum.ac.uk

The Tank Museum, Bovington

One of the largest and most comprehensive collections of armoured fighting vehicles in the world, including some of the earliest examples. Incorporates the Royal Tank Regiment Museum. Tel: 01929 405096; Web: www.tankmuseum.co.uk

The D Day Museum, Southsea

Detailed displays covering the D Day Landings and the campaign in Normandy. The Embroidery is a modern counterpart to the Bayeux Tapestry and tells the full story of D Day in 34 panels. Tel: 023 9282 7261; Web: www.ddaymuseum.co.uk

Index

• *H* •

• *I* •

• *K* •

British Military History For Dummies

Major Wars Fought by the British Army

War of Spanish Succession, 1701–14

War of Austrian Succession, 1740–48

French and Indian War in North America, 1754–63

Seven Years' War, 1756–63

American War of Independence, 1775–86

French Revolutionary and Napoleonic Wars, 1792–1815

Peninsula War, 1807–14

Anglo-American War, 1812–14

Waterloo Campaign, 1815

First Afghan War, 1839–42

First Sikh War, 1845–46

Second Sikh War, 1846–48

Crimean War, 1854–55

Indian Mutiny, 1857–58

Second Afghan War, 1878–80

Zulu War, 1879

First Boer War, 1880–81

Arabi Pasha' Rebellion in Egypt, 1882

Sudan Campaigns, 1883–98

North-West Frontier, 1897

Second Boer War, 1899–1902

First World War, 1914–18

Second World War, 1939–45

Korean War, 1950–53

Falklands War, 1982

First Gulf War, 1990–91

Second Gulf War, 2003–

Afghanistan, 2003–

British Army Ranks and Responsibilities

Field Marshal: Army Group

General: Army

Lieutenant General: Corps

Major General: Division

Brigadier (Brigadier General up and including World War I): Brigade

Colonel: Second in command of Brigade

Lieutenant Colonel: Infantry Battalion, Armoured Battalion, or Royal Artillery, or Royal Engineers Regiment

Major: Second in command to Lt Colonel, or Company, Squadron, or Battery commander

Captain: Second in command to Major

Lieutenant: Platoon or Troop

Second Lieutenant: Platoon or Troop

Regimental Sergeant Major: Discipline within battalion or regiment

Regimental Quartermaster Sergeant: Equipment and supply, assistant to regimental Quartermaster

Company/Squadron/Battery Sergeant Major: Discipline within unit

Company/Squadron/Battery Quartermaster Sergeant: Equipment and supply

Sergeant: Second in command to Lieutenant or Second Lieutenant

Corporal, or Bombardier in Royal Artillery: Second in command to Sergeant

Lance Corporal, or Lance Bombardier in Royal Artillery: Second in command to Corporal or Bombardier

Private in many infantry battalions and administrative corps, exceptions as below:

Guardsman (the Brigade of Guards); Rifleman (Rifle Regiments); Fusilier (Fusilier Regiments); Gunner (Royal Artillery); Trooper (SAS, armoured and cavalry regiments); Sapper (Royal Engineers); Craftsman (Royal Electrical and Mechanical Engineers)

For Dummies: Bestselling Book Series for Beginners

British Military History For Dummies®

Cheat Sheet

Famous Battles Fought by British Armies

Medway, AD 43
Mons Graupius, AD 84
Mount Badon, c. 500
Brunanburgh, 937
Maldon, 991
Stamford Bridge, 1066
Hastings, 1066
Falkirk, 1298
Bannockburn, 1314
Halidon Hill, 1333
Crecy, 1346
Poitiers, 1356
Agincourt, 1415
Towton, 1461
Bosworth, 1485
Flodden, 1513,
Edgehill, 1642
Marston Moor, 1644
Naseby, 1645
Preston, 1648
Worcester, 1651
The Boyne, 1690
Blenheim, 1704
Ramillies, 1706
Oudenarde, 1708
Malplaquet, 1709
Preston, 1715
Dettingen, 1743
Fontenoy, 1745
Prestonpans, 1745
Falkirk, 1746
Culloden, 1746
Lexington, 1775
Bunker Hill, 1775
Quebec, 1775
Long Island, 1776
Princeton, 1777
Saratoga, 1777
Brandywine, 1777
Germantown, 1777
Monmouth, 1778
Savannah, 1779
Charleston, 1780
Camden, 1780
Cowpens, 1781
Guilford Court
   House, 1781
Yorktown, 1781

Gibraltar, 1779–83
Malta, 1798
Vinegar Hill, 1798
Alexandria, 1801
Assaye, 1803
Maida, 1806
Vimeiro, 1808
Talavera, 1809
Busaco, 1810
Fuentes de Onoro, 1811
Albuera, 1811
Cuidad Rodrigo, 1812
Badajoz, 1812
Salamanca, 1812
Queenston Heights, 1812
Vittoria, 1813
Stony Creek, 1813
Chateaugay River, 1813
Chippewa, 1814
Lundy's Lane, 1814
Bladensburg, 1814
New Orleans, 1815
Quatre Bras, 1815
Waterloo, 1815
Jellalabad, 1841–42
Mudki, 1845
Ferozshah, 1845
Aliwal, 1846
Chilianwallah, 1849
Gujerat, 1849
The Alma, 1854
Balaklava, 1854
Inkerman, 1854
Delhi, 1857
Lucknow, 1857
The Betwa, 1858
Jhansi, 1858
Gwalior, 1858
Taku Forts, 1860
Abyssinia, 1867
Amoaful, 1874
Isandhlwana, 1879
Rorke's Drift, 1879
Kambula, 1879
Ulundi, 1879
Charasia, 1879
Sherpur, 1879
Maiwand, 1880

Kandahar, 1880
Laing's Nek, 1881
Majuba Hill, 1881
Tel el Kebir, 1882
Abu Klea, 1884
El Teb, 1884
Tamai, 1884
The Atbara, 1898
Omdurman, 1898
Mafeking, 1899–1900
Kimberley, 1899–1900
Ladysmith, 1899–1900
Stormberg, 1899
Magersfontein, 1899
Colenso, 1899
Spion Kop, 1900
Paardeberg, 1900
Peking, 1900
Mons, 1914
Le Cateau, 1914
The Marne, 1914
The Aisne, 1914
First Ypres, 1914
Second Ypres, 1915
Loos, 1915
Ctesiphon, 1915
Gallipoli, 1915–16
Kut-al-Amara, 1915–16
The Somme, 1916
Romani, 1916
Baghdad, 1916–17
First Gaza, 1917
Second Gaza, 1917
Third Gaza/Beersheba,
   1917
Arras/Vimy Ridge, 1917
Third Ypres
   (Passchendaele), 1917
Cambrai, 1917
Ludendorff Offensives,
   1918
Le Hamel, 1918
Megiddo, 1918
Amiens, 1918
Arras, 1940
Dunkirk, 1940
Sidi Barrani, 1940
Bardia, 1941

Tobruk, 1941
Beda Fomm, 1941
Crete, 1941
Operation Crusader, 1941
Malaya, 1941–42
Singapore, 1942
Gazala/Knightsbridge,
   1942
First Alamein, 1942
Alam Halfa, 1942
Dieppe, 1942
Milne Bay, 1942
Kokoda Trail, 1942
Second Alamein, 1942
Tebourba Gap, 1942
Mareth Line, 1943
Pichon/Fondouk, 1943
Longstop Hill, 1943
Sicily, 1943
Salerno, 1943
Admin Box, 1944
Monte Cassino, 1944
Gustav Line, 1944
Anzio, 1944
Hitler Line, 1944
Kohima, 1944
D-Day, 1944
Imphal, 1944
Caen, 1944
Falaise Pocket, 1944
Scheldt Estuary, 1944
Arnhem, 1944
Nijmegen, 1944
Gothic Line, 1944
Mandalay, 1945
Reichswald, 1945
Meiktila, 1945
Rhine Crossings, 1945
Argenta Gap, 1945
Pusan Perimeter, 1950
Imjin River, 1951
Suez Landings, 1956
Goose Green, 1982
Port Stanley, 1982
Kuwait, 1991
Basra, 2003–
Helmand, 2006–